Courts and Diversity

Brill's Asian Law Series

VOLUME 12

The titles published in this series are listed at *brill.com/asla*

Courts and Diversity

Twenty Years of the Constitutional Court of Indonesia

Edited by

Bertus de Villiers, Saldi Isra and Pan Mohamad Faiz

BRILL | NIJHOFF

LEIDEN | BOSTON

Library of Congress Cataloging-in-Publication Data

Names: De Villiers, B. (Bertus), editor. | Isra, Saldi, editor. | Faiz, Pan Mohamad, editor.
Title: Courts and diversity : twenty years of the constitutional court of Indonesia / edited by Bertus de Villiers, Saldi Isra, and Pan Mohamad Faiz.
Description: Leiden ; Boston : Brill/Nijhoff, 2024. | Series: Brill's Asian law series, 2214-6547 ; volume 12 | Includes index.
Identifiers: LCCN 2024001520 (print) | LCCN 2024001521 (ebook) | ISBN 9789004691681 (hardback) | ISBN 9789004691698 (ebook)
Subjects: LCSH: Constitutional courts–Indonesia. | Indonesia. Mahkamah Konstitusi. | Cultural pluralism.
Classification: LCC KNW2620 .C68 2024 (print) | LCC KNW2620 (ebook) | DDC 347.598/035–dc23/eng/20240129
LC record available at https://lccn.loc.gov/2024001520
LC ebook record available at https://lccn.loc.gov/2024001521

Typeface for the Latin, Greek, and Cyrillic scripts: "Brill". See and download: brill.com/brill-typeface.

ISSN 2214-6547
ISBN 978-90-04-69168-1 (hardback)
ISBN 978-90-04-69169-8 (e-book)
DOI 10.1163/9789004691698

This book is printed on acid-free paper and produced in a sustainable manner.

Contents

Figures, Maps and Tables

Figures

Maps

Tables

Notes on Contributors

Yance Arizona

is a lecturer at the Department of Constitutional Law, Universitas Gadjah Mada, Indonesia. He accomplished his PhD studies the Van Vollenhoven Institute for Law, Governance and Society, Leiden University, the Netherlands. Prior to his PhD, Yance obtained a master's in constitutional law from the University of Indonesia and Master of Arts from International Institute for the Sociology of Law, Spain. He has published many articles regarding the constitution, agrarian and natural resources, and indigenous communities' rights in Indonesia. Currently, he is the chair of the Centre for Democracy, Constitution and Human Rights at the Faculty of Law, Universitas Gadjah Mada.

George Barrie

is Emeritus Professor of the University of Johannesburg. Previously he was State Advocate of the High Court of South Africa; Senior Law Adviser of the Department of Foreign Affairs; Dean of the Faculty of Law of the Rand Afrikaans University and a Visiting Professor at the Free University of Brussels. From 1995 to 1999 he served on the National Advisory Council of Correctional Services. He is the author of *Topical International Law* and numerous articles in legal journals. He was on the International Advisory Board of the *South African Journal of International Law*.

Bisariyadi

is a researcher at the Constitutional Court of the Republic of Indonesia who assists judges at the Court and conducts research to help the Judge in dealing with constitutional cases. Bisar has spent fifteen years at the Court soon after graduating from Law School at Universitas Indonesia for his Bachelor degree (2003). During his years at the Court, he was awarded a scholarship to have a Master of Laws at Melbourne University (2010). Bisar is also keen to write and publish scholarly articles on constitutional and human rights issues. His essays published in nationally accredited Law Reviews as well as a number of short pieces as a contributor in the Court's monthly bulletin. He manages a compilation of his writing where you can read and download from bisariyadi.wordpress. com. He is available for writing and research projects. You can reach him at bisariyadi@mahkamahkonstitusi.go.id.

Ann Black
is a Professor of Law at the TC Beirne School of Law, The University of Queensland, Australia, and Executive Director (Comparative Law) of its Centre for Public, International and Comparative Law. Her research analyses the intersection of law, religion and secularism, including the operation of Sharia in the Sultanate of Brunei Darussalam and in secular Australia. In addition to journal articles and chapters, her publications include *Modern Perspective of Islamic Law* (with Nadir Hosen & Hossein Esmaeili), *Law and Legal Institutions of Asia* (with Gary Bell) and *Religious Freedom in Secular States* (with Jahid Hossain Bhuiyan).

Miriam Cohen
is an Associate Professor and Canada Research Chair on Human Rights and International Reparative Justice at Université de Montréal Faculty of Law. She is the award-winning author of "Realizing Reparative Justice for International Crimes: From Theory to Practice" (Cambridge University Press), recipient of the 2022 Scholarly Book Award of the Canadian Council on International Law and the First Prize of the Legal Competition of the Quebec Bar Foundation. Dr. Cohen is the founder of the *Human Rights and International Justice Laboratory*, funded by the *Canada Foundation for Innovation* (CFI) and the *Government of Quebec*. She has previously worked in legal advisory roles at the International Court of Justice and the International Criminal Court, and she has appeared as Counsel before the International Tribunal for the Law of the Sea and the Supreme Court of Canada. Recipient of several awards, fellowships and grants, including major research grants from the *Social Sciences and Humanities Research Council of Canada* (SSHRC), Dr. Cohen is the author of over 40 papers and monographs on human rights and international law published in English, French, Portuguese and Spanish, in leading law journals and books around the world. She holds graduate degrees from Harvard Law School, Cambridge University, Université de Montréal and Leiden University, where she obtained her PhD in international law. She is both an international lawyer (member of the Quebec Bar) and an accredited mediator.

Pan Mohamad Faiz
is a Constitutional Law Expert. He works as a Senior Expert Assistant to Justice at the Indonesian Constitutional Court. Faiz received his Doctor of Philosophy in Constitutional Law from TC Beirne School of Law, the University of Queensland, Australia. Currently, he lectures in constitutional law on Legal Theory, Law and Constitution, Comparative Constitutional Law, Constitutional Court, Procedural Law of the Constitutional Court, and Election

Dispute Resolutions at several universities, among others, the University of Brawijaya, Universitas Gadjah Mada, and the University of Indonesia. Faiz is also an External Research Fellow at the Center for Public, International and Comparative Law at the University of Queensland. Faiz serves as Secretary of the Research and Publication Department at the Association of Constitutional Law and State Administrative Law Lecturers, and Coordinator at the Association of Indonesian Legal Journal Management. In addition, Faiz has attended professional training in the ProCuria Program for Legal Officers from The Hague University of Applied Science, The Netherlands (2017) and Leadership in Court Governance from the Singapore Judicial College (2017). He also passed the Education and Training Program for Researchers (Advanced Level) held by the Indonesian Institute of Sciences (LIPI). Faiz is also known for his academic writings on legal and constitutional issues that have become references for many law students and academics. Currently, Faiz is the Editor-in-Chief of *Constitutional Review*, a Scopus-indexed international journal published by the Center for Research and Case Analysis of the Indonesian Constitutional Court.

Robert Shenton French AC

served as Chief Justice of Australia from 1 September 2008 until 29 January 2017. He is a graduate of the University of Western Australia in science and law. He served as a Judge of the Federal Court of Australia from November 1986 until his appointment as Chief Justice of the High Court on 1 September 2008. Since his retirement as Chief Justice, Mr French has been appointed as a Non-Permanent Justice of the Hong Kong Court of Final Appeal (May 2017), as an International Judge of the Singapore International Commercial Court (January 2018) and as a Judge of the Court of Appeal of the Dubai International Financial Centre (June 2019). He was elected as Chancellor of the University of Western Australia in December 2017.

Saldi Isra

is a Constitutional Law Professor at the Faculty of Law of Andalas University in Padang, West Sumatra, and the Deputy Chief Justice of the Constitutional Court of Indonesia. Prior to his appointment to the Constitutional Court in 2017, he was Director of the Center for Constitutional Studies (PUSaKO) at the Faculty of Law of Andalas University from 2005–2017. He chaired the Faculty of Law's Doctoral Program from 2011–2016. Saldi is a prolific writer, having contributed more than 600 articles to Indonesian national newspapers, including the *Kompas* daily, *Media Indonesia* and *The Jakarta Post*. He is the author of over 20 books and some 50 articles published in national and international scientific journals. His international academic activities have included: External

Examiner for Ph.D. in Law at Maastricht University (December 2017); Constitutional Dialogue at the State Administrative Tribunal in Perth in collaboration with Curtin University, Germany's Max Planck Foundation and Andalas University (Australia, March 2017); Participant in the Joint Study for Legislative Practice in Japan (Osaka, February 2017); Joint Study on Legislation in the Netherlands (November 2016); Visiting Scholar at Gakushuin University (Tokyo, October 2011); Participant in Rule of Law Forum in Dallas, Washington and New York (USA, September–October 2009); Chevening Fellowship at University of Birmingham (UK, January–April 2006); Participant in Law and Governance in Developing Countries at Van Vollenhoven Institute Faculty of Law, Leiden University, (September–December 2003); and Researcher of the Indonesian-Netherlands Studies on Decentralization of the Indonesian Rechtsstaat in collaboration with several Indonesian universities and the Van Vollenhoven Institute of Leiden University (2003–2007).

Tove H. Malloy
is a Professor of European Studies at the Europa-Universität Flensburg, Germany, and an External Lecturer at Roskilde University, Denmark. She formerly served as the Director of the European Centre for Minority Issues in Flensburg, Germany, and was a member of the Council of Europe's Advisory Committee on the Framework Convention for the Protection of National Minorities, where she was elected Gender Equality Rapporteur (2011–2018). Her background is in political theory, specializing in the political and legal aspects of national and ethnic minority rights in international relations and international law, particularly in the European context. She is the author of *National Minority Rights in Europe* (OUP, 2005) and has co-edited a number of volumes on minority rights protection and non-territorial autonomy as well as two textbooks. She serves as consultant with the Council of Europe, the OSCE and the Raoul Wallenberg Institute. She holds a PhD in Government from Essex University, UK.

I D.G. Palguna
is an expert in international law and constitutional law. He is presently a lecturer at the Faculty of Law of Udayana University in Bali (Indonesia), where he also lectures at the Notary Masters Program, the Masters in Government Law Program and the Doctoral Program at the Postgraduate School. He served as a member of the Election Supervisory Committee for Bali Province in Indonesia's historic 1999 general election and in the same year he was elected by the Bali Provincial Legislative Assembly as one of Bali's Regional Representatives in the People's Consultative Assembly (MPR). At the MPR, he first served as Secretary

of the Ad Hoc Committee II of the MPR Working Committee (1999–2000) and then became a member of the Ad Hoc Committee I (2000–2002), which was tasked with drafting amendments to Indonesia's 1945 Constitution. In 2003, a year before the expiration of his term as a member of the MPR, he was elected as one of three justices appointed by the House of Representatives to Indonesia's newly formed Constitutional Court. Thus, he became part of the nine-member bench for the Constitutional Court's first period (2003–2008). Later, after a gap of six years, he was again selected as a Constitutional Justice (2015–2020), this time as one of three justices chosen by the President. Palguna has authored numerous books, including *Pengaduan Konstitusional: Upaya Hukum terhadap Pelanggaran Hak-hak Konstitusional Warga Negara* (*Constitutional Complaint: Legal Remedies for Violations of Citizens' Constitutional Rights*, 2013), *Mahkamah Konstitusi dan Dinamika Politik Hukum di Indonesia* (*The Constitutional Court and Political Dynamics of Law in Indonesia*, 2020).

Nico Steytler
is the Director of the Community Law Center at the University of the Western Cape, a research and advocacy institute that works to uphold the democratic values and human rights outlined in South Africa's Constitution. He has been actively involved in the development of the new constitutional order over the past decade. He served as a technical advisor to the Constitutional Assembly during the drafting of the 1996 Constitution (1995–1996) and advised the Western Cape Provincial Legislature on the development of a provincial constitution (1996–1997). In recognition of his contributions, he was appointed the South African Research Chair in Multi-Level Government, Law and Policy by the National Research Foundation (2013–2017). His primary research focus lies in intergovernmental relations and local government. His research interests are Constitutional design and the multi-level government system, comparative federalism, and local government.

Bertus de Villiers
is a Visiting Professor of the Law School of the University of Johannesburg and a Member of the State Administrative Tribunal of Western Australia. He is a Fellow of the Alexander von Humboldt Stiftung (Germany). He specializes in the areas of minority and indigenous rights, decentralization, human rights, and land reform. Professor De Villiers has undertaken research and lectured on constitutional and political developments in various countries, including Ethiopia, Sudan, South Sudan, Indonesia, and the Philippines. He received in 2016 the Alexander von Humboldt Stiftung award for *Innovative Research Networking*. During his career, Prof. De Villiers contributed to the South African

constitution drafting process by providing advice and research. He also served on the Commission for the Demarcation of the Provinces. In recent years, he has been cooperating with the Constitutional Court of Indonesia since 2017 as a visiting academic. His most recent works include *Indigenous Rights in the Modern Era – Regaining What Has Been Lost* (Brill, 2023); *Navigating the Unknown – Essays on Selected Case Studies about the Rights of Minorities* (Brill, 2022); and as co-editor of *Litigating the Rights of Minorities and Indigenous Peoples in Domestic and International Courts* (Brill, 2021).

Christie S. Warren
is Professor of the Practice of International and Comparative Law and Director of the Center for Comparative Legal Studies & Post-Conflict Peacebuilding at William & Mary Law School. Her areas of expertise include Comparative Law, Comparative Constitutional Law, Post-Conflict Justice and the Rule of Law, Public International Law, International Human Rights Law and Islamic Law. She has designed, implemented, monitored and assessed academic, constitutional, judicial and legal development and training projects in more than 58 countries throughout Africa, Central and East Asia, Latin America and the Caribbean, Central and Eastern Europe, the Middle East, Russia and the Newly Independent States, the Balkans and East Timor. Her research and publications are in the fields of Comparative Constitutional Law, Post-Conflict Reconstruction and Islamic Law. Warren served as the 1998–1999 Supreme Court Fellow at the Supreme Court of the United States and the 2010 Senior Expert in Constitutional Issues on the Mediation Support Unit Standby Team within the United Nations Department of Political Affairs. She was named the 2016–2017 Fulbright-Schuman Distinguished Chair at the European University Institute in Florence, Italy and served as a 2019 Visiting Professor of Constitutional Law at the Universidad Autónoma de Madrid and a 2021 Visiting Professor of International Law at Sapienza University in Rome. She is the recipient of the Administration of Justice Award from the Supreme Court Fellows Alumni Association, given "In Recognition of Significant Contributions to the International Administration of Justice."

CHAPTER 1

Constitutionalism and Diversity: Setting the Scene

Bertus de Villiers

Abstract

This chapter introduces the theme transformative constitutionalism and the role of highest courts to utilise constitutional provisions to transform society into greater fairness and equality. The challenges faced by emerging or aspiring democracies differ to those of established democracies, but a commonality often shared is the role of the highest court to adjudicate disputes under the banner of constitutionalism. Constitutionalism requires the highest court to be independent and to function without fear or threat of interference by government. Governments are often reluctant to submit to the authority of the highest court when contentious judgements are handed down. The chapter speaks about the highest court being a protection against government interference, but also the risk of it becoming an agent of government. Reference is made to transformative judgements in South Africa, the USA, Germany, and Australia. In the case of Indonesia, the Constitutional Court has become a keystone in the transformation of the country. A fine balance is sought since Indonesia is so complex in terms of population composition, legal plurality, and geographical size. Caution is expressed that the transformative role of the courts does not end with laudable, transformative judgements but little practical effect. The impacts of judgements are ultimately assessed by the practical change they bring to society.

Keywords

post-conflict societies – constitutionalism – transformative – noken – decentralisation – native title – Mabo – law of diversity – bundestreue – ubuntu – indigenous rights – free – prior and informed consent – Pancasila – democratisation

The 20th anniversary of a constitutional court is a major milestone for any country. In modern, liberal democratic governance, constitutionalism has become a vital aspect of political practices since the seminal judgement of the Supreme Court of the United States in Marbury v Madison.[1] The notion of constitutionalism reinforces the supremacy of the law, with the highest court declaring the law, and renders parliament and government to the constitution subservient to the constitution. It is *the* essential ingredient for contemporary democratic theory and practice. Achieving majoritarian government through the popular vote is relatively simple, but for a majority to accept and abide by the independence of the judiciary and the supremacy of the constitution is often a bridge too far for young and emerging democracies. In this respect, Warren provides an insightful overview of some of the challenges experienced by constitutional courts in post-conflict societies. Introducing constitutionalism requires a deep consensus and legitimacy, as well as maturity and respect by each organ of government for the responsibilities of other organs and the separation of powers. A common denominator shared by aspiring democracies and established democracies is that the independence of the judiciary is an essential requirement for constitutionalism and democratic stability. The judiciary can on the one hand be a sword to defend freedom and a bulwark against governmental excess and abuse of powers, but on the other hand the judiciary can also become a pawn in the hands of a majority and hence an instrument to perpetuate the dominance of minorities.

The Constitutional Court of Indonesia is a prime example of what is referred to in literature as 'transformative constitutionalism'. By using the principles contained in the Constitution, the Court has not only provided guidance to the nation, but has also encouraged tolerance, recognised the rights of indigenous people, celebrated civil liberties, steered through challenging circumstances, and transformed Indonesian society. The following chapters highlight some of the Court's essential judgements in response to the diversity of Indonesia, which ranges from the composition of the population, to different faiths, interactions between secular and religious society, conflict between modernism and custom, and the protection of individual rights vis-a-vis community demands and interests.

As Steytler explains, Indonesia's asymmetrical approach to the decentralisation of powers and functions to regional and local governments brought about unique challenges to the Constitutional Court to develop uniform standards, whilst at the same time allowing for pragmatism and asymmetry in its decentralisation. In a similar vein, the recognition of *noken* (a local method for casting votes in parts of Papua), as discussed by De Villiers, is comparable in its impact to the recognition of native title in the seminal Mabo judgement

1 Marbury, Marbury v. Madison, 5 U.S. (1 Cranch) 137 (1803), (1803).

in Australia. Black highlights how the demands to manage respect for faith and secularism have been addressed, while Barrie, Cohen and Arizona reflect on the competing demands for access to land. The Constitutional Court has played a leading and transformative role in assisting Indonesian society to respond to the complexity of these issues. Although the journey of constitutionalism and transformation embarked upon by the Constitutional Court is ongoing, two decades of operations is a laudable achievement.

For young and emerging democracies, 20 years of judicial independence signifies a major step of maturity. The ideals of constitutionalism and the rule of law are terms that are often heard during liberation struggles and civil war as an ideal, but to achieve and sustain those ideals *after* a transition, is a major feat. This is because the very might that gave rise to the overthrow of a despotic system, must as an outcome of the transition to constitutionalism bow the knee to constitutional supremacy and the independence of the judiciary. Such a transition is not as simple as it may seem in theoretic discourse. The supremacy of the law, and the credibility and legitimacy that flow from it, are essential elements to solidify a liberal democracy, but many aspiring democracies stumble at this hurdle. Warren explains how some constitutional courts have been activist, whilst others have been mindful of potential political interference and therefore failed to discharge their duties as guardians of the constitution and the rule of law. She also emphasises that the creation and functioning of a constitutional court must be assessed within context and the demands placed on a particular society at a particular time. In this regard, she refers to Sachs, who has noted that the nature and impact of a judgement may be seen purely technical or profoundly transformative, depending on the topic and the circumstances.

The past two decades of constitutionalism in Indonesia demonstrate what can be achieved if there is political will, leadership, public support, and intellectual capacity to attain the goal of judicial independence. However, the judiciary alone cannot transform a society, nor can it be the sole defender of democratic norms, standards, and fundamental rights. Comparative experiences have shown that the judiciary's independence can only be effective if each organ of government discharges its functions properly in accordance with the constitution. Only when the legislature, executive, and judiciary cooperate and respect each other's functions can the governmental system serve the interests of the people. The doctrine of separation of powers, as discussed by Isra and Faiz, embodies the importance of respecting the responsibilities of each organ of government, while recognising the common obligation to serve the people in discharging their functions. In this regard, Malloy's proposal on the notion of non-territorial autonomy and what she calls the Law of Diversity is noteworthy. She emphasises that the Law of Diversity requires greater pragmatism, a plurality of legal resources, and negotiation of content within the context of each nation. She refers to different case studies to highlight that the accommodation of diversity is not solely a matter for the individual rights debate, but may also require arrangements that allow for the collective exercise of rights to ensure democratic stability and legitimacy. The recognition of *noken* by the Constitutional Court could be seen as a reflection of Malloy's proposes. As explained by De Villiers, at face value there is little constitutional justification for the application of *noken* in elections, and yet the Constitutional Court accepted the cultural practice for voting purposes, despite the disenfranchisement of individuals living under the *noken* system.

However, the courts have limitations in their functions. This can be frustrating for the population, as the courts are often seen as the most responsive organ of government to address concerns of minorities. Emerging democracies often experience a plethora of litigation since the courts are perceived as more accessible than the political process. Issues that are dealt with by way of popular debate, policy development and legislation in established democracies often become the topic of litigation in emerging democracies.[2] But therein lies the dilemma. Courts cannot create work, build houses, clean the environment, or bring peace to violent ethnic or religious conflicts. The courts are part of a team, which includes the executive and the legislature, as well as an active civil society and free media. The courts in emerging democracies often find themselves in what Klug calls 'lawfare' as they are seen as the principal or perhaps only organ to which minority interests can resort to defend their rights against a majority or to achieve certain policy outcomes.[3] But all societal ills cannot be cured with litigation. One can agree with the observation that the 'interests of the disadvantaged cannot only be advanced through successful litigation ... courts need the cooperation of both the legislature and the executive in order to ensure respect for their decision' (Gargarella, Domingo, and Roux 2006, 273). Judicial power, in the wrong hands, can become a barricade to freedom, whilst judicial power in the right hands can be applied with surgical

2 Note for example the litigation in India pursuant to the Directive Principles of State Policy aimed at bringing greater equity and fairness to the poor, homeless and workers. Bertus De Villiers, "Directive Principles of State Policy and Fundamental Rights: The Indian Experience," *South African Journal on Human Rights* 8 (1992): 29–49.

3 H. Klug, "Towards a Sociology of Constitutional Transformation: Understanding South Africa's Post-Apartheid Constitutonal Order" (Legal Studies Research Paper Series No. 1373, Wisconsin Law School, 2016). https://papers.ssrn.com/sol3/papers.cfm?abstract_id=2729460.

precision in the service of individual and minority freedoms and rights. Albie Sachs comments how in South Africa, the judiciary had moved from being a barricade to freedom under *apartheid,* to a transformative institution that represents freedom under the new Constitution. He puts it as follows:

> And far from the law constituting a barricade of injustice that had to be stormed and torn down for freedom to be achieved [under *apartheid*], it became the primary instrument accomplishing a peaceful revolution [under the new constitution].[4]

Transformation is therefore best achieved if, and when, all parts of the team work in unison. In the absence of strong institutions and an active civil society, the demanding role placed on the judiciary to effect change is however often undermined by a 'bottleneck' of weak policy implementation.[5] Courts may hand down judgements that are poetic and reflect the most noble principles, but if those judgements do not translate into practically enforceable policies and implementation, the spectre of ivory tower-judgements prevails. Ultimately, the 'judiciary cannot substitute policy making through political institutions'.[6]

The transformative role of the courts therefore does not end with laudable, transformative judgements. The impacts of judgements are ultimately assessed by the practical change they bring to society. Therein lies the challenge. South Africa, which is universally applauded for its liberal, socially responsible and equitable constitution, its peaceful transition, and particularly the independence of its Constitutional Court and the transformative role of the Court, suffers some of the starkest inequality, poverty, corruption, and crime in the world.[7] Regardless of the recognition of social and economic rights in the South African Constitution, ground-breaking judgements on social rights such as in the Grootboom-case,[8] and the use of the notion of Ubuntu to give content to fundamental

---

4 A. Sachs, *The Strange Alchemy of Life and Law* (London: Oxford University Press, 2009), 2–3.

5 A. Von Bogdandy et al., "Ius Constitutionale Commune En America Latina: A Regional Approach to Transformative Constitutionalism" (MPIL Research Paper Series, Heidelberg, MPIL, 2016), 9.

6 Ibid., 11.

7 Gini Index, "Gini Index (World Bank Estimate) South Africa," Washington DC, World Bank, 2022, https://worldpopulationreview.com/country-rankings/gini-coefficient-by-country.

8 Grootboom-case, Government of the Republic of South Africa and Others v. Grootboom and Others (CCT11/00) [2000] ZACC 19; 2001 (1) SA 46; 2000 (11) BCLR 1169 (4 October 2000) (2000).

rights,[9] the country's socio-economic realities and widespread corruption at a scale described as 'state capture',[10] are a drag on transformation and reduce and erode the effectiveness of court judgements. The same challenges are faced by many other emerging and young democracies, including Indonesia.

The judiciary is tasked to turn the sterile words of a constitution into reality. The judiciary fills in the gaps; it identifies implied terms; and it gives direction. It is a life-giving task. There is, of course, a fine balance to be struck between a judiciary giving life to a constitution that reflects the values and aspirations of the society it serves, and a judiciary that pursues its own social-policy agenda and, in the process, loses track of its core functions, its duty towards its people, its obligation to uphold the constitution, its obligation to respect its own limited powers, and in doing so exceeds its powers and encroaches on the separation of powers. As is explained by Palguna, Isra and Faiz, the Constitutional Court of Indonesia must operate within a highly pluralistic environment that accommodates and reflects the country's cultural, religious and regional diversity, recognising the rights of indigenous people and accommodating minorities.[11]

The highest courts have transformed many nations, for example the abolition of the doctrine of separate but equal education in the USA,[12] the endorsement of *Bundestreue* as an essential value for cooperative federalism in Germany (BVerfGE 1 56), the use of directive principles of state policy to give content to fundamental rights in India,[13] the abolition of capital punishment in South Africa,[14] and the recognition of the *noken* indigenous electoral system in Indonesia.[15] Barrie reflects on universal standards concerning consultation

---

9 Bertus De Villiers, "Does a Constitution Have a Soul? The Role of Bundestreue in Germany and Ubuntu in South Africa to Give Life and Identity to a Constitutional Text," in *Navigating the Unknown – Essays on Selected Case Studies about the Rights of Minorities* (Leiden: Brill, 2022), 163–214.

10 R.M.M. Zondo, "Judicial Commission of Inquiry into Allegations of State Capture, Corruption and Fraud in the Public Sector Including Organs of State" (Pretoria: Judicial Commission, 2022), https://www.statecapture.org.za/site/files/announcements/649/Judicial_Commission_of_Inquiry_into_State_Capture_Report_Part_3-1.pdf.

11 Bertus De Villiers, Saldi Isra, and Z. Mochtar, "Asymmetry in a Decentralised, Unitary State: Lessons to Be Drawn from the Experiences of Decentralisation to the Special Regions of Indonesia," *Journal on Ethnopolitics and Minority Issues in Europe* 18 (2019): 43–71.

12 Brown-case, Brown v. Board of Education, 347 U.S. 483 (1954) (SC 1954).

13 Chandra Bhawan-case, Chandra Bhawan Boarding and Lodging Bangalore v. The State of Mysore 1970 SCR 600 (1970).

14 Makwanyane-case, S v. Makwanyane 1995 3 SA 391 (CC) (1995).

15 Noken-case, Constitutional Court No 47-18 / PHPU.A / VII / 2009 (Constitutional Court 2009). Whilst some critics view the recognition of the noken-system in Papua as 'incompatible' with the Constitution and contemporary democratic norms (T.

with indigenous people when activities are embarked upon that affect their traditional lands. Considering developments in international law and practice, he examines the concept of free, prior and informed consent (FPIC). He poses the question whether FPIC has evolved into a principle of international customary law, and if not, what the standards of consultation it implies. Barrie applies these international law developments to consultation practices in Indonesia and concludes that the country's jurisprudence on consultation obligations with indigenous people is consistent with jurisprudence arising from Australia, Canada, the Americas and southern Africa. Additionally, Cohen and Arizona demonstrate how the Constitutional Court has recognised the plurality of legal systems in Indonesia, particularly in the area of the right to land and recognition of traditional laws and customs.

Judiciaries often test the balance of societal and constitutional tolerance. Albie Sachs writes as follows:

> In an open and democratic society, political compromise based on the principle of give-and-take rather than the idea of winner-takes-all, was to be applauded. Yet judges were unsuited to take decisions on houses, hospitals, schools, and electricity. They just did not have the know-how and the capacity to handle those questions. But judges did know about human dignity, about oppression and about things that reduced a human being to a status below that which a democratic society would regard as tolerable.[16]

Efriandi, O. Couwenberg, and R.L. Holzhacker, "The Noken System and the Challenge of Democratic Governance at the Periphery," in *Challenges of Governance: Development and Regional Integration in Southeast Asia*, ed. R.L. Holzhacker and W.G.Z. Tan (Springer, 2021), 68.), the Constitutional Court has described it as an essential element of cultural pluralism without which conflict may arise at a local level (Noken-case 2009; Noken-case 2015, 14). Pamungkas describes the Noken system as a 'bridge' between traditional and modern political systems (C. Pamungkas, "Noken Electoral System in Papua: Deliberative Democracy in Papuan Tradition," *Jurnal Masyarakat and Budaya* 19 (2017): 220.). Yunus suggests that the noken system is comparable to the Electoral College system in the United States (A. Yunus, "Multilayered Democracy in Papua: A Comparison of "Noken" System and Electoral College System in the United States," *Hasanuddin Law Review* 6 (2020): 232–39.). The noken-system has given rise to polarising descriptions, for example, on the one hand, that it should be abolished; that it causes manipulation of votes; and that it conflicts with the democratic principles of the Constitution; whilst on the other hand that it is a bridge between traditional and modernity; that it is consistent with the plurality of Indonesia; that it encourages local involvement and participation; and that it recognises indigenous law and customs. For a more detailed discussion see chapter by De Villiers below.

16 Sachs, *The Strange Alchemy of Life and Law*, 170–71.

The composition, powers, and functions of the judiciary, especially the highest court, often resemble a tug of war in post-conflict societies. The design of governance institutions, including the judicial system, in deeply divided and heterogenous societies remains a challenge. The constitutional drafting process is often a shot in the dark.[17] This is illustrated by Isra and Faiz in their analysis of the time it took for the Indonesian Constitutional Court to come into being. The creation of a constitutional court, as Warren highlights, must be supported by a broad consensus to ensure the independence of the court. Essential questions that need to be addressed relate to the powers and functions of the constitutional court, the appointment of judges, and perhaps the most controversial issue: the recall of judges. Isra and Faiz explain how justices of the Constitutional Court can be recalled, and whilst this option may have political merit, it is likely to inhibit the confidence by which justices perform their functions. However, the art of political compromise in Indonesia demanded that the concern about justices not being accountable be balanced with the possibility of recall.

Despite the progress made in international law, comparative constitutional law and political science, including measures to protect the rights of individuals, minorities and indigenous people, the design of institutions for a particular country remains imbued with risk, challenges, and uncertainty. Comparative constitutional law often looks retrospectively at past events, with experts eloquently analysing the reasons for the success or failure of constitutions and governmental systems. However, the same science is weak when it comes to looking prospectively to determine what will work and what will fail in a particular country. Institutional design remains a mixture of guesswork and hope. So much depends on the subjective circumstances and leadership of countries. A case in point is South Africa: without the leadership of Nelson Mandela, F.W. De Klerk and Desmond Tutu, the door to the 1996 settlement may not have opened, and without the subsequent commitment to uphold the settlement and the independence of the Constitutional Court, the door on democratisation may have closed abruptly. Recent events in the Russian Federation show how a democratisation process that started with much promise in the early 1990s under Gorbachev has lost its track. The same can be said about the challenges to democratisation processes in Hungary, Poland, South Sudan, Ethiopia, the Maldives, Sri Lanka, and many other young, emerging, and aspiring democracies. Several emerging democracies arising from the

17 Bertus De Villiers, "The Design of Institutions in Response to Diversity: A Shot in the Dark or a Fine Art?" in *Navigating the Unknown – Essays on Selected Case Studies about the Rights of Minorities* (Leiden: Brill, 2022), 1–37.

post-1990 democratisation wave[18] have been faltering. The outcome of democratisation is never guaranteed. Likewise, the independence of the judiciary is not a given.

Indonesia commenced its independence journey in 1945 with great hope, but it soon experienced similar challenges as many young and emerging democracies. Since 1945, Indonesia has had four constitutions, commencing with liberal democracy, then reverting to authoritarianism, then again to liberal democracy, and finally (so one hopes) to stable liberal democracy. Isra and Faiz provide insight into the complexity Indonesia faced to complete the democratic transition. It therefore took some time for the Constitutional Court, which was foreshadowed in the constitution-drafting process but only established in 2003, to find its voice. Continuous commitment to trustworthy leadership will be required for that voice to retain its strength, independence and credibility. Isra and Faiz shed light on the longwinded process to establish the Constitutional Court and the rationale for establishing a separate constitutional court rather than integrating its functions with the Supreme Court. Most of the chapters in this book highlight unique aspects of the jurisprudence emanating from the Constitutional Court.

The Constitutional Court of Indonesia functions within a family of constitutional courts internationally. Warren highlights how justices of these courts interact in international forums, exchange ideas, develop themes, and exert informal influence upon each other. This is not limited to emerging or young constitutional courts. The Mabo judgement in Australia was profoundly influenced by events in international law. In essence, courts learn from each other and share knowledge. Whilst the Indonesian Constitutional Court has often referred to international jurisprudence during its 20-year tenure, the Court has also contributed to the body of jurisprudence on diversity that is available to the global community. As highlighted by De Villiers, the approach adopted by the Court in regard to recognition of *noken* is unique and merits further review and analysis by courts where modernity intersects with traditionalism. Steytler also demonstrates how asymmetry has allowed the Court to accommodate the diversity of traditional systems of governance while still adhering to national norms of accountability and representation. The Constitutional Court is, however, still in a process of 'consolidation'.[19]

---

18 S.P. Huntington, "Democracy's Third Wave," *Journal of Democracy* Spring (1991): 12–34.

19 Rudy, R. Perdana, and R. Wijaya, "The Recognition of Customary Rights by Indonesian Constitutional Court," *Academic Journal for Interdisciplinary Studies* 10 (2021): 310.

The principle of Pancasila has been an underlying feature of the Indonesian democratisation process, akin to the use of the word *Ubuntu* in South Africa.[20] Pancasila is a non-defined, value-laden principle that refers to belief in God, a civilized and just humanity, nationalism, democracy and social justice.[21] While the Indonesian Constitutional Court does not often rely on Pancasila in resolving disputes, unlike the South African Constitutional Court's reliance on *Ubuntu*, there is however a risk that such an undefined principle can become ideologized and a mechanism to enforce artificial unity or conformity. It is not surprising that the term has been described as a double-edged sword since it embodies a deeply held respect for pluralism, whilst it may also be used as a mechanism of control. Black highlights the role of the concept Pancasila in Indonesian society and how it has impacted on the reasoning of the Constitutional Court. She demonstrates how Indonesia has sought to find a balance between the demands of a secular state, a state in which freedom of religion is respected, and a state where the Islamic faith is predominant. She discusses judgements of the Constitutional Court in which a balance between seemingly competing objectives is sought, including through the recognition of traditional beliefs. She also shows that as a guardian of the Constitution, the Constitutional Court has played a pivotal role in ensuring that national legislation complies with constitutionally guaranteed rights and freedoms. In a nation where belief in Almighty God is a pre-eminent constitutional tenet, the Constitutional Court is called on to uphold the religious and spiritual rights of all Indonesians, whether Muslim, followers of the other five recognised religions, or animism believers. Guided by the unifying spirit of the Pancasila, the Constitutional Court has adopted an integrative approach.

International events teach us that even in the oldest of democracies, the political pressures on courts sometimes become unbearable, risking the court becoming a player in a disruptive political game. The appointment and recall processes of justices of a constitutional court often become more political as the review powers of the court widen. Recent experiences in the United States regarding the Supreme Court's judgements on gun control, abortion, and other social issues, highlight how easily the highest court can be drawn into a mire of political debate, both during the appointment process and, if a recall is possible, during the circumstances leading to the removal of a justice. The Constitutional Court of Indonesia is not immune to these challenges, and

---

20 De Villiers, "Does a Constitution Have a Soul?".

21 H.P. Wiratraman and D.A.H. Shah, "Indonesia's Constitutional Responses to Plurality," in *Pluralism Constitutions in Southeast Asia*, ed. J.L. Neo and B. Ngoc Son (London: Hart Publishing, 2019), 118.

it will in time also be exposed to political pressures and other challenges to its independence and authority. The possibility of recalling justices may not only lead to abuse, it may also prevent justices from fulfilling their duties properly. On the other hand, there may be reasonable concerns that justices may become detached from society due to a lack of accountability. The real test for young democracies is how they deal with and respond to the independence of their judiciary, and how the judiciary applies its own powers.

Indonesia is a kaleidoscope of humanity and diversity, facing numerous challenges, such as colonial history, population diversity, vast territory, religious diversity, poverty, unemployment, traditional and modern governmental systems, and more. Palguna provides valuable insight into the scope and depth of Indonesia's diversity, which in many respects resembles the face of many nations, and yet functions under a single constitution amid shared patriotism. Indonesia contains within its boundaries all the challenges that many modern democracies must scale, including radicalism and fundamentalism, competition for limited resources, climate change, and a struggle between the ideals of the rule of law and populism. With around 300 ethnic and linguistic groups, a population of over 270 million, six major religions plus many traditional beliefs, and a territory spread over more than 17,000 islands, Indonesia is more diverse than the entire European continent. And each of those European democracies is experiencing its unique challenges that plurality of population brings.[22] Indonesia in many respects embodies the fears, hopes, challenges, and aspirations of humanity. The Constitutional Court is required to resolve disputes within this kaleidoscope of diversity and plurality with flexibility, pragmatism, asymmetry, and wisdom. Whilst national minimum norms are important for nation-building, recognition of local customs, diversities and indigenous systems are equally important to protect the territorial integrity of Indonesia and ensure local peace and stability. The Constitutional Court, which is expected to represent the unity of Indonesia, operates in a highly

22 A comparison between institutional arrangements in Indonesia and those in the 27 or more states of the European continent highlights the limitations of comparative analysis. Whilst constitutional theorists tend to analyse and comment on the Indonesian system as a single constitutional arrangement and then expect uniformity of institutions across the vast nation, in Europe there are 27 constitutions with many sub-arrangements to provide for the rights of ethnocultural minorities. Those sub-arrangements include specialised electoral systems; quotas; local autonomies; special power-sharing arrangements; advisory bodies; collective rights; and special funding – all aimed at the protection of ethnocultural minorities. One should therefore not be surprised if in Indonesia there is asymmetry, pragmatism and accommodation of unique regional and local arrangements that reflect the diversity of the nation.

diverse, pluralist, and decentralised society where a one-size-fits-all approach may lead to centrifugal forces that threaten the very unity the Court is supposed to symbolise. Therefore, the asymmetry referred to by Malloy applies not only to self-governing arrangements within the context of public law, but also to asymmetry in regard to the multitude of local laws and customs adhered to by Indonesians at a societal level. Whilst non-territorial autonomy in the context of public law arrangements may not be suitable to all of Indonesia's diversities, the concept is applicable in civil and private fields whereby communities are allowed to manage their own affairs through their traditional laws and customs.

The progress made by Indonesia in democratisation, particularly in the functioning of the Constitutional Court, is often overlooked by international constitutional and political studies due to the relative lack of comparative works on the Court's jurisprudence. Language barriers further complicate the matter, making it difficult for experts in comparative law to gain insight into Indonesian jurisprudence. This book seeks to share with readers the wealth and richness of a few landmark judgements handed down by the Court, placing them in the context of comparative jurisprudence. The book is not intended to provide a general overview of all important judgements. Rather, it focuses on specific judgements that deal with diversity, asymmetry and plurality – issues that often cause emerging and young democracies to stumble. In their respective chapters, Barrie, Cohen and Arizona discuss the challenges faced by contemporary society in acknowledging and accommodating the rights of indigenous people, particularly in regard to their traditional lands and customary law, as it is often the remote lands that are most severely impacted upon by new developments. They highlight how the Constitutional Court must ensure some uniformity and consistency across the vastness of Indonesia while also being mindful of the plurality, diversity, and asymmetry without which the very fabric on which Indonesia stands would be torn away. This interface between modernity and indigeneity makes for fascinating analysis and is a valuable contribution by Indonesia to the region in which it finds itself.

Many advanced and stable democracies, even those of nation-states in Europe, are also being tested by the reality of population diversity, religious conflict, cultural demands, radicalism, populism, and deepening societal divisions. Migration has resulted in vast numbers of people on the move. Some as regulated immigrants and some unregulated as refugees. However, they all share one common demand: equal citizenship rights in the new country where they reside, while often wanting to retain their own culture and traditions. And this is where the challenge often lies. The principles underlying the nation-state in Europe are being replaced by a state based on pluralism and diversity.

Malloy highlights that while international standards allow for the recognition of plurality, there is no positive obligation on states to support or promote plurality. The topic cannot, however, be ignored. It forces itself onto the agenda. Emerging democracies once looked to stable democracies in Europe and North America for insights into the protection of individual rights, electoral systems, decentralization and federalism. In future, those established democracies will in turn look at countries such as Indonesia, South Africa, India and Brazil to gain insights into the management of population diversity and measures to respond to the challenges that arise from ethnic pluralism. In this regard, it is particularly relevant to see how Indonesia deals with religious plurality as discussed by Black; indigenous rights as analysed by Barrie, Cohen and Arizona; asymmetry in decentralisation as analysed by Steytler; and the use of *noken* for electoral purposes as analysed by De Villiers. It is notable, however, as discussed by Warren, that Indonesia has not been able to adopt a truth and reconciliation process to deal with past injustices, as some other post-conflict countries have done. Indonesia has much to potentially gain from amnesty and reconciliation processes in countries such as South Africa, Chile, Brazil, Germany, and Spain. Whilst this book primarily comments on Indonesian jurisprudence, we also hope to provide Indonesia with an opportunity to share its experiences with the world.

The independence of the judiciary in general and the Constitutional Court, as one of the highest courts, is not to be taken for granted. The courts in many young and emerging democracies find themselves in political crosswinds, exposed to executive interference, and under public pressure. Warren gives an overview of how courts have succeeded and failed to establish legitimacy. Whilst constitutional transformation is often lauded as an ability of the judiciary to use its powers to transform a country, the converse is unfortunately also true, namely that political interference has caused many a high court to become the voice of the oppressor, rather than offering hope to the oppressed. Although this book reflects on the past 20 years of the Constitutional Court of Indonesia, we caution Indonesians that the independence of the Court should not be taken for granted. The Court, along with all other agencies of the government, must persist in its efforts to ensure and maintain its independence. The Court must be the embodiment of a fighting or 'militant' democracy (known as *streitbare Demokratie* in German), where it never ceases to defend its autonomy, independence, and the constitutional supremacy under which it operates.[23]

---

23 K. Loewenstein, "Militant Democracy and Fundamental Rights," *American Political Science Review* 31 (1937): 417–32.

In this book we have gathered prominent international scholars in their respective fields to give a comparative commentary on some of the landmark judgements of the Constitutional Court of Indonesia. We have selected themes that not only celebrate the diversity of Indonesia but also reflect challenges faced by other countries. We trust the reader will delight in the window opened by the book as far as Indonesian jurisprudence is concerned, and that the comparative element of each chapter adds to the wealth of international jurisprudential insights. Whilst each chapter is written in the unique style of its author(s), we have attempted to structure the chapters consistently, where practicable, on the following basis: (a) an introduction to the specific theme, (b) a summary of the relevant judgement of the Constitutional Court, (c) a critical assessment of the judgement considering international jurisprudence, and (d) any insights, recommendations and observations.

On a personal note: Those who have had the pleasure and honour of working with the Constitutional Court of Indonesia, its justices, and staff, can attest to their ongoing attempts to honour the Constitution; to serve their people, and to declare the law in an independent, just, reasonable, correct, and proper manner. I have experienced on multiple occasions since my first visit to the Constitutional Court in 2017 the thirst of those serving in the Court to gain insight from international jurisprudence, and to declare justice in an unbiased and fair manner. This book not only celebrates the Constitution Court as an institution, but also the dedication and hard work of the people who serve in it.

Bibliography

Brown-case. Brown v. Board of Education, 347 U.S. 483 (1954) (SC 1954).

BVerfGE 1 56. BVerfGE 1 56 (n.d.).

Chandra Bhawan-case. Chandra Bhawan Boarding and Lodging Bangalore v. The State of Mysore 1970 SCR 600 (1970).

De Villiers, B., Saldi Isra, and Z. Mochtar. "Asymmetry in a Decentralised, Unitary State: Lessons to Be Drawn from the Experiences of Decentralisation to the Special Regions of Indonesia." *Journal on Ethnopolitics and Minority Issues in Europe* 18 (2019): 43–71.

De Villiers, Bertus. "Directive Principles of State Policy and Fundamental Rights: The Indian Experience." *South African Journal on Human Rights* 8 (1992): 29–49.

De Villiers, Bertus. "Does a Constitution Have a Soul? The Role of Bundestreue in Germany and Ubuntu in South Africa to Give Life and Identity to a Constitutional Text." In *Navigating the Unknown – Essays on Selected Case Studies about the Rights of Minorities*, 163–214. Leiden: Brill, 2022.

De Villiers, Bertus. "The Design of Institutions in Response to Diversity: A Shot in the Dark or a Fine Art?" In *Navigating the Unknown – Essays on Selected Case Studies about the Rights of Minorities*, 1–37. Leiden: Brill, 2022.

Efriandi, T., O. Couwenberg, and R.L. Holzhacker. "The Noken System and the Challenge of Democratic Governance at the Periphery." In *Challenges of Governance: Development and Regional Integration in Southeast Asia*, edited by R.L. Holzhacker and W.G.Z. Tan, 65–85. Springer, 2021.

Gargarella, R., P. Domingo, and T. Roux. "Courts, Rights and Social Transformation: Concluding Reflections." In *Courts and Social Transformation in New Democracies*, edited by R. Gargarella, P. Domingo, and T. Roux, 255–82. Hampshire: Ashgate, 2006.

Gini Index. "Gini Index (World Bank Estimate) South Africa." Washington DC: World Bank, 2022. https://worldpopulationreview.com/country-rankings/gini-coefficient-by-country.

Grootboom-case. Government of the Republic of South Africa and Others v Grootboom and Others (CCT11/00) [2000] ZACC 19; 2001 (1) SA 46; 2000 (11) BCLR 1169 (4 October 2000) (2000).

Huntington, S.P. "Democracy's Third Wave." *Journal of Democracy* Spring (1991): 12–34.

Klug, H. "Towards a Sociology of Constitutional Transformation: Understanding South Africa's Post-Apartheid Constitutional Order." Legal Studies Research Paper Series No. 1373, Wisconsin Law School, 2016. https://papers.ssrn.com/sol3/papers.cfm?abstract_id=2729460.

Loewenstein, K. "Militant Democracy and Fundamental Rights." *American Political Science Review* 31 (1937): 417–32.

Makwanyane-case. S v Makwanyane 1995 3 SA 391 (CC) (1995).

Marbury. Marbury v. Madison, 5 U.S. (1 Cranch) 137 (1803), (1803).

Noken-case. Constitutional Court Case No. 31/PUU-XII/2014, 11 March 2015 (Constitutional Court 2015).

Noken-case. Constitutional Court No 47–18 / PHPU.A / VII / 2009 (Constitutional Court 2009).

Pamungkas, C. "Noken Electoral System in Papua: Deliberative Democracy in Papuan Tradition." *Jurnal Masyarakat and Budaya* 19 (2017): 219–35.

Rudy, R. Perdana, and R. Wijaya. "The Recognition of Customary Rights by Indonesian Constitutional Court." *Academic Journal for Interdisciplinary Studies* 10 (2021): 308–18.

Sachs, A. *The Strange Alchemy of Life and Law*. London: Oxford University Press, 2009.

Von Bogdandy, A., E. Gregor, M. Antoniazzi, and X. Soley. "Ius Constitutionale Commune En America Latina: A Regional Approach to Transformative Constitutionalism." MPIL Research Paper Series. Heidelberg: MPIL, 2016.

Wiratraman, H.P., and D.A.H. Shah. "Indonesia's Constitutional Responses to Plurality." In *Pluralism Constitutions in Southeast Asia*, edited by J.L. Neo and B. Ngoc Son, 115–42. London: Hart Publishing, 2019.

Yunus, A. "Multilayered Democracy in Papua: A Comparison of "Noken" System and Electoral College System in the United States." *Hasanuddin Law Review* 6 (2020): 232–39.

Zondo, R.M.M. "Judicial Commission of Inquiry into Allegations of State Capture, Corruption and Fraud in the Public Sector Including Organs of State." Pretoria: Judicial Commission, 2022. https://www.statecapture.org.za/site/files/announcements/649/Judicial_Commission_of_Inquiry_into_State_Capture_Report_Part_3-1.pdf.

CHAPTER 2

Indonesia's Diversity: A Brief Constitutional Perspective

I D.G. Palguna and Bisariyadi

Abstract

This chapter examines Indonesia's diversity from a constitutional perspective. It highlights the country's multifaceted nature and the challenges of maintaining unity in such a pluralistic society. The chapter also provides a historical overview of Indonesia's constitutional framework, with a focus on different constitutional frameworks and regional autonomy policies that have been experimented with to accommodate diversity. The constitutional history is divided into five periods: revolutionary (1945–1949), constitutional democracy (1949–1957), guided democracy (1957–1965), New Order (1965–1998), and reform (1998–present). The chapter suggests that throughout the course of the Indonesian history, the diversity has been sustained by strong political figures rather than a stable system of government or institutions. Ultimately, the chapter argues that Indonesia's identity as a nation should be shaped by the diversity of its citizens, and the country's constitution should serve as a unifying legal document that recognizes and protects diversity.

Keywords

archipelago – constitutions – diversity – history of Indonesia – system of government

> So which one is called our homeland, our motherland?
> In geopolitical terms, Indonesia is our homeland.
> Indonesia that is whole, not just Java, not just Sumatra, or Borneo, or Celebes, or Ambon, or Maluku,
> but of all the islands designated by Allah SWT

DOI:10.1163/9789004691698_003

as a united territory between two continents and two oceans, that is our motherland![1]

SOEKARNO

1 Introduction

Many people perceive Indonesia as a country with a vast area, stretching from Sabang to Merauke, made up of large and small islands. This perception is affirmed in the Indonesian Constitution, which states, "The Unitary State of the Republic of Indonesia is an archipelagic state having an Archipelagic (*Nusantara*) character with a territory, the borders and rights of whose territory is stipulated by law." Indonesia takes great pride in its identity as an archipelagic nation, where thousands of islands form a cohesive unit that embodies the national motto of *Bhinneka Tunggal Ika* (Unity in Diversity).[2]

However, the essence of a state cannot be viewed solely from a territorial perspective; it also encompasses its people, who are the inhabitants and citizens of the state.[3] Indonesia's identity as a nation is shaped by the diversity of its citizens, who belong to various ethnic groups with different racial characteristics. With about 18,110 islands and islets (of which about 6,000 are inhabited), Indonesia is the world's largest archipelagic state. Its total area, including its exclusive economic zone, is estimated at 9.8 million sq km, comprising 1.9 million sq km of land and 7.9 million sq km of sea.[4] The country is home

1 Speech by Indonesian founding father and future President Soekarno on Pancasila during the Meeting of the Investigative Body for Preparatory Work for Independence (BPUPK) on 1 June 1945.

2 *Bhinneka Tunggal Ika* is a phrase from the ancient Javanese *Kakawin Sutasoma*, a poem by Mpu Tantular written in Balinese script in the 14th century. The quote 'Unity in Diversity' comes from pupuh 139, stanza 5, of *Kakawin Sutasoma*. See Dick van der Meij, *Indonesian Manuscripts form the Islands of Java, Madura, Bali and Lombok* (Leiden: Brill, 2017), 567.

3 The Indonesian Constitution distinguishes between "citizens" and "residents". Article 26 (1) and (2) of the Constitution states: (1) Those who become citizens are native Indonesian people and people of other nations who are legalized by law as citizens. (2) Residents are Indonesian citizens and foreigners residing in Indonesia.

4 Ministry of Foreign Affairs of Indonesia, "Indonesia at a Glance," Embassy of the Republic of Indonesia in Vancouver, accessed January 22, 2023, https://kemlu.go.id/vancouver/en/pages/indonesia_at_a_glance/2016/etc-menu#!.

to more than 300 ethnic groups and cultures, with 742 living local languages.[5] Its people embrace five mainstream religions (Islam, Christianity, Hinduism, Buddhism, Confucianism), along with dozens of local and indigenous beliefs that are collectively known as *aliran kepercayaan kepada Tuhan* (traditional belief in God). The majority of Indonesians practice Islam, which is adhered to by more than 86.7% of the population.[6]

In addition, it has long been observed that in a pluralistic society, such as Indonesia, maintaining the concept of unity can be challenging due to various factors.[7] These include (i) segmentation in the form of groups with subcultures that often differ significantly with one another; (ii) a social structure that is divided into non-complementary institutions; (iii) a lack of consensus on some basic values among members; (iv) relatively frequent conflicts between groups; (v) social integration that is based largely on coercion and economic interdependence among groups; (vi) the domination of a certain group over others.[8] Furthermore, the structure of Indonesian society is unique in both horizonal and vertical aspects. Horizontally, it comprises numerous social entities formed and developed on the basis of ethnicity, custom, religion, and region. Vertically, there are relatively sharp differences between the upper and lower classes within the society.[9]

The quotation by Soekarno, which opens this chapter, reflects the ideas and efforts of Indonesia's founding fathers to instill and disseminate ideas on nationalism as the spirit of unity. It should be noted that the *zeitgeist* of

---

5 Umi Farisiyah and Zamzani, "Language Shift and Language Maintenance of Local Languages toward Indonesian," (paper presented for International Conference of Communication Science Research (ICCSR)), 2018.

6 According to the Religious Affairs Ministry, referring to data from Statistics Indonesia available at https://data.kemenag.go.id/agamadashboard/statistik/umat, retrieved on January 14, 2023, the religious composition of the Indonesian population is: 86.7% Muslims, 10.72% Christians (7.6% Protestants, 3.12% Roman Catholics), 1.7% Hindus, 0.77% Buddhists, 0.03% Confucians, 0.05% others. See also Saldi Isra and Pan Mohamad Faiz, "The Role of Constitutional Court in Protecting Minority Rights: A Case on Traditional Beliefs in Indonesia," in Bertus de Villers, et al., *Litigating the Rights of Minorities and Indigenous Peoples in Domestic and International Courts* (Leiden: Brill, 2021), 125.

7 Elisabeth Pisani, *Indonesia Etc.: Exploring the Improbable Nation* (Jakarta: The Lontar Foundation, 2014), 9. In this book, Pisani, a British-American epidemiologist, journalist and author, notes the challenges of unifying a diverse nation like Indonesia, with its many islands and different cultures. She writes, "When the flamboyant nationalist leader Soekarno proclaimed the independence of Indonesia, he was liberating a nation that didn't really exist, imposing a notional unity on a ragbag of islands that had only a veneer of shared history and little common culture."

8 Nasikun, *Sistem Sosial Indonesia* [*Social System of Indonesia*] (Jakarta: Rajawali Pers, 2001), 33.

9 Ibid.

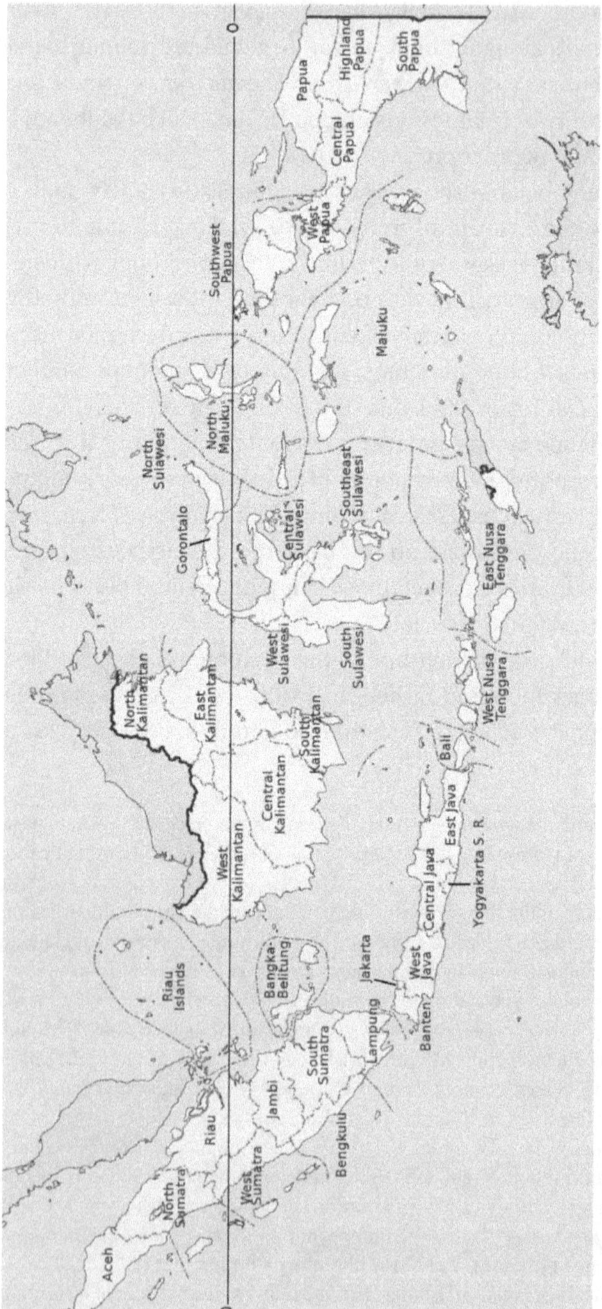

MAP 1.1 Current map of Indonesia

Indonesia's independence in 1945 was strongly influenced by the international context of nations fighting to liberate themselves from colonialism.[10]

Now, 78 years since the declaration of independence, Indonesia has experienced various transformations. A positive outlook that is often expressed today is that Indonesia has tremendous potential for progress and success as a great nation. One of many factors supporting this projection is demographic bonus[11] that Indonesia is set to experience in the near future. Whether Indonesia can achieve such expectations of greatness is not the main focus of this chapter. Given the vast scope of the issue and the need for expertise from many fields to answer this question, the focus of this chapter is instead to provide a comprehensive constitutional perspective of Indonesia's diversity.

The aim of this chapter is to explore Indonesia's diversity from the perspective of its constitution. As a fundamental legal document, the constitution links the nation's history with its aspirations for the future. Furthermore, it seeks to unify the nation while simultaneously recognizing and protecting the diversity of its people.

In providing a comprehensive constitutional perspective of Indonesia, this chapter is divided into two main sections. The first section describes Indonesia by looking from a historical angle at the idea of Indonesia in the past and in relation to the goals of the state as outlined in the constitution. The second section focuses on the constitutional arrangement of the state with its citizens and the authority of state institutions. The section will describe the unique characteristics of Indonesia's constitutional arrangement, which is influences by the legal traditions of other countries. The chapter pays particular attention to the Indonesian legal system's branch of judicial power, including a description of the Constitutional Court. Both sections will conclude with a summary of the key points discussed.

2 The Idea of Indonesia: a Perspective of Constitutional History

The word "Indonesia" was not coined until 1850. It was first introduced in ethnological studies by George Samuel Windsor Earl, who used the term "Indu-nesians" to describe the Polynesian race inhabiting the Indian islands.

---

10 Phillip C. Jessup, *The Birth of Nations* (New York: Columbia University Press, 1974), 56.

11 Adrian Hayes and Diahhadi Setyonaluri, *Taking Advantage of the Demographic Dividend in Indonesia: A Brief Introduction to Theory and Practice* (Jakarta: UNFPA Indonesia, 2015), https://indonesia.unfpa.org/sites/default/files/pub-pdf/Buku_Policy_Brief_on_Taking_Advantage_on_Demographic_Dividend_02c_%282%29_0.pdf.

However, Earl faced a dilemma between using the terms "Indu-nesians" or "Malay-nesians". He ultimately chose the term "Malayu-nesians".[12] The term "Indu-nesians" was later adopted by Earl's colleague, James Richardson Logan, founder of *The Journal of the Indian Archipelago and Eastern Asia*, where the word "Indonesia" was mentioned in 1850.[13]

George Alexander Wilkens, a prominent Dutch ethnologist who was also a professor at Leiden University, was inspired by Logan to use the word "Indonesia".[14] Following Wilkens' lead, successive Dutch scientists used the word "Indonesia" in the titles of their scientific articles published between 1911 and 1925. These included works by Johan Hendrik Caspar Kern, George Karel Niemann and Christiaan Snouck Hurgronje.[15]

The idea of an independent nation represented by the word "Indonesia" was later embraced by students and figures in the then-Dutch East Indies who envisioned the independence movement. Adrian Vickers notes that,

> By 1920 the most intriguing of words appeared in the parties' vocabulary: 'Indonesia' ... Previously the Youth Alliances had talked about a separate Balinese nation, Javanese nation, Sumatran nation and so on; now 'Indonesia' spoke of a single people.[16]

However, the movement for Indonesian independence did not only involve the Dutch government. In 1942, Japan invaded and expanded its power in Southeast Asia, including Indonesia.[17] The Japanese occupation of Indonesia did not last long, but it brought major changes, including in the use of daily language. Anthony J.S. Reid analyzed that,

> The Japanese were, for example, ignorant and contemptuous of the Dutch language. In contrast to Malaya and Burma the use of the old colonial language was banned in Indonesia, and the formerly Dutch-speaking

12 Russell Jones, "George Windsor Earl and 'Indonesia'," *Indonesia Circle* 22, no. 64 (August 2007): 279–290, https://doi.org/10.1080/03062849408729825.

13 Ibid., see also Robert Edward Elson, *The Idea of Indonesia: A History* (Cambridge: Cambridge University Press, 2008); Akira Nagazumi, "Indonesia and Indonesians: Semantics in Politics," *Asian Profile* 1, no. 1 (1973): 91–102.

14 Elson, *The Idea*, 4.

15 Ibid., 11.

16 Adrian Vickers, *A History of Modern Indonesia* (Cambridge: Cambridge University Press, 2005), 79.

17 Malcolm Caldwell and Ernst Utrecht, *Indonesia: An Alternative History* (Sydney: Alternative Publishing Co-operative Ltd, 2008), 61.

> élite had to team to communicate in Indonesian. This gave a tremendous boost to the national language, whose status was never questioned after the war.[18]

In addition, Japan's attitude toward the Indonesian independence movement showed little effort to impede it. In fact, the Japanese even facilitated the movement with the establishment of the Investigative Body for Preparatory Work for Independence (*Badan Penyelidik Usaha Persiapan Kemerdekaan*, BPUPK) in March 1945. BPUPK held its first meeting in May 1945, when Indonesia was still in its embryonic stage, but the composition of its 62 members was dominated by nationalist groups and failed to represent the diversity of the future nation.[19] In July 1945, facing imminent defeat in World War II, Japan promised that Indonesian independence would be granted on 7 September 1945;[20] however, Japan announced its surrender to the Allied forces on 15 August 1945.

In essence, the concept of Indonesia as a nation was accomplished with the declaration of independence on 17 August 1945. The narrative of "Indonesia" as an independent nation entitled to self-government was establish with a unified territory that stretched across the vast regions formerly occupied by the Dutch and the Japanese. The idea of independence was also enshrined in the Preamble to the 1945 Constitution, which declared: "Whereas Independence is the inalienable right of all nations; therefore, colonialism must be abolished." The drafters of the Preamble were eager to encourage other nations under colonialism to boldly declare themselves as independent countries on the basis of equality.

Furthermore, the next paragraph in the Preamble includes the following statement: "By the blessings of Almighty God and motivated by the noble desire to live a free national life, the people of Indonesia hereby declare their independence." This statement contains two elements that served as the impetus for the independence declaration. First, that freedom is an endowment from God. Therefore, in the administration of government, the greater power of God's sovereignty should not be forgotten. Second, that independence is a manifestation of the desire to live in a free nation. These elements show that the concepts of independence and freedom were significant considerations in the drafting of the Preamble.

18 Anthony J.S. Reid, *The Indonesian National Revolution 1945–1950* (Hawthorn: Longman Australia, 1974), 10–11.

19 Ibid., 19–20.

20 Ibid., 21.

It has been well documented that the newly-formed republic faced a challenging period after the independence declaration. George McTurnan Kahin referred to the time between 1945 and 1949, which marked the transition from independence to the enforcement of a new constitution, the Constitution of the Republic of the United States of Indonesia (*Konstitusi Republik Indonesia Serikat 1949*), as the revolutionary period.

To better understand the chronological order of events and the phases of Indonesian history under different constitutions, it is necessary to compile a periodization. This chapter divides the period after the declaration of independence into five distinct phases: (1) the revolutionary period (1945–1949); (2) the constitutional democracy period (1949–1957); (3) the guided democracy period (1957–1965); (4) the New Order era, (1966–1998); and (5) the reform period (1998–present).

2.1 *The Revolutionary Period, 1945–1949*

The era after declaration was called the revolutionary period, characterized by the major overhaul in the system of government following the Japanese occupation era. The Constitution drafted by BPUPK as further developed by the Preparatory Committee for Indonesian Independence (*Panitia Persiapan Kemerdekaan Indonesia*, PPKI) came into effect the day after the declaration, with the understanding that it was provisional. At the same time, the PPKI appointed Soekarno as President and Mohammad Hatta as Vice President.[21] PPKI did not only decide the first President and Vice President, but also the territorial division of the new nation. This took shape on 19 August 1945, when the PPKI issued a decree dividing Indonesia into eight provinces: West Java, Central Java, East Java, Sumatra, Kalimantan, Sulawesi, Maluku and *Sunda Ketjil* (Lesser Sundas).

On 29 August 1945, Soekarno transformed the PPKI into the Central Indonesian National Committee (*Komite Nasional Indonesia Pusat*, KNIP) and expanded its membership to 135 people. However, KNIP was not designed as a parliament with legislative functions, but rather as an advisory body to the President in national policy-making. Additionally, KNIP were not formed only at the national level but also at the provincial level to provide assistance and assessments to the governors.

Concurrently, the government took steps for the formation of a national army by disarming and reorganizing the armed forces that had been formed

21 George McTurnan Kahin, *Nationalism and Revolution in Indonesia* (Ithaca: Cornell University Press, 1952).

during the Japanese occupation. The government established the People's Peace Preservation Corps (*Badan Keamanan Rakyat*, BKR). Then, on 5 October 1945 the BKR was renamed the People's Peace Preservation Army (*Tentara Keamanan Rakyat*, TKR).

On 31 August 1945, the President formed a cabinet of 16 ministers, with 10 of them assigned to handle foreign affairs, domestic affairs, justice, economic affairs, finance, education, social affairs, information, health, and communications. The remaining ministers were appointed without any specific portfolio.[22]

Despite the establishment of essential institutions for the government's administration, its performance fell short of expectations due to the unstable political situation. Meanwhile, the process of disarming the Japanese troops was still ongoing, being conducted by Allied forces led by the British who entered Indonesian territory. However, the disarmament was met with resistance in many areas, and the presence of Dutch armed forces accompanying Allied troops further complicated the situation.

In addition to facing external threats, the young Indonesian government also experienced internal political instability. The KNIP, initially established as an advisory body to the President, sought to expand its powers to legislative functions, including drafting and enacting laws. It also initiated a move to change the governmental system from presidential to parliamentary. To accomplish these changes, the KNIP appointed Sutan Sjahrir and Amir Syarifuddin to lead a Working Committee.

The Working Committee introduced a multi-party to replace the existing one-party system, and scheduled general elections for January 1946 to establish a parliament that would succeed the KNIP. As a result of this initiative, numerous political parties emerged, including the Indonesian National Party (*Partai Nasional Indonesia*, PNI) founded by Soekarno and Hatta, the Indonesian Muslim Syuro Council Party (*Partai Majelis Syuro Muslimin*, Masyumi), the Socialist Party, the Catholic Republican Party of Indonesia, the Indonesian Communist Party (*Partai Komunis Indonesia*, PKI), and the Indonesian Labor Party.[23] However, due to the unstable political climate, the elections were postponed.

In response to armed conflicts with Dutch forces, which had joined the Allied convoys in disarming the Japanese, the Indonesian government engaged in several diplomatic meetings with the Dutch. These negotiations resulted in the Linggajati, Renville, and Roem-van Royen agreements. However, controversy

22 Ibid., 139.

23 Ibid., 155–160.

surrounded these accords due to dissent among political groups, which was echoed by the representatives of the political parties. These Dutch used these negotiations as part of their strategy to break up Indonesia's territorial integrity by introducing the concept of a federal government. Lt. Governor General H.J. van Mook proposed the creation of 15 regions, six of which were states while the others were autonomous regions, under the control of the Dutch royal government.[24] These new states and autonomous regions were incorporated into a Dutch organization named the Meeting for Federal Consultation (*Bijeenkomst voor Federal Overleg,* BFO).

Van Mook's initiative to create a federal Indonesian state under Dutch control sparked a political divide. The republicans were devoted to the idea of a unitary state, while the federalists joined the BFO.[25] This division between the two political groups became significant in subsequent negotiations that ultimately led to the Round Table Conference, which marked a turning point in the Indonesian state administration.

The Round Table Conference, held from August to 2 November 1949, was preceded by a series of meetings aimed at drafting a new constitution for Indonesia. The conference was attended by three parties: the Royal Dutch government, the Republic of Indonesia, and the BFO representing the member states of the federation.

The conference led to the transfer of sovereignty and recognition of the Indonesian government as a federal state. The following key points were agreed upon:[26]

1. The Kingdom of the Netherlands unconditionally and irrevocably transfers complete sovereignty over Indonesia to the Republic of the United States of Indonesia, thereby recognizing it as an independent and sovereign state.
2. The Republic of the United States of Indonesia accepts this sovereignty on the basis of the provisions of its Constitution, which as a draft has been brought to the knowledge of the Kingdom of the Netherlands.
3. The transfer of sovereignty shall take place at the latest on 30 December 1949.

---

24 Audrey R. Kahin, ed., *Regional Dynamics of the Indonesian Revolution: Unity From Diversity* (Honolulu: University of Hawaii Press, 1985), 8.

25 Amry Vandenbosch, "The Netherlands-Indonesian Union," *Far Eastern Survey* 19, no. 1 (1950): 3–4.

26 "Charter of the Transfer of Sovereignty over Indonesia, Signed at the Round Table Conference, The Hague, 2 November 1949," *International Organization* 4, no. 1 (February 1950): 176–177.

The conference also introduced the new constitution, the Constitution of the United States of Indonesia. Under the agreement and the new constitution, the territory of the United States of Indonesia was defined as follows:

> The United States of Indonesia covers the entire territory of Indonesia, namely the following regions:
> a. The Republic of Indonesia, with areas according to the status quo as stated in the Renville agreement dated 17 January 1948: East Indonesia State; Pasundan State, including Jakarta Federal District; East Java State; Madura State; East Sumatra State, with the understanding that the status quo of South Asahan and Labuhan Batu in relation to East Sumatra State remains in effect; South Sumatra Country.
> b. Self-supporting state units: Central Java; Bangka; Belitung; Riau; West Kalimantan (special region); Dayak Besar; Banjar area; Southeast Kalimantan; and East Kalimantan. The regions of a and b have the right to determine their own destiny and are united in the federation of the Republic of the United States of Indonesia, based on what is stipulated in this Constitution.
> c. The rest of Indonesia that is not part of the regions of a and b.

Close examination of the agreement shows that the regions included in the United States of Indonesia are referred to as the "Republic of Indonesia". This republic was recognized as a member of the federal state. Consequently, the 1945 Constitution, which was promulgated on 18 August 1945, remains the valid constitution of the Republic of Indonesia as a state. However, the newly drafted constitution resulting from the conference pertains to the United States of Indonesia as a federal state. Therefore, while the 1945 Constitution is still enforced in the Republic of Indonesia as a member state with its capital city in Jogjakarta, the newly drafted constitution applies to the United States of Indonesia as a federal state.

2.2 *The Constitutional Democracy Period, 1949–1957*

As a follow-up to the conference's agreement, a state ceremony was held on 27 December 1949 to symbolize the of transfer of sovereignty. The ceremony consisted of three processes:[27]

---

27 Homer G. Angelo, "Transfer of Sovereignty Over Indonesia," *The American Journal of International Law* 44, no. 3 (July 1950): 572.

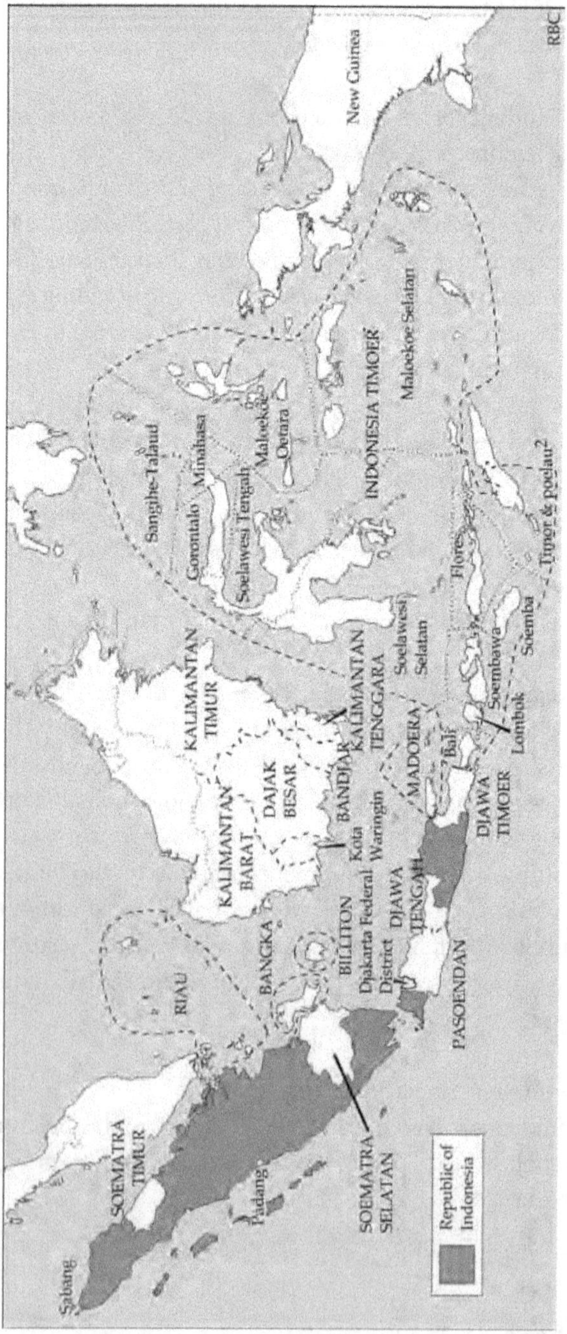

MAP 1.2 Federal Indonesia, 1948–1949
SOURCE: ROBERT CRIBB AND AUDREY KAHIN, HISTORICAL DICTIONARY OF INDONESIA, 2ND EDITION, 2004, P. XXXVIII

1. First, the Prime Minister of the Netherlands and the Prime Minister of the Republic of the United States of Indonesia signed a Protocol, which acknowledged the relevant provisions of the Netherlands Constitution and the acceptance of the Covering Resolution by the 16 Indonesian territories. It stated that both parties had accepted the draft agreements and exchange of letters, thereby establishing "the new order of law".
2. Second, the Queen of the Netherlands proclaimed her assent and that of the Netherlands Cabinet to the new order, transferring sovereignty by an Act of Confirmation.
3. Third, the Act of Transfer of Sovereignty and Recognition was promulgated and accepted.

Accordingly, a new chapter began for the nascent federal government in the form of the United States of the Republic of Indonesia (*Republik Indonesia Serikat*), and Soekarno was appointed as President. The newly adopted presidential system stipulated that "the President and Ministers together constitute the Government".[28] However, the President may appoint a Prime Minister as follows,[29]

1. The President, in agreement with the representatives of the regions referred to in Article 69, appoints three Cabinet members.
2. In accordance with the recommendations of the three Cabinet members, the President appoints one of them as Prime Minister and appoints other Ministers.

Hatta was appointed the first prime minister but his government did not last long, nor did the cabinets of the other prime ministers during this period. Herbert Feith notes there were at least seven cabinet changes during this period: (1) Mohammad Hatta, from December 1949 to August 1950; (2) Muhammad Natsir, from September 1950 to March 1951; (3) Sukiman, from April 1951 to February 1952; (4) Wilopo, from April 1952 to June 1953; (5) Ali Sastroamidjojo (first cabinet), from July 1953 to July 1955; (6) Burhanuddin Harahap, from August 1955 to March 1956; and (7) Ali Sastroamodjojo (second cabinet), from March 1956 to March 1957.[30]

Despite the frequent changes in the cabinet, Feith argued that the period was still one of constitutional democracy in Indonesia. He stated,

28 Article 68(1) of the 1949 Constitution of the Republic of the United States of Indonesia.

29 Article 74 of the 1949 Constitution of the Republic of the United States of Indonesia.

30 Herbert Feith, *The Decline of Constitutional Democracy in Indonesia* (Jakarta: Cornell University Press, 1962), 69.

> Was this, then, a period of constitutional democracy? I have argued that it was, in a particular sense. The system of politics which operated in those years and finally broke down had six distinct features characteristic of constitutional democracy. Civilians played a dominant role. Parties were of very great importance. The contenders for power showed respect for "rules of the game" which were closely related to the existing constitution. Most members of the political elite had some sort of commitment to symbols connected with constitutional democracy. Civil liberties were rarely infringed. Finally, governments used coercion sparingly. This represented, at the very least, an attempt to maintain and develop constitutional democracy.[31]

The Hatta administration was tasked with establishing the new government soon after the transfer of sovereignty. However, halfway through the administration's term, the federation formed by the Dutch, comprising various states and regions, proved incapable of containing insurgencies within their domains. Consequently, these entities declared themselves dissolved and joined the state of the Republic of Indonesia. The climax was the dissolution of East Indonesia State, which had more essential elements of statehood compared to other regions in the federation.[32] This dissolution was preceded by a rebellion led by Captain Andi Abdul Azis in Makassar in April 1950.

The idea of merging into a unitary state under the Republic of Indonesia began to gain traction. After several days of negotiation, an agreement was reached on 19 May 1950 between the Mohammad Hatta, the Prime Minister of the United States of Indonesia, and Abdul Halim, the Prime Minister of the Republic of Indonesia. The two agreed:

31 Ibid.

32 Ibid., 65. For further history on the East Indonesia State, particularly on Bali as part of the state, see Palguna's epilogue to the biography of Tjokorde Gede Raka Soekawati in Arya Suharja et al., *Laksana Manut Sasana* (Denpasar: Sarwa Tattwa Pustaka, 2021). According to Soekawati's account, Bali's inclusion in the East Indonesia State was proposed as a means to prevent further bloodshed. Although there was an attempt in the Linggajati accord to expand the boundary of the Republic of Indonesia to include Bali, it was not successful. The states created by van Mook's proposal, including Bali, ultimately chose to remain within the Republic of Indonesia. The idea of a federal state for Indonesia was temporary, as the states were reluctant to be tied together in the form of a United States.

> to implement in cooperation and in the shortest possible time the formation of a Unitary State which shall be a materialization of the Republic of Indonesia based on the Proclamation of 17 August 1945.[33]

Based on the above accord, a committee of 14 members was set up to draft a constitution for the new unitary state government. The committee had seven members representing the United States of Indonesia and seven representing the Republic of Indonesia. After almost two months of work, the committee succeeded in drafting a new constitution that did not deviate much from the 1949 Constitution of the United States of Indonesia. This was because the May 19th accord emphasized that the Constitution for the formation of the Republic of Indonesia as unitary state was temporary in nature. As a result, a Constituent Assembly would be formed through an election to draft a permanent Constitution.

The mechanism for approving the draft of the new constitution for the unitary state required submission to the respective parliaments of the United States of Indonesia and the Republic of Indonesia, but these parliaments were not given authority to alter the draft. This caused strong protests by each parliament when the draft was submitted at the end of July 1950. However, after long negotiations, each parliament ratified the draft on 17 August 1950, coinciding with the fifth anniversary of Indonesia's Independence's Day. In the parliament of the United States of Indonesia, the draft was approved by the House of Representatives with 18 votes and a unanimous vote in the Senate. Meanwhile, in the parliament of the Republic of Indonesia, the draft was approved by 31 votes to 2, with 7 members abstaining.[34] In terms of regional division, the national government established 10 provinces: North Sumatera, Middle Sumatra, South Sumatra, West Java, Middle Java, East Java, Lesser Sundas, Borneo, Celebes and Moluccas.

The adoption of the new constitution and the shift to a unitary state led to the end of the Hatta administration. The change from a federal to a unitary form of government caused a deviation from the Round Table conference agreement, which stipulated a federal government. However, this significant political shift did not receive much attention.

Hatta had previously expressed his preference for a federal form of government for Indonesia. However, given the history of Dutch colonial rule and the political developments that ensued, many Indonesians became wary of

33 Ministry of Information, Special Region of Yogyakarta, Republic of Indonesia, Jakarta, Ministry of Information, 1953, as quoted in Feith, *The Decline*, 69.

34 Ibid., 99.

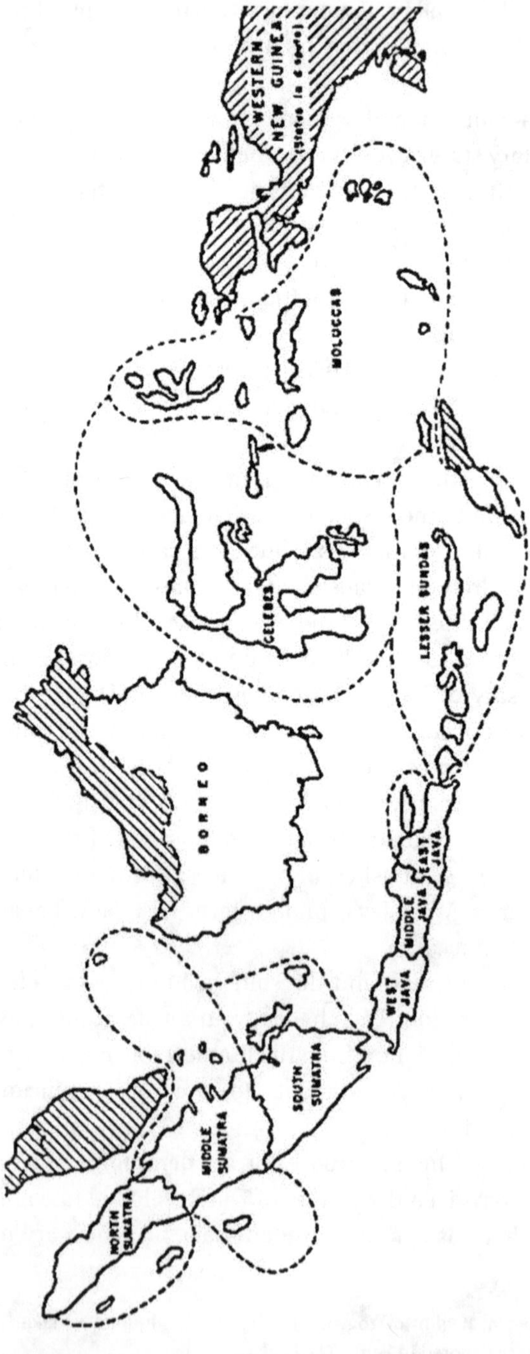

MAP 1.3 Indonesia in 1950
SOURCE: GEORGE MCTURNAN KAHIN, NATIONALISM AND REVOLUTION IN INDONESIA, 1952, P. 452

federalism. It was therefore deemed necessary to adopt a unitary form of government as an interim measure until the Constituent Assembly could draft a more permanent Constitution. Hatta himself wrote,

> Although a federal system is, in fact, suitable for such a far-flung archipelago as Indonesia, and might be expected to strengthen the feeling of unity, the manner and timing of the move by the Netherlands Indies Government had aroused such antipathy toward ideas of federation that it was found necessary to make the change from a federal to a unitary state before a constituent assembly could be formed to draw up a definitive constitution.[35]

The enactment of the 1950 Provisional Constitution established a provisional parliament, which Miriam Budiardjo noted consisted of regional representatives as well as political representatives. She stated,

> At its establishment it counted 236 members: 146 and 31 respectively from the House and Senate of the former federal Parliament, and 46 and 13 respectively from the Parliament and the Supreme Advisory Council of the Jogja Republic.[36]

However, the composition of political representation in the provisional parliament exacerbated the disparity between the political parties. As a result, mechanisms of parliamentary control over the government were often used as a tool to bring down the cabinet. Budiardjo commented that,

> Two cabinets have been defeated as a result of motions. The Masjumi-dominated Cabinet of Natsir fell in consequence of the Hadikusumo (Nationalist) motion on the structure of the regional councils (February-March 1951). The fall of the Wilopo (Nationalist-Masjumi) Cabinet was precipitated by a motion on illegal land occupation in Tandjung Morawa (near Medan) moved by Sidik Kertapati of the Progressive Unity Group and supported in Parliament by the Prime Minister's own Nationalist Party (April-June 1953).[37]

35 Mohammad Hatta, "Indonesia's Foreign Policy," *Foreign Affairs* 31, no. 3 (1953): 449.

36 M.S. Budiardjo, "The Provisional Parliament of Indonesia," *Far Eastern Survey* 25, no. 2 (1956): 17.

37 Ibid., 19.

Despite the cabinet's efforts, its proposed agendas often faced obstacles in the parliament. As Logemann pointed out, there was still a lingering ideological competition in the parliament, which was a remnant from the revolutionary period. While the cabinet prioritized running the government, the parliament focused on imposing its ideological notions on the cabinet. As Logemann noted,

> Under present conditions in Indonesia, we do not find a cabinet guiding the affairs of Parliament in implementing a political programme which has been approved by the nation, but rather a Parliament struggling to impose its ideological notions on the Ministry. Indeed, this attitude of Parliament seems to be in keeping with the conception of democracy as it evolved during the long struggle for independence. Broadly speaking, Parliament is still striving for the early and radical completion of revolution, whereas the Government is worried by the practical day-to-day issues which arise at every turn.[38]

One crucial issue during this period was the drafting of the Election Law. The purpose of holding elections was not only to establish a new parliament as a legislative institution, but also to install a Constituent Assembly with the power to draft a new permanent Constitution. The idea of drafting an election law had existed since the Hatta administration, but the draft law was only approved and promulgated on 17 October 1952.[39] Elections were scheduled to be held on 29 September 1955.[40]

According to Herbert Feith, the 1955 elections may not have resulted in the desired political stability. Nevertheless, these elections had a significant impact on the political landscape of Indonesia. As he noted,

> elections have had other consequences hoped for by the Indonesian leadership. Their value as political education was enormous; understanding of national-level politics by the people of Indonesia's villages was greatly increased. They have also produced greater understanding of village Indonesia in Djakarta and exposed a number of political and

---

38 J.H.A. Logemann, "The Indonesian Parliament," *Parliamentary Affairs* 6, no. 4 (August 1953): 350.

39 Herbert Feith, "Toward Elections in Indonesia," *Pacific Affairs* 27, no. 3 (1954): 245.

40 Elections were scheduled to be held on two days, 29 September and 29 November, 1955, with the latter date chosen to anticipate places that were difficult to reach. However, based on available data, the elections on 29 September were carried out in approximately 85% of the 95,532 polling stations, Feith, *The Decline*, 425.

> sociological myths previously accepted by social planners as well as politicians in the capital. They have tapped new sources of leadership and afforded representation to a number of social groups which previously had none. They have helped to strengthen all-Indonesian consciousness, by affording large group of people a sense of participating in the affairs of the nation. They have also been valuable from a foreign publicity point of view. The fact that they were held at all, and that they were carried through successfully, represents an important vindication of the case of the Indonesian nationalist against those who insisted that Indonesians were incapable of self-government.[41]

Nonetheless, despite the successful election, the adoption of the parliamentary system in Indonesia led to the emergence of seeds of distrust in political institutions, particularly political parties, which were founded not on ideologies but on the charisma of their leaders. As put by Ruslan Abdulgani,

> The political parties of the present time are centred more in the personalities of their leaders than in ideologies. In the attitude they take towards the national government, our political parties are often still guided by an oppositional attitude, a relic of ways of thinking in dealing with the colonial regime. The efforts of political parties at this time seem to be centred mainly in struggles in Parliament and the cabinet. They still pay too little attention to activities among the people themselves.[42]

In the same vein, Sjahrir stated,

> Political divisions between groups in Indonesia do not arise from differences in ideas on economic and social issues. On the contrary, the reason for the classification is personal enmity between individuals with followers from everywhere.[43]

In 1956, Soekarno put forward the idea of guided democracy as a solution to Indonesia's political instability. In making his proposal in a speech famously

41 Herbert Feith, *The Indonesian Election of 1955* (Ithaca, NY: Cornell Modern Indonesia Project, Interim Reports Series, 1957), 89–90.

42 Ruslan Abdulgani as quoted in Logemann, "The Indonesian," 350.

43 Sjahrir, quoted in R.E Elson, *The Idea of Indonesia* (Cambridge: Cambridge University Press, 2008), 183.

titled "Let Us Burry the Parties", he suggested the parties were hindering the nation's progress, so a new system of governance was necessary.

> the democracy I crave for Indonesia is not a liberal democracy such as exists for Western Europe. No! What I want for Indonesia is a guided democracy, a democracy with leadership. A guided democracy, a guided democracy, something which is guided but still democracy.... Our situation with respect to the party system is one of complete disruption. It is not healthy; it must be transformed entirely. Especially, if we want to build as people have in other countries I have seen, for example, in the Chinese People's Republic, we must transform the party system completely. At the very least we must rationalize it and make it healthy.[44]

At the end of his speech, Soekarno said he had a "conception" that would be offered as a replacement for the parliamentary system. That conception will be discussed in the next section.

2.3 *Guided Democracy Period, 1957–1965*

On 14 March 1957, at 10.00 am, Ali Sastroamidjojo, the prime minister, returned the government's mandate to the president. Just half an hour later, President Soekarno declared a state of emergency. Regarding this declaration, Legge wrote,

> At the end of 1957 a new State of Emergency Law was passed to replace the existing Dutch measure under which Soekarno had declared a state of siege and war in March of that year. The state of emergency itself was extended by Parliament for a further year.[45]

After Ali Sastroamidjojo's resignation, the political landscape in Indonesia was dominated by four main players: (1) the PKI, (2) President Soekarno, (3) the Army's central leadership, and (4) the civilian military movement at the local level. Meanwhile, all of the political parties, except the PKI, had lost public trust at this point.[46] Later, Soekarno explained his "conception" of government in response to his previous address. He first criticized the existence of

---

44 As quoted in Herbert Feith and Lance Castles (eds), *Indonesian Political Thinking 1945–1965* (Ithaca: Cornell University Press, 1970), 81.

45 Legge, J.D., "Guided Democracy and Constitutional Procedures in Indonesia," *Australian Outlook* 13, no. 2 (1959): 93.

46 Feith, *The Decline*, 548.

opposition in the government, arguing that it was a model of democracy that was not in accordance with the Indonesian personality.

> In this Western parliamentary democracy, we find the idea of the opposition, and it is this idea of the opposition which has made us go through hardships for eleven years, because we have interpreted this idea of opposition in a way which does not accord with the Indonesian spirit.[47]

Soekarno further explained that his conception of guided democracy would consist of two institutions, the Mutual Cooperation (*Gotong Royong*) Cabinet and the National Council. He said the *Gotong Royong* Cabinet would be a government that "should include all political parties and groups represented in parliament which have obtained a certain quotient of votes in the election". The National Council, on the other hand, would have the objective "to assist the Cabinet with advice, whether such advice is requested or not, because the National Council is composed of representatives of or persons from functional groups in our society. Therefore, I regard the Council as a reflection of our society, while the Cabinet would be a reflection of Parliament".[48]

The National Council would consist of functional representatives from community groups. Soekarno explained,

> the National Council shall include a representative of or a person from labor circles, ...; a representative of or a person from the peasants, ...; from the intelligentsia, ...; a representative of or a person from the group of national entrepreneurs, ...; a representative of or a person from the Protestant group; a representative of or a person from the Catholic group; two representatives of the Alim Ulama; a representative of or a person from the women's group; a representative of or a person from the youth; a representative of or a person from the 1945 Generation; a representative of or a person from the group which can express or set forth the problems of the regions. And ..., I want this National Council to include the Chief of Staff of the Army, the Chief of Staff of the Navy, the Chief of Staff of the Air Force, the Chief of the State Police, the Attorney General, and several Ministers who hold important portfolios.[49]

---

47 Feith and Castles (eds), *Indonesian Political*, 84–85.

48 Ibid., 87–88.

49 Ibid.

He also rejected the existence of a multi-party system and aimed at a one-party system, taking the example of the Soviet Union.[50] Furthermore, Soekarno distanced himself from the adoption of the party system in the past.

> On the matters of parties ... I am not responsible. I wash my hands of all wrong, because it wasn't I who ordered the existence of parties. Not I. In November 1945, a decree was issued to establish parties. Thank God, it wasn't Soekarno who signed that decree.[51]

From a sociological perspective, Selo Soemardjan discussed the link between cultural influence and leadership characteristics. He argued the Soekarno's notion of guided democracy, which led to a strong personal leadership, is in fact in accordance with the moral order of Indonesian society. Compared to the parliamentary democracy model, which emphasizes the separation of powers, Soemardjan asserted that guided democracy was more attuned to Indonesian culture.

> The history of Indonesia is replete with kings, sultans, rajahs, and other absolute rulers whom society regarded as the mediators between this world and the cosmological powers that control the life of man and society. Thus, society entrusted to them all powers – social, religious, and political – and expected that the powers would be applied for the welfare of the society ... In the cultural context of this belief system it was hard for the less sophisticated and non-Western-educated groups of Indonesian society to adjust to the Western democratic system of collective government, which imposed upon them a cabinet or an executive council composed of members representing political parties alien to the indigenous population.[52]

Soekarno's guided democracy model was opposed by Hatta, who wrote an article headlined "Our Democracy" in the *Pandji Masyarakat* daily newspaper on 1 May 1960. Hatta argued that Soekarno's ideas and actions clearly violated the constitution. According to Hatta, the first violation was that the President, who under the 1950 Constitution was not accountable and was not

---

50 Daniel S. Lev, *The Transition to Guided Democracy, Indonesian Politics, 1957–1959* (Ithaca, NY: Cornell University Press, 1966), 74–75.

51 Ibid., 72.

52 Selo Soemardjan, "Some Social and Cultural Implications of Indonesia's Unplanned and Planned Development," *The Review of Politics* 25, no. 1 (1963): 89.

beyond criticism, appointed himself to form a cabinet. In doing so, he carried out a responsible act of government without bearing the responsibility for it. Soekarno justified this by citing an "emergency situation". The second violation, according to Hatta, was when Soekarno dissolved the Constituent Assembly, which had been chosen by the people, before it could finish producing a new constitution. Soekarno then promulgated a return to the 1945 Constitution by Presidential Decree on 5 July 1959. Hatta viewed these actions as violations of the constitution and a *coup d'etat*.

In the final part of his article, Hatta revealed details of a debate he had with Soekarno regarding guided democracy. Hatta admitted that he was willing to give Soekarno's system a reasonable opportunity to prove its effectiveness or inadequacy. Hatta conceded, "It seems good to me that Soekarno should be given a fair chance within a reasonable time to see if his system will succeed or fail. I have taken this position ever since our unsuccessful negotiations about two years ago."

Hatta's article can be viewed in the context of constitutional history. In 1957, after Ali Sastroamidjojo's resignation, Soekarno declared a state of emergency under the 1950 Provisional Constitution, which was in effect at that time. The Constituent Assembly, which was tasked with drafting a definitive Constitution, had not succeeded at that point. Soekarno appointed Djuanda as the Prime Minister and formed the Working Cabinet (*Kabinet Karya*). Open discussions were held between the President and cabinet members in December 1958 and January 1959 to formulate the parliament's composition, influenced by Soekarno's concept of class representation in the National Council. Meanwhile, the idea of reverting to the 1945 Constitution was also openly discussed. On 19 February, the Working Cabinet decided to adopt the notion of returning to the 1945 Constitution and amending the electoral law to enable functional representation in Parliament.[53]

The 1945 Constitution was considered a more suitable legal basis for implementing Soekarno's ideas because of its flexible nature. There are four very loosely defined systems of governance in the 1945 Constitution. First, the President is granted enormous power, including the power to make laws. Second, the House of Representatives (DPR) is a legislative body but does not have the power to impeach the President. Third, the People's Consultative Assembly (*Majelis Permusyawaratan Rakyat*, MPR), an expansion of the DPR's membership, embodies the people's sovereignty. The MPR convenes every five years and has the power to enact State Guidelines (*Garis-Garis Besar Haluan*

53 J.D, "Guided Democracy," 97.

Negara, GBHN). Fourth, the Supreme Advisory Council (*Dewan Pertimbangan Agung*, DPA) is an adviser to the President, with its members appointed by the President.[54]

2.4 *The New Order, 1966–1998*

The guided democracy era came to an end with the failed coup attempt in early hours of October 1, 1965, blamed on the PKI. While historians have extensively analyzed this incident and its fatal impact, this chapter focuses on the perspective of constitutional history. Following the failed coup attempt, Soekarno's position as President became increasingly uncertain due to political pressure amid the ensuing liquidation of the PKI. On 11 March 1966, Soekarno issued a mandate to Soeharto to restore political stability and security. This mandate is the starting point of a controversy and debate that have continued to this day. Despite the controversy, on 12 March 1967, Soeharto was appointed acting president by the Provisional MPR. On 27 March 1968, Soeharto was sworn in as the definitive President, and the New Order era began.

In an effort to gain legitimacy, the Soeharto administration held elections in 1971. Soeharto used an organization of so-called Functional Groups (*Golongan Karya*, Golkar) as his political vehicle. Golkar had been formed by the military to counter the influence of the PKI during the Guided Democracy period.[55] In terms of the Constitution, there was no desire from Soeharto to amend the 1945 Constitution. In fact, the New Order launched a campaign to enforce the 1945 Constitution as firmly and authentically as possible.

From a constitutional perspective, power arrangements can be interpreted in various ways, including to perpetuate power. The 1945 Constitution does not clearly state the model of government, whether it is a presidential or parliamentary system. This ambiguity is inherent in the 1945 Constitution because the constitutional system was designed based on the notion of the supremacy of the MPR. This uniqueness in the Indonesian constitutional design has give rise to many peculiarities, including what are known as "constitutional antics".

The supremacy of the MPR is reflected in the Article 1 (2) of the 1945 Constitution, which states, "Sovereignty is in the hands of the people and is fully exercised by the People's Consultative Assembly." The meaning of this provision is further described in the Elucidation of the 1945 Constitution, which states,

---

54 J.A.C. Mackie, "Indonesian Politics Under Guided Democracy," *Australian Outlook* 15, no. 3 (1961): 265.

55 Dirk Tomsa, *Party Politics and Democratization in Indonesia: Golkar in the Post-Soeharto Era* (London: Routledge, 2008), 35.

> People's sovereignty is held by an institution, the People's Consultative Assembly, as the embodiment of all Indonesian people (*Vertretungsorgan des Willens des Staatsvolkes*). The Assembly establishes the Constitution and determines the guidelines of state policy. The Assembly appoints the Head of State (President) and Deputy Head of State (Vice President). It is this assembly that holds the highest state power, while the President must carry out state policy according to the guide set by the Assembly. The President appointed by the Assembly is subject to and responsible to the Assembly. He is the "*mandatarist*" of the Assembly. He is obliged to carry out the decisions of the Assembly. The President is not "*neben*" (equal), but "*untergeordnet*" (subordinate) to the Assembly.[56]

In essence, the supremacy of the MPR means it is the highest state institution, serving as the focal point of all state power and representing the entirety of the Indonesian people as the holder of sovereignty.

Furthermore, the Elucidation of the 1945 Constitution mentions that although the President is not responsible to the House of Representative (DPR), but rather to the MPR, the position of the DPR is strong (*kuat*). The President must pay serious attention to the opinions and aspirations of the DPR. As elaborated in the Elucidation,

> The position of the House of Representatives is strong. The House cannot be dissolved by the President (unlike the parliamentary system). In addition, all the members of the House are concurrently members of the People's Consultative Assembly. Therefore, the DPR can always monitor the actions of the President and if the DPR considers that the President has seriously violated the state policy directives established by the Constitution or by the People's Consultative Assembly, then the Assembly can be invited to convene a special session in order to hold the President accountable.[57]

The design of the governmental system according to the 1945 Constitution had the consequence of posing a threat to presidential power, in that the President could potentially be dismissed by the MPR midway through his/her term of office. Therefore, the president must have an interest in taming, or even

56 Elucidation of the 1945 Constitution on the System of State Administration, no. III.

57 Ibid., VII.

completely eliminating, this threat. Significantly, the Constitution provides avenues for the President to subdue the MPR through political maneuvering antics.

Article 2 (1) of the 1945 Constitution states, "The People's Consultative Assembly consists of members of the House of Representatives plus delegates from the regions and groups, according to the rules stipulated by law." This provision implies that the president's ability to control or eliminate the threat emanating from the MPR to his/her power depends on his/her proficiency in controlling the members of the MPR. This is possible because the President holds the power to make laws. As stated in Article 5 (1) of the 1945 Constitution, "The President holds the power to draft laws with the approval of the House of Representatives." Therefore, if the President is able to overcome the DPR, he/she need not worry about any political threats from the MPR to his/her power. To achieve this, the President must first bring the political parties under his/her control, as the DPR membership is derived from political parties. Such tactics are permissible under the 1945 Constitution.

The situation described above was reflected by President Soeharto's New Order regime. Soeharto was able to maintain his grip on power for more than three decades by using the "constitutional antics" avenue. One of his strategies was to reduce the number of political parties, allowing only two parties to participate in elections, along with Golkar, which was not classified as a political party. Soeharto engineered the coupling of a number of Islamic parties into the United Development Party (*Partai Persatuan Pembangunan*, PPP) and non-Islamic parties into the Indonesian Democratic Party (*Partai Demokrasi Indonesia*, PDI), while ensuring that neither party would become too powerful. With this arrangement, the government used its power to suppress genuine opposition, so PPP and PDI were never able to win an election under Soeharto.

The New Order managed to limit the number of political parties within the constitutional sphere by taking advantage of the 1945 Constitution's silence on the issue. However, the Soeharto administration did not stop there. To further ensure the President's control over the Parliament, Soeharto appointed former military members to the MPR. Moreover, MPR members from regional and group representatives were also under the President's influence. This was due to the arrangements of MPR membership being engineered by the government's election law proposals. In short, this manipulation was a key component of the constitutional antics employed by the New Order.

2.5 *The Reform Era, 1998–Present*

In 1998, Soeharto resigned from the presidency, largely due to the people's growing demands for political reform amid a devastating financial crisis. One of the demands was to amend the Constitution.[58] In response, the MPR amended the 1945 Constitution, with several substantial considerations in mind: (1) maintaining the unaltered Preamble; (2) preserving the unitary state; (3) strengthening the presidential government system; (4) annulling the Elucidation and incorporating its substantial matters into the articles; and (5) adopting an addendum approach for the amendment process.[59]

Despite the efforts to preserve some elements of the original 1945 Constitution, the amendments were ultimately considered a fundamental revision due to the significant increase in the number of provisions[60] and the introduction of new state institutions.[61] As a result, the amendments had a significant impact on the constitutional system, which will be discussed in the next section by comparing it to the system in the 1945 Constitution before the amendments.

---

58 There were six demands for reform that gained strength before and especially after the fall of President Soeharto in 1998, namely: (1) Amendments to the 1945 Constitution; (2) Abolition of the dual function of the Armed Forces; (3) Upholding the rule of law, respecting human rights, and eradicating corruption, collusion and nepotism; (4) Decentralization and fair relations between the Center and the Regions (regional autonomy); (5) Realizing freedom of the press; and (6) Realizing democratic life; see People's Consultative Assembly of the Republic of Indonesia, *Panduan Dalam Memasyarakatkan Undang-Undang Dasar Negara Republik Indonesia Tahun 1945* [*Guidelines for Popularizing the 1945 Constitution of the Republic of Indonesia*] (Jakarta: General Secretariat of the People's Consultative Assembly of the Republic of Indonesia, n.d.), 6.

59 Ibid., 25. Jakob Tobing, who served as the Chair of the Ad Hoc Committee I of the MPR Working Committee responsible for preparing the draft amendment to the 1945 Constitution, referred to the five points of agreement as a "gentlemen's agreement" reached among the various factions within the MPR at that time; see Rofiqul-Umam Ahmad et al. (editors), *Building the Road to Democracy: A Collection of Jakob Tobing's Thoughts on the Amendment of the 1945 Constitution* (Jakarta: Constitution Press, 2008), 182.

60 The pre-amendment 1945 Constitution consisted of 16 chapters, 37 articles, 49 paragraphs, and 4 articles of Transitional Rules and 2 paragraphs of Additional Rules. The post-amendment 1945 Constitution consists of 21 chapters, 73 articles, 170 paragraphs, 3 Articles of Transitional Rules, and 2 paragraphs of Additional Rules, see Ibid., 77–78.

61 There are several new state institutions explicitly or implicitly mentioned in the post-amendment Constitution. Those mentioned explicitly include the Regional Representatives Council, the Constitutional Court, and the Judicial Commission. Implicitly mentioned institutions include the General Election Commission, the central bank, and the Presidential Advisory Council.

3 The Indonesian Constitutional Arrangement

The amendments to the 1945 Constitution, made by the MPR over 1999 to 2002, fundamentally changed Indonesia's constitutional system. This is evident in the alteration of Article 1(2) of the Constitution. The amendments were not just editorial changes, as the original text read, "Sovereignty is in the hands of the people and fully exercised by the People's Consultative Assembly." The amended text now reads, "Sovereignty is in the hands of the people and is implemented according to this Constitution." This signifies a conscious decision by the MPR to alter the system from one based on the supremacy of the MPR to one based on the supremacy of the Constitution.

In the realm of theory and scholarship, the supremacy of the MPR has given rise to differing opinions and interpretations.[62] In constitutional practice, the MPR holds an Annual Session, where the main state institutions (the President, DPR, Supreme Advisory Council, State Audit Agency and Supreme Court) report to the MPR. This annual convention indicates that the MPR is the nucleus of all state power and distributes its power to subordinate state institutions.

Close scrutiny of the Elucidation of the 1945 Constitution reveals contradictory notions. On the one hand, the Elucidation rejects the idea of absolutism or unlimited power. On the other hand, it allows the MPR to have unlimited power beyond the control of any institution. The fact is that absolutism occurs not only when unlimited power is grasped by a person but also when it is held by a group of people.

62 Padmo Wahjono concluded that the People's Consultative Assembly is the only state institution that exercises the people's sovereignty; see Padmo Wahjono (editor), *Masalah Ketatanegaraan Indonesia Dewasa Ini* [*Current Issues of Indonesian Statehood*] (Jakarta: Ghalia Indonesia, 1984), 78–79. See also Padmo Wahjono, *Beberapa Masalah Ketatanegaraan di Indonesia* [*Several Issues of Statehood in Indonesia*] (Jakarta: CV Rajawali, 1984), 83–84. Hamid Attamimi indirectly refuted Padmo Wahjono's opinion above. In his dissertation, Hamid Attamimi said, referring to Soepomo's opinion at the BPUPK session of 13 June 1945, that the people's sovereignty in the hands of the MPR was transferred to the President. Thus, in fact the President is the embodiment of the sovereignty of the people. This is because the power of state 'overnment which originates from the sovereignty of the people (which is fully implemented by the MPR) "flows" through the mandate given by the peo'le (MPR) to the President. This was also mentioned by Harun Al Rasyid in his inaugural speech as Associate Professor at the Faculty of Law, University of Indonesia, 29 July 1995; see Harun Alrasid, *Pemilihan Presiden dan Penggantian Presiden dalam Hukum Positif Indonesia* [*Presidential Election and Replacement in Indonesian Positive Law*] (Jakarta: Yayasan Lembaga Bantuan Hukum Indonesia, 1997), 26–27.

According to Hamid Attamimi, the MPR has two qualities: as an institution that has the power to enact the Constitution and as the holder of the people's sovereignty. Attamimi argues that, in terms of the former, the MPR is above the Constitution. Whereas in the latter quality, because it implements the 1945 Constitution, the position of the MPR is under the Constitution.[63]

Attamimi's opinion raises significant concerns over the interpretation of the phrase "above the constitution", as it could be misconstrued to imply that the MPR is not bound by the Constitution. In reality, the Constitution establishes a constitutional structure that centers on the supreme power held by the MPR, which fully implements people's sovereignty, but lacks proper checks and balances in state institutions. As a result, the power of the MPR is essential for the power of the government but appears to be disconnected from the will of the people.[64]

It is worth noting that Attamimi's opinion may be directed to the vision of the state (*staatsidee*), particularly in relation to the notion of an integralistic state put forward by Soepomo.[65] This notion may have been influenced by Rudolf Smend's integration theory[66] and associated with organicism.[67]

During Soeharto's reign, there was an attempt to reconcile the interpretation of the 1945 Constitution with the view of an integralistic state. This can be seen, in an example, in a book published by the State Secretariat on the Minutes of Meeting of the BPUPK. After publishing Soepomo's speech in full,

63 A. Hamid S. Attamimi, "Peranan Keputusan Presiden Republik Indonesia dalam Penyelenggaraan Pemerintahan Negara Suatu Studi Analisis mengenai Keputusan Presiden yang Berfungsi Pengaturan dalam Kurun Waktu Pelita I-Pelita IV" [The Role of the President of the Republic of Indonesia in the Administration of the State: A Study and Analysis of Presidential Decisions that Function as Regulations During the Period of Pelita I–IV] (Dissertation, Faculty of Law, University of Indonesia, 1990), 8.

64 Among them are the non-recognition of the people's sovereignty in the hands of the people themselves and the formation of a totalitarian government; see Simanjuntak, 253–254.

65 Saafroedin Bahar et al. (editors), *Risalah Sidang Badan Penyelidik Usaha-Usaha Persiapan Kemerdekaan Indonesia (BPUPKI), Panitia Persiapan Kemerdekaan Indonesia (PPKI) 29 Mei 1945 – 19 Agustus 1945* [*Minutes of the Meetings of the Investigative Body for Preparatory Efforts for Indonesian Independence (BPUPKI) and the Preparatory Committee for Indonesian Independence (PPKI) May 29, 1945 – August 19, 1945*] (Jakarta: Sekretariat Negara Republik Indonesia [State Secretariat of the Republic of Indonesia], 1992), 26–36.

66 Werner S. Landecker, "Smend's Theory of Integration," *Social Forces* 29, no. 1 (1950): 39–48.

67 David Bourchier, *Illiberal Democracy in Indonesia: The Ideology of the Family State* (Routledge: Abingdon, 2015).

the book's editorial team deemed it necessary to provide notes on Soepomo's speech.[68] One of the notes states that,

> The application of the concept of a corporatist state and an integralistic state in Western Europe shows excesses, namely the emergence of opportunities for authoritarianism and totalitarianism. This is clearly contrary to the concepts of kinship and togetherness, as well as harmony and balance, that are deeply rooted in Indonesian culture itself. As a result, the concept of an integralistic state underwent modifications when applied to the draft of the 1945 Constitution. Among the important modifications were the recognition of the rights of citizens and the right to regional autonomy.
>
> Therefore, in the training material on the Guidelines for Understanding and Practicing Pancasila, the National BP-7 [Agency for the Development of Education and the Implementation of the Guidelines for the Understanding and Practice of Pancasila] uses the term "Indonesian integralistic" to distinguish it from "German integralistic" understanding.[69]

The claim that the modification of the integralistic state ideology includes protection of citizens' rights and granting regional autonomy is merely a facade. In reality, fundamental rights and local autonomy are not adequately protected or guaranteed. Despite the regional autonomy policy, an integralistic view is evident in the centralized management of state power. The New Order government implemented a centralized system, giving the central government complete control over policies and decision-making in the regions. Local governments had limited authority in managing governance and development affairs in their territory.

The New Order also adopted a uniformity policy in regional development, disregarding cultural, custom and socio-economic differences in regional territories and local communities. This policy was reflected in the Regional Government Law of 1974 and Village Administration Law of 1979. However, the amendments to the 1945 Constitution paved the way for more detailed local government arrangements. The post-amendment Constitution states, "The local governments exercise wide-ranging autonomy". The impact has been extraordinary, leading to a growing interest in establishing new local governments in many regions. Anne Booth has noted,

---

68 This note is entitled "Editor's Notes About: Prof. Mr. Dr. Soepomo Regarding the Rights of Citizens and Integralistic States." See Bahar, et.al., 36–37.

69 Ibid., 37.

> When Soeharto left office in May 1998, there were 27 provinces in Indonesia, compared with 12 in the early 1950s. Since 1998, one province (East Timor) has achieved independence, and seven new provinces have been created, all but one outside Java. Between 1995 and 2009, 37 new urban districts (*kota*) and 168 new rural districts (*kabupaten*) emerged.[70]

The emergence of a large number of new regions has resulted in a more diverse regional political situation. Nevertheless, this diversity may also lead to stagnation in the administration of local governance. As Horowitz has pointed out,

> Indonesia is a thoroughly heterogeneous country, and local political balances are highly variable. The party fragmentation prevailing at the national level is often replicated, but in varying configurations, at the regional level. The task of a district head or mayor in multiparty regions is to put together a coalition that enables the executive to deal with what may be a plurality of competing interests in the region. Some such interests can render the devolved government ineffective.[71]

Given the high level of diversity in Indonesia, it is worth considering whether the Constitution can serve as a unifying element. One way to achieve this could be through the Constitution's Preamble. By emphasizing a number of statements that outline the government's agenda or declare specific principles,[72] a preamble can play a role in unifying a population. A preamble often provides important guidance on a nation's objectives and background, particularly in terms of how the constitution should be interpreted. In many cases, the political values formulated in the preamble are then reflected in the constitutional norms.

The Preamble of the 1945 Constitution contains a legal concept (*rechtsidee*) that consists of four important points. First, "The State protects the nation and all of Indonesia's citizens based on the principle of unity by in order to achieve social justice for all its people." This notion recognizes the importance of a unified state that covers and protects the entire nation, transcending individual

70 Anne Booth, "Splitting, Splitting and Splitting Again: A Brief History of the Development of Regional Government in Indonesia since Independence," *Bijdragen tot de Taal-, Land- en Volkenkunde* 167, no. 1 (2011): 32.

71 Donald L. Horowitz, *Constitutional Change and Democracy in Indonesia* (Cambridge: Cambridge University Press, 2013), 135–136.

72 Henc van Maarseveen and Ger van der Tang, *Written Constitution: A Computerized Comparative Study* (New York: Oceana Publication Inc.-Sijthoff & Nordhoff, 1978), 252.

and group distinctions. According to the Preamble, the state requires unity encompassing the entire nation as one. This is a foundational principle of the state that should not be forgotten.

Second, the state's objective to provide social justice. Third, the Preamble emphasizes that the state is founded the principles of democracy and acknowledge the people's sovereignty through deliberations. Therefore, the governmental system in the Constitution must be based on democracy and representative deliberations that align with the nature of Indonesian society.

The fourth main idea in the Preamble is that the state is based on the belief in One God, in accordance with a just and civilized humanity. Therefore, the Constitution must impose an obligation on the government and state institutions to preserve noble human values and uphold the moral ideals of the people.

The four key principles in the Preamble of the Indonesian Constitution form the foundation of the country's governance. They are crucial to building a strong, just and prosperous nation that protects its citizens. The Preamble reflects the shared dream of many Indonesians for a unified and prosperous nation, despite their diversity. By upholding these principles, the Indonesian government can work toward building a more equitable and inclusive society.

Furthermore, the Constitutional Court's role to sustain unity amidst pluralism in Indonesia cannot be overlooked. The Court which was established after the Constitutional Amendments has many contributions to the idea of consolidation through its decisions. This section will not discuss at length decisions of the Court in this regard since there will be another chapter in this book dedicated to it. But, at the very least 2 decisions that may be considered to serve as examples in the involvement of the Court. The first is in a decision on the constitutionality of law that prohibit former members of the Indonesian Communist Party from running for public office. The second is decision relating to state recognition of the status of a citizen who adheres to beliefs outside the religions formally stated in legislation.

At the beginning of the reform, lawmakers still adopted requirement to fill public office that were often asserted during the New Order. The law stated in terms of running for members of the DPR shall be prohibited for former members of the outlawed Indonesian Communist Party, including members of its mass organizations.[73] This requirement was challenge to the Court. In

73 See Article 60 (g) of Law No 12/2003 on Election for Members of House of Representatives, Regional Representatives Council, and Regional House of Representatives. The provision triggered judicial review case submitted by not only former members of the Indonesian Communist Party but also prominent figures like the late Ali Sadikin, former beloved

its decision, the Court ruled that the requirement in the article was unconstitutional.[74] The Court says, among others, that the provision is a denial to human rights. It is a form of discrimination based on political consideration. The Court also express,

> the provision in Article 60 (g) of Law No 12 of 2003 ... must be seen as no longer relevant to national reconciliation effort that had been the common determination of the Indonesian people towards a more democratic and just future. Hence, despite the majority of the Indonesian people believe on the involvement of the Indonesian Communist Party in the G.30.S incident in 1965 ... the individual persons of the former Indonesia Communist Party's and its subordinate mass organizations' members must be equally treated without discrimination.[75]

The second example of the Court ruling is on the recognition of local belief. There are thousands of Indonesians who adhere various local or indigenous beliefs. Despite legally there seems no problem yet they tend to be treated unfairly officials, especially in regions where conservative views prevail. This is worsen with the requirement in the law on Demographic Administration.[76] Petition for judicial review was filed by parties who were the adherents of local beliefs. The party claimed that the provision had cause to unfair and discriminative treatments. The identity documents, ID Card and Family Paper, were needed to access public services, such as education, social service, and health

---

Jakarta Governor and outspoken opposant to President Suharto and his New Order regime; historian cum educator, the late Deliar Noer; senior politician, Sri Bintang Pamungkas and many others who put a deep concern on the issue.

74 See the Constitutional Court Decision No. 011-017/PUU-I/2003.

75 Ibid., p. 37.

76 See Law No. 23/2006 (then amended by Law No. 24/2014) on Demographic Administration, especially provisions contained in Article 61 paragraphs (1) and (2) and Article 64 paragraph (1) and (5).

Article 61 (1) contained provision which regulates that every Family Card (*Kartu Keluarga*) consists of list, one of which concerning (status of) religion. Meanwhile, paragraph (2) of the Article ruled that residents whose religions had not yet recognized according to legislations or those who adhered local beliefs, the (status of) religion should be left blank or unfilled but they must still be serve and their data are included in resident database. Furthermore, Article 64 (1) contained provision on information that must be filled in Electronic Identification Card (E-KTP), one of which was religion. While, paragraph (5) of this Article contained provision that was similar to provision in Article 61 paragraph (2) saying that status of religion in E-KTP for residents whose religion had not yet recognized according to legislations or those who adhered local beliefs must be left blank or unfilled but they must still be served and included in resident database.

care. The status of religion must be recorded and shall not be left blank. Yet, this caused people who adhered local belief unable to access governmental services unless they filled the list with one of the state recognized religions, which are Islam, Christianity, Hinduism, Buddhism, and Confucianism.

The Court ruled that the term "religion" contained in identity documents list must be read as included local beliefs. The Court says, among others, that when the Constitution recognizes freedom of religion and belief, the implication is that to adhere religion and belief is an inherent right for everyone. Further, the Court also emphasize that the Constitution govern two things on religion, first is on religion as fundamental right and the other is on the State's role to protect it.[77]

4 Conclusion

The idea of Indonesia as an independent nation has been a century-long journey that has culminated in its emergence as a strong and developing country. This idea was born from the desire to stand on one's own feet and was fostered by nationalists in the early 20th century, including by those who became the nation's founding fathers. Despite its diversity of cultures, races and religions, Indonesia stands upright as a melting pot with primordial sentiments, geographical continuity and religious ties serving as unifying elements, rather than as elements of division.

Throughout its history, Indonesia has experimented with various constitutional frameworks to accommodate its diversity. One way this has been achieved is by ensuring representation in political institutions that reflects the country's diversity. Another way has been through experiments with the form of the state, such as considering the options of a federal or unitary state. Additionally, the country has implemented regional autonomy policies, including the expansion of new autonomous regions, to further accommodate the diversity of its population.

The big task ahead is to maintain this awareness and cultivate the spirit of Indonesia's founding principles. Indonesia's history has been marked by a tendency to rely on charismatic leaders, known as *Ratu Adil* (a just ruler), to guide the people to peace and prosperity from times of crisis. This reliance on charismatic leaders has often resulted in the neglect or lack of development of strong political institutions. As a result, political institutions have not developed a

77 See The Constitutional Court Decision No. 97/PUU-XIV/2016.

strong identity in the constitutional system. State institutions often change with the different systems that come and go. Moreover, political institutions are very dependent on their leaders. Consequently, when a leader is replaced, the institutional identity also shifts. This perception needs to change because institutional identity is much more important than maintaining a figure. Political institutions should be built to stand the test of time, lasting longer than a human generation.

Safeguarding the Constitution is vital in unifying the people and recognizing diversity. The Constitution should not be treated as a sacrosanct document, rather, it must remain to open interpretation, enabling sustainable implementation. As the highest law of the land, the Constitution is essential for maintaining Indonesia's unity and stability, while upholding its diversity.

Bibliography

Ahmad, Rofiqul-Umam, et al., eds. *Membangun Jalan Demokrasi: Kumpulan Pemikiran Jakob Tobing tentang Perubahan UUD 1945 [Building the Road to Democracy: A Collection of Jakob Tobing's Thoughts on the Amendment of the 1945 Constitution]*. Jakarta: Konstitusi Press, 2008.

Alrasid, Harun. *Pemilihan Presiden dan Penggantian Presiden dalam Hukum Positif Indonesia [Presidential Election and Presidential Substitution in Indonesian Positive Law]*. Jakarta: Yayasan Lembaga Bantuan Hukum Indonesia, 1997.

Angelo, Homer G. "Transfer of Sovereignty Over Indonesia." *The American Journal of International Law* 44, no. 3 (July 1950): 572.

Attamimi, A. Hamid S. "Peranan Keputusan Presiden Republik Indonesia dalam Penyelenggaraan Pemerintahan Negara Suatu Studi Analisis mengenai Keputusan Presiden yang Berfungsi Pengaturan dalam Kurun Waktu Pelita I-Pelita IV [The Role of Presidential Decrees of the Republic of Indonesia in the Administration of State Government An Analysis Study of Presidential Decrees Functioning in the Period of Pelita I-Pelita IV]." PhD diss., Faculty of Law, University of Indonesia, 1990.

Ave, M.B. "Tentang Asal-Usul dan Pemakaian Istilah Indonesia [About the Origin and Use of Indonesian Terms]." Bintang Timur, published August 23, 1964.

Bahar, Saafroedin, et al., eds. *Risalah Sidang Badan Penyelidik Usaha-usaha Persiapan Kemerdekaan Indonesia (BPUPKI), Panitia Persiapan Kemerdekaan Indonesia (PPKI) 29 Mei 1945 – 19 Agustus 1945 [Minutes of the Meetings of the Investigative Body for Preparatory Efforts for Indonesian Independence (BPUPKI) and the Preparatory Committee for Indonesian Independence (PPKI) May 29, 1945 – August 19, 1945]*. Jakarta: Sekretariat Negara Republik Indonesia, 1992.

Booth, Anne. "Splitting, Splitting and Splitting Again: A Brief History of the Development of Regional Government in Indonesia since Independence." *Bijdragen tot de Taal-, Land- en Volkenkunde* 167, no. 1 (2011): 32.

Bourchier, David. *Illiberal Democracy in Indonesia: The Ideology of the Family State.* Abingdon: Routledge, 2015.

Budiardjo, M.S. "The Provisional Parliament of Indonesia." *Far Eastern Survey* 25, no. 2 (1956): 17.

Caldwell, Malcolm and Ernst Utrecht. *Indonesia: An Alternative History.* Sydney: Alternative Publishing Co-operative, 2008.

"Charter of the Transfer of Sovereignty over Indonesia, Signed at the Round Table Conference, The Hague, 2 November 1949." *International Organization* 4, no. 1 (February 1950): 176–177.

Cribb, Robert and Audrey Kahin. *Historical Dictionary of Indonesia.* Lanham: Scarecrow Press, 2004.

Elson, Robert Edward. *The Idea of Indonesia: A History.* Cambridge: Cambridge University Press, 2008.

Farisiyah, Umi and Zamzani. "Language Shift and Language Maintenance of Local Languages toward Indonesian." Paper, 2018.

Feith, Herbert and Lance Castles, eds. *Indonesian Political Thinking 1945–1965.* Ithaca: Cornell University Press, 1970.

Feith, Herbert. "Toward Elections in Indonesia." *Pacific Affairs* 27, no. 3 (1954): 245.

Feith, Herbert. *The Decline of Constitutional Democracy in Indonesia.* Ithaca: Cornell University Press, 1962.

Feith, Herbert. *The Indonesian Election of 1955.* Ithaca: Cornell Modern Indonesia Project, Interim Reports Series, 1957.

Hatta, Mohammad. "Indonesia's Foreign Policy." *Foreign Affairs*, 31, no. 3 (1953).

Hayes, Adrian and Diahhadi Setyonaluri. *Taking Advantage of the Demographic Dividend in Indonesia: A Brief Introduction to Theory and Practice.* Jakarta: UNFPA Indonesia, 2015. eBook.

Horowitz, Donald L. *Constitutional Change and Democracy in Indonesia.* Cambridge: Cambridge University Press, 2013.

Isra, Saldi and Pan Mohamad Faiz. "The Role of Constitutional Court in Protecting Minority Rights: A Case on Traditional Beliefs in Indonesia." In Bertus de Villers, et al., *Litigating the Rights of Minorities and Indigenous Peoples in Domestic and International Courts.* Leiden: Brill, 2021.

Jessup, Phillip C. *The Birth of Nations.* New York: Columbia University Press, 1974.

Jones, Russell. "George Windsor Earl and 'Indonesia'." *Indonesia Circle* 22, no. 64 (August 2007): 279–290, https://doi.org/10.1080/03062849408729825.

Kahin, Audrey R., ed. *Regional Dynamics of the Indonesian Revolution: Unity from Diversity.* Honolulu: University of Hawaii Press, 1985.

Kahin, George McTurnan. *Nationalism and Revolution in Indonesia*. Ithaca: Cornell University Press, 1952.

Landecker, Werner S. "Smend's Theory of Integration." *Social Forces* 29, no. 1 (1950): 39–48.

Legge, J.D. "Guided Democracy and Constitutional Procedures in Indonesia." *Australian Outlook* 13, no. 2 (1959): 93.

Lev, Daniel S. "The Transition to Guided Democracy." *Indonesian Politics* 1957–1959: 74–75.

Logemann, J.H.A. "The Indonesian Parliament." *Parliamentary Affairs* 6, no. 4 (August 1953): 350.

Maarseveen, Henc van and Ger van der Tang. *Written Constitution, A Computerized Comparative Study*. New York: Oceana Publication, 1978.

Mackie, J.A.C. "Indonesian politics under guided democracy." *Australian Outlook* 15, no. 3 (1961): 265.

Meij, Dick van der. *Indonesian Manuscripts form the Islands of Java, Madura, Bali and Lombok*. Leiden: Brill, 2017.

Ministry of Foreign Affairs of Indonesia. "Indonesia at a Glance." Embassy of the Republic of Indonesia in Vancouver. Accessed January 22, 2023. https://kemlu.go.id/vancouver/en/pages/indonesia_at_a_glance/2016/etc-menu#!.

Nagazumi, Akira. "Indonesia and Indonesians: Semantics in Politics." *Asian Profile* 1, no. 1 (1973): 91–102.

Nasikun. *Sistem Sosial Indonesia* [*Social System of Indonesia*]. Jakarta: Rajawali Pers, 2001.

People's Consultative Assembly of the Republic of Indonesia. *Panduan Dalam Memasyarakatkan Undang-Undang Dasar Negara Republik Indonesia Tahun 1945* [*Guidelines for Popularizing the 1945 Constitution of the Republic of Indonesia*]. Jakarta: General Secretariat of the People's Consultative Assembly of the Republic of Indonesia, 2022.

Pisani, Elisabeth. *Indonesia Etc.: Exploring the Improbable Nation*. Jakarta: The Lontar Foundation, 2014.

Reid, Anthony J.S. *The Indonesian National Revolution 1945–1950*. Hawthorn: Longman Australia, 1974.

Sjahrir. "Political Conditions in Indonesia." In R.E. Elson, *The Idea of Indonesia: A History*. Cambridge: Cambridge University Press, 2008.

Soemardjan, Selo. "Some Social and Cultural Implications of Indonesia's Unplanned and Planned Development." *The Review of Politics* 25, no. 1 (1963): 89.

The 1949 Constitution of the Republic of the United States of Indonesia.

Tomsa, Dirk. *Party Politics and Democratization in Indonesia, Golkar in the Post-Soeharto era*. London: Routledge, 2008.

Vandenbosch, Amry. "The Netherlands-Indonesian Union." *Far Eastern Survey* 19, no. 1 (1950).

Vickers, Adrian. *A History of Modern Indonesia*. Cambridge: Cambridge University Press, 2005.

Wahjono, Padmo. *Beberapa Masalah Ketatanegaraan di Indonesia* [*Some State Administration Problems in Indonesia*]. Jakarta: Rajawali, 1984.

Wahjono, Padmo. *Masalah Ketatanegaraan Indonesia Dewasa Ini* [*Indonesian Constitutional Problems Today*]. Jakarta: Ghalia Indonesia, 1984.

CHAPTER 3

The Indonesian Constitutional Court: An Overview

Saldi Isra and Pan Mohamad Faiz

Abstract

This chapter presents a general description of the Indonesian Constitutional Court, exploring its emergence, development, powers, responsibilities, and the process for appointing its Justices. Although Indonesia declared independence in 1945, its Constitutional Court was not born until 2003. This chapter explains the Court's long gestation period, its sudden birth and how it has exercised its powers. The Court has been instrumental in safeguarding the supremacy of the Constitution, protecting Indonesian citizens' fundamental human rights, and ensuring that the government adheres to the rule of law. Its decisions have also had a significant impact on a wide range of issues, ranging from election disputes to recognition of minority religions. Furthermore, this chapter looks the role of Pancasila as the foundation of the Indonesian Constitution and its importance in guiding the Constitutional Court. The methodology used in this chapter is a qualitative analysis of the Court's functions and secondary sources, including scholarly literature. This chapter concludes with a brief assessment of the Court's performance and future challenges, such as the need to enhance the quality of its decisions while ensuring its independence from political influences. This independence is critical to preserving the Court's integrity and legitimacy as an impartial arbiter of constitutional issues. By examining the Court's history and functions, this chapter explains the Court's vital functions in maintaining Indonesia's diversity and its democratic system.

Keywords

constitutional court – diversity – Indonesia – judicial review – Pancasila

1 Introduction

The Indonesian Constitutional Court has played a critical role in upholding the rule of law, protecting citizens' rights, and ensuring that the government's actions are in line with the country's Constitution. This chapter will provide

 | DOI:10.1163/9789004691698_004

an overview of the Constitutional Court's origins and evolution, powers, functions and its Justice selection mechanism.

The chapter aims to shed light on the role of the Court in strengthening Indonesia's democratic institutions, promoting the rule of law, and safeguarding citizens' rights. With this objective in mind, it will begin by discussing the historical context that led to the establishment of the court and the factors that influenced its design and operations. It will then examine the court's powers and functions, including a look at the number and types of cases it has handled. It also provides an overview of the development of the Court's powers during the first twenty years of its establishment.

This is followed by an explanation of the processes for the appointment and dismissal of the Constitutional Court's nine Justices. This is an important matter as it is one of the factors that can influence the Court's independence. Finally, the chapter concludes by briefly assessing the Court's performance and its future challenges.

> By providing an in-depth analysis of the Indonesian Constitutional Court, this chapter seeks to contribute to the broader understanding of the role of the Court in consolidating democracy, upholding the rule of law, and promoting human rights, which will be elaborated in the further chapters.

2 Background

One of the goals of the amendments to Indonesia's inaugural 1945 Constitution, conducted over 1999 to 2002, was to improve the basis of democratic and modern governance of the state. These improvements included a more explicit distribution of power, a system of checks and balances, and the establishment of new institutions to accommodate the nation's evolving needs after decades of authoritarian rule. At the same time, there was also a restructuring of the authority of existing state institutions and the creation of new ones, as part of efforts to strengthen Indonesia as a constitutional democracy.

One of the new state institutions introduced by the amended Constitution is the Indonesian Constitutional Court, which is one of the holders of judicial power. Article 24(2) of the Constitution states: "The judicial power is exercised by a Supreme Court with its subordinated judicial bodies within the form of general courts, religious courts, military courts, administrative courts, and by a Constitutional Court." Although both the Supreme Court and the Constitutional Court hold judicial power and have the status of "independent" state institutions, they possess different authorities, and there is no hierarchical relationship between them.

In the development of Indonesia's constitutional history, the idea of establishing a Constitutional Court or an institution with the authority to examine laws against the constitution was proposed by one of Indonesia's founders during the preparation of the first constitution of independent Indonesia in the meetings of the Investigating Committee for Preparatory Work for Independence (BPUPK). At that time, Muhammad Yamin proposed that a mechanism be provided for comparing laws.[1] Referring to it as the *Balai Agung* (Supreme Hall), he suggested the institution be given the authority to evaluate the work of political institutions that produce legal products in the form of laws. Although he did not refer to it as a Constitutional Court, Yamin wanted the *Balai Agung*'s mandate to be like that of a constitutional court with the authority to review laws against the constitution.

Yamin's idea was not discussed deeply in the BPUPK because it was rejected by Soepomo, a fellow member of BPUPK and one of the architects of Indonesia's first constitution. Soepomo had at least two objections to Yamin's proposal. First, the Indonesian Constitution was not based on Montesquieu's theory of the separation of powers (*trias politica*). Second, there were not enough legal experts in the early days of independence to compare (*membanding*) or review laws as intended by Yamin. Additionally, Soepomo argued that a comprehensive comparative study of experiences from countries such as Austria and Czechoslovakia, the first two countries that established constitutional courts, both in 1920, was necessary to grant a *Balai Agung* the authority to compare laws.[2] Another reason for Soepomo's objection was that giving judges the authority to compare laws would have contradicted the concept of supremacy of the People's Consultative Assembly (MPR) adopted by the 1945 Constitution.

Although Yamin's proposal was not included in the final version of the 1945 Constitution, the concept of judicial review was still recognized as a part of the judiciary's power in Indonesia. This recognition is based on the philosophical

1 Saafroedin Bahar et al., *Risalah Sidang Badan Penyelidik Usaha-Usaha Persiapan Kemerdekaan Indonesia (BPUPKI) dan Panitia Persiapan Kemerdekaan Indonesia (PPKI) 29 Mei 1945, 19 Agustus 1945* [Minutes of Meeting of the Investigating Committee for Preparatory Work for Independence (BPUPKI) and the Preparatory Committee for Indonesian Independence (PPKI) 29 May 1945, 19 August 1945] (Jakarta: State Secretariat of the Republic of Indonesia, 1992), 299. Compare with Muh. Yamin, *Naskah Persiapan Undang-Undang Dasar 1945* [Preparatory Manuscripts of the 1945 Constitution] (Jakarta: Yayasan Prapanca, 1959), 341.

2 Bahar et al., *Risalah Sidang*, 341–342.

principle of an independent and free judiciary, which is stated in Article 24 of the 1945 Constitution and its Elucidation.[3] In principle, the authority to conduct judicial review cannot be separated from an independent judiciary because it is a fundamental aspect of its implementation.[4] Such arguments can be justified, for example, by referring to the experience of the United States (US) Supreme Court in the case of Marbury vs Madison,[5] where the authority of judges to perform judicial review was not explicitly stated in the Constitution, but was an interpretation of the power of an independent judiciary. This case was a milestone in the history of the judiciary in the practice of judicial review because for the first time, the US Supreme Court invalidated a law made by the US Congress. The influence and concept of reviewing laws, known as judicial review, quickly spread to many other parts of the world.

The idea of establishing a judicial review mechanism in Indonesia gained momentum during the sessions of the Constituent Assembly over 20 May to 13 June 1957. In a plenary session focused on collecting essential materials for a new constitution, several members of the Constituent Assembly revived Yamin's proposal for judicial review. These included Soeripto of the Indonesian National Party (PNI), Oei Tjoe Tat, Siauw Giok Tjohan and Yap Thiam Hien of the Indonesian Council of Deliberation (Baperki), Hermanu Kartodiredjo of the Indonesian Communist Party (PKI), Penda Saroengalo of the Indonesian Christian Party (Parkindo), and members of the Indonesian Judges Association (IKAHI). The members proposed that an article be included in the Constitution stipulating that a law would not apply if it contradicts the Constitution.[6] The Constituent Assembly's efforts to create a new constitution were ultimately unsuccessful, as founding president Soekarno dissolved the assembly in 1959 and introduced his concept of Guided Democracy, centralizing authority under the president's guidance.[7]

---

3 See Saldi Isra, "Hak Menguji Materiil Mahkamah Agung Menurut Hukum Positif Indonesia [The Substance Review of the Supreme Court According to Indonesian Positive Law]," *Jurnal Yustisia* 5 (1997).

4 Adnan Buyung Nasution, "Ke arah Berfungsinya Hak Uji Materiil Mahkamah Agung [Toward the Functioning of the Supreme Court's Substantive Review]," *Analisa CSIS* Year XXII 5 (September 1993): 445.

5 Marbury v. Madison, 5 U.S. 137, 138 (1803).

6 Tim Penyusun, *Naskah Komprehensif Perubahan Undang-Undang Dasar Negara RI Tahun 1945: Buku IV Kekuasaan Kehakiman* [Comprehensive Manuscript of Amendments to the 1945 Constitution of the Republic of Indonesia: Book IV Judicial Power] (Jakarta: Sekretariat Jenderal Mahkamah Konstitusi, 2010), 24–25.

7 For further discussion on the dissolution of the Constituent Assembly, see Adnan Buyung. *Aspirasi Pemerintahan Konstitusional Indonesia. Study Sosio-Legal atas Konstituante*

Despite setbacks, the development of Indonesia's constitutional law reflects that, over time, Yamin's ideas were gradually incorporated into various legal products, even though the authority for judicial review of laws against the constitution was not yet established. This process began with the enactment of Law No. 14 of 1970 on the Basic Provisions of Judicial Power, which granted the Supreme Court the power to declare regulations below the level of law invalid on the grounds of inconsistency with higher regulations. Subsequently, the Third People's Consultative Assembly Decree of 1978, commonly referred to as Tap MPR No III/MPR/1978, further expanded the Supreme Court's authority to include the material review of the substance of regulations below the law. This was followed by the passage of Law No. 14 of 1985 on the Supreme Court, which granted the Supreme Court the power to conduct substantive review of regulations below the law, but only on the grounds of inconsistency with the law, not the with the Constitution.

In 1998, a massive wave of demonstrations culminated in the resignation of President Soeharto, who had held power for 32 years. Following his fall, the 1945 Constitution underwent a four-stage amendment process that resulted in a profound recalibration of Indonesian politics toward liberal democracy and significantly enhanced the effectiveness of power distribution among various state institutions.[8] This constitutional reform was based on four fundamental principles: constitutional supremacy, separation of powers with checks and balances, constitutional democracy, and protection of citizens' fundamental rights.[9] The changes to these fundamental principles were so significant that, according to Richard Albert, the event could be described more accurately as a constitutional dismemberment rather than a mere constitutional amendment.[10]

Soeharto's resignation marked a significant turning point in reviving Yamin's idea of reviewing laws against the constitution. During the 1998 MPR Special Session, the legal basis for reform was discussed, including changes to the judiciary's power as outlined in the 1945 Constitution. The push for judicial reform was motivated by a desire to uphold the independence of the judiciary and enable the authority to review laws, not just regulations under the law, but

1956–1959 [Aspirations of Indonesian Constitutional Governance. Socio-Legal Study of the Constituent Assembly 1956–1959] (Jakarta: Pustaka Utama Grafiti, 2001).

8 Simon Butt and Tim Lindsey, *Indonesian Law* (Oxford: Oxford University Press, 2018), 8.

9 Pan Mohamad Faiz, "The Role of the Constitutional Court in Securing Constitutional Government in Indonesia" (PhD diss., University of Queensland, 2016), 2.

10 Richard Albert, "Constitutional Amendment and Dismemberment," *The Yale Journal of International Law* 43, no. 1 (2018): 29–59.

also the laws themselves.[11] As changes to the 1945 Constitution were made, the prospect of achieving judicial reform moved closer to reality.

Upon examination of the minutes of the amendments to the 1945 Constitution, it is clear that the discussion about granting the judiciary the authority to review laws first emerged in relation to the Supreme Court's power. For instance, during the sixth meeting of the Ad-Hoc Committee III of the Working Body (PAH BP) of the MPR on 12 October 1999, the proposed text of Article 24 (3) of "Chapter IX on the Supreme Court" stated the Supreme Court is authorized to conduct substantive reviews on laws and regulations under the law.[12] However, a key part of this power would subsequently be transferred to a new institution called the "Constitutional Court," which was raised during the discussion at the PAH BP MPR meeting on 1 March 2000.

After the Second Amendment of the 1945 Constitution in 2000, the discussions regarding the reform of the judicial power were concluded in the Third Amendment of 2001. The Third Amendment finalized the institutional design, powers, and appointment process of the judiciary. It introduced the design of the judicial power as outlined in the Constitution's Chapter IX on Judicial Power, which is elaborated in Articles 24, 24A, 24B and 24C, including the establishment of the Constitutional Court.[13] The construction of Article 24C underscores that the establishment of the Constitutional Court was a response to the idea and desire of creating a system of judicial review of laws. Furthermore, the Constitutional Court was established to empower the judiciary to conduct judicial review of laws against the constitution, which was not possible earlier.[14]

Although the design and arrangements for the Constitutional Court had been completed when the MPR established the Third Amendment on 9 November 2001, the Constitutional Court itself had not yet been formally established. It was not until the MPR made the Fourth Amendment on 10 August 2002, that the Constitutional Court began to take shape. However, progress was slow, prompting the MPR to agree on a transitional arrangement at the constitutional level. Article III of the Transitional Provisions of the Indonesian Constitution stipulated the Constitutional Court must be established no later than 17 August 2003. Until then, all of its authorities would be

---

11 Ibid., 27.

12 Ibid., 62–63.

13 Saldi Isra and Pan Mohamad Faiz, *Indonesian Constitutional Law: Selected Articles on Challenges and Developments in Post-Constitutional Reform* (Depok: Rajawali Pers, 2021), 8.

14 Moh. Mahfud MD, *Perdebatan Hukum Tata Negara Pascaamandemen Konstitusi* [Post-Amendment Constitutional Law Debate] (Jakarta: Rajawali Pers, 2011), 74.

held by the Supreme Court. This provision provided a clear deadline for the establishment of the Constitutional Court, and exceeding it was not allowed. Despite the Constitutional Court not yet being established, its authority was exercised by the Supreme Court, underscoring its importance.

To meet the 17 August 2003 deadline for establishing the Constitutional Court, the government and the House of Representatives (DPR) agreed to approve the Bill on the Constitutional Court at an Extraordinary Plenary Session of the DPR on the sidelines of the MPR 2003 session, on 13 August 2003, just over a year after the Fourth Amendment of the 1945 Constitution. President Megawati Soekarnoputri on that day signed it into law as Law No. 24 of 2003. This event is considered special, not only because of the approval between the government and the DPR, but also due to its enactment and promulgation in the State Gazette on the same day. Indonesia was the 78th country to establish a Constitutional Court and the first to do so in the 21st century.[15] The approval and enactment of Law No. 24 of 2003 on 13 August 2003, is widely regarded as the birth of the Indonesian Constitutional Court. Consequently, 13 August 2023 marks the 20th anniversary of the Constitutional Court's birth.

The process did not stop at the enactment of Law No. 24 of 2003. The next step was the appointment of nine judges, more formally known as justices, to serve on the Constitutional Court. In accordance with Article 24C(3) of the Indonesian Constitution, the state institutions entrusted with proposing Constitutional Court justices, namely the DPR, the President, and the Supreme Court, each recruited three people for the positions. Each institution then proposed its selections to be appointed by the President. Through Presidential Decree No. 147/M of 2003, dated 15 August 2003, President Megawati appointed nine Constitutional Court justices, who then took their oath of office at the Presidential Palace on 16 August 2003. As stipulated in the Constitutional Court Law, the Chief Justice and Deputy Chief Justice of the Constitutional Court are selected from among the Constitutional justices, rather than being chosen by other branches of government.[16]

---

15 Jimly Asshiddiqie and Mustafa Fakhri, *Mahkamah Konstitusi: Kompilasi Ketentuan Konstitusi, Undang-Undang, dan Peraturan di 78 Negara* [Constitutional Court: Compilation of Constitutional Provisions, Laws, and Regulations in 78 Countries] (Jakarta: Center for Constitutional Law Studies, Faculty of Law, University of Indonesia).

16 For further discussion on the background of the formation of the Indonesian Constitutional Court, see I D.G. Palguna, Saldi Isra, and Pan Mohamad Faiz, *The Constitutional Court and Human Rights Protection in Indonesia* (Depok: Rajawali Pers, 2022), xv-xxiii; Petra Stockman, *The New Indonesian Constitutional Court: A Study into Its Beginnings and First Years of Work* (Jakarta: Hanns Seidel Foundation, 2007); Hendrianto, "Institutional Choice

3 Powers and Functions

Before discussing the powers of the Constitutional Court as outlined in Article 24C(1) and (2) of the Indonesian Constitution, it is important to first understand the Constitutional Court's role in the design of judicial power. As stated in Article 24(1) of the Constitution, "The judicial power is an independent authority in organizing the judicature for the sake of law enforcement and justice." This principle is central to the concept of the rule of law, which emphasizes the necessity of judicial power being independent as an absolute requirement for a constitutional democratic state.[17] The idea of judicial power as a separate and independent authority was first introduced by Montesquieu, who developed the doctrine of the separation of powers, also known as the *trias politica*. Montesquieu believed that oversight was necessary to prevent abuse of power, and that this oversight had to be conducted through or by means of power. His statement forms the basis of his belief that it is important to separate the powers within the state, and not allow them to be consolidated in one hand.[18]

In addition, Montesquieu emphasized the significance of an independent judiciary, free from the influence of other branches of government, as the judiciary plays a pivotal role in the event of confrontation between the government, the law and individuals. Thus, the judiciary must function as a primary barrier to government actions that disregard the law. To achieve this, Montesquieu suggested that judges should be selected from the community, and their terms of office should be limited.[19] With regard to the establishment of Indonesia's Constitutional Court, this highlights the essential need for judicial independence since the Constitutional Court's power is closely tied to the processes and outcomes of political institutions. Given the intimate relationship between its powers and the political process, the Constitutional Court can also be referred to as a "political court". As the court has jurisdiction over various cases related to politics, the resolution of political cases is known as the "judicialization of politics".[20]

---

and the New Indonesian Constitutional Court," in *New Courts in Asia*, ed. Andrew Harding and Penelope Nicholson (London: Routledge, 2010).

17 I D.G. Palguna, *Mahkamah Konstitusi & Dinamika Politik Hukum di Indonesia* [Constitutional Court & Dynamics of Political Law in Indonesia] (Jakarta: Rajawali Pers, 2020), 181–182.

18 Ibid.

19 Ibid., 182–183.

20 See Ran Hirschl, *The Judicialization of Politics* (Oxford: Oxford University Press, 2008), 119; Pan Mohamad Faiz, "Judicialization of Politics," *The Jakarta Post*, 8 November 2011, 6.

In addition to the aforementioned guarantee of independence, judicial power in Indonesia is not exercised by a single institution as it was before the amendment of the 1945 Constitution, or like the US Supreme Court or the High Court in Australia. In terms of the design of the holders of the judicial power, Article 24 (2) of the Constitution states: "The judicial power is exercised by a Supreme Court with its subordinated judicial bodies within the form of general courts, religious courts, military courts, administrative courts, and by a Constitutional Court." The phrases "by a Supreme Court" and "by a Constitutional Court" indicate judicial power in Indonesia is exercised by two institutions with different authorities, in an equal position, and with different jurisdictions.[21]

Compared to other countries' state institutions with the power of judicial review, the Indonesian Constitutional Court tends to follow the European[22] or Kelsenian model.[23] This model is a centralized system of constitutional review, which is centered on a single institution called the Constitutional Court or *Verfassungsgerichtshof*.[24] In contrast, the model of constitutional review introduced in the United States does not establish a separate institution with the power of constitutional review, but rather vests this power in the Supreme Court, which then acts as the guardian and protector of the Constitution.[25]

As one of the judicial powers in Indonesia, the authority of the Constitutional Court differs from that of the Supreme Court. Article 24C,(1) and (2) of the Constitution state:

1. The Constitutional Court has the authority to adjudicate at the first and final level, whose decision is final to review laws against the Constitution, to adjudicate on authority disputes of state institutions whose authorities are given by the Constitution, to adjudicate on the dissolution of a political party, and to adjudicate on disputes regarding the result of a general election.

21 M. Luthfi Chakim, "Institutional Improvement of the Indonesia Constitutional Court: Based on Comparative Study with South Korea and Germany" (Master Thesis, Graduate School of Seoul University College of Law, Seoul, 2020), 9.

22 Victor Ferreres Comella, "The European Model of Constitutional Review of Legislation: Toward Decentralization?" *International Journal of Constitutional Law* 2, no. 3 (2004): 461.

23 Hans Kelsen, "Judicial Review of Legislation," *The Journal of Politics* 4, no. 2 (1942): 183. See also Christoph Bezemek, "A Kelsenian Model of Constitutional Adjudication: The Austrian Constitutional Court," *Austrian Journal of Public Law* 67 (2012): 117.

24 Jimly Asshiddiqie, *Model-Model Pengujian Konstitusional di Berbagai Negara* [Models of Constitutional Review in Other Countries] (Jakarta: Sinar Grafika, 2010), 44.

25 Ibid., 45.

2. The Constitutional Court shall render a decision on the opinion of the House of Representatives regarding an alleged violation by the President and/or Vice-President according to the Constitution.

Article 24C(1) confers four powers to the Constitutional Court: (1) reviewing laws against the Constitution, (2) adjudicating disputes over authority between state institutions, (3) ruling on the dissolution of political parties, and (4) deciding on contested election results. Additionally, as specified in Article 24C(2), the Constitutional Court has another authority, which, while framed as a duty by I D.G. Palguna, is to render a decision on the opinion of the DPR on alleged violations by the President and/or Vice President in accordance with the Constitution. These powers can be attributed to the Constitutional Court's function of constitutional review, which upholds the principles of a constitutional democratic state.[26] Therefore, the phrase "shall render a decision" in Article 24C (2) should not be construed as an obligation of the Constitutional Court because it cannot be dissociated from the time limit given to the Court to decide on the DPR's opinion for legal certainty on allegations of violations committed by the President and/or Vice President. The following section elucidates the five powers of the Constitutional Court outlined in Article 24C (1) and (2).

In implementing its powers and functions, the Constitutional Court has been guided by Pancasila, the philosophical foundation of the Indonesian state which has five key principles: belief in the One and only God, just and civilized humanity, unity of Indonesia, democracy through representation and social justice for all Indonesians. One example of Pancasila's influence on the Court is the way it interprets the national motto of Unity in Diversity (*Bhinneka Tunggal Ika*) which is seen as a fundamental value of Indonesian society. The Court has used this principle to protect Indonesian diversity.

The Constitutional Court's five powers establish its role as the defender of the constitution and democracy, as well as the safeguard of human rights and citizens' constitutional rights. These authorities will be expounded upon in the subsequent section.

3.1 *Reviewing Laws against the Constitution*

Upon examining Article 24C(1) of the Indonesian Constitution, it is clear that the authority to review laws against the Constitution is the primary power

26 I D.G. Palguna, *Mahkamah Konstitusi: Dasar Pemikiran, Kewenangan, dan Perbandingan dengan Negara Lain* [Constitutional Court: Rationale, Authority, and Comparison with Other Countries] (Jakarta: Konstitusi Press, 2018), 146.

of the Constitutional Court. This is hardly surprising, as the review of laws against the Constitution was the primary reason for the establishment of the Constitutional Court. Initially, Law No. 24 of 2003 on the Constitutional Court restricted the laws that could be tested or assessed for their constitutionality by the Constitutional Court. Article 50 of Law No. 24 of 2003 stated that only laws enacted after the amendment of the Constitution could be subjected to review. The Elucidation of Article 50 of Law No. 24 of 2003 further specified that "after the amendment of the Constitution" referred to the first amendment of the Constitution on 19 October 1999. Consequently, this provision implies that all laws enacted before that date were beyond the purview of the Constitutional Court's constitutional review. However, Article 24C(1) of the Constitution does not impose any such limitations and merely refers to "laws" that are against the Constitution.

If the limitation in the Elucidation of Article 50 of Law No. 24 of 2003 is justified, then it is reasonable to argue that laws enacted before 19 October 1999 do not fall within the jurisdiction of the Constitutional Court to examine them. However, laws enacted before 19 October 1999 are very likely to be contrary to the Constitution. This creates a gap in the institution authorized to examine, adjudicate and decide on requests to review laws enacted before the first amendment, namely before 19 October 1999.

Regarding the limitation, the Constitutional Court, which is obligated to examine and adjudicate cases submitted to it, made a breakthrough in Decision No. 004/PUU-I/2003 dated 30 December 2003, by "setting aside" Article 50 of Law No. 24 of 2003. In its legal considerations, the Constitutional Court stated that it has the authority to declare law that is not in line or even contradictory to the Constitution, as not bound by the said law.[27] This effectively removed the limitation on reviewing laws that were enacted before the First Amendment to the 1945 Constitution. Stefanus Hendrianto referred to the examination of Article 50 of Law No. 24 of 2003 as a "standing battle".[28] After the ruling, the Constitutional Court was able to review all existing laws without being bound by the limitation of when they were enacted.[29]

In addition to the normative limitations that have been set aside, the authority of the Constitutional Court is also limited to reviewing only laws against the Constitution. Reviewing regulations lower than laws, against laws,

---

27 Constitutional Court Decision No. 004/PUU-I/2003, 30 December 2003, 13–14.

28 Stefanus Hendrianto, *Law and Politics of Constitutional Courts: Indonesia and the Search for Judicial Heroes* (New York: Routledge, 2018), 136.

29 Simon Butt and Tim Lindsey, *The Constitution of Indonesia: A Contextual Analysis* (Oxford: Hart Publishing, 2012), 108–109.

is the authority of the Supreme Court, under Article 24A(1) of the Constitution. Consequently, the jurisdiction of the Constitutional Court is narrow. The division and, at the same time, limitation of the reviewing authority between two different institutions is similar to the reviewing system model in the Constitutional Court of South Korea.[30] However, in practice, the separation of the jurisdiction of reviewing laws by the Constitutional Court and reviewing regulations under laws by the Supreme Court can create problems and legal uncertainty.[31]

Despite the division of authority between the Constitutional Court and the Supreme Court, reviewing laws against the Constitution provides an avenue for the judiciary to correct any legislative processes or materials that are in conflict with the Constitution. This is based on the understanding that laws, as a result of political compromise, have the potential to produce oppressive or despotic provisions.[32] Legal and political philosopher Jeremy Waldron even expressed concern "that legislation and legislatures have a bad name in legal and political philosophy, a name sufficiently disreputable to cast doubt on their credentials as respectable source of law".[33] This suspicion, combined with the possibility of laws conflicting with the constitution, makes the assessment of the constitutionality of laws necessary as part of the checks and balances process.[34]

The assessment of the constitutionality of a law pertains not only to its material or substantive aspects but may also be carried out on the validity of its formalities. Sri Soemantri asserts that a law may be assessed either materially (*materiele toetsing*) or formally (*formele toetsing*).[35] Formal review pertains to the procedures for drafting a law. If the review involves alleged procedural errors or deliberate bypassing of procedures in law-making, the process is called formal review. Conversely, if what is being reviewed is the material

30 Simon Butt, *The Constitutional Court and Democracy in Indonesia* (Leiden: Brill-Nijhoff, 2018), 31.

31 Pan Mohamad Faiz, "Legal Problems of Dualism of Judicial Review System in Indonesia," *Jurnal Dinamika Hukum* 16, no. 2 (2016): 187–195. See also Saldi Isra, "Legitimasi Perubahan Konstitusi [Legitimacy of Constitutional Amendments]," *Harian Kompas*, 3 January 2020, 6.

32 John Agresto, *The Supreme Court and Constitutional Democracy* (London: Cornel University Press, 1984), 31.

33 Jeremy Waldron, *The Dignity of Legislation* (Cambridge: Cambridge University Press, 1999), 1.

34 Saldi Isra and Khairul Fahmi, *Pemilihan Umum Demokratis: Prinsip-Prinsip dalam Konstitusi Indonesia* [Democratic General Elections: Principles in the Indonesian Constitution] (Depok: Rajawali Pers, 2019), 88.

35 Sri Soemantri, *Hak Uji Materil di Indonesia* [Substantive Review Rights in Indonesia] (Bandung: Alumni, 1997), 39.

content of the law because it is alleged to be in conflict with the Constitution, it is called substantive review.

Formal review is a useful tool for evaluating at least four aspects of the constitutionality of laws, namely: (1) whether the format of the law conforms to the Constitution or laws derived from it; (2) the extent to which the procedures followed during the law-making process were observed; (3) whether the institutions involved in creating the law were actually authorized to do so; and (4) whether the procedures for enacting and implementing the law comply with the provisions outlined in the Constitution or laws based on the Constitution.[36] The distinction in review yields different consequences. Substantive review, if upheld, may result in some or even all of the content of the law being deemed in conflict with the Constitution and declared devoid of binding force. In contrast, if formal review is upheld, the legal effect of the law as a whole is deemed to be in conflict with the Constitution and is declared to have no binding legal force.

Although Article 24C (1) of the Constitution states the Constitutional Court has the authority to review laws against the Constitution, in practice, a Government Regulation in Lieu of Law, also known as an Interim Emergency Law (*Peraturan Pemerintah Pengganti Undang-Undang*, Perppu), can also be reviewed for its constitutionality by the Constitutional Court. This 'expansion' of authority is based on Constitutional Court Decision No. 138/PUU-VII/2009, dated 8 February2010. The basis of the Constitutional Court's consideration stems from the understanding that a Perppu is not the same as a government regulation, as stipulated in Article 5 (2) of the Constitution. In this case, the purpose of government regulations is to carry out laws as they should be, while a Perppu is regulated in the Constitution's Chapter VII on the DPR, where the DPR holds the power to form laws. Thus, Perppu material should be material that, according to the Constitution, is regulated by law and not material that enforces the law as referred to in Article 5 (2) of the Constitution.[37] Furthermore, the Constitutional Court considers that in situations where the substance of a law has not been processed in accordance with established procedures or provisions, a legal vacuum may occur. In such cases, urgent legal needs may arise that require immediate action. To address such needs, Article 22 of the Constitution authorizes the President to issue a Perppu. This special provision enables the President to address the urgent matter and fill the legal vacuum without going through the time-consuming process of creating a law

36 See Jimly Asshiddiqie, *Pengujian Formil Undang-undang di Negara Hukum* [Formal Review of Laws in the Law-Based State] (Jakarta: Konstitusi Press, 2020).

37 Constitutional Court Decision No. 138/PUU-VII/2009, 8 February 2010, 18–19.

through the usual process, which involves the submission of a draft law by the DPR or the President.[38]

The Constitutional Court's decision not only established the differences between Perppu and government regulations and confirmed that Perppu is substantively a form of law, but it also clarified the meaning of "in the event that exigencies compel", in other words, when there is an urgent situation, as a condition for issuing a Perppu, as outlined in Article 22 (1) of the Constitution. The determination of this requirement is significant as there had been no prior legal interpretation of the term. Prior to this ruling, debates regarding the issuance of Perppu and its requirement were mainly based on doctrine or expert opinions. The Constitutional Court identified three criteria that must be satisfied for a situation to be considered urgent or compelling and thus warrant the issuance of a Perppu, namely:

1. There is a compelling situation that demands a timely resolution of a constitutional legal issue.
2. Either there is no law in place to address the matter, creating a legal vacuum, or an existing law is insufficient to deal with the urgent legal problem.
3. The legal vacuum cannot be overcome by creating a law through the usual procedure, as it would take a considerable amount of time, while the urgent situation requires prompt resolution.[39]

Based on those three criteria, the Constitutional Court clarified that the "compelling exigency" concept should not be interpreted only as a state of danger, as referred to in Article 12 of the Constitution. Although the presence of danger may hinder the regular law-making process, it is not the sole circumstance that qualifies as a compelling exigency under Article 22(1) of the Constitution. In its legal reasoning, the Constitutional Court explained that a Perppu could establish legal norms with the same binding force as a law. Therefore, the Constitutional Court has the authority to assess whether the norms outlined in a Perppu conflict materially with the Constitution.[40]

The Constitutional Court's jurisdiction includes constitutional review cases, which are more frequent than other cases. As of the end of 2022, the Constitutional Court had ruled on 1,603 cases involving law and Perppu reviews, with 297 cases either partially or entirely granted. This translates to an annual

38 Ibid., 19.
39 Ibid.
40 Ibid., 20–21.

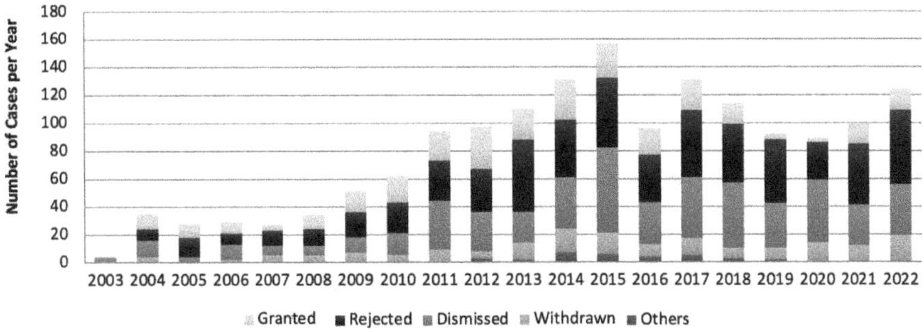

FIGURE 3.1 Recapitulation of law review decisions (2003–2022)
SOURCE: SECRETARIAT GENERAL AND REGISTRAR OFFICE OF THE CONSTITUTIONAL COURT

grant rate of around 18.41% for law review cases. Figure 3.1 provides further details on the verdicts in all law review cases decided by the Constitutional Court between 2003 and 2022.

3.2 *Adjudicating on Authority Disputes between State Institutions*

Textually, Article 24C(1) of the Constitution grants the Constitutional Court the authority to "to adjudicate on authority disputes of state institutions whose authorities are given by the Constitution". Regarding this authority, the phrase provides two main elements, namely "authority disputes of state institutions" and "whose authorities are given by the Constitution". This means that only matters of authority, not other disputes, can be disputed in the Constitutional Court. Furthermore, state institutions that can file disputes are those whose authority is granted by the Constitution. Therefore, the phrase "whose authorities are given by the Constitution" serves as an attributive authority.[41]

The phrase "to adjudicate on authority disputes of state institutions whose authorities are given by the Constitution" has been the subject of study by the Consortium for National Law Reform, which has examined the constitutional limits contained in the phrase. The consortium stated in its research on this matter:

41 Ichsan Anwary, *Lembaga Negara dan Penyelesaian Sengketa Kewenangan Konstitusional Lembaga Negara* [State Institution and Settlement of Constitutional Disputes of State Institutions] (Yogyakarta: Genta Publishing, 2018), 167.

> With respect to disputes that fall under the jurisdiction of the Constitutional Court, the Constitution sets a clear and specific limit. First and foremost, the dispute must pertain to issues of authority. Disputes over authority are the primary matters that can be brought before the Constitutional Court; all other disputes are outside its purview. The contested authority may stem from either the Constitution or other laws. Second, only state institutions with authority granted by the Constitution may be parties in such disputes. Thus, state institutions that derive their authority from sources other than the Constitution cannot file requests for the resolution of disputes over authority between state institutions from the Constitutional Court.[42]

In fact, the construction of norm formulation in the phrase "adjudicate on authority disputes of state institutions whose authorities are given by the Constitution" essentially involves constitutional authority disputes that arise from the implementation of authority granted by the Constitution. However, the phrase "whose authorities are given by the Constitution" can have a broader meaning than the authority granted by the Constitution. The term "constitution" itself theoretically has a broader meaning than "constitutional law". Constitutional law scholar Jimly Asshiddiqie, who was the inaugural chief justice of the Indonesian Constitutional Court, formulates a dispute of constitutional authority as follows:

> Therefore, the Constitutional Court's authority to resolve disputes concerning the authority of state institutions with authority granted by the Constitution can be referred to more simply as inter-institutional constitutional authority disputes. There are two elements to the notion of constitutional authority disputes: (i) the existence of constitutional authority as defined in the Constitution; and (ii) the emergence of disputes in the implementation of constitutional authority due to varying interpretations among two or more related state institutions.[43]

The Constitution does not explicitly identify which state institutions may bring disputes before the Constitutional Court, apart from the phrase "to

---

42 Firmansyah Arifin et al., *Lembaga Negara dan Sengketa Kewenangan Antar Lembaga Negara* [State Institutions and Disputes of Authority Between State Institutions] (Jakarta: KRHN and MKRI, 2005), 123.

43 Jimly Asshiddiqie, *Sengketa Kewenangan Antarlembaga Negara* [State Institutions' Authority Disputes] (Jakarta: Konstitusi Press, 2005), 15.

adjudicate on authority disputes of state institutions whose authorities are given by the Constitution". According to Achmad Roestandi, state institutions whose authority is granted by the Constitution can be classified into three groups. The first group consists of institutions whose form, name and authority are specified in the Constitution, such as the MPR, DPR and the Regional Representative Council (DPD). The second group comprises institutions whose form and name are not specified in the Constitution, but whose authority is granted by law, including the Presidential Advisory Council and the General Elections Commission (KPU). Last, the third group encompasses institutions whose form, name and authority are not specified in the Constitution, but are granted by law, such as the central bank and other bodies whose functions are related to the power of the judiciary.[44]

In fact, the debate regarding "state institutions" and "authorities given by the Constitution" in the phrase "adjudicate on authority disputes of state institutions whose authorities are given by the Constitution" could have been clarified during the drafting of Law No. 24 of 2003 on the Constitutional Court. However, the wording of the law does not provide much help in resolving the debate. Article 61(1) of Law No. 24 of 2003 states: "The petitioner is a state institution whose authority is granted by the Constitution and has a direct interest in the disputed authority." The construction of the norm in this provision still does not explicitly state which state institutions can file a dispute to the Constitutional Court.

In general, when examining the norm construction governing disputes of authority in Law No. 24 of 2003, three requirements must be met for a dispute of authority between state institutions to fall under the jurisdiction of the Constitutional Court. First, the dispute must concern authority between state institutions. Second, the authority must be granted by the Indonesian Constitution. Third, the state institution in question must have a direct interest in the disputed authority.[45] Initially, Law No. 24 of 2003 limited the state institutions that could become parties in a dispute of authority before the Constitutional Court. Article 65 of the Law states the Supreme Court cannot be a party in a dispute of authority between state institutions in the Constitutional Court. However, in Law No. 8 of 2011, which amended Law No. 24 of 2003, the restriction on the Supreme Court was lifted, and this institution can now be a party in disputes of authority before the Constitutional Court.

---

44 Luthfi Widagdo Eddyono, *Penyelesaian Sengketa Kewenangan Lembaga Negara oleh Mahkamah Konstitusi* [Settlement of State Institutions' Authority Disputes by the Constitutional Court] (Yogyakarta: Insigna Strat, 2013), 48.

45 Anwary, *Lembaga Negara*, 5. See also Arifin et al., *Lembaga Negara*, 124.

In its development, the Constitutional Court has played a significant role in interpreting and defining the phrase "adjudicate on authority disputes of state institutions whose authorities are given by the Constitution". The Constitutional Court Decision No. 004/SKLN-IV/2006, dated 12 July 2006, is considered one of the most important decisions in explaining the meaning of disputes over state institutions' authorities. There are at least three basic explanations concerning disputes over state institutions' authorities. First, it is essential to determine if there are specific authorities (*objectum litis*) granted by the Constitution, and then to which agency those authorities are granted (*subjectum litis*). Second, in determining the content and limits of the authority that becomes the *objectum litis* of a dispute over authority, the Constitutional Court does not solely rely on the textual interpretation of the provisions of the Constitution that grant authority to a particular agency. The Constitutional Court also considers the possibility of implicit authority that may be used to carry out the main authority.[46] Furthermore, in Decision No. 3/SKLN-X/2012, dated 19 September 2012, the Constitutional Court held that disputed authority does not necessarily have to be explicitly stated (*expressis verbis*) in the Constitution. The authority in question can also include delegated authority derived from the attributed authority mentioned in the Constitution. In this regard, the most important factor to assess is whether the state agency in dispute has been granted authority by the Constitution.[47]

Meanwhile, constitutional law professor Ni'matul Huda has identified several causes of constitutional disputes over the authorities of state institutions. First, disputes can arise due to overlapping of authority between two or more state institutions as regulated in the pre-amendment Constitution and the post-amendment Constitution. Second, a state institution may ignore the authority of another state institution, which is obtained from the pre-amendment Constitution or the post-amendment Constitution. Third, a state institution may carry out authority obtained from the pre-amendment Constitution or the post-amendment Constitution that is designated for another state institution, and so on.[48]

Compared to the review of laws, the number of cases regarding disputes over state institutions' authorities brought to the Constitutional Court is relatively small. This is due to the very limited number of state institutions

---

46 Eddyono, *Penyelesaian Sengketa*, 131.

47 Constitutional Court Decision No. 004/SKLN-IV/2006, 12 July 2006, 90–91.

48 Ni'matul Huda, *Sengketa Kewenangan Lembaga Negara dalam Teori dan Praktik di Mahkamah Konstitusi* [Disputes on the Authority of State Institutions in Theory and Practice at the Constitutional Court] (Yogyakarta: FH UII Press, 2016), 179–180.

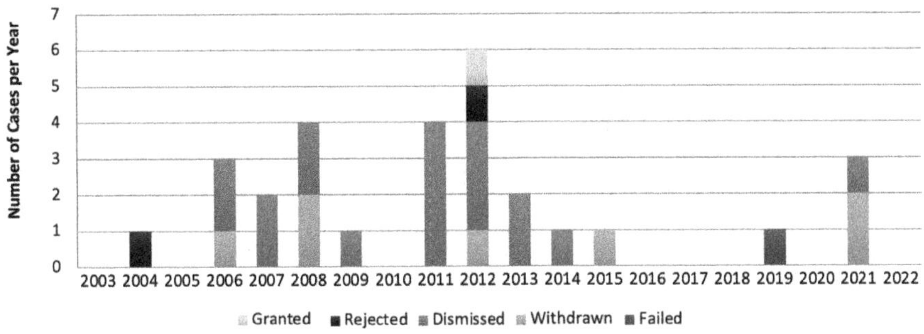

FIGURE 3.2 Recapitulation of decisions on authority disputes between state institutions
SOURCE: SECRETARIAT GENERAL AND REGISTRAR OFFICE OF THE CONSTITUTIONAL COURT

that can become parties to disputes over state institutional authority in the Constitutional Court. By the end of 2022, the Constitutional Court had decided on 29 cases of disputes over state institutional authority. Of all these cases, only one case was granted, namely Case No. 3/SKLN-X/2012, which concerned a dispute between the KPU and the Papuan People's Representative Council.[49] The details of the rulings on all disputes over state institutional authority are outlined in Figure 3.2.

3.3 *Deciding on the Dissolution of Political Parties*

The Constitutional Court's authority to decide on the dissolution of political parties is closely linked to the objective of preventing arbitrary actions that could infringe upon citizens' rights to organize and associate. To this end, the Venice Commission has established guidelines that uphold the principle of every person's right to form and join political parties. The prohibition or forced dissolution of political parties is only permissible in cases where a party employs violence to undermine the democratic order that guarantees individual rights and freedoms.[50] The dissolution of a political party cannot be initiated solely because of the errant actions of individual members, if such actions were not mandated by the party. Prohibition or dissolution of political parties

49 Constitutional Court Decision No. 3/SKLN-X/2012, 19 September 2019.

50 Pan Mohamad Faiz, "The Dissolution of Political Parties in Indonesia: Lessons Learned from the European Court of Human Rights," *Journal of Legal, Ethical and Regulatory Issues* 22, no. 4 (2019): 5.

should be determined by the Constitutional Court or other judicial institutions while ensuring due process, transparency and a fair trial.[51]

In those instances, where political parties may be banned, there is usually a review of some sort by the highest court, given the final and binding nature of the decision to dissolve. The primary authority for the dissolution of political parties is the Constitutional Court. Many countries with a Constitutional Court, such as Albania, Armenia, Austria, Azerbaijan, Chile, Croatia, the Czech Republic, Georgia, Germany, Hungary, Macedonia, Moldova, Poland, Portugal, Romania, Slovakia, Slovenia, South Korea, Spain, Taiwan, Thailand and Türkiye, have conferred the authority to dissolve political parties within their jurisdiction to the Constitutional Court.[52]

Just like the aforementioned countries, the Indonesian Constitutional Court has the authority to dissolve political parties, as granted under Article 24C(1) of the Constitution. However, the Constitution does not outline the specific requirements for dissolution. Instead, the requirements for dissolving a party are set forth in Law No. 2 of 2008, as amended by Law No. 2 of 2011 on Political Parties. In accordance with this law, a political party may be dissolved by the Constitutional Court if it violates the prohibitions stated in Article 40(2), which include engaging in activities that are against the Constitution and other regulations, or engaging in activities that endanger the integrity and safety of the Unitary State of the Republic of Indonesia.

The Constitutional Court is authorized to dissolve political parties, but Law No. 24 of 2003 does not specify the requirements for political parties that can be dissolved. However, the law establishes that the applicant for the dissolution of a political party is the central government. According to Article 68, (2) of Law No. 24 of 2003, the applicant must clearly outline in its request the ideology, principles, goals, programs and activities of the political party in question, which are deemed to be in conflict with the Constitution. To provide clarity on these requirements, Constitutional Court Regulation No. 12 of 2008 on Procedures for the Dissolution of Political Parties contains two alternative reasons for the Constitutional Court to dissolve a political party. First, if the ideology, principles, goals or programs of the political party are in conflict with the Constitution. Second, if the activities of the political party are in conflict with the Constitution, or if the consequences of these activities are in conflict with the Constitution. Meanwhile, Constitutional Court Decision No. 53/

51 M. Ali Safaat et al., *Hukum Acara Mahkamah Konstitusi* [Constitutional Court Procedural Law] (Jakarta: Sekretariat Jenderal Mahkamah Konstitusi, 2020), 359.

52 Ibid., 360.

PUU-IX/2011, dated 3 January 2013, states that a political party can be proposed for dissolution through a Constitutional Court decision if:

1. The political party has engaged in activities that are contrary to the Constitution and other laws and regulations, after previously being subject to a temporary suspension.
2. The political party engages in activities that endanger the integrity and safety of the Unitary State of the Republic of Indonesia, after having previously been subject to temporary suspension.
3. The political party adheres to and promotes the teachings or doctrines of communism/Marxism-Leninism.

One of the issues that is often debated with regard to the dissolution of political parties is the restriction in Article 68(1) of Law No. 24 of 2004, as amended by Law No. 7 of 2020, which stipulates that only the central government is allowed to initiate the dissolution of political parties. The Constitutional Court's ruling supports this provision, citing that Article 24C of the Constitution does not specify which parties are entitled to file a case on the dissolution of political parties to the Constitutional Court. The Court argues that designating the government as the applicant in cases of dissolving political parties is a choice made by the lawmakers (the DPR and the President) when formulating and establishing procedural legal provisions of the Constitutional Court under the Constitutional Court Law.[53]

It is worth noting that while the Constitutional Court's authority to dissolve political parties is stipulated in Article 24C(1) of the Constitution, several laws have also established requirements or grounds for the dissolution of political parties, and procedural laws have been arranged accordingly. However, as of the end of 2022, the Constitutional Court has never received a petition for the dissolution of a political party. This means that the legal instrument regarding the dissolution of political parties has not yet been put to the test. As argued by the petitioner in Case No. 53/PUU-IX/2011, it is quite possible that the restriction in Article 68(1) of Law No. 24 of 2003, which limits the petitioner to only the government, specifically the central government, becomes a safeguard against the exercising the power provided by the Constitution to dissolve political parties.

53 Constitutional Court No. 53/PUU-IX/2011, January 3, 2013, 51–52.

3.4 *Deciding Disputes Over General Election Results*

The constitution drafted by the Indonesian state's founders did not explicitly regulate elections as a mechanism for selecting the President or legislative members. The pre-amendment 1945 Constitution only stipulates that the President and Vice President are to be elected by the MPR. Meanwhile, the process of selecting MPR and DPR members is not clearly regulated in the Constitution but rather delegated to be regulated by law.[54] This choice was likely made intentionally to avoid lengthy debates on the formulation of the basic law due to limited time. However, in addition to this possibility, the founders of the state at that time may not have viewed elections as an urgent constitutional instrument for organizing democracy.[55]

As part of constitutional reform during Indonesia's reform era, the principle of constitutional democracy was emphasized and strengthened.[56] In line with this principle, the implementation of democracy through general elections was also strengthened, as shown by the adoption of regulations on the basic principles of organizing general elections in the Constitution. Chapter VIIB of the Constitution regulates the principles of organizing general elections, the types of positions elected, and the institutions responsible for conducting general elections. The Constitution aims to ensure that general elections are conducted democratically according to the general guidelines set out in Article 22E, (1), which includes being "direct", "general", "free", "secret", "honest", "fair", and "periodic".[57] Although the Constitution delegates detailed regulations on the conduct of general elections to the law, the general election laws must still adhere to the principles of general election administration set out in the Constitution.[58]

Elections serve as an important means to fill political positions in state institutions, but more fundamentally, they are a tangible expression of the people's sovereignty. As Jimly Asshiddiqie suggests, the purposes of elections are to

---

54 Hendarmin Ranadireksa, *Dinamika Konstitusi Indonesia* [Indonesian Constitutional Dynamics] (Bandung: Fokus Media, 2009), 44.

55 Isra and Fahmi, *Pemilihan Umum Demokratis*, 4.

56 Jimly Asshiddiqie, *Konsolidasi Naskah UUD 1945 Setelah Perubahan Keempat* [Consolidation of the Manuscripts of the 1945 Constitution After the Fourth Amendment] (Jakarta: Center for Constitutional Law Studies, Faculty of Law, University of Indonesia, 2002), 3.

57 Pan Mohamad Faiz, "Memperkuat Prinsip Pemilu yang Teratur, Bebas, dan Adil Melalui Pengujian Konstitusionalitas Undang-Undang [Strengthening the Principle of Regular, Free and Fair Elections Through Constitutional Review]," *Jurnal Konstitusi* 14, no. 3 (2017): 672.

58 Isra and Fahmi, *Pemilihan Umum Demokratis*, 6.

ensure the peaceful and orderly transfer of leadership; to enable the replacement of officials who represent the interests of the people in representative institutions; to uphold the principle of popular sovereignty; and to uphold the principles of human rights and citizenship.[59] The right to vote is a crucial safeguard of citizens' rights in the practice of governance, and citizens must be treated fairly to ensure that their right to vote is protected in the electoral process.

One central issue in conducting elections is how to ensure the election results are fair and just. To address this, the International Institute for Democracy and Electoral Assistance (International IDEA) popularized the term "electoral justice" as a paradigm to uphold citizens' right to vote.[60] Electoral justice encompasses the ways and mechanisms available, whether at the country, community, regional, or international level, to ensure that every action, procedure, and decision related to the election process complies with the legal framework. It aims to protect or restore the right to vote and enables citizens (voters) whose right to vote has been violated to file a complaint, attend a trial, and obtain a decision.[61]

Instruments for upholding electoral justice are implemented through the enforcement of election laws with a legal design that effectively regulates dispute resolution mechanisms. According to International IDEA, there are seven principles in the resolution of election disputes, namely: (i) transparency, clarity and simplicity in developing arrangements for resolving election disputes; (ii) effective and comprehensive resolution; (iii) freedom and reasonable cost; (iv) a legal framework; (v) the right to defend or be heard in the legal process; (vi) full and timely enforcement of judgments and rulings; and (vii) consistency in the interpretation and application of election laws.[62]

In relation to electoral justice, according to Article 24C(1) of the Indonesian Constitution, the Constitutional Court is given the authority to "decide disputes concerning the results of general elections". This authority is in line with the research findings of Ginsburg and Versteeg on 204 countries for the period 1781–2011, which showed that the formation of ae constitutional court is highly

59 Jimly Asshiddiqie, *Pengantar Ilmu Hukum Tata Negara* [Introduction to Constitutional Law] (Jakarta: Rajawali Pers, 2013), 418.

60 International IDEA, *Electoral Justice: The International IDEA Handbook* (Jakarta: International IDEA-Cetro-Bawaslu RI, 2011), 5.

61 Ibid.

62 Jesus Orozco-Henriques, *Electoral Justice: The International IDEA Handbook* (Stockholm: International IDEA, 2010), 119–131.

influenced by domestic electoral politics.[63] Textually, the dispute over the results is generally understood as a settlement based on the numbers derived from the vote count. In addition, the results of the general election are also defined as the final outcome of the election process. Furthermore, based on Article 75 of Law No. 24 of 2003, the main issues that must be submitted to the Constitutional Court in filing a dispute resolution application over the election results are: first, an error in the vote count announced by the KPU and the correct vote count according to the applicant. Second, a request to annul the vote count announced by the KPU and to establish the correct vote count according to the applicant. This qualification indeed provides an interpretation that the phrase "results of general elections" in Article 24C(1) of the Constitution is only limited to the quantity or numbers of the vote count.

The narrow interpretation of the phrase "the results of general elections" as solely referring to disputes over the national election results announced by the KPU has been criticized as a weakness in the electoral process. This narrow interpretation has led to the Constitutional Court being called a "calculator court" in settling disputes over election results, rather than fulfilling its role as the guardian of democracy, including ensuring the principles of direct, general, free, secret and fair elections as outlined in Article 22E(1) of the Constitution.[64]

Furthermore, the electoral disputes brought to the Constitutional Court are limited to matters that can have an impact, such as the election of candidates for the Regional Representative Council, the determination of presidential and vice-presidential candidates who enter a second round of voting, the election of the president and vice-president, and the acquisition of seats by political parties participating in the elections in a certain electoral district. In fact, in many cases, the issue of candidates who have won seats within political parties is often submitted as a dispute application to the Constitutional Court. In this regard, the experience of disputes over the determination of seats within political parties during the 2019 legislative elections was also resolved through the dispute settlement mechanism of the Constitutional Court.

The development of handling electoral disputes in the Constitutional Court is not just about determining the numerical results of the election obtained by

63 See Tom Ginsburg and Mila Versteeg, "Why Do Countries Adopt Constitutional Review?" *The Journal of Law, Economic, and Organization* 30, no. 3 (2013): 587–622.

64 Harry Setya Nugraha, "Redesain Kewenangan Mahkamah Konstitusi dalam Penyelesaian Sengketa Perselisihan Hasil Pemilihan Umum Presiden dan Wakil Presiden di Indonesia [Redesigning the Authority of the Constitutional Court in Settlement of Presidential and Vice Presidential Election Disputes in Indonesia]," *Jurnal Hukum Ius Quia Iustum* 22, no. 3 (2015): 422.

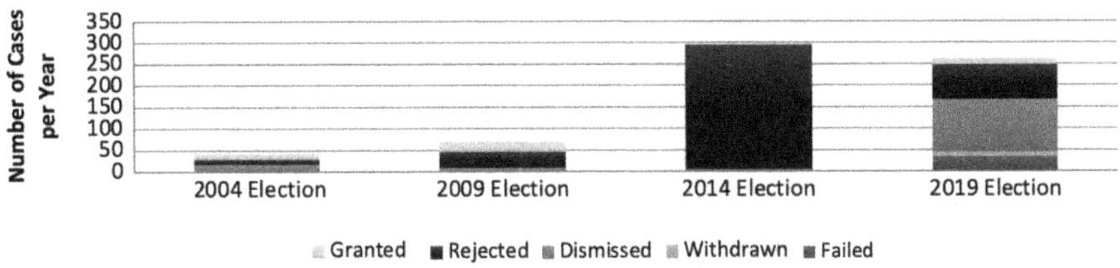

FIGURE 3.3 Recapitulation of legislative election dispute decisions
SOURCE: SECRETARIAT GENERAL AND REGISTRAR OFFICE OF THE CONSTITUTIONAL COURT

contestants or participants, but also concerns the quality of the election process.[65] Therefore, the Constitutional Court not only reviews quantitative issues (numerical election results), but also assesses the qualitative aspects (the fulfilment of constitutional principles) of the election process.[66]

According to the Constitutional Court's decisions, disputes related to the quality of the election process are a concern for the Constitutional Court only if the principles specified in Article 22E,(1) and (5) of the Constitution are violated. For example, in Case No. 062/PHPU-B-II/2004, it was stated that the Constitutional Court, as a constitutional guard, is obligated to ensure that the election process is qualitatively carried out in accordance with the principles set forth in Article 22E,(1) and (5) of the Constitution. Therefore, in several Constitutional Court decisions, there have been orders for election organizers (KPU, provincial KPU, district/city KPU, the Independent Election Commission of Aceh) to conduct a recount or even a revote if the Court finds that these principles have been violated.[67] Specifically for legislative elections, if the settlement of disputes over the results from the 2004 to 2019 elections is tracked, a total of 671 applications have been filed. Of these, 53 applications were granted (10.3%), with various verdicts, such as orders for a revote, vote recount, determination of the number of political party votes, and others. The Constitutional Court's decisions related to the settlement of legislative election disputes can be seen in Figure 3.3.

Similarly, in the case of presidential and vice-presidential elections, since the first direct presidential election in 2004 until the 2019 presidential election,

65 Safaat et al., *Hukum Acara*, 394.
66 Constitutional Court Decision No. 062/PHPU-B-II/2004, August 9, 2004.
67 Ibid., 396.

there have been five requests for disputes over the presidential election results submitted to the Constitutional Court. All five requests were rejected. Despite that, there were also no requests for disputes over the election results that were deemed inadmissible (*niet onvankelijke verklaard* or NO), meaning that the requests were dismissed due to not meeting the formal requirements for submission. Until now, all such requests submitted in relation to presidential elections were rejected because they were not legally justified (Figure 3.4).

In addition to disputes over the election results of legislative members (DPR, DPD, and DPRD) and presidential and vice-presidential election results, the Constitutional Court also has the authority to settle disputes over the results of regional head elections, namely the election of governors and vice governors, regents and vice regents, as well as mayors and deputy mayors. The Constitutional Court began settling disputes over the results of regional head elections in 2008. Previously, Article 106 of Law No. 32 of 2004 on Regional Governance stated that objections to the determination of the results of regional head elections could be submitted to the Supreme Court. Specifically, objections to the results of regent and vice-regent as well as mayor and deputy mayor elections, the Supreme Court delegated its authority to the provincial high court with jurisdiction over the area where the dispute occurred.

With the development of electoral laws in Indonesia, Article 106 of Law No. 32 of 2004 was further amended by Article 236C of Law No. 12 of 2008, which states, "The handling of disputes over the vote count of regional head elections by the Supreme Court is transferred to the Constitutional Court no later than 18 months after this law is enacted." To meet this deadline, on 29 October 2008, the Chief Justice of the Supreme Court and the Chief Justice of the Constitutional Court signed a Record of Transfer of Jurisdiction to Adjudicate.

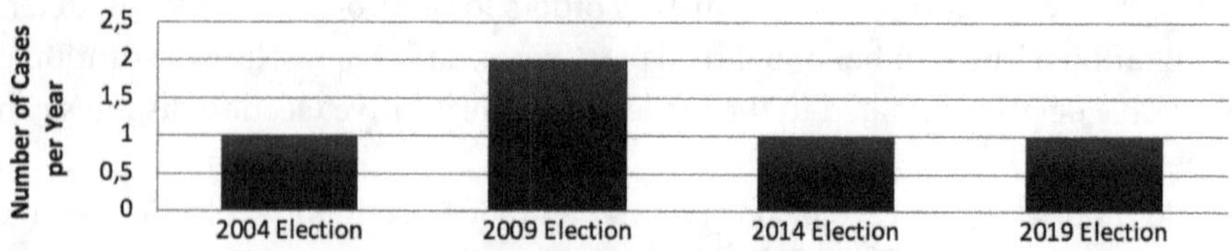

FIGURE 3.4 Recapitulation of presidential election dispute decisions (requests rejected)
SOURCE: SECRETARIAT GENERAL AND REGISTRAR OFFICE OF THE CONSTITUTIONAL COURT

This event marked the beginning of the Constitutional Court's authority to handle disputes over regional head elections.

Looking back, the transfer of authority for resolving disputes over the results of local head elections from the Supreme Court to the Constitutional Court was also influenced by Law No. 22 of 2007 on the Organization of General Elections. As the first to regulate general elections after the amendment of the Constitution, it introduced the notion that local head elections are part of general elections. Article 1 number 4 of Law No. 22 of 2007 states that "elections for local heads and deputy local heads are general elections to directly elect local heads and deputy local heads within the Unitary State of the Republic of Indonesia based on Pancasila and the Constitution of the Republic of Indonesia." In addition, it explicitly states that one of the tasks of the election organizers is to hold local head and deputy head direct elections by the people.

Even before the existence of Law No. 12 of 2008, Constitutional Court Decision No. 72–73/PUU-II/2004, dated 22 March 2005, essentially interpreted that constitutionally, the legislator can ensure that the direct election of regional heads is an expansion of the understanding of elections as stipulated in Article 22E of the Constitution, so that disputes over the results of regional head elections become the authority of the Constitutional Court in accordance with the provisions of Article 24C(1) of the Constitution.[68] This Constitutional Court decision marked the beginning of a change in the way many parties, especially legislators, categorized regional head elections as part of general elections.

However, through Decision No. 97/PUU-XI/2013, dated 19 May 2014, the Constitutional Court changed its position from its previous decision by stating that its authority to adjudicate disputes over the results of regional head elections by expanding the meaning of general elections in Article 22E of the Constitution was unconstitutional. The Constitutional Court's decision in No. 97/PUU-XI/2013 was not unanimous, as three justices of the Court expressed a dissenting opinion from the majority of other justices. In the latest development, the Court has issued Decision No. 85/PUU-XX/2022, dated 29 September 2022, which essentially states there is no longer a distinction between the conduct of general elections and regional head elections. This is because the Court has affirmed its authority to resolve disputes over the results of regional head elections in the simultaneous elections in 2024. This decision ends the debate about whether or not a special court should be established to replace

68 For more, read the legal considerations of Constitutional Court Decision No. 72–73/PUU-II/2004, especially page 115.

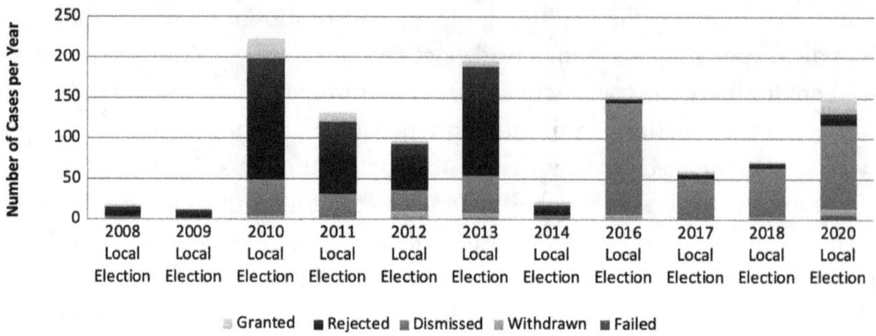

FIGURE 3.5 Recapitulation of regional head election dispute decisions
SOURCE: SECRETARIAT GENERAL AND REGISTRAR OFFICE OF THE CONSTITUTIONAL COURT

the Constitutional Court's authority in resolving disputes over the results of regional head elections.

Despite the academic debates surrounding the direct election of regional heads and deputy regional heads, since the authority for resolving disputes over the election of regional heads has been transferred to the Constitutional Court, 982 cases have been decided. Of these, 63 petitions, or about 6.4%, were granted with various orders, such as orders for a recount, a revote, and others, as detailed in Figure 3.5.[69]

3.5 *Decide on the DPR's Opinion Regarding Alleged Violations of the Constitution by the President and/or Vice President*

Article 24C,(2) of the 1945 Constitution of the Republic of Indonesia states that the Constitutional Court is required tow provide a ruling on the opinion of the DPR regarding alleged violations of the Constitution by the President and/or Vice President, commonly known as impeachment. In this regard, Article 7A of the Constitution states that the President and/or Vice President may be dismissed during their term of office by the MPR upon the proposal of the DPR on the grounds of proven violations of the law in the form of treason against the state, corruption, bribery, other serious crimes, or reprehensible conduct; and if it is proven that they no longer meet the qualifications as President

69 For further discussion on the settlement of regional head election result disputes at the Constitutional Court, see Pan Mohamad Faiz *et al.*, eds., *Menegakkan Keadilan Pemilu, Menjaga Kemurnian Suara Rakyat. Dinamika Penyelesaian Sengketa Hasil Pilkada di Mahkamah Konstitusi* [Upholding Election Justice, Maintaining the Purity of the People's Voice. Dynamics of Regional Election Result Dispute Resolution at the Constitutional Court] (Depok: Rajawali Pers, 2021).

and/or Vice President. Even if the DPR believes that the President and/or Vice President have fulfilled these reasons, the DPR cannot directly propose the dismissal of the President and/or Vice President to the MPR. Constitutionally, the DPR must first submit the matter to the Constitutional Court, and the Constitutional Court is obliged to provide a ruling on the opinion of the DPR.

Under Article 7A and Article 7B of the Constitution, the process for impeachment of the President and/or Vice President goes through three stages: first in the DPR, second in the Constitutional Court, and third in the MPR. The first stage is the proposal stage carried out by the DPR as one of its supervisory functions. The second stage is in the Constitutional Court. If the DPR's opinion on a violation of the law or a condition that does not meet the requirements of the President and/or Vice President has been approved in accordance with the above requirements, the DPR will then submit the opinion to the Constitutional Court which will examine, adjudicate, and decide fairly within a certain period of time. The Constitutional Court will decide whether the DPR's opinion is proven or not.

As noted by I D.G. Palguna, in this context, the function of the Constitutional Court is related to its task in maintaining the functioning of the principle of checks and balances, in this case, to maintain the functioning of the presidential system of government. On the one hand, the Constitutional Court must consider that the President (and Vice President) are elected for a definite term through direct legitimacy from the people, namely through general elections. On the other hand, the Constitutional Court must also consider, constitutionally, that the DPR has the authority to oversee the governance led by the President (and Vice President).[70] In addition, the process carried out by the Constitutional Court is a continuation of the political process, precisely assessing the political process carried out by the DPR, and therefore the Constitutional Court is obliged to make a decision within a certain period of time.

Upon the request of the DPR to the Constitutional Court, there are three possible verdicts that can be delivered. First, if the Constitutional Court considers that the request from the DPR does not meet the requirements from the applicant and the request, the verdict states that the request cannot be accepted (*niet ontvankelijke verklaard*). Second, if the Constitutional Court decides that the President and/or Vice President have not been proven to have committed a legal violation or to no longer meet the requirements as stated in the DPR's opinion, the verdict of the Constitutional Court is to reject the request. Third,

70 Palguna, *Mahkamah Konstitusi*, 150.

if the Constitutional Court decides that the President and/or Vice President have been proven to have committed a legal violation or to no longer meet the requirements as stated in the DPR's opinion, the verdict of the Constitutional Court is to approve the DPR's opinion.[71] If the Constitutional Court approves the DPR's opinion in its verdict, the DPR will then request the MPR to hold a Special Session to carry out the process of removing the President and/or Vice President. Therefore, in this case, the Constitutional Court's verdict still needs to be followed up by the DPR and MPR as the final stages of the impeachment of the President and/or Vice President.[72]

Similar to the dissolution of political parties, although the Constitutional Court's authority to rule on the DPR's opinion regarding alleged violations by the President and/or Vice President has been regulated in Article 24C(2) of the Constitution, up until time of writing, the Constitutional Court has never handled such a case. This means that the legal instrument regarding the Constitutional Court's authority to rule on the DPR's opinion on alleged violations of the Constitution by the President and/or Vice President has not been tested. Nevertheless, if placed within the framework of the presidential system of government and the experiences of the removal of President Soekarno (1967) and President Abdurrahman Wahid (2001), the Constitutional Court's authority as stipulated in Article 24C(2) of the Constitution can be considered part of the design to strengthen the presidential system of government.

4 Appointment Mechanism for Justices

Article 24C(3) of the Constitution states, "The Constitutional Court is composed of nine members of constitutional justices who are designated by the President, of whom three are nominated by the Supreme Court, three by the House of Representatives, and three by the President." Following this provision, Article 24C(5) of the Constitution stipulates the requirements for Constitutional justices, including having integrity and an impeccable character, be fair, be a statesperson with mastery of the constitution and constitutionalism, and not concurrently hold any position as a state official. However,

---

71 Safaat et al., *Hukum Acara*, 446–447.

72 Compare this with the impeachment mechanism of the President in South Korea, where the South Korean Constitutional Court's decision does not need to be discussed again in parliament to dismiss the President. See Jin Wook Kim, "Korean Constitutional Court and Constitutionalism in Political Dynamics: Focusing on Presidential Impeachment," *Constitutional Review* 4, no. 2 (2018): 222.

Article 24C(6) of the Constitution delegates the appointment and dismissal of Constitutional justices, procedural laws, and other provisions related to the Constitutional Court to be regulated by law.

The number and composition of Constitutional Court justices in Indonesia are similar to those of South Korea. Article 111(2) of the 1987 South Korean Constitution states, "The Constitutional Court shall be composed of nine adjudicators qualified to be court judges, and they shall be appointed by the President." Furthermore, Article 111(3) states, "Among the adjudicators referred to in (2), three shall be appointed from persons selected by the National Assembly, and three appointed from persons nominated by the Chief Justice [of the Supreme Court]."

Meanwhile, Article 112(2) of the South Korean Constitution of 1987 requires that Constitutional Court judges are not members of a political party or involved in political activities. Although the Indonesian Constitution has set stricter requirements for becoming a Constitutional Court justice, compared to South Korea, the provision of Article 24C(6) of the Indonesian Constitution still delegates further regulation to the law regarding the appointment and dismissal of Constitutional Court justices, procedural law, and other provisions related to the Constitutional Court.

The delegation under Article 24C(6) of the Constitution was first implemented through Law No. 24 of 2003. Chapter IV of this law regulates the appointment and dismissal of Constitutional justices. Regarding the requirements, Law No. 24 of 2003 sets three important aspects: requirements to be met as a Constitutional justice, requirements to be met as a candidate for appointment as a Constitutional justice, and a prohibition on holding multiple positions while serving as a Constitutional justice. The three aspects related to the appointment of Constitutional justices are regulated in Articles 15, 16(1), and 17 of Law No. 24 of 2003, as last amended by Law No. 7 of 2020. Article 15(1) of Law No. 7 of 2020 states, "Constitutional justices must meet the requirements: (a) possess integrity and a respectable character; (b) be fair; and (c) be a statesman who has a mastery of the constitution and state administration." Furthermore, Article 15(2) of Law No. 7 of 2020 states that to be appointed as a Constitutional justice, a candidate must meet the following requirements:

a. Indonesian citizen;
b. Hold a doctoral degree (level three) based on a bachelor's degree in the field of law;
c. Pious and of good moral character;

d. At least 55 years old;[73]
e. Physically and mentally capable of carrying out duties and obligations;
f. Never sentenced to imprisonment based on a final and binding court decision;
g. Not declared bankrupt based on a court decision; and
h. Has at least 15 years of work experience in the legal field and/or for prospective judges from the Supreme Court environment, currently serving as a high-level justice or as a supreme justice.

In addition to the aforementioned requirements, Law No. 24 of 2003 also includes prohibitions for Constitutional justices, specifically regarding holding multiple positions. Article 17 of Law No. 24 of 2003 states that Constitutional justices are prohibited from holding concurrent positions as: (a) other state officials; (b) members of political parties; (c) entrepreneurs; (d) lawyers; or (e) civil servants. In a broader context, this prohibition is common in the appointment of public officials. When related to the phrase "not holding concurrent positions as state officials" in Article 24C(5) of the Constitution, the prohibition in Article 17 of Law No. 24 of 2003 provides an interpretation and expands the intended meaning of the phrase. However, in the context of the judicial institution, the prohibition of holding multiple positions is crucial to the position of the Constitutional Court as an independent judiciary. Similarly, the requirements for a candidate for a Constitutional justice in Law No. 24 of 2003 are necessary because Article 24C of the Constitution only regulates the requirements for a Constitutional justice, and not the requirements for becoming a candidate for the position.

In addition to the qualifications, the process of appointing Constitutional justices is also regulated in more detail in Law No. 24 of 2003. In this regard, Article 19 of Law No. 24 of 2003 states that the nomination of Constitutional justices shall be carried out in a transparent and participatory manner. Furthermore, Article 20(1) of Law No. 24 of 2003 states that the provisions regarding the selection, election, and submission of Constitutional justices shall be regulated by each authorized institution, namely the Supreme Court,

73 Regarding the minimum age requirement for Constitutional justice candidates, there have been two changes to the Constitutional Court Law, from an initial requirement of a minimum age of 40, then changed to a minimum age of 47, and most recently changed to 55. Lawmakers reasoned that maturity of age is necessary for someone to be appointed as a Constitutional justice, so the minimum age limit for candidates has always been increased. However, at the time of writing this chapter, the DPR plans to revise the Constitutional Court Law again by lowering the minimum age limit for Constitutional justice candidates to 50 years.

the DPR, and the President. Subsequently, Article 20(2) of Law No. 24 of 2003 states that the selection of Constitutional justices shall be conducted objectively and accountably. Based on these provisions, the recruitment process for Constitutional justice candidates requires transparency and public participation. In fact, the explanation of Article 19 of Law No. 24 of 2003 requires that candidates be published in the mass media so that the public has the opportunity to provide input on the respective Constitutional justice candidates. Thus, the process of selecting Constitutional justice candidates will be conducted objectively and accountably.

Although Article 20(1) of Law No. 24 of 2003 mandates that proposing institutions regulate the selection, nomination, and submission procedures for Constitutional Court justices, the implementation of Article 20(1) of Law No. 24 of 2003 is only reflected in the DPR's Code of Conduct, which pertains to the DPR's authority to elect and propose three Constitutional Court justice candidates to be appointed by the President. Meanwhile, the Supreme Court and the President have not issued any specific regulations regarding the selection of Constitutional Court justice candidates. Therefore, every time the position of Constitutional Court justice is filled from a source proposed by the President and the Supreme Court, problems always arise because there are no standardized criteria used as a reference in the recruitment process for Constitutional Court justices.[74]

As cited by I D.G. Palguna, the fulfillment of the requirements for becoming a constitutional justice mandated by the Constitution consists of two major components: capacity and integrity. The capacity component refers to the fulfillment of requirements for mastery of the constitution and state governance, while the integrity component refers to the fulfillment of requirements for integrity and an unblemished character, fairness, and statesmanship.[75] Within reasonable limits, both of these components can be traced and examined if the recruitment of constitutional judge candidates is conducted transparently and participatively and the process is objective and accountable. This means that the requirements that must be met by Constitutional justice candidates, along with a transparent and participatory selection process that is objective and accountable, are a *conditio sine qua non* in recruiting Constitutional justices as required by Article 24C(5) of the Constitution.

---

74 Pan Mohamad Faiz, "Critical Analysis of Judicial Appointment Process and Tenure of Constitutional Justice in Indonesia," *Hasanuddin Law Review* 2, no. 2 (2016): 152–169; Achmad Edi Subiyanto, 2019, *Pengisian Jabatan Hakim Konstitusi* [Selection of Constitutional Justices] (Rajawali Pers: Jakarta, 81).

75 I D.G. Palguna, *Mahkamah Konstitusi*, 86.

5 Reasons for Dismissal of Constitutional Justices

Although the Constitution does not specify the term of office for Constitutional justices, Article 22 of Law No. 24 of 2003 initially regulated that the term of office for Constitutional justices was five years and could be re-elected for only one more term. During the five-year term, a Constitutional justice may be dismissed before the end of their term. However, the periodicity of the term of office was eliminated after the enactment of Law No. 7 of 2020, which amended some provisions in Law No. 24 of 2003. Article 23(1) of Law No. 7 of 2020 specifies the grounds for the honorable dismissal of a Constitutional justice, which are:

a. Deceased;
b. Resignation at one's own request submitted to the Chief Justice of the Constitutional Court;
c. Has reached the age of 70 years;
d. (deleted);[76] or
e. Physically or mentally ill continuously for three months, making it impossible to carry out duties, as evidenced by a doctor's certificate.

In addition to regulating honorable dismissal, Article 23(2) of Law No. 7 of 2020 also regulates the dismissal of Constitutional justices without honor if they:

a. have been sentenced to imprisonment based on a legally binding court decision for committing a crime punishable by imprisonment;
b. committed dishonorable acts;
c. did not attend the hearing that is their duty and obligation for five consecutive times without valid reasons;
d. violated oaths and pledges of office;
e. deliberately obstructed the Constitutional Court from issuing a ruling within the time specified in Article 7B(4) of the Constitution.[77]
f. hold multiple positions as referred to in Article 17;
g. no longer meet the requirements as a constitutional justice; and/or

---

76 This provision previously regulated the reason "has ended their term", but the provision has now been deleted because the term periodization has been eliminated, so the term of office is now based on the retirement age of constitutional judges, which is 70 years old.

77 Article 7B(4) of the Constitution regulates the authority of the Constitutional Court to examine allegations of violations committed by the President and/or Vice President. The content of the provision states that "the Constitutional Court must examine, judge, and decide fairly on the request from the DPR within a maximum of 90 days after it is received by the Constitutional Court."

h. violate the Code of Ethics and Guidelines for the Conduct of Constitutional justices.

Regarding the non-honorable dismissal, Article 23(3) of Law No. 7 of 2020 stipulates that a request for non-honorable dismissal on the grounds of committing a despicable act, failing to attend a hearing for five consecutive times without a valid reason, violating oaths and promises of office, intentionally obstructing the Constitutional Court in deciding on the DPR's opinion regarding alleged violations by the President and/or Vice President, violating the prohibition on holding multiple positions, no longer meeting the qualifications as a Constitutional justice, and/or violating the code of ethics and guidelines of Constitutional justice behavior, shall be carried out after the concerned party is given the opportunity to defend themselves before the Ethics Council (*Majelis Kehormatan*) of the Constitutional Court (MKMK).

Regarding the enforcement of the code of ethics and behavior for judges, the Constitutional Court has ratified Constitutional Court Regulation No. 1 of 2023 on the Ethics Council of the Constitutional Court as a follow-up to Law No. 7 of 2020. The purpose of the Ethics Council is to maintain and uphold the honor, dignity, and behavior of judges, as well as the code of ethics and guidelines for the behavior of constitutional justices (*Sapta Karsa Hutama*). The membership of the Ethics Council consists of three people, with the composition being one Constitutional Court justice, one community figure, and one academic with a background in law. This membership can be permanent for a three-year term or *ad hoc* as determined in the Council of Justices' Meeting. In the event of a suspected violation of the code of ethics and guidelines for the behavior of constitutional judges, the Ethics Council may impose sanctions on constitutional justices in the form of oral reprimands, written reprimands, or dismissal without honor.

6 Conclusion

In the context of a constitutional democracy, the Indonesian Constitutional Court is an essential institution. In reaching its 20th anniversary, the Constitutional Court has made significant contributions to strengthening the state system in Indonesia, particularly in protecting human rights and consolidating democracy.[78] As experienced by other constitutional courts in other

78 Marcus Mietzner, "Political Conflict Resolution and Democratic Consolidation in Indonesia: The Role of the Constitutional Court," *Journal of East Asian Studies* 10, no. 3 (2010): 417.

countries, the Indonesian Constitutional Court has had ups and downs in its performance and effectiveness. One of its main challenges currently is how to strengthen the quality of its decisions with adequate legal considerations, so that it can contribute to the development of constitutional theory and practice in Indonesia. In the implementation of the Constitutional Court's powers and function, Pancasila has been a significant influence in shaping the Court's approach to protecting citizens' rights and freedoms. The Court has relied on Pancasila's principles to interpret the Constitution and ensure that its decisions align with the country's values.

The Constitutional Court is viewed as an important institution for protecting citizens' rights and upholding the rule of law in the country. It has gained the trust of the Indonesian people, particularly due to its efforts to increase transparency and ensure due process in its decision-making process. However, there have also been instances where the Court's decisions have been questioned or criticized, particularly when decisions are deemed too progressive, such as a case concerning the recognition of traditional beliefs to be added to mandatory identity cards, or the recognition of the 'noken' voting system as a traditional right of Papuan people in elections. The Court has also faced criticism from some legislators for deeming some laws to be unconstitutional or conditionally unconstitutional.

Therefore, it is crucial for the Indonesian Constitutional Court to maintain its independence and autonomy in examining, adjudicating, and deciding cases, without any external intervention. The legislature, judiciary, and executive branches must respect the Constitutional Court's authority and not attempt to undermine its independence. This is necessary to ensure that the Court can uphold the Constitution and protect citizens' rights, free from any vested interests or political pressures. By upholding the principles of judicial independence, the Constitutional Court can serve as a safeguard against abuses of power and ensure that constitutional justice is served fairly and impartially. Furthermore, the Constitutional Court does not need to base its decisions on populist opinions. Instead, the Constitutional Court must adhere to constitutional values that serve as the basic guidelines in governing the state.

Bibliography

Agresto, John. *The Supreme Court and Constitutional Democracy*. London: Cornel University Press, 1984.

Albert, Richard. "Constitutional Amendment and Dismemberment." *The Yale Journal of International Law* 43, no. 1 (2018): 1–84.

Anwary, Ichsan. *Lembaga Negara dan Penyelesaian Sengketa Kewenangan Konstitusional Lembaga Negara* [State Institution and Settlement of Constitutional Disputes of State Institutions]. Yogyakarta: Genta Publishing, 2018.

Arifin, Firmansyah, et al. *Lembaga Negara dan Sengketa Kewenangan Antar Lembaga Negara* [State Institutions and Disputes of Authority Between State Institutions]. Jakarta: KRHN and MKRI, 2005.

Asshiddiqie, Jimly and Mustafa Fakhri. *Mahkamah Konstitusi: Kompilasi Ketentuan Konstitusi, Undang-Undang, dan Peraturan di 78 Negara* [Constitutional Court: Compilation of Constitutional Provisions, Laws, and Regulations in 78 Countries]. Jakarta: Pusat Studi Hukum Tata Negara Fakultas Hukum Universitas Indonesia.

Asshiddiqie, Jimly. *Konsolidasi Naskah UUD 1945 Setelah Perubahan Keempat* [Consolidation of the Manuscripts of the 1945 Constitution After the Fourth Amendment]. Jakarta: Pusat Studi Hukum Tata Negara, Fakultas Hukum Universitas Indonesia, 2002.

Asshiddiqie, Jimly. *Model-Model Pengujian Konstitusional di Berbagai Negara* [Models of Constitutional Review in Other Countries]. Jakarta: Sinar Grafika, 2010.

Asshiddiqie, Jimly. *Pengantar Ilmu Hukum Tata Negara* [Introduction to Constitutional Law]. Jakarta: Rajawali Pers, 2013.

Asshiddiqie, Jimly. *Pengujian Formil Undang-Uundang di Negara Hukum* [Formal Review of Laws in the Law-Based State]. Jakarta: Konstitusi Press, 2020.

Asshiddiqie, Jimly. *Sengketa Kewenangan Antarlembaga Negara* [State Institutions' Authority Disputes]. Jakarta: Konstitusi Press, 2005.

Bahar, Saafroedin, et al. *Risalah Sidang Badan Penyelidik Usaha-Usaha Persiapan Kemerdekaan Indonesia (BPUPKI) dan Panitia Persiapan Kemerdekaan Indonesia (PPKI) 29 Mei 1945, 19 Agustus 1945* [Minutes of Meeting of the Investigating Committee for Preparatory Work for Independence (BPUPKI) and the Preparatory Committee for Indonesian Independence (PPKI) 29 May 1945, 19 August 1945]. Jakarta: Sekretariat Negara Republik Indonesia, 1992.

Bezemek, Christoph. "A Kelsenian Model of Constitutional Adjudication: The Austrian Constitutional Court." *Austrian Journal of Public Law* 67 (2012): 115–28.

Butt, Simon and Tim Lindsey. *Indonesian Law.* Oxford: Oxford University Press, 2018.

Butt, Simon and Tim Lindsey. *The Constitution of Indonesia: A Contextual Analysis.* Oxford: Hart Publishing, 2012.

Butt, Simon. *The Constitutional Court and Democracy in Indonesia.* Leiden: Brill-Nijhoff, 2018.

Chakim, M. Luthfi. "Institutional Improvement of the Indonesia Constitutional Court: Based on Comparative Study with South Korea and Germany." Master Thesis, Graduate School of Seoul University College of Law, Seoul, 2020.

Comella, Victor Ferreres. "The European Model of Constitutional Review of Legislation: Toward Decentralization?" *International Journal of Constitutional Law* 2, no. 3 (2004): 461–91.

Constitutional Court Decision Number 004/PUU-I/2003, December 30, 2003.

Constitutional Court Decision Number 004/SKLN-IV/2006, July 12, 2006.

Constitutional Court Decision Number 062/PHPU-B-II/2004, August 9, 2004.

Constitutional Court Decision Number 138/PUU-VII/2009, February 8, 2010.

Constitutional Court Decision Number 3/SKLN-X/2012, September 19, 2019.

Constitutional Court Decision Number 53/PUU-IX/2011, January 3, 2013.

Constitutional Court Decision Number 72–73/PUU-II/2004, March 22, 2005.

Eddyono, Luthfi Widagdo. *Penyelesaian Sengketa Kewenangan Lembaga Negara oleh Mahkamah Konstitusi* [Settlement of State Institutions' Authority Disputes by the Constitutional Court]. Yogyakarta: Insigna Strat, 2013.

Faiz, Pan Mohamad et al. Eds. *Menegakkan Keadilan Pemilu, Menjaga Kemurnian Suara Rakyat. Dinamika Penyelesaian Sengketa Hasil Pilkada di Mahkamah Konstitusi* [Upholding Election Justice, Maintaining the Purity of the People's Voice. Dynamics of Regional Election Result Dispute Resolution at the Constitutional Court]. Depok: Rajawali Pers, 2021.

Faiz, Pan Mohamad. "Critical Analysis of Judicial Appointment Process and Tenure of Constitutional Justice in Indonesia." *Hasanuddin Law Review* 2, no. 2 (2016).

Faiz, Pan Mohamad. "Judicialization of Politics." *The Jakarta Post*, November 8, 2011.

Faiz, Pan Mohamad. "Legal Problems of Dualism of Judicial Review System in Indonesia." *Jurnal Dinamika Hukum* 16, no. 2 (2016): 187–195.

Faiz, Pan Mohamad. "Memperkuat Prinsip Pemilu yang Teratur, Bebas, dan Adil Melalui Pengujian Konstitusionalitas Undang-Undang [Strengthening the Principle of Regular, Free and Fair Elections Through Constitutional Review]." *Jurnal* Konstitusi 14, no. 3 (2017): 672–700.

Faiz, Pan Mohamad. "The Dissolution of Political Parties in Indonesia: Lessons Learned from the European Court of Human Rights." *Journal of Legal, Ethical and Regulatory Issues* 22, no. 4 (2019): 1–10.

Faiz, Pan Mohamad. "The Role of the Constitutional Court in Securing Constitutional Government in Indonesia." PhD diss., University of Queensland, 2016.

Ginsburg, Tom and Mila Versteeg. "Why Do Countries Adopt Constitutional Review?" *The Journal of Law, Economic, and Organization* 30, no. 3 (2013): 587–622.

Hendrianto, Stefanus. *Law and Politics of Constitutional Courts: Indonesia and the Search for Judicial Heroes*. New York: Routledge, 2018.

Hendrianto. "Institutional Choice and the new Indonesian Constitutional Court." In *New Courts in Asia*, edited by Andrew Harding and Penelope Nicholson, 158–77. London: Routledge, 2010.

Hirschl, Ran. *The Judicialization of Politics*. Oxford: Oxford University Press, 2008.

Huda, Ni'matul. *Sengketa Kewenangan Lembaga Negara dalam Teori dan Praktik di Mahkamah Konstitusi* [Disputes on the Authority of State Institutions in Theory and Practice at the Constitutional Court]. Yogyakarta: FH UII Press, 2016.

International IDEA. *Electoral Justice: The International IDEA Handbook.* Jakarta: International IDEA-Cetro-Bawaslu RI, 2011.

Isra, Saldi and Khairul Fahmi. *Pemilihan Umum Demokratis: Prinsip-Prinsip dalam Konstitusi Indonesia* [Democratic General Elections: Principles in the Indonesian Constitution]. Depok: Rajawali Pers, 2019.

Isra, Saldi and Pan Mohamad Faiz. *Indonesian Constitutional Law: Selected Articles on Challenges and Developments in Post-Constitutional Reform.* Depok: Rajawali Pers, 2021.

Isra, Saldi. "Hak Menguji Materiil Mahkamah Agung Menurut Hukum Positif Indonesia [The Right to Substance Review of the Supreme Court According to Indonesian Positive Law]." *Jurnal Yustisia* 5 (1997).

Isra, Saldi. "Legitimasi Perubahan Konstitusi [Legitimacy of Constitutional Amendments]." *Harian Kompas*, January 3, 2020.

Kelsen, Hans. "Judicial Review of Legislation." *The Journal of Politics* 4, no. 2 (1942): 183–200.

Kim, Jin Wook. "Korean Constitutional Court and Constitutionalism in Political Dynamics: Focusing on Presidential Impeachment." *Constitutional Review* 4, no. 2 (2018): 222–248.

Mahfud MD, Moh. *Perdebatan Hukum Tata Negara Pascaamandemen Konstitusi* [Post-Amendment Constitutional Law Debate]. Jakarta: Rajawali Pers, 2011.

Marbury v. Madison, 5 U.S. 137, 138 (1803).

Mietzner, Marcus. "Political Conflict Resolution and Democratic Consolidation in Indonesia: The Role of the Constitutional Court." *Journal of East Asian Studies* 10, no. 3 (2010): 397–24.

Nasution, Adnan Buyung. "Ke arah Berfungsinya Hak Uji Materiil Mahkamah Agung [Toward the Functioning of the Supreme Court's Substantive Review]." *Analisa CSIS Tahun XXII* 5 (September 1993).

Nasution, Adnan Buyung. *Aspirasi Pemerintahan Konstitusional Indonesia. Study Sosio-Legal atas Konstituante 1956–1959* [Aspirations of Indonesian Constitutional Governance. Socio-Legal Study of the Constituent Assembly 1956–1959]. Jakarta: Pustaka Utama Grafiti, 2001.

Nugraha, Harry Setya. "Redesain Kewenangan Mahkamah Konstitusi dalam Penyelesaian Sengketa Perselisihan Hasil Pemilihan Umum Presiden dan Wakil Presiden di Indonesia [Redesigning the Authority of the Constitutional Court in Settlement of Presidential and Vice Presidential Election Disputes in Indonesia]." *Jurnal Hukum Ius Quia Iustum* 22, no. 3 (2015): 440–441.

Orozco-Henriques, Jesus. *Electoral Justice: The International IDEA Handbook.* Stockholm: International IDEA, 2010.

Palguna, I D.G. *Mahkamah Konstitusi & Dinamika Politik Hukum di Indonesia* [Constitutional Court & Dynamics of Political Law in Indonesia]. Jakarta: Rajawali Pers, 2020.

Palguna, I D.G. *Mahkamah Konstitusi: Dasar Pemikiran, Kewenangan, dan Perbandingan dengan Negara Lain* [Constitutional Court: Rationale, Authority, and Comparison with Other Countries]. Jakarta: Konstitusi Pres, 2018.

Palguna, I D.G., Saldi Isra, and Pan Mohamad Faiz. *The Constitutional Court and Human Rights Protection in Indonesia.* Depok: Rajawali Pers, 2022.

Ranadireksa, Hendarmin. *Dinamika Konstitusi Indonesia* [Indonesian Constitutional Dynamics]. Bandung: Fokus Media, 2009.

Safaat, M. Ali, et al. *Hukum Acara Mahkamah Konstitusi* [Constitutional Court Procedural Law]. Jakarta: Kepaniteraan dan Sekretariat Jenderal Mahkamah Konstitusi RI, 2020.

Soemantri, Sri. *Hak Uji Material di Indonesia* [Substantive Review Rights in Indonesia]. Bandung: Alumni, 1997.

Stockman, Petra. *The New Indonesian Constitutional Court: A Study into Its Beginnings and First Years of Work.* Jakarta: Hanns Seidel Foundation, 2007.

Subiyanto, Achmad Edi. *Pengisian Jabatan Hakim Konstitusi* [Selection of Constitutional Justices]. Depok: Rajawali Pers, 2019.

Tim Penyusun. *Naskah Komprehensif Perubahan Undang-Undang Dasar Negara RI Tahun 1945: Buku IV Kekuasaan Kehakiman* [Comprehensive Manuscript of Amendments to the 1945 Constitution of the Republic of Indonesia: Book IV Judicial Power]. Jakarta: Sekretariat Jenderal Mahkamah Konstitusi, 2010.

Waldron, Jeremy. *The Dignity of Legislation.* Cambridge: Cambridge University Press, 1999.

Yamin, Muhammad. *Naskah Persiapan Undang-Undang Dasar 1945* [Preparatory Manuscripts of the 1945 Constitution]. Jakarta: Yayasan Prapanca, 1959.

CHAPTER 4

The Law of Diversity and Indonesia's Village Law: Creating Procedures for Completeness in Diverse Societies

Tove H. Malloy

Abstract

This chapter explores the "Law of Diversity," a conceptual framework promoting inclusive, deliberative, and reflective democracy in law-making, with a focus on Indonesia's Constitutional Court. It examines the principles of asymmetry, pluralism of sources, and negotiation of content, highlighting their role in developing more legitimate and effective laws. The Village Law process in Indonesia serves as a compelling case study, involving diverse entities such as indigenous communities, civil society groups, elected officials, and the Constitutional Court. Asymmetry grants indigenous peoples a unique position, enabling significant influence on the law-making process. Emphasizing pluralism of sources and subjects, the Village Law process engages diverse legal sources and stakeholders, fostering mutual recognition, trust, and cooperation. Deliberative and reflective approaches challenge existing norms and facilitate continuous change. The pivotal role of Indonesia's Constitutional Court becomes evident through its review of the 1999 Forestry Law, recognizing the rights of indigenous communities and ultimately leading to the passage of the Village Law. In conclusion, the Law of Diversity offers a comprehensive and effective framework for law-making in Indonesia, promoting social idealism and inclusive self-creation of societies while prioritizing authentic, reflective, and negotiated democratic processes.

Keywords

constitutional court – indigenous communities – Indonesia – law of diversity – village law

 | DOI:10.1163/9789004691698_005

1 Introduction

For decades, societies worldwide have worked on improving respect for diversity within their communities, including within post-colonial contexts such as Indonesia. The goal has been to adapt political and legal systems to differences among individuals and groups. Inclusive democratic practices necessitate the development of policies that can effectively embrace the natural variations in identities within a society, which is particularly relevant given Indonesia's diverse cultural landscape. To achieve this, discursive and participatory models of democracy have emerged, allowing room for alterity and otherness to be acknowledged. Moreover, human rights ideals emphasize the importance of equality and equity, often requiring the implementation of special rights to foster societal integration. Certain post-colonial societies have adopted systems respecting indigenous and plural normative and legal approaches. However, the process of adapting law-making and court systems to be more receptive to diversity has faced challenges, and the Indonesian Constitutional Court has played a significant role in addressing these challenges.

Legal philosophy, traditionally leaning toward positivistic rules, expects judges to rigidly adhere to a prescribed code, functioning like a "calculating machine."[1] While judges are expected to accommodate exceptions within these rules, the emergence of the 'interpretive turn' has softened positivism, allowing for a broader understanding of what the law encompasses. This understanding may include "not just the extant sources, but also what follows from those sources, or what provides the best justification for those sources."[2] However, the trade-off in law between predictability and fairness is not a given in all legal systems. This is problematic when seeking equality and equity in diverse societies. A legal approach that respects both established and newly evolving diversity by incorporating diverse sources and approaches is essential. This chapter explores a recent conceptualization of a 'law of diversity.'

The Law of Diversity to be examined is not a law itself, but rather a philosophical perspective on law-making. It challenges pre-established positions in law-making by blurring the distinction between rules and exceptions, making this differentiation increasingly difficult, if not obsolete. This perspective enables differentiation in the legal standing of societal groups, allowing for pluralism concerning both legal and non-legal sources. Furthermore, it facilitates the renegotiation of the status of actors in specific societal relationships, which is

1 Leonard Lawlor citing Jacques Derrida, 'Jacques Derrida.' *Stanford Encyclopedia* 2005/2021.

2 Richard Holton, 'The Exception Proves the Rule.' *Journal of Political Philosophy* 18, Vol. 4 (2010), 369–388.

particularly relevant in the context of the Indonesian Constitutional Court's role in recognizing and protecting indigenous rights.

By challenging the traditional distinction between rule and exception, the Law of Diversity draws upon the philosophical notion that law is formed through a dialectic process of law-making, which requires an ongoing and infinite dialogue on justice.[3] Emphasizing the pluralism of sources, it expands the foundational scope of law-making and broadens the profile of actors involved in this process. By advocating for the renegotiation of actors' statuses, it allows for participatory approaches to law-making. In sum, the Law of Diversity is a systematic process of social exchange, driven by a pragmatism that employs a relational logic to uncover the essence of the law.

After presenting the key elements of the Law of Diversity, this chapter will explore each element through relevant philosophical theories. This involves seeing law-making as a dialectic process of deconstruction and undecidability as proposed by Jacques Derrida. Philip Allott's social idealism, which examines humanity's ability to actualize social objectives in self-organizing societies, will also be introduced. Additionally, John Dryzek's arguments for discursive democracy, based on deliberative and reflective processes, will be discussed. To provide a practical perspective on the Law of Diversity, the chapter will introduce the United Nations' policy of participatory law-making. This will set the stage for analysing the law-making process of the Indonesian 2014 Village Law, an example of participatory law-making embodying the main tenets of the Law of Diversity. The active civil society participants in the process leading to the adoption of the Village Law were traditional indigenous communities. Through deliberation in the public sphere and utilizing new constitutional provisions and participatory rights, they influenced the law-making. The example of the Village Law process demonstrates that participatory law-making is multi-dimensional, involving a pluralism of sources and inclusive negotiations, in line with the vision of the Law of Diversity. This goes beyond being a mere procedural aspect of law-making; it represents a conceptualization of completeness.

---

3 Jacques Derrida, 'Force of Law: The 'Mystical Foundation of Authority'' in *Deconstruction and the Possibility of Justice*, ed. Drucilla Cornell, Michel Rosenfeld and David Gray Carlson. (London: Routledge, 1992), 3–67.

2 The Law of Diversity

The Law of Diversity was originally presented by two constitutional scholars, Francesco Palermo and Jens Woelk, as a procedure for law-making in multi-ethnic and multicultural societies.[4] Their objective is to provide a legal approach that allows for differentiation in the legal positions of ethno-cultural minority groups.[5] The focus is on conceptualizing a procedure that determines common ground rather than promoting an ideological bias associated with systems of justice. Instead, the Law of Diversity acts as a detached regulator, akin to a "referee,"[6] leaving the substantive details to be influenced and determined by the participation of non-dominant groups in collaboration with local, regional, and state governments under their jurisdiction. In the Indonesian context, the Constitutional Court, through its interpretative role, plays a crucial role in guiding these collaborative efforts, ensuring that the law respects and protects the rights of minority groups.

In the spirit of collaborative decision-making, the involved actors collectively address substantive issues through cooperation, much like collaborative shop owners in a busy city square. Cooperation is paramount for the Law of Diversity to function effectively, requiring the willingness of all parties to work together and become mutually integrated. This approach also aims to encourage the dominant majority to recognize the complexity of their society and the need for comprehensive solutions. In other words, simple rules are not sufficient when dealing with law-making in multi-ethnic and multicultural societies, such as Indonesia.

The Law of Diversity is characterized by three main elements:

> *asymmetry* regarding its application as well as the single instruments (differentiation in the legal position of the groups thus becomes the rule); *pluralism* of legal sources and of subjects (creating the obligation of mutual recognition, consideration of the position and interests of others and, in the end, mutual acceptance; mutual trust and cooperation are the most important non-legal preconditions for the acceptance of the single solutions) as well as the *negotiation* of its content in a quasi-contractual framework, i.e., going beyond pre-established majority and

---

4 The Law of Diversity was first framed by Francesco Palermo and Jens Woelk in 'From Minority Protection to a Law of Diversity? Reflections on the Evolution of Minority Rights.' *European Yearbook of Minority Issues*. Vol. 3 (2003/4), 5–14.

5 Palermo and Woelk, 'Law of Diversity,' 12.

6 Ibid., 13.

minority positions (and making the distinction between rule and exception increasingly difficult if not obsolete).[7]

The Law of Diversity necessitates flexibility in law-making and societal engagement, where status, position, and identity do not determine one's right to be heard and included, resonating with the principles upheld by the Indonesian Constitutional Court to ensure equal access to justice for all, irrespective of background. Emphasizing the importance of deliberation and reflection, the Law of Diversity envisions an environment free from coercion by power structures that disregard diversity. The following sections will describe in more detail the elements of the Law of Diversity, exploring their connections with post-modern and contemporary philosophical perspectives of law and politics for the first time.

3 Asymmetry in Application

The argument that asymmetry defines the application of the Law of Diversity is interesting for a number of reasons. First, with regard to applicability, it challenges the formal equality approach that has characterized the liberal paradigm of law for decades. Second, it implies that applying corporate rights to groups could be necessary. Third, it implies a conceptual challenge to the universal buttresses of international human rights law by which human rights are seen as belonging to all humankind. However, asymmetry poses a number of conceptual problems in law-making inasmuch as asymmetric rights in legal theory are special institutional rights that give members of society particular entitlements to a range of benefits subject to meeting certain well-defined criteria.

The British moral philosopher Onora O'Neill highlights the challenges of asymmetric relationships, as they require moral justification for the granted rights and ethical value in the supporting political institutions.[8] Special obligations within such relationships necessitate ethical reasoning at two levels, questioning both the ethical claims arising within these relationships and the background practices and institutions enabling them.[9] The Indonesian Constitutional Court, for instance, has been instrumental in addressing

7 Ibid., 12.

8 Onora O'Neill, *Towards Justice and Virtue: A Constructive Account of Practical Reasoning* (Cambridge University Press, Cambridge, 1998).

9 O'Neill, *Towards Justice and Virtue,* 148.

asymmetric rights in the context of ethno-cultural diversity. Essentially, this means that justifying asymmetric rights demands evidence of moral justification for imposing duties on others and ethical behaviour among the rights-holders. For ethno-cultural minority rights, this entails demonstrating both the benefit of receiving special group protection and the worthiness of such protection. Without this, the political will to establish asymmetric rights is unlikely to materialize.

4 Pluralism of Sources

Pluralism of sources in law-making is not a question of reconciling divergent values but of reconciling divergent factual existences in an ethical manner, as exemplified by the Indonesian Constitutional Court's role in upholding diverse legal foundations. This requires a set of non-legal preconditions for the acceptance of solutions. These preconditions must include mutual recognition, consideration of the position and interests of others, mutual trust and cooperation, as well as acceptance.[10] Thus, the notion of a fixed or singular perfect model of justice representing common values is simply not feasible.

The Canadian political philosopher James Tully has explained the need for pluralism of sources, or what he calls multiplicity of voices, as a process of collective reasoning through an intercultural multilogue that gives a voice to all groups in society. Intercultural multilogue entails ongoing negotiations among diverse groups within self-organizing societies,[11] viewing constitutionalism as flexible and constantly renegotiated to adapt to societal changes. Tully names this "common constitutionalism" as opposed to the contemporary imperial constitutionalism of liberal democracy, which he argues is unable to adjust to multiple diversity. Tully builds his theory upon three cornerstone concepts or conventions of intercultural multilogue: mutual recognition, consent and continuity. By *mutual recognition*, Tully means the principle of equality of self-governing groups as espoused by the treaty system that regulated the relations between the aboriginal peoples of North America and the British Crown.[12] The second convention of trust, that of *consent*, is derived from the Roman law principle of *quod omnes tangit, ab omnibus comprobetur* (what touches all must be agreed to by all) and later articulated by the British philosopher

10 Palermo and Woelk, 'Law of Diversity,' 12.

11 James Tully, *Strange Multiplicity: Constitutionalism in an Age of Diversity* (Cambridge University Press, Cambridge, 1995).

12 Tully, *Strange Multiplicity*, 117.

John Locke.[13] The third convention of trust, *continuity*, refers to the principle of respect, implying that the ways and customs of diverse groups and peoples serve as evidence of their free agreement. Therefore, the continuity of the group's culture in terms of norms, values and traditions should be respected.[14] According to Tully, these three conventions should be seen as preconditions for a reasonable system of accommodation in divided societies. But they are not only preconditions; they are principles that diverse groups must follow in their intercultural multilogue – a mode of communication rooted in the ethical principle of *audi alteram partem*, meaning 'the duty to listen to the other side'.[15] By combining these three conventions and the principle of multilogue, Tully argues that it is possible to negotiate common constitutional arrangements in divided societies.

5 Negotiation of Content

In practice, the Law of Diversity approach stems from the principles of procedural republic, constitutionalism, communicative action and representative government. Jürgen Habermas, the German philosopher and sociologist, highlights the significance of proceduralism in a procedural democracy, where law serves as the defining structure.[16] However, procedural democracy is also discursive. Discursive democracy refers to the ideal of reaching agreement through communicative action. The rules that guide discursive democracy are procedural inasmuch as they set a standard for how the deliberation process should be ordered. Hence, ethical considerations are regulated by the procedures of law, which are collectively agreed upon through communicative action. Unlike being solely influenced by universal liberal ideology or particularistic communitarian tradition, the rules in discursive democracy are shaped by a discourse principle that seeks impartial justification for norms of action. The approach empowers the state based on the discursive nature of public reasoning.

13 Ibid., 122.

14 Ibid., 125.

15 James Tully 'The Crisis of Identification: The Case of Canada.' *Political Studies*, 42 (1994), 77–96 at 84.

16 Jürgen Habermas, *The Theory of Communicative Action*, I, trans. Thomas McCarthy (London: Heinemann, 1984) and II, trans. Thomas McCarthy (Cambridge: Polity Press, 1987).

Habermas perceives law as the conduit through which public reasoning translates into administrative power, emphasizing the empirical relevance of democratic ideals embraced by citizens. Proceduralism, according to Habermas, fuses the juridical and the political, forming a composite model of the constitutional and political state.[17] While the constitutional state upholds rights through institutions and procedures, the political state operates in the public sphere where groups engage and interpret collective goals and goods. This model of proceduralism suggests mediation by just personalities who are able to disengage any self-interest in that process. By doing so, trust is fostered among the deliberating parties and in the final outcome. Essentially, citizens openly debate and deliberate on the rights they consider equitable and essential for safeguarding both individual liberties and public participation.

The Indonesian Constitutional Court has similarly played a role in fostering trust and deliberation by ensuring that the discourse principle is upheld. Its decisions and interpretations have contributed to the shaping of constitutional and legal principles that resonate with the diverse voices within the Indonesian society. The Court's engagement exemplifies the core principles of the Law of Diversity. The three components of this legal perspective – namely, asymmetry, pluralism of sources, and negotiation – can be examined within a broader theoretical framework of metaphysics, encompassing doctrines of being, identity and change. Beyond law-making, these concepts are relevant in the creation, maintenance and development of societies, posing challenges for humanity across various domains in handling diversity. A brief review of three approaches to understanding human diversity will enhance our comprehension of these challenges.

6 The Dialectics of Law

The key notion proposed by the Law of Diversity is that law-making should not be seen as a static and inflexible process. This view has been advocated by the French political philosopher, Jacques Derrida, who argued that the road to justice is non-static and unsettled in that it is constantly renegotiated through a dialectic process among the people to whom it pertains.[18] Derrida's concept

17 Jürgen Habermas, "Struggles for Recognition in the Democratic Constitutional State", in *Multiculturalism,* ed. Amy Gutmann (Princeton: Princeton University Press, 1994), 107–149. See also, Melissa S. Williams, 'Justice Toward Groups. Political Not Juridical.' Vol. 23, Issue 1, *Political Theory* (1995), 67–91.

18 Jacques Derrida, 'Force of Law,' 12.

of dialectic entails a departure from deriving ethical imperatives from factual realities; instead, it compels us to perceive justice not merely as an ethical mandate (ought) but as a possibility (could). In this sense, the dialectic process elicits "could" from "is." Through negotiating conceptions of justice, the aim is to establish what we could support, rather than what we ought to endorse. This approach avoids absolutism and emphasizes the importance of individual capacity for critical practical reasoning. By replacing "ought" with "could," the normative idealization of our world is tempered, creating a foundation for negotiations grounded in factual considerations rather than ideological values.

Derrida further explains that good law-making encounters two paradoxes, signifying the dialectic nature of the process. The first paradox involves the deconstruction of the rule, which leads to its re-institution. According to Derrida, a judgment that merely adheres to the letter of the law may be correct but not inherently just. To achieve true justice, a judge must re-institute the decision through a fresh and possibly alternative judgment. Consequently, a decision seeking justice is both governed by established norms and free from their constraints. In a single verdict, the law is both dismantled or temporarily set aside and simultaneously preserved.[19] For Derrida, the re-institution of the law in a decision may seem like a form of violence since it does not conform perfectly to the instituted codes. As such, a violent act or a deconstruction of existing orders occurs and sets the stage for a new view of justice to emerge. The re-institution of the law through deconstruction, therefore, means that justice is always in the making.

The fact that law is always in the making is the second paradox. Derrida refers to this as the undecidability of law. This means that when a case does not fit the established codes, a decision about it seems to be impossible. Thus, the decision-maker experiences undecidability, even after gathering background knowledge and engaging in interpretation. Despite this challenge, the decision-maker must undergo the process of undecidability to ensure that the decision remains free. The crux of the issue lies in the aftermath of the ordeal; once concluded, the decision aligns itself with a rule, and in doing so, it loses its inherent justice. While the decision may be right, it does not necessarily embody justice. Consequently, justice remains perpetually in the future, never fully present. No moment arises when a decision can be deemed wholly just in the present. It faces a predicament: either it disregards a rule, rendering it unjust, or it adheres to a rule that lacks a solid foundation, leading to injustice. Even if it follows a rule, it falls short of justice as it fails to account for the

19 See, Lawlar, 'Jacques Derrida,' Section 5.

uniqueness of the case. This unyielding injustice underscores that the ordeal of the undecidable is never relegated to the past.

Even though the elements of the Law of Diversity are not based on ideological foundations, the dialectic search for just laws helps us understand the aims of the Law of Diversity. It shows that making the distinction between rule and exception is increasingly difficult and that the aim of law-making is finding the solutions that are feasible. Feasibility is, therefore, a key presupposition of the Law of Diversity. The Indonesian Constitutional Court similarly engages in the dialectic process of law, reshaping interpretations and guiding the complex interactions of diverse societal perspectives to seek just outcomes. This mirrors the dynamic and evolving nature of law-making within the framework of the Law of Diversity.

7 Social Idealism

Feasibility depends on many aspects of society, not least humanity's ability to cooperate and become mutually integrated. British legal theorist and long-time adviser to the British Foreign Office, Philip Allott, has eloquently explained that "humanity is a self-ordering system within the ordering of the universe of all-that-is finds intermediate self-ordering in the structure-system of society and in the structure-system of each individual human being."[20] The self-creating structure-system, Allott further explains, is guided by its own laws, or what he calls "its law-for-itself."[21] Society's law-for-itself is its legal system, while the individual's law-for-itself is human consciousness, and humanity's law-for-itself is the consciousness that facilitates its self-creation within the order of the universe. The amalgamation of individuals, society, and the universe is theoretically feasible due to the inherent opportunities, and in practice, these entities must survive and thrive. Calling these processes the pure and practical theories of social idealism, Allott summarizes that "society is the collective self-creating of human beings" and "law is the continuing structure-system of human socializing."[22]

Social idealism is thus a philosophy that believes in "the capacity of the human mind to transcend itself in thought, to take power over the human future, to choose the human future, to make the human future conform to our

20 Philip Allott, *Eunomia. New Order for a New World* (Oxford: Oxford University Press, 1990), 410, Section 19.23.

21 Allott, *Eunomia*, 410, Section 19.24.

22 Ibid., 411, Section 19.27.

ideals, to our best ideas of what we are and what we might be."[23] This self-constituting of humanity informs the Law of Diversity in that it allows for the contradiction of consensus thinking. It does not seek an absolute truth, but it obliges us to speak truly.[24] It also speaks to the notion of the city square where the owners of the shops decide on the substantive issues of cooperation. Social idealism, therefore, helps us understand why the Law of Diversity requires us to engage in deliberation and reflection. The Indonesian Constitutional Court also resonates with the essence of social idealism through its role in upholding the evolving legal framework that reflects the dynamic interplay of societal values and aspirations, embodying the self-ordering nature of a nation's legal structure-system.

8 Deliberative and Reflective Democracy

The need to adjust to and improve the exchange of opinions and ideas, has become a demand of democratic institutions with a view to ensure respect for diversity in our societies. Inclusive processes are now expected, if not always secured, and the scope of actors is expanded to include non-governmental and non-official agents and agencies. New technologies have promoted options for greater participation and knowledge sharing, for better or for worse, and the art of deliberation has entered spaces where it would previously not be allowed or welcomed. Theorists speak of the 'deliberative turn' in democratizing, and processes of decision-making have enjoyed greater democratic legitimacy.[25] Despite certain obstacles that could be pointed out, such as the inability of large segments of societies that cannot participate for reasons of lack of human capital, or access, or direct and indirect exclusion on the basis of 'otherness' or disabilities, deliberation has increasingly become the essence of democracy.

The British-Australian political theorist, John Dryzek, has pointed out that deliberation is seen in contradistinction to traditional democratic tools, such

---

23 Philip Allott, *The Health of Nations. Society and Law beyond the State* (Cambridge: Cambridge University Press, 2002), x.

24 Philip Allott, *Eutopia. New Philosophy and New Law for a Troubled World* (Cheltenham: Edward Elgar, 2016), 139, Section 7.61.

25 The deliberative turn rides on the back of many liberal democracy theories, from Edmund Burke and John Stuart Mill to John Rawls and Jürgen Habermas. One of the first to coin the phrase was John Drzyek in *Discursive Democracy. Politics, Policy, and Political Science* (Cambridge: Cambridge University Press, 1990).

as voting, interest aggregation, constitutional rights, or even self-government.[26] He does not advocate eliminating these institutions; rather, he emphasizes the focus on deliberation in relation to them. Dryzek defines deliberation as the "ability or opportunity to participate in effective deliberation on the part of those subject to collective decisions."[27] He underscores that effective deliberation involving the concerned actors necessitates reflection. In other words, decisions taken collectively must be accepted as long as such "decisions have been justified to these people in terms that, on reflection, they are capable of accepting. The reflective aspect is critical, because preferences can be transformed in the process of deliberation."[28] Thus, Dryzek further argues, "deliberation as a social process is distinguished from other kinds of communication in that deliberators are amenable to changing their judgements, preferences, and views during the course of their interactions, which involve persuasion rather than coercion, manipulation, or deception."[29] In summary, the deliberative turn in democratic theory has led to a notable enhancement in the authenticity of democracy, ensuring that processes focus on substantive issues rather than mere symbolic rhetoric.

In practical application, the implementation of deliberative and reflective democracy requires not only novel processes but also alternative platforms. Social movements have been hailed as the foremost evidence of alternatives to established democratic structures. Some scholars highlight that educational institutions, family units, friendship circles, and even "deliberative mini-publics" such as citizens' juries and assemblies, comprising randomly chosen individuals, could play vital roles as deliberative and reflective arenas.[30] Dryzek has additionally contended that extensive mediation processes, such as regulatory negotiations and other pre-policy settings, could be regarded as platforms for deliberation.

To explain how such processes and forums might work, Dryzek has theorized what he calls "discursive designs," arguing that these are "social institutions around which the expectations of a number of actors converge."[31] A discursive design serves as a space where people are aware that they can

26 John S. Dryzek, *Deliberative Democracy and Beyond: Liberals, Critics, Contestations* (Oxford: Oxford University Press, 2000), 1.

27 Dryzek, Deliberative Democracy and Beyond, 1.

28 Ibid.

29 Ibid.

30 Rebecca Willis, Nicole Curato and Graham Smith, 'Deliberative democracy and the climate crisis.' *Climate Change*, Vol. 13, Issue 2 (2022), 759.

31 Dryzek, *Discursive Democracy*, 43.

meet for recurrent communicative interaction, and which is defined by certain parameters. For instance,

> [I]ndividuals should participate as citizens, not as representatives of the state or any other corporate and hierarchical body. No concerned individuals should be excluded, and if necessary, some educative mechanism should promote the competent participation of persons with a material interest in the issues at hand who might otherwise be left out. The focus of deliberations should include, but not be limited to, the individual or collective needs and interests of the individuals involved. Thus the institution is oriented to the generation and coordination of actions situation within a particular problem context. But complicity in state administration should be avoided. As long as a state is present, discursive designs should be located in, and help constitute, a public space within which citizens associate and confront the state. Within the discursive design, there should be no hierarchy or formal rules, though debate may be governed by informal canons of free discourse. A decision rule of consensus should obtain.[32]

In addition to these practical criteria, Dryzek has emphasized that it is the obligation of the state to ensure that conditions for discursive designs are promoted and protected. States should create environments where political interactions are egalitarian, uncoerced, competent, and free from delusion, deception, power, and strategy. In a parallel vein, the Indonesian Constitutional Court has also been instrumental in nurturing a sense of trust and promoting thoughtful deliberation. This has been accomplished through the Court's commitment to upholding the discourse principle in its rulings and interpretations. As a result, the Court's decisions have significantly influenced the development of constitutional and legal frameworks that harmonize with the diverse voices present within Indonesian society. The link to the aims of the Law of Diversity is not difficult to see. Deliberative and reflective democracy speaks to the elimination of the status quo of pre-established majority and minority positions by extending inclusivity to a wide range of actors.

32 Ibid.

9 Participatory Law-Making

Inclusive deliberative and reflective democracy processes, however uncoerced they may be, must be supported by a structural framework in which to operate. To that effect, many states have recognized the right to participate in public affairs and decision-making on public policy while some have even enshrined this right in constitutional law. Moreover, international standards on this are very clear. In 2018, the United Nations (UN) Human Rights Council affirmed that participation,

> plays a crucial role in the promotion of democracy, the rule of law, social inclusion and economic development. It is essential for reducing inequalities and social conflict. It is also important for empowering individuals and groups and is one of the core elements of human rights-based approaches aimed at eliminating marginalization and discrimination.[33]

Effective participation furthermore requires an environment where rights to freedom of opinion and expression as well as to freedom of peaceful assembly and association are fully respected and enjoyed by all individuals. According to the Council, the right to participate in public affairs is closely linked to the full realization of the right of access to information, which is an enabler of participation and a prerequisite that ensures the openness, transparency and accountability of government decisions. In addition, a structure for participating in public decision-making would also require that the life, physical integrity, liberty, security and privacy of all members of society are protected. Specifically, concerning the phase when a decision is in the preparatory stages and still open, the Council advises public authorities against making any formal, irreversible decisions prior to the initiation of the process. It also requires that no steps be taken that would undermine public participation in practice. For instance, refraining from making large investments in the direction of one option, or commitments to a certain outcome, including agreements with another party or another state.

In this context, the Indonesian Constitutional Court offers a pertinent example. Recent challenges to its independence have brought to the fore the importance of maintaining an environment conducive to participatory law-making, free from interference. The Court's role in fostering trust and deliberation by

33 OHCHR, *Guidelines for States on the effective implementation of the right to participate in public affairs.* https://www.ohchr.org/sites/default/files/Documents/Issues/PublicAffairs/GuidelinesRightParticipatePublicAffairs_web.pdf.

upholding the discourse principle through its rulings and interpretations has contributed to the shaping of deliberative processes in Indonesia. This underscores the interconnectedness of various mechanisms that collectively foster inclusivity and effective governance, especially when dealing with the intricacies of participatory law-making.

In 2021, the UN Food and Agriculture Organization (FAO) developed guidelines specifically aimed at promoting participatory law-making for the recognition of legitimate tenure rights.[34] According to the FAO, robust citizen participation in law-making can help to protect pre-existing legitimate tenure rights and address citizens' tenure challenges. Specifically, governments must ensure widespread knowledge of and compliance with the law and empower citizens to demand that new laws are implemented. These recommendations build on previous guidelines from 2012 aimed at consultation and participation by engaging with and seeking the support of those who, having legitimate tenure rights, could be affected by decisions. Ideally, governments should engage prior to decisions being taken and respond to the contributions of the holders of the tenure rights. More importantly, governments must take into consideration existing power imbalances between different parties and ensure active, free, effective, meaningful and informed participation of individuals and groups in associated decision-making processes.[35] After a decision has been taken, governments should ensure participation in monitoring and evaluation. This should be considered as a continuum and include the use of social accountability tools, such as social audits, public expenditure tracking surveys, community score cards, transparency portals, community media and public hearings.

Participatory law-making is thus much more practical than the theoretical construct of deliberative and reflective democracy but must conform to the rules of deliberative democracy. Participatory law-making speaks to the Law of Diversity in that it shows how complex the negotiations can be and how important it is to ensure a plurality of sources.

10 Indonesia's 2014 Village Law

The Law of Diversity, along with dialectic law-making, social idealism, and deliberative democracy, is intertwined with the recommendations for

34 FAO, *Promoting participatory law-making for recognition of legitimate tenure rights*. July 2021. https://www.fao.org/3/cb4490en/cb4490en.pdf.

35 FAO, *Voluntary Guidelines on the Responsible Governance of Tenure of Land Fisheries and Forests in the Context of National Food Security* (VGGT), 2012.

participatory law-making put forth by the UN and the FAO. These elements serve as a backdrop for comprehending the evolution that Indonesian society underwent during the 2010s with the formulation of the Village Law in 2014.[36] The legislation provided for a new framework for local territorial management, extending opportunities for indigenous peoples to be recognized under the concept of *adat* (indigenous) villages, with more cultural-based criteria than previous laws and regulations.

The Village Law grants indigenous communities communal land rights, allowing them to adhere to their customary *adat* law. Consequently, the government is obliged to honour both the land and cultural rights of these customary indigenous groups. While the Village Law holds significance as a groundbreaking legal document in Indonesia,[37] its interest for our study lies in the developmental process that led to its adoption. Particularly noteworthy is the journey up to the pivotal point in 2012, when the Indonesian Constitutional Court ruled in favour of the indigenous groups contesting the status quo.[38] Although criticism has arisen regarding the deficient implementation of the Village Law post-adoption,[39] the development process of this legislation signifies a novel phase in Indonesian democracy, aligning with the tenets of the Law of Diversity.

The feasibility of participatory law-making involving indigenous communities in Indonesia began with the demise of the Suharto regime in 1998. As part of the democratization process, Indonesia's legislators amended the Constitution, recognizing the rights of indigenous peoples to safeguard their culture and traditional communities. Subsequently, new legislation on law-making provided for participation of civil society groups through the National Program for Legislation (*Program Legislasi Nasional*, Prolegnas). The Prolegnas is jointly determined by the president and the parliament at the start of a newly elected parliament's five-year term and is adapted before each year's session. If civil society organizations seek to promote a certain law or seek changes to a law, they will need to get approval from parliament and the president that

36 Law of The Republic of Indonesia, No. 6 of 15 January 2014 concerning Village. *State Gazette of The Republic of Indonesia* (2014), No 7.

37 The Village Law has been hailed as "revolutionary" by observers. See, Jacqueline Vel, Yando Zakari, and Adriaan Bedner, Law-Making as a Strategy for Change: Indonesia's New Village Law. Asian Journal of Law and Society, Vol. 4 (2017), 447–471.

38 Decision 35/PUU-X/2012, reviewing Law 41 of 1999 on Forestry, issued 20 March 2013 (*Traditional Forest Community case*) (2012).

39 See for instance, Mirza Satria Buana, 'Understanding indigenous cultural rights in Indonesia,' in *Non-Territorial Autonomy and Decentralization. Ethno-Cultural Diversity Governance*, eds. Tove H. Malloy and Levente Salat (London: Routledge, 2021), 195–214.

their proposal be included in the Prolegnas. Only then does it make sense to start lobbying for the actual changes, and, of course, inclusion in the Prolegnas is not a guarantee that the proposal will become legislation. Next, a rather general academic document (*naskah akademik*) is drawn up to outline the parameters of the law and the problems that it should seek to resolve. This is the starting point of actual influence, as it also represents the beginning of the drafting period.

During the drafting period civil society groups will have to deal with many obstacles. Whether the drafting is organized by the government's offices or the parliament, civil society groups should try to get one of their own experts involved. This is feasible, especially in those cases where the government offices are understaffed and lacking expertise in specific areas of policy. When the drafting process is opened up for debate in the parliament, it gets more difficult for civil society groups to have direct involvement. They will usually have to depend on good relations with members of parliament. Once a bill is adopted, civil society organizations will furthermore have to find ways to continue monitoring the implementation of the law. This is because Indonesian legislation is often rather general and seldom includes directions for implementation. Thus, the guidelines issued by the FAO on civil society involvement especially after adoption of legislation seem very relevant for Indonesia.

The process of lobbying for the 2014 Village Law began in 2005–06 when civil society groups expressed their dissatisfaction with decentralization legislation. This legislation had notably augmented the budget allocated for village-level programs, yet villages were only granted decision-making authority over the allocation. Six distinct civil society groups united behind a shared objective. They effectively translated their overarching policy objectives into concrete demands and proposed articles to be incorporated into a new law. These articles were eventually promoted by legislators involved in the debates about the Village Law Bill in the special committee of the parliament assigned to the drafting. While this portrayal simplifies the process, the observers of this process noted the involvement of both private and public interests related to village management. Among these interests was the National Association of Indigenous Communities (AMAN), which simultaneously sought to advocate for the recognition and protection of indigenous communities.[40] This secondary cause eventually contributed to advancing the primary cause beyond the committee stage.

---

40 Jacqueline Vel, Yando Zakari, and Adriaan Bedner, Law-Making as a Strategy for Change, 459.

Parallel to the process of lobbying for improving village management, AMAN, alongside two indigenous communities,[41] had been involved in another process resulting from the constitutional recognition of indigenous customary law communities.[42] As a number of laws had to be amended due to the elevation of indigenous rights to the constitutional level, it became clear that the laws were lacking enforcement mechanisms. AMAN mobilized on the basis of prior cases in which the government had treated customary forests as state-owned forest. This, they claimed, was possible because the 1999 Forestry Law categorized traditional forests as 'state forests,' thereby subjecting them to state control.

Rather than lobbying the parliament for a new law, AMAN leveraged the new constitutional provisions recognizing indigenous rights to take the matter to the Constitutional Court directly. AMAN argued that the 1999 Forest Law had allowed the state to award rights over traditional forests to commercial entities without obtaining the agreement of the traditional indigenous communities that used or occupied those forests, and without being required to compensate them. The result was that traditional indigenous communities were being excluded from forestry resources they had used for generations. AMAN asked the Court to invalidate the provisions that defined state forests to include forests traditionally used and accessed by indigenous communities, and to reformulate provisions that breached their constitutional rights.[43] The Court agreed with the applicants' principal arguments and, by issuing declarations of conditional constitutionality, amended the 1999 Forestry Law to remove indigenous forests from the definition of state forest. Notwithstanding the criticism of the Court's power to influence law-making,[44] and the difficulties that many indigenous communities will encounter when trying to lobby or take issues to court, the Court's review of the 1999 Forest Law has been hailed as a turning point in the value of participatory law-making because it influenced the parallel process in the parliament to hash out a law on village management.[45] Collectively, these endeavours ultimately paved the way for the enactment of the 2014 Village Law.

---

41 Kuntu State Indigenous Community Union and Kasepuhan Cisitu Indigenous Community Union.

42 See, Simon Butt, 'Traditional Land Rights before the Indonesian Constitutional Court', *Law, Environment and Development Journal*, Vol, 10, No. 1 (2014), 57, http://www.lead-journal.org/content/14057.pdf.

43 Decision 35/PUU-X/2012, reviewing Law 41 of 1999 on Forestry, issued 20 March 2013 (*Traditional Forest Community case*) (2012).

44 Butt, 'Traditional Land Rights,' 71.

45 Buana, Understanding indigenous cultural rights in Indonesia, 197.

Observers of the law-making process have explained that to "turn an idea into a Bill and a Bill into a law requires quite distinct steps."[46] It entails getting into the Prolegnas via the *naskah akademik* so that a draft legislation emerges and gets discussed on the floor of the parliament. In that regard, the split between government drafts and parliament drafts is significant. In the case of the draft Village Law, the government at one point halted the process, forcing civil society groups to get together with an activist-turned-legislator, who could put pressure on the government to resume drafting by threatening to have parliament take over the initiative. This, in a sense, outmanoeuvred the government. Moreover, due to sustained lobbying, civil society groups succeeded in forcing the government to accept a law that was completely different from the draft the government had presented at the beginning. Although the Village Law was eventually presented as a government product, observers argue that it was the civil society organizations that kept the momentum and pushed the process using demonstrations, legal debate, political campaigns during election times, and active lobbying at times sponsored by international donor organizations. As one observer put it, "their success is that the law lent itself to unite a diversity of policy agendas and the communities pushing them."[47] Such a statement validates the argument that the process to find the Village Law sustains the tenets of the Law of Diversity. The final discussion below will explore the link between the two.

11 Applying the Law of Diversity

While the process of formulating the Village Law is perhaps not representative of law-making processes in Indonesia in general, it provides a good illustration of the three main components of the Law of Diversity, which this chapter examines. First, it involves *asymmetry* in application by allowing differentiation in the legal position of the groups. On one side, these groups are objects of the case, and on the other side, they function as subjects or participants in the law-making process. Granted, the legal position and rights of indigenous peoples in Indonesia now enjoy constitutional protection. However, by involving these groups in the law-making process, their asymmetrical position becomes solidified as a standard. The dialectics of law-making have proved beneficial for Indonesia's indigenous communities.

46 Vel, Zakari and Bedner, Law-Making as a Strategy for Change, 466.

47 Ibid.

Second, the process of the Village Law exemplifies the principle of *pluralism* of legal sources and subjects. In terms of legal sources, it entailed the Constitution, the assessment of a case determined by the Constitutional Court, legislation pertaining to participatory law-making, and administrative regulations concerning legislative preparation. In terms of subjects, it encompassed elected officials, administrators, experts, civil society organizations, and beneficiaries. According to the Law of Diversity, when pluralism is observed, it carries an obligation of mutual recognition, consideration of each other's positions and interests, and ultimately, mutual acceptance. Therefore, the most vital non-legal prerequisites for adopting solutions are mutual trust and cooperation.

Third, the process of formulating the Village Law exemplifies the principle of *negotiating* content within a quasi-contractual framework. Participating in discussions with official law bodies may seem non-committed but is in fact quasi-contractual insofar that there is legislation in place securing access to participation in policy-making. Petitioning a court is usually also quasi-contractual in that the option is guaranteed any individual or civil society group that may have grievances. The Law of Diversity further expects that negotiations of content would go beyond pre-established majority and minority positions, thus making the distinction between rule and exception increasingly difficult if not obsolete. The Court's decision on the 1999 Forestry Law did precisely this. By establishing the violations in the interpretation of what constitutes a state forest, the Court reversed the roles of state and traditional indigenous communities in regard to the use of forests in Indonesia. It gave power back to the disadvantaged. It did not only make an exception; it made a new rule and thus changed, at least in a prescriptive way, the guidelines for territorial management in local areas.

12 Conclusions

This chapter's main objective was to introduce and elucidate the principles of the Law of Diversity, and to illustrate their application through the lens of the participatory law-making process surrounding Indonesia's Village Law of 2014. Notably, this example not only showcases the tenets of participatory law-making but also highlights the significant role played by the Indonesian Constitutional Court in shaping the legal landscape.

The Village Law process serves as a compelling illustration of the multifaceted nature of participatory law-making, underpinned by principles like asymmetry, pluralism, and deliberation, which are core components of the Law of

Diversity. By allowing various stakeholders to engage in the process, the Village Law experience emphasizes the importance of inclusive negotiations and diverse sources in shaping comprehensive legal frameworks.

Of equal importance is the transformative role played by the Indonesian Constitutional Court. Its involvement in reviewing the 1999 Forestry Law marked a pivotal juncture, redefining the relationship between the state and indigenous communities in terms of forest management. This landmark decision not only rectified historical injustices but also instigated a paradigm shift in the guidelines for local territorial management.

The participatory law-making process leading to the Village Law also underlines the significance of an approach that fosters deliberation and reflection throughout the negotiation process. This emphasis on inclusive dialogue underscores the notion that society's self-formation thrives on the integration of diverse perspectives, an imperative that all societies should uphold.

In conclusion, the Law of Diversity is perhaps more than a procedure; it is a conceptualization of completeness. This framework encapsulates a comprehensive conceptualization that finds tangible expression in the complex interplay of actors, institutions, and legal mechanisms, as exemplified by the Village Law case. Furthermore, the symbiotic interaction between participatory law-making and the Indonesian Constitutional Court exemplifies the intricate dynamics that drive legal evolution and societal progress.

In conclusion, the Law of Diversity emerges as a framework that transcends mere procedural considerations. It encapsulates a comprehensive conceptualization that finds tangible expression in the complex interplay of actors, institutions, and legal mechanisms, as exemplified by the Village Law case. Furthermore, the symbiotic interaction between participatory law-making and the Indonesian Constitutional Court exemplifies the intricate dynamics that drive legal evolution and societal progress.

Bibliography

Allott, Philip, *Eunomia. New Order for a New World.* Oxford: Oxford University Press, 1990.

Allott, Philip, *Eutopia. New Philosophy and New Law for a Troubled World.* Cheltenham: Edward Elgar, 2016.

Allott, Philip, *The Health of Nations. Society and Law beyond the State.* Cambridge: Cambridge University Press, 2002.

Brunkhorst, Hauke, "Dialectical snares: human rights and democracy in the world society." *Ethics & Global Politics*, Vol. 2, Issue 3 (2009): 219–239.

Buana, Mirza Satria, "Understanding indigenous cultural rights in Indonesia," in *Non-Territorial Autonomy and Decentralization. Ethno-Cultural Diversity Governance* edited by Tove H. Malloy and Levente Salat. London: Routledge, 2021.

Butt, Simon, "Traditional Land Rights before the Indonesian Constitutional Court." *Law, Environment and Development Journal* 10, No. 1 (2014), http://www.lead-journal.org/content/14057.pdf.

Czapanskiy, Karen Syma and Rashida Manjoo, "The Right of Public Participation in the Law-Making Process and the Role of Legislature in the Promotion of this Right." *Duke Journal of Comparative & International Law*. Vol. 19 (2008): 1–40.

Decision 35/PUU-X/2012, reviewing Law 41 of 1999 on Forestry, issued 20 March 2013 (*Traditional Forest Community case*) (2012).

Derrida, Jacques, "Force of Law: The 'Mystical Foundation of Authority,'" in *Deconstruction and the Possibility of Justice,* edited by Drucilla Cornell, Michel Rosenfeld and David Gray Carlson, 3–67. London: Routledge, 1992.

Dryzek, John S., *Deliberative Democracy and Beyond: Liberals, Critics, Contestations.* Oxford: Oxford University Press, 2000.

Drzyek, John S., *Discursive Democracy. Politics, Policy, and Political Science.* Cambridge: Cambridge University Press, 1990.

FAO, *Promoting Participatory Law-making for Recognition of Legitimate Tenure Rights.* July 2021. https://www.fao.org/3/cb4490en/cb4490en.pdf.

FAO, *Voluntary Guidelines on the Responsible Governance of Tenure of Land Fisheries and Forests in the Context of National Food Security* (VGGT), 2012.

Glendinning, Simon, "Derrida and the Philosophy of Law and Justice." *Law Critique,* Vol. 27 (2016): 187–203.

Habermas, Jürgen, "Struggles for Recognition in the Democratic Constitutional State," in *Multiculturalism* edited by Amy Gutmann, 107–149. Princeton: Princeton University Press, 1994.

Habermas, Jürgen, *The Theory of Communicative Action I*, trans. Thomas McCarthy. London: Heinemann, 1984.

Habermas, Jürgen, *The Theory of Communicative Action II*, trans. Thomas McCarthy. Cambridge: Polity Press, 1987.

Holton, Richard. "The Exception Proves the Rule." *Journal of Political Philosophy* 18, No. 4 (2010): 369–388.

Koivurova, Timo and Leena Heina¨ma¨ki, "The participation of indigenous peoples in international norm-making in the Arctic." *Polar Record*, Vol. 42 (221) (2006): 101–109.

Law of The Republic of Indonesia, No. 6 of 15 January 2014 concerning Village. *State Gazette of the Republic of Indonesia* of 2014, No 7.

Lawlor, Leonard, "Jacques Derrida." *Stanford Encyclopedia* (2005/2021), https://plato.stanford.edu/entries/derrida/.

Lukito, Ratno, *Legal Pluralism in Indonesia:Bridging the Unbridgeable*. Taylor & Francis Group, 2012. ProQuest Ebook Central, http://ebookcentral.proquest.com/lib/kbdk/detail.action?docID=995686.

McCormick, John P., "Derrida on Law; Or, poststructuralism gets serious." *Political Theory*, Vol. 29, No. 3 (2001): 395–423.

O'Neill, Onora, *Towards Justice and Virtue: A Constructive Account of Practical Reasoning*. Cambridge: Cambridge University Press, 1998.

OHCHR, *Guidelines for States on the effective implementation of the right to participate in public affairs*. https://www.ohchr.org/sites/default/files/Documents/Issues/PublicAffairs/GuidelinesRightParticipatePublicAffairs_web.pdf.

Palermo, Francesco and Jens Woelk, "From Minority Protection to a Law of Diversity? Reflections on the Evolution of Minority Rights." *European Yearbook of Minority Issues*, Vol. 3 (2003/4): 5–14.

Rose, Gillian R., *Dialectic of Nihilism. Post-Structuralism and Law*. Oxford: Basil Blackwell, 1984.

Tamma, Sukri and Timo Duile, "Indigeneity and the State in Indonesia: The Local Turn in the Dialectic of Recognition." *Journal of Current Southeast Asian Affairs*, Vol. 39, Issue 2 (2020): 270–289.

Tully, James, "The Crisis of Identification: the Case of Canada." *Political Studies*, 42 (1994): 77–96.

Tully, James, *Strange Multiplicity: Constitutionalism in an Age of Diversity*. Cambridge: Cambridge University Press, 1995.

Vel, Jacqueline, Yando Zakari, and Adriaan Bedner, "Law-Making as a Strategy for Change: Indonesia's New Village Law." *Asian Journal of Law and Society*, 4 (2017): 447–471.

Widiati, Ekawestri Prajwalita, "Efficient Public Participation in the Local Law-Making Process." *Yuridika*, Vol. 33, No. 3 (September 2018): 389–401.

Williams, Melissa S., "Justice Toward Groups. Political Not Juridical." *Political Theory*, 23, No. 1 (1995): 67–91.

Willis, Rebecca, Nicole Curato and Graham Smith, "Deliberative democracy and the climate crisis." *Climate Change*, Vol. 13, Issue 2 (2022): 759.

CHAPTER 5

The Constitutional Court of Indonesia as a Post-Conflict Institution

Christie S. Warren

Abstract

In post-conflict settings, constitutional courts have important roles to play despite complex and often competing challenges they face to institutionalize their legitimacy and entrench the rule of law while attempting to build bridges from conflict to peace. By processing political conflict through legal means, constitutional courts can shift the tenor of public dialogue and provide a less inflammatory platform for analyzing conflicts that have divided societies. This article analyzes two seminal cases decided by the Constitutional Court of Indonesia in the aftermath of post-Suharto conflict and finds that despite its young age, the Court addressed lustration issues and a Truth and Reconciliation scheme in ways that were consistent with approaches taken by other post-conflict apex courts, concluding that the Constitutional Court of Indonesia has solidified its position among modern constitutional bodies. Instead of relying only on its own decisions or those of the Supreme Court, it has demonstrated its ability to carry out comprehensive global comparative analysis, referring to cases from other constitutional and international courts to help shape its jurisprudence. In this way, the Indonesian Court is ahead of a number of other apex courts in its willingness to consider constitutional issues through a global lens.

Keywords

constitutional court – political conflict – post-conflict – transitional justice – truth and reconciliation – post-conflict reconstruction – amnesties – lustration

1 Post-Conflict Indonesia

In 1998, following sustained periodic conflict driven in part by ethnoreligious divisions, regional separatist movements, the influence of the Indonesian Communist Party and top-down authoritarian leadership, President

DOI:10.1163/9789004691698_006

Suharto – who himself had taken control of the country by way of a coup – resigned, and the period known as *Era Reformasi* (the Reform Era) began.[1] This period brought about economic stabilization and initiated focus on democratic principles, more open free speech and political debate and, in general, increased liberal political and social policies. Incoming President B.J. Habibie's administration introduced a range of political reforms, including legislation increasing the number of permissible political parties, which had previously been limited to three under the Suharto regime. Over the course of the Reform Era, the 1945 Constitution was amended in four stages between 1999 and 2002. Human rights were strengthened, and a Bill of Rights modeled on the Universal Declaration of Human Rights was introduced in reaction to gross violations that had occurred at the end of the previous regime.[2]

A new institution to protect human and constitutional rights in the post-conflict recovery period was considered necessary. Simply augmenting the powers of the Supreme Court was not regarded as a viable option given widespread diminished confidence in the institution following years of corruption and neglect.[3] The third set of constitutional amendments included Article 24c, which created a new constitutional court with jurisdiction to review the constitutionality of legislation, resolve disputes over the authority of state institutions created by the Constitution, decide issues relating to the dissolution of political parties, resolve electoral disputes and rule on issues relating to constitutional violations committed by the President and Vice President.

On August 13, 2003, the Law on the Constitutional Court was signed by President Megawati Soekarnoputri, and Indonesia became the 78th country with an established constitutional court (The Constitutional Court of the Republic of Indonesia). The selection process for seating the nine justices allowed the three branches of government – the national Parliament, the President, and the Supreme Court – to each choose three judges.[4] Following the election of Dr. Jimly Asshiddiqie, a professor of Constitutional Law at the University of Indonesia, as Chief Justice and Dr. H. M. Laica Marzuki as Deputy Chief Justice, cases were transferred to the Constitutional Court from

1 The Asia Foundation, "Indonesia – The State of Violence and Conflict in Asia," *The Asia Foundation*, October 2017, https://asiafoundation.org/wp-content/uploads/2017/10/Indonesia-StateofConflictandViolence.pdf.

2 Simon Butt, "Indonesia's Constitutional Court: Conservative Activist or Strategic Operator?" Law Explorer, KnowledgeBase, October 8, 2016, https://lawexplores.com/indonesias-constitutional-court-conservative-activist-or-strategic-operator/.

3 Ibid.

4 Ibid.

the Supreme Court, where they had previously been heard pursuant to Article III of the Transitional Provisions of the 1945 Constitution, and the work of the Constitutional Court officially began.

2 Emergence of Post-Conflict Constitutional Jurisprudence

The new court did not shy away from challenge; in fact, despite its young age, it proved able to engage in thorough comparative analysis, aligning its methodology with that of other contemporary post-conflict constitutional courts grappling with similar issues. Within the first three years of the Court's existence, it issued two seminal decisions directly addressing the earlier period of conflict.

In Case No. 011–017/PUU-I/2003, the Court dealt with the issue of vetting actors allegedly implicated in the conflict by virtue of their past membership in the Communist Party and prohibiting them from running for office. Individuals and leaders of various organizations and committees filed a petition against the government, alleging that Article 60(g) of Law No. 12 of 2003, which prohibited former members of the Indonesian Communist Party from running for office in local, regional, and national elections, violated Article 27 of the Constitution. The plaintiffs argued that any restrictions of Article 27, requiring that all citizens be treated equally under the law, together with Article 28, which gives every citizen the right to take part in public affairs, including the right to vote and be elected, must be reasonable and proportionate. The Constitutional Court agreed, and, relying in part on the Universal Declaration of Human Rights and the International Covenant on Civil and Political Rights, held that MPRS Decree Number XXV/MPRS/1966 on the Dissolution of *Partai Komunis Indonesia* (Indonesian Communist Party), which had previously declared the Party a prohibited organization, in no way restricted the right of former Communist Party members to vote or run for elected office. Article 60(g), the Court held, constituted an abridgement of rights based on political belief and was therefore a violation of the Indonesian Constitution.

Three years later, in Case Br 006/PUU-IV/2006, the Constitutional Court addressed the issue of amnesties in the context of the Indonesian transitional justice scheme. The plaintiffs, individuals and members of organizations representing missing persons and victims of forced kidnappings, disappearances and violence that took place between 1997 and 1998, argued that Law No. 27 of 2004, which established the Truth and Reconciliation Commission, was unconstitutional in that it conditioned the rights of victims to rehabilitation and compensation on granting amnesty to perpetrators, thereby violating the victims' constitutional human rights. The Court agreed, holding that the statutory scheme granting amnesty to perpetrators of gross human rights abuses precluded resubmitting claims to the ad hoc human rights court established by Law 26/ 2000 and eliminated the state's right to prosecute, violating both the Constitution and international human rights law. The Court also found that requiring the physical presence of perpetrators unfairly burdened victims' inherent rights to recovery. Since Law No. 27 was at the core of the national transitional justice scheme, the entirety of the law establishing the Truth and Reconciliation Commission was invalidated.

3 Roles and Challenges of Post-Conflict Constitutions and Constitutional Courts

In order to contextualize the significance of the granting of jurisdiction and holdings in Cases 011–017/PUU-I/2003 and Br 006/PUU-IV/2006, an understanding of specific roles, functions and challenges faced by post-conflict constitutions and constitutional courts is useful. Although Indonesia's Constitution is not per se a post-conflict document, the four amendment stages that took place between 1999 and 2002 were in direct response to periods of violence and instability preceding Suharto's resignation. The need for a new constitutional court was rooted in political disputes and conflicts accompanied by ambiguous laws that threatened to upend the democratization process.[5] As had been the case in post-war Germany, processing political conflict via legal means and a new constitutional court shifted the tenor of public dialogue and provided a less inflammatory platform for analyzing the conflict that had plagued the country.[6]

3.1 *Post-Conflict Constitutions*

Constitutional courts in general are of comparatively recent origin and are the product of Hans Kelsen's theories that led to the creation of the Austrian Constitutional Court in 1920. This institutional innovation caused a fundamental shift in the adjudication of constitutional claims.[7] Constitutions created or

5 Ibid.

6 Anuscheh Farahat, "The German Federal Constitutional Court," in *Constitutional Adjudication: Institutions*, Vol. III (Oxford: The Max Planck Handbooks in European Public Law, Oxford University Press, 2020), 281.

7 Lech Garlicki, "Constitutional Courts versus Supreme Courts," *International Journal of Constitutional Law* 5, no. 1 (January 2007): 44–68; Farahat, "The German Federal Constitutional Court, 283."

amended as part of peacebuilding efforts are of even more recent origin. In the modern era, Germany's 1949 constitution is considered one of the earliest post-conflict constitutions, and since 1989, post-conflict constitution building processes have been undertaken throughout Latin America, Africa, Eastern Europe and Asia.[8] Although constitutions need not follow conflict to be considered transformative,[9] and although amendment processes themselves can lead to democratic backsliding,[10] post-conflict constitutional processes are now part of many peacebuilding strategies as countries seek to create new blueprints for the future based on democratic principles.[11] These processes may include utilizing interim constitutions designed to facilitate transitions to

8 Kimana Zulueta-Fülscher, "Interim Constitutions: Peacekeeping and Democracy-Building Tools," International IDEA, October 2015, 10, https://www.idea.int/sites/default/files/publications/interim-constitutions-peacekeeping-and-democracy-building-tools.pdf.

9 Courts can be transformative even if they are not established after conflict. See, for example, the Constitutional Court of India, whose role and jurisprudence in many ways are surprisingly similar to those of the Constitutional Court of Germany (See Michaela Hailbronner, "Rethinking the Rise of the German Constitutional Court: From Anti-Nazism to Value Formalism," *International Journal of Constitutional Law* 12, no. 3 (July 2014): 626–49). Transformative constitutionalism presents issues relating to social utopias and upliftment, which can be at odds with desires for legal certainty (See Hailbronner, "Rethinking the Rise," 645). See also Commentary by Justice Albie Sachs, who recounts early visits to the new Constitutional Court of South Africa by India's former Chief Justice and Attorney General, whose descriptions of their own Supreme Court caused the South African justices to reconsider the role of their court (See Albie Sachs, "Karl Klare: The Person Who Helped Us See the Tree for the Wood," Northeastern University School of Law. Northeastern University School of Law, June 17, 2022, https://law.northeastern.edu/karl-klare-testimonial/ and Jackie Dugard, "Courts and Structural Poverty in South Africa: To What Extent Has the Constitutional Court Expanded Access and Remedies to the Poor?" in *Constitutionalism of the Global South: The Activist Tribunals of India, South Africa, and Colombia*, edited by Daniel Bonilla Maldonado, 329 (Cambridge: Cambridge University Press, 2013), https://doi.org/10.1017/CBO9781139567114.011).

10 In recent years, constitutional amendment processes have resulted in democratic backsliding in Hungary, Venezuela, Honduras, Ecuador and Nicaragua (see Landau, "Constitutional Backsliding: Colombia," 499). Some courts have restricted amendment processes if the amendments would undermine core constitutional principles (see Landau, "Constitutional Backsliding: Colombia, 500)" and Yaniv Roznai, "Unconstitutional Constitutional Amendments—The Migration and Success of a Constitutional Idea," *The American Journal of Comparative Law* 61, no. 3 (2013): 657–719. http://www.jstor.org/stable/43668170.

11 Vivien Hart, "Democratic Constitution Making." (Special Report 107. United States Institute of Peace, July 2003), https://www.usip.org/publications/2003/07/democratic-constitution-making.

more just democratic political orders based on fundamental human rights or, as in the case of Indonesia, amending pre-existing constitutions.[12]

Because of their nature, post-conflict constitutions tend to focus on values such as human dignity, reconciliation and national unity. In Germany's constitution, drafted in the aftermath of World War II, peace is mentioned fifteen times; Article 1 states that human dignity shall be inviolable and that it shall be the duty of state authorities to respect and protect it. The 1978 Constitution of Spain, drafted after forty years of dictatorship and inspired by constitutional processes that had taken place in Germany, Italy and France, created a new regime of rights, freedoms and democratic principles designed to break from international isolation that resulted from the Franco dictatorship.[13] In South Africa, the epilogue to the post-apartheid constitution emphasizes the fundamental role of national unity and reconciliation and states that the Constitution is meant to serve as an "historic bridge between the past of a deeply divided society characterized by strife, conflict and untold suffering and injustice, and a future founded on the recognition of human rights, democracy and peaceful co-existence and development opportunities for all South Africans, irrespective of colour, race, class, belief or sex".[14] The Preamble to the post-conflict constitution of Kosovo similarly focuses on peace, envisioning Kosovo as a "free, democratic and peace-loving country that will be a homeland to all of its citizens … (and) a dignified member of the family of peace- loving states of the world".[15]

3.2 *Post-Conflict Constitutional Courts*

Just as post-conflict constitutions differ from those created under less turbulent circumstances, constitutional courts created in the aftermath of conflict also face unique challenges. Sapiano analyzes factors that distinguish the jurisprudence of post-conflict constitutional courts from that of other courts.[16] The

12 Fülscher, "Interim Constitutions," 3; Albie Sachs, "War, Violence, Human Rights, and the Overlap between National and International Law: Four Cases before the South African Constitutional Court," *Fordham International Law Journal* 28, no. 2 (January 2005): 432–476.

13 Marian Ahumada Ruiz, "The Spanish Constitutional Court," in *Comparative Constitutional Reasoning*, ed. András Jakab, Arthur Dyevre, and Giulio Itzcovich, 604 (Cambridge: Cambridge University Press, 2017), https://doi.org/10.1017/9781316084281.018.

14 Sachs, "War, Violence, Human Rights," 435.

15 The Constitution of Indonesia, although not post-conflict in its entirety, contains similar language, promoting "a world order based on freedom, perpetual peace and social justice".

16 Jenna Sapiano, "Courting Peace: Judicial Review and Peace Jurisprudence," *Global Constitutionalism* 6, no. 1 (2017): 138, https://doi.org/10.1017/S2045381716000253.

authoritative bases of post-conflict constitutional courts can differ from other courts as well; the post-war German Constitutional Court achieved a large measure of authority from public reaction to the Nazi regime.[17]

Other unique aspects of post-conflict courts are discussed by Tushnet, who identifies strategies that can be undertaken by new constitutional courts to enhance the legitimacy of peace agreements and related legislation by invalidating some of their provisions without overtly legitimizing or discarding the rest.[18] Ran Hirschl's description of constitutional courts as engaged in "mega-politics" – the resolution of high-stakes controversies dealing with core questions of national identity and immediate political leadership – resonates even more strongly in the immediate aftermath of conflict than in times of peace.[19]

Post-conflict constitutions and constitutional courts are not always able to avoid controversy, however, given the competing roles they are asked to assume. Vicki Jackson describes the paradox of constitution-making in post-conflict environments when constitutions serve as both political pacts towards peace and foundational legal documents serving more typical ultra vires functions.[20] In Spain, the preeminent post-dictatorship impulse was to normatize the Constitution as a binding legal framework and establish standards to harmonize prior law with the new Constitution in order to avoid legislative gaps and inconsistencies.[21] Peace agreement constitutions also bear the heavy burden of moving societies beyond existing divisions toward stability while accommodating warring factions that may bear residual reluctance to achieve a united national identity.[22]

Post-conflict constitutions may be pulled into political territory as well when addressing thorny transitional justice issues, including the granting of amnesties, reparations for violations of human rights and vetting processes to prohibit actors who were involved in past conflict from serving in public office. This was the case in Germany, where constitutional drafters were largely

---

17 Hailbronner, "Rethinking the Rise of the German Constitutional Court," 628.

18 Mark Tushnet, and Beatriz Botero Arcila, "Conceptualizing the Role of Courts in Peace Processes," *International Journal of Constitutional Law* 18, no. 4 (December 2020): 1290–1302.

19 Ran Hirschl, "The Judicialization of Mega-Politics and the Rise of Political Courts," *Annual Review of Political Science* 11, no. 1 (June 1, 2008): 94. https://doi.org/10.1146/annurev.polisci.11.053006.183906.

20 Vicki C Jackson, "What's in a Name? Reflections on Timing, Naming, and Constitution-Making," *William & Mary Law Review* 49, no. 4 (March 1, 2008): 1249.

21 Ruiz, "The Spanish Constitutional Court," 607.

22 Sapiano, "Courting Peace: Judicial Review," 137.

concerned with issues addressing the composition of state institutions and ways to render them less susceptible to authoritarian capture in the future.[23]

3.2.1 Establishing Legitimacy

Among the primary challenges newly created constitutional courts must confront is establishing their own legitimacy and embedding the rule of law in societies where it may have been undermined or eradicated.[24] Over the decades, constitutional courts have sought public legitimacy through a variety of means. Debates in post-war Germany preceding the creation of the German court, for example, included the idea of appointing lay justices in order to solidify public confidence.[25] In Italy, the Constitutional Court has sought to neutralize hostility from lower courts through the novel strategy of refraining from selecting and imposing one interpretation of a challenged law and instead simply eliminating one or more possible interpretations, leaving lower courts free to choose the one they believe to be correct from among several legitimate alternatives.[26] Another feature utilized by the Italian Court is the abrogative referendum (*referendum abrogativo*), whereby the Court reviews the constitutionality of requests for citizens to vote whether to repeal a statute.[27]

By contrast, the Constitutional Court of Bosnia and Herzegovina, created by Annex IV of the Dayton Peace Accords, suffered from an initial lack of legitimacy since it was the creation of external international actors and was not authoritatively ratified by any state institution.[28] The Court's legitimacy was further compromised by its unpopular hybrid nature, which featured international judges sitting jointly on panels with Bosnian counterparts in an effort to balance presumed political biases of local judges.[29]

---

23 Hailbronner, "Rethinking the Rise of the German Constitutional Court," 630.

24 The contours of the theory of institutional legitimacy in the context of the South African Constitutional Court are analyzed by Gibson, see Gibson, "The Evolving Legitimacy."

25 Farahat, "The German Federal Constitutional Court," 285.

26 Vincenzo Vigoriti, "Italy: The Constitutional Court," *The American Journal of Comparative Law* 20, no. 3 (1972): 413. https://doi.org/10.2307/839312.

27 Clare Tame, and Sarah Pasetto, trans, "The Italian Constitutional Court," Constitutional Court of Italy, March 2020, https://www.cortecostituzionale.it/documenti/download/pdf/lacorte_depliant_EN.pdf.

28 David Feldman, "Developments," *International Journal of Constitutional Law* 3, no. 4 (October 2005): 651; James C. O'Brien, "The Dayton Constitution of Bosnia and Herzegovina," in *Framing the State in Times of Transition*, 332–49 (United States Institute of Peace, 2010). https://www.usip.org/sites/default/files/Framing%20the%20State/Chapter12_Framing.pdf.

29 Alex Schwartz, "International Judges on Constitutional Courts: Cautionary Evidence from Post-Conflict Bosnia," *Law & Social Inquiry* 44, no. 1 (February 2019): 1.

Although some post-conflict courts – such as the South African Constitutional Court – are purposely activist, in other contexts judicial activism can compromise legitimacy in the eyes of the public. The German Court's post-conflict jurisprudence rendered it susceptible to allegations of activism; between 1951 and 2011, the Court invalidated 640 laws and administrative regulations.[30] The Corte Suprema de Justicia of El Salvador avoided risking controversy by declaring its incompetence to determine the constitutional validity of amnesty laws on the basis that the issue violated the political question doctrine.[31]

Dangers associated with the erosion of legitimacy are illustrated by the example of Hungary in 2009, when the populist Fidesz party amended the constitution in an attempt to undermine the Constitutional Court, eliminating the Court's jurisdiction over fiscal and budgetary matters in response to a decision the Court had recently issued in those areas. Two years later, the party succeeded in replacing the constitution with an entirely new document.[32]

Direct access of ordinary citizens to constitutional courts can enhance the courts' legitimacy in the eyes of the public. When people have direct access, free of cost, to petition courts when they perceive their rights to have been violated, confidence and trust are strengthened. This is especially true in post-conflict settings when populations often harbor mistrust resulting from previous governmental misfeasance.[33] In post-war Germany, the constitutional complaint doctrine became an important means of instilling public confidence in the government's commitment to move past the Nazi period by providing individuals with free direct access to the Constitutional Court.[34] In Spain, the *recurso de amparo* was introduced in 1978 to provide direct judicial access to individuals whose human rights were violated.[35] In Colombia, the *tutela* was introduced in the 1991 Constitution, giving citizens access to a rapid avenue

---

30 Donald P. Kommers and Russel A. Miller, *The Constitutional Jurisprudence of the Federal Republic of Germany 3rd ed* (Duke University Press Books, 2012).

31 Massimon Starita, "Amnesty for Crimes against Humanity: Coordinating the State and Individual Responsibility for Gross Violations of Human Rights," *Italian Yearbook of International Law* 9 (1999): 86–112.

32 David Landau, "Constitutional Backsliding: Colombia," in *Constitutionalism in Context*, ed. David S. Law, 3 (Cambridge: Cambridge University Press, 2022), https://doi.org/10.1017/9781108699068.023.

33 Petra Stockmann and Hanns-Seidel-Stiftung, "The New Indonesian Constitutional Court: A Study into Its beginnings and First Years of Work" (2007): 11.

34 Uwe Kranenpohl, "Decision Making at the German Federal Constitutional Court," in *Constitutional Courts in Comparison: The US Supreme Court and the German Federal Constitutional Court* (Berghahn Books, 2016), https://www.jstor.org/stable/j.ctt1btbw22.11 and Kommers and Miller, "*The Constitutional Jurisprudence*," 12.

35 Ruiz, "The Spanish Constitutional Court," 612.

to challenge actions impacting their fundamental rights.[36] Article 113(7) of Kosovo's post-conflict constitution authorizes individuals to refer violations of their rights and freedoms to the Constitutional Court after exhausting all other legal remedies. Exhaustion of all other remedies is similarly required by the Spanish *recurso de amparo.*

3.2.2 Embedding the Rule of Law

Newly established constitutional courts also bear responsibility for entrenching the rule of law, which may have been undermined in previous regimes and may have contributed to conflict. In Spain, the judicial system played a key role in political repressions of the Franco era.[37] In post-war Germany, legislators were concerned with questions of separating the operation of law and politics and resolving tensions between representative democracy and constitutional review.[38] In South Africa, the Constitutional Court, established in the immediate post-apartheid era, bolstered the rule of law by endorsing legal analysis of issues that could otherwise have been construed as political.[39] Gibson describes the growing legitimacy of the South African Constitutional Court as the result of a process of promoting public acceptance that the court had the moral authority and duty to decide if it was to perform its democratic role.[40]

The Constitutional Court of Colombia offers an example of a powerful post-conflict court created as part of an overall political movement to reform institutions that had lost legitimacy due to violence and corruption. Over time, the court built independence, credibility and respect that later allowed it to rebuff two attempts by a powerful president to extend his term limits.[41] Popularity of the court emanates in part from the *tutela* process described above. The appointment process for justices, whereby the President, the Supreme Court and the Council of State each select candidates for one third of the seats, has further solidified the court's legitimacy.[42]

---

36 Landau, "Constitutional Backsliding: Colombia," 7.

37 Paloma Aguilar, "The Spanish Amnesty Law of 1977 in Comparative Perspective: From a Law for Democracy to a Law for Impunity," in *Amnesty in the Age of Human Rights Accountability: Comparative and International Perspectives*, edited by Francesca Lessa and Leigh A. Payne, 317 (Cambridge: Cambridge University Press, 2012), https://doi.org/10.1017/CBO9781139177153.016.

38 Hailbronner, "Rethinking the Rise of the German Constitutional Court," 630 and Kommers and Miller, "*The Constitutional Jurisprudence*," 33.

39 Tushnet and Arcila, "Conceptualizing the Role of Courts in Peace Processes," 1294.

40 Gibson, "The Evolving Legitimacy," 229–66.

41 Landau, "Constitutional Backsliding: Colombia," 5.

42 Landau, "Constitutional Backsliding: Colombia," 7.

The Constitutional Court of Kosovo provides another example of a court's post-conflict commitment to strengthen the rule of law. Soon after the new constitution was enacted, the Constitutional Court publicized its vision and mission statement on its public website: to serve as a "professional, competent, and independent institution that is establishing a new tradition of judicial impartiality and full accountability in the service of the citizens of Kosovo. … (and serve as a) transparent institution that vindicates the rights and fundamental freedoms of the citizens and communities of Kosovo, by adjudicating in a fair and transparent manner within its jurisdiction, and overseeing fairness in the exercise and use of powers vested in it by the Constitution. … (and serving as the) final authority of the constitutional order of the country, thereby ensuring and supporting the transition of Kosovo toward prosperity, democracy, and rule of law."[43]

3.2.3 Navigating Relationships with Other Apex Courts

Newly created constitutional courts face additional challenges when their competencies were previously held by other apex courts, including Supreme Courts.[44] In these situations, tensions between the two apex courts can be difficult to negotiate. This was the case in post-war Germany, when the new constitutional court found itself in competition with ordinary courts and in particular with the Federal Supreme Court, or Bundesgerichtshof.[45] In the end, the need for a new judicial institution became clear because the Nazis, who had been elected by the people, had abused rights; the new court was considered necessary to establish a legitimate bridge to a new era.[46] In post-dictatorship Spain, the Constitutional Court had to defend its normative power to the Supreme Court and other high level courts as late as four years after the Constitution entered into force.[47] In Italy, tensions between the Constitutional Court and Court of Cassation, another apex court, arose when the Constitutional Court introduced new interpretations of law that contradicted earlier decisions of the Court of Cassation.[48]

---

43 "2010 Annual Report," Constitutional Court of Kosovo, 2011, https://gjk-ks.org/wp-content/uploads/2017/11/Annual-Report-2010.pdf.

44 Lech Garlicki argues that it is nearly impossible to completely separate the jurisdictions of dual apex courts. See Garlicki, "Constitutional Courts versus Supreme Courts."

45 Farahat, "The German Federal Constitutional Court," 28.

46 Hailbronner, "Rethinking the Rise of the German Constitutional Court," 626.

47 Ruiz, "The Spanish Constitutional Court," 606.

48 Vigoriti, "Italy: The Constitutional Court," 413.

4 Contextualizing Transitional Justice: Comparative Post-Conflict Jurisprudence

It is in the context of the particular challenges faced by post-conflict constitutions and constitutional courts that Indonesia's post-conflict jurisprudence should be considered. The relevant analysis can best be undertaken by comparing whether and how other post-conflict constitutional courts became involved in transitional justice issues, specifically questions relating to lustration and amnesties, and whether their decisions served the goals of contributing to peace and stronger democratic processes.

4.1 *Lustration*

In addition to Indonesia, a number of countries emerging from conflict, including Belgium, France and the Netherlands, have addressed legacies of war through lustration – that is, processes designed to purge political and other influences that led or contributed to the conflict. The most prominent lustration case study is Germany.

In early post-war Germany, the newly formed Constitutional Court directly addressed the country's post-war legacy in a series of decisions. One of the first dealt with banning political parties associated with Nazi ideology.

On November 22, 1951, the federal government requested a determination by the Federal Constitutional Court that the West German Communist Party was unconstitutional under Article 21(2) of the Basic Law. On November 28, the same request was made with respect to the Socialist Reich Party, an extreme right-wing, neo-Nazi type political party.[49] The Court soon ruled that although the German Basic Law guaranteed free establishment and freedom of action for political parties, those guarantees did not apply to parties seeking to abuse formal democratic instruments in order to abolish the free democratic order.[50] Both parties were banned since neither maintained internal structures conforming to basic democratic principles, and the Court found that both endangered the existence of the Federal Republic of Germany.[51]

---

49 Petersberg Agreement, 1 BVerfGE 351 (German Federal Constitutional Court 1952).

50 "Statement by the Press Office of the Federal Constitutional Court," The Federal Constitutional Court, October 23, 1952, https://www.bundesverfassungsgericht.de/SharedDocs/Pressemitteilungen/EN/1952/bvg52-059.html and Edward McWinney, "The German Federal Constitutional Court and the Communist Party Decision," *Indiana Law Journal* 32, no. 3 (Spring 1957): 295–312.

51 "Government Commits to Seeking a Ban of the Extreme Right-Wing National Democratic Party of Germany (NPD)," *German Law Journal* 1, no. 2 (2000): E3. https://doi.org/10.1017/S2071832200003102. Decisions in the Socialist Reich Party Case and the Communist

In 2017, the Constitutional Court issued a long-awaited third decision on the issue of political parties associated with the former Nazi regime. Contrary to the two earlier decisions, the Court found that although the Nationaldemokratische Partei Deutschlands (NPD) advocated political ideologies aimed at destroying the free democratic order, there was no indication at that time that it would be able to achieve its unconstitutional goals.[52] On this basis the Court declined to ban the party. This outcome might be viewed as protecting freedom of association instead of furthering lustration goals, indicating that the need for post-conflict lustration expires after the passage of time.

4.2 *Amnesties*

The issue of amnesties in post-conflict societies can be contentious and often involves separation of powers issues. Criticisms of amnesties following conflict include that they entrench impunity and prevent even minimal investigation and accountability, thereby discouraging justice.[53] Although the United Nations Human Rights Committee has condemned amnesties, amnesty laws have been enacted in a number of countries, including Chile, Brazil, Uruguay, Argentina, Nicaragua, Honduras, El Salvador, Haiti, Peru, Guatemala, Côte d'Ivoire, South Africa, Algeria, Sierra Leone, and Liberia pursuant to the argument that they are effective to uncover the truth and lead to national healing.[54] For the purposes of this discussion, the issue of note is which branches of government in post-conflict contexts have addressed amnesties, and whether this issue is appropriately addressed at all by the judicial branch and, in particular, by constitutional courts.

Party Case can be found at: http://www.uni-wuerzburg.de/dfr/bv002001>www.uni-wuerzburg.de/dfr/bv002001 and http://www.uni-wuerzburg.de/dfr/bv005085>www.uni-wuerzburg.de/dfr/bv005085. The approach of the German Constitutional Court in reckoning with the past is in contrast to that taken by the Hungarian Constitutional Court in 1989. Second and third generation European constitutional courts, such as the Hungarian court, tend not to completely abolish former political institutions but instead seek to maintain institutional continuity while achieving radical new beginnings (Sólyom 2020, 363).

52 "Proceedings for the Prohibition of Political Parties." German Federal Constitutional Court, n.d. https://www.bundesverfassungsgericht.de/EN/Verfahren/WichtigeVerfahrensarten/Parteiverbotsverfahren/parteiverbotsverfahren_node.html.

53 Ronald Slye, "The Cambodian Amnesties: Beneficiaries and the Temporal Reach of Amnesties for Gross Violation of Human Rights," *WIS. INT'L L. J.* 22 (January 1, 2004): 99, https://digitalcommons.law.seattleu.edu/faculty/552.

54 Simon Chestermann, "Justice and Reconciliation: The Rule of Law in Post-Conflict Territories," in *You, The People: The United Nations, Transitional Administration, and State-Building*, 159 (Oxford University Press, 2004).

4.2.1 Germany

In post-war Germany, Parliament held the power to legislate amnesties; the Constitutional Court ultimately weighed in and upheld its ability to do so.[55] This followed a period of reluctance on the part of the judiciary to become involved in amnesties, which was attributed to a high degree of continuity in the judicial system following the dissolution of the Nazi regime.[56]

4.2.2 Italy

The 1947 Constitution of Italy established that powers relating to grants of amnesty were held by the executive branch.[57] However, these powers were limited by the legislature to crimes committed after the Constitution was enacted; therefore, amnesty could not be granted for crimes committed during the war.[58]

In 2014, the Constitutional Court affirmed its jurisdiction over the issue of German immunity for crimes committed in Italian territory during World War II, including claims by Italian citizens who had been sent to German concentration camps. In Judgment No. 238/2014, the Court ruled that legislation compelling compliance with decisions from the International Court of Justice (ICJ) was unconstitutional, thereby in effect ruling against German immunity and paving the way for lawsuits in Italian courts brought by surviving victims of violations of humanitarian law committed by the Nazi regime during World War II.[59] This decision was significant in that the Constitutional Court asserted its authority to decide whether international norms interpreted by the ICJ could be applied within the Italian domestic order.[60]

4.2.3 Spain

The 1977 Amnesty Law provided amnesty for political crimes committed prior to December 15, 1976, crimes committed before June 15, 1977, whose purpose

---

55 Norbert Frei and Joel Golb, "The Amnesty Law of 1954," in *Adenauer's Germany and the Nazi Past: The Politics of Amnesty and Integration*, 75 (Columbia University Press, 2002), http://www.jstor.org/stable/10.7312/frei11882.9.

56 Frei and Golb, "The Amnesty Law," 67–68.

57 In 1992, the Constitution was amended to permit Parliament to grant amnesties following approval of two thirds of both Houses (Amendment to Article 79 1992).

58 "Legge Costituzionale 6 marzo 1992, n. 1.," Legge Costituzionale 6 marzo 1992, n. 1. (1992): 1–1.

59 Italy's Diplomatic, 2014.

60 Maria Elena Gennusa, "Constitutionalising the International Legal Order through Case Law – Judgment No. 238/2014 from the Italian Constitutional Court," *Cambridge Journal of International and Comparative Law* 5, no. 1 (2016): 144.

was restoring autonomy to Spain, and political crimes not involving threats to life committed before October 6, 1977.[61] Recently, in Auto 80/2021 de 15 de Septiembre de 2021, the Constitutional Court denied a petition for *recurso de amparo* alleging that crimes committed by a member of the secret police between 1964 and 1974 constituted violations of international and domestic law.[62] Aguilar argues that this outcome was influenced by the absence of strong social demand for truth and justice following Franco's death. The fact that both sides in the Spanish Civil War committed atrocities led to an intense need for mutual and reciprocal forgiveness and ultimately allowed the Constitutional Court to approve the 1977 Amnesty Law.[63] In Spain, reconciliation is inextricably tied to "forgetting," "erasing," "burying" and "overcoming."[64]

4.2.4 South Africa

The Constitutional Court of South Africa considered itself a transformational institution from the outset of its existence. Within its first few years, the Court issued a series of decisions addressing structural inequalities that had buttressed the apartheid era.[65] The issue of amnesties was addressed in Azanian Peoples' Organization (AZAPO) v. President of the Republic of South Africa, in which the Court held that the Committee on Amnesty could grant amnesty to perpetrators of politically motivated crimes. As a result of the granting of amnesty, perpetrators would not be held civilly or criminally liable. The constitutionality of Section 20(7) of the Promotion of National Unity and Reconciliation Act 34 of 1995 was upheld by reference to the epilogue to the Constitution (National Unity and Reconciliation), which stated that the "Constitution provides a historic bridge between the past of a deeply divided society characterized by strife, conflict, untold suffering and injustice, and a future founded on the recognition of human rights, democracy and peaceful co-existence and development opportunities for all South Africans, irrespective of colour, race, class, belief or sex. The pursuit of national unity, the well-being of all South African citizens and peace require reconciliation between the people of South Africa and the reconstruction of society." The Court's judgment was issued over the objection

---

61 Law 46/1977 of 15 October 1977 Of Amnesty (1977): 1–5.

62 Order 80/2021, No. 5781–2018 (Constitutional Court of Spain September 15, 2021).

63 Aguilar, "The Spanish Amnesty Law," 316–18.

64 Ibid., 331.

65 Drew Cohen, "A Constitution at a Crossroads: A Conversation with the Chief Justice of the Constitutional Court of South Africa," *Northwestern Journal of Human Rights* 12, no. 2 (April 1, 2014): 132. https://scholarlycommons.law.northwestern.edu/njihr/vol12/iss2/1.

that providing amnesties to perpetrators of crimes would necessarily negatively impact victims' fundamental rights.[66]

In State v. Basson, following the conclusion of a trial against a former employee of the South African National Defence Force charged with conspiracy to commit 67 counts of murder, fraud, and various other crimes, the government appealed to the State Court of Appeal, challenging certain rulings that had been made during trial. The appeal was rejected on both procedural and substantive grounds; the government then applied to the Constitutional Court for leave to appeal against the judgment of the State Court of Appeal. The Constitutional Court held hearings to determine whether constitutional issues were at stake as a precursor to deciding whether it had jurisdiction to accept the case.[67] Further cementing its role as an activist court, the Court accepted jurisdiction in the first prosecution of apartheid crimes that had reached it.[68] In his concurring opinion, Justice Sachs highlighted the significance of the Court's granting of jurisdiction in the case:

> The questions before us have to be determined in the complex historical and jurisprudential situation in which the South African State had moved from perpetrating grave breaches of international humanitarian law to providing constitutional protection against them. Issues which in another context might appear to be purely technical concerning the interpretation of a statute or the powers of a court on appeal, took on profoundly constitutional dimensions in the context of war crimes.[69]

4.2.5 Cambodia

Domestic Cambodian courts have been only minimally involved in the issue of amnesties. In 1994, decades after the fall of the Khmer Rouge, the Cambodian government passed legislation banning the group and providing amnesty to Khmer Rouge guerrillas who defected to the government between certain specific dates. After the law was passed, the King retained discretion to decide who would benefit from amnesties.[70] Although some commentators argued that the 1994 law was not passed in compliance with the Constitution, at least one Cambodian court disagreed.[71]

---

66 Sachs, "War, Violence, Human Rights," 437.
67 Sachs, "War, Violence, Human Rights," 449.
68 Mia Swart, "The Wouter Basson Prosecution: The Closest South Africa Came to Nuremberg?" *Heidelberg Journal of International Law* 68 (2008): 209.
69 Sachs, "War, Violence, Human Rights," 450.
70 Slye, "The Cambodian Amnesties," 101.
71 Ibid.

4.2.6 Bosnia and Herzegovina

According to a 1997 amendment to the 1995 Constitution, the President holds the power to grant pardons for crimes other than war crimes, crimes against humanity, and genocide. The Constitutional Court has only marginally been involved in the issue of amnesties. In Case No. U 44/03 of 23 September 2003, it held that a right to amnesty is not included in the list of rights under Article II (3) of the Constitution of Bosnia and Herzegovina and is not provided for by the European Convention for the Protection of Human Rights and Fundamental Freedoms and its Protocols.[72]

4.2.7 Argentina

Courts in Argentina, including the Supreme Court, have taken active roles in amnesty issues. Beginning in 2001, lower domestic courts began to strike down amnesty laws enacted after the Dirty War, which had taken place between 1976 and 1983. In 2005, the Supreme Court confirmed lower court rulings holding the amnesty laws unconstitutional, citing as binding authority a 2001 Peruvian case in which the Inter-American Court of Human Rights declared that two amnesty laws introduced by the Fujimori government in 1995 were incompatible with the American Convention on Human Rights and therefore without legal effect.[73] The decision by the Supreme Court of Argentina impacted the validity of amnesty laws in other Latin American countries, including Chile, Uruguay and Colombia.[74]

4.2.8 Timor Leste

Perhaps because the post-conflict Constitution of Timor Leste was created with input primarily from common law advisors, it does not provide for a constitutional court. Instead, Article 124 states that the Supreme Court of Justice is the highest court and shall administer justice on juridical, constitutional and electoral matters. Article 95(3)(g) assigns to Parliament the power to grant amnesties, while Article 149 allows the President to request anticipatory review by the Supreme Court of Justice of any bill, including those relating to amnesties, submitted to him or her for promulgation.

---

72 "Admissibility: As to the Prima Facie (Manifestly) Ill-Founded." Constitutional Court of Bosnia and Herzegovina, n.d. https://www.ustavnisud.ba/en/as-to-the-prima-facie-manifestly-ill-founded.

73 Human Rights Watch. "Argentina: Amnesty Laws Struck Down," June 14, 2005. https://www.hrw.org/news/2005/06/14/argentina-amnesty-laws-struck-down.

74 The Supreme Court of Chile had previously limited the application of Chile's amnesty law in 1999, holding that it did not apply in cases of disappearances (Slye, "The Cambodian Amnesties").

The power to grant amnesties was also given to the Commission for Reception, Truth, and Reconciliation, which was established in 2001. After holding hearings on crimes committed between April 25, 1974, and October 25, 1999, the Commission was to report its findings to Parliament along with recommendations. Its power to grant amnesties was limited to minor crimes committed by individuals who admitted to them and performed community service.[75]

4.2.9 Kosovo

Article 65(15) of the Constitution of Kosovo permits the Assembly to enact amnesty laws that are approved by a two-thirds vote. The Law on Amnesty (04/L-209) was passed in 2013, providing amnesty for a group of criminal offenses committed before June 20, 2013, with the exception of violations of international humanitarian law and crimes resulting in serious bodily harm or death.

In Case No. KO 108/13, applicants argued that the Law on Amnesty violated their right to a legal remedy, as guaranteed by Article 32 of the Constitution. The Constitutional Court upheld the constitutionality of the statute but held that broad amnesties for some crimes, including arson, would undermine the objective of reconciliation; amnesties for those crimes were therefore deemed unconstitutional.

4.2.10 Colombia

In 2006, the Constitutional Court of Colombia ruled on the constitutionality of Law 975, known as the Justice and Peace Law, which addressed criminal and civil liability of recently demobilized paramilitary groups.[76] In general, the Court upheld the law while setting constitutional limitations on its application to ensure victims' ability to participate in proceedings to determine eligibility of former combatants to receive reduced sentences and other concessions. The Court voiced concern that criminal penalties should not be lightened unless whole truths were factually uncovered without relying solely on defendants' confessions. The Court also held that former members of paramilitary groups would lose the benefits of the law if they failed to compensate their victims.[77]

---

75 "Truth Commission: Timor-Leste (East Timor)," United States Institute of Peace, February 7, 2002. https://www.usip.org/publications/2002/02/truth-commission-timor-leste-east-timor.

76 Constitutional Case No. C-370/06 (Constitutional Court of Colombia 2006).

77 Tushnet, and Beatriz Botero Arcila, "Conceptualizing the Role of Courts in Peace Processes," 1298.

5 Contextualizing the Indonesian Cases

Against the backdrop of approaches taken by other constitutional courts that have addressed transitional justice issues, the decisions in Cases No. 011–017/PUU-I/2003 and 011–017/PUU-I/2003, decided by the Constitutional Court of Indonesia, are not outliers but are instead consistent with outcomes and analytical approaches taken by similar courts. In addition to conducting constitutional analysis and limiting standing in appropriate ways, the Indonesian Court carried out comparative studies of caselaw from other post-conflict constitutional courts that were asked to rule on the constitutionality of legislation and rules relating to lustration and amnesties.

In Case No. 006/PUU-IV/2006, the Court considered the issue of applicants' standing and issued a nuanced, well-considered ruling that in order to sustain claims of standing, petitioners must demonstrate that (1) their rights are protected in the Constitution; (2) their rights have been impaired; (3) impingement on their rights is specific and actual, or at least potential; (4) there is a causal relationship between the alleged action and harm; and (5) the Court's action will remedy any continued harm. Over the objection of two justices, the Court held that individuals and associations who were impacted by the Truth and Reconciliation Law had standing to file their petitions.

The substance of the Court's decision in this case, that the principles and objectives of the challenged law could not be carried out because the law failed to provide legal certainty – both in the formulation and implementation of norms – with respect to remedies for victims, was reached after careful consideration of reparations schemes in South Africa, Argentina, Colombia and Timor Leste, along with provisions of the International Covenant on Civil and Political Rights. In its decision, the Court, consistent with positions taken by other post-conflict constitutional courts, acknowledged that this case involved political as well as legal issues. The Court found persuasive authority for deeming the entirety of the Truth and Reconciliation Law unconstitutional – as opposed to only parts of its provisions – in Article 45 of the South Korean Constitutional Court Law, which states that if an entire statute cannot be enforced when one of its provisions is found to be unconstitutional, the whole statute may be ruled unconstitutional.

The outcome of this case has been criticized in that it left victims of human rights violations without a legal remedy.[78] Although the Constitutional Court

78 Saivol Virdaus, Nasrulloh Ali Munif, and Zainal Arifin, "The Urgency of the Truth and Reconciliation Commission (KKR)," 560–67 (Atlantis Press, 2021), https://doi.org/10.2991/assehr.k.211112.073.

proposed alternative methods for resolving past violations of human rights via legal or political means and ordered the government to draft a new law within two years, none of these actions have been undertaken since Case No. 006/PUU-IV/2006 was decided.[79]

In Case No. 011–017/PUU-I/2003, it was the dissent that found authority through comparative analysis. The legal issue in that case was the constitutionality of Article 60(g) of the Election Law, which banned former members of the Indonesian Communist Party from running for legislative office. The majority opinion held that the law was based only on political considerations and that it contained nuances of political punishment aimed at former Communist Party members. Stating that Article 60(g) constituted an impermissible denial of rights and discrimination on the basis of political belief, the Court held that the law was contrary to human rights guaranteed by the Constitution and therefore had no binding legal force.

The dissent disagreed, arguing that post-war Germany presented an analogous context with a different outcome. Citing expert testimony presented during hearings in the Indonesian case, the dissenting justice argued that at the beginning of the era of the Federal Republic of Germany (1949–1953), several actions were taken to conduct de-Nazification, including restricting former members of the Nazi party from occupying certain government positions. These restrictions were not permanent, the dissenting opinion argued, but were progressively loosened over time and were finally ended in 1956.

Case No. 011–017/PUU-I/2003 represented another example of the way constitutional courts may be asked to address issues that intertwine individual and political rights with security concerns of the state. As Mietzner states, the decision in this case was of enormous symbolic importance and highlighted the Court's protection of individual rights even at the risk of alienating large segments of the population who remained deeply opposed to the Communist Party, and in spite of harsh criticism from the armed forces.[80]

---

79 In January 2023, the news outlet Inside Indonesia criticized the President for not moving forward redrafting the Truth and Reconciliation Law as mandated by the Constitutional Court in Case No. 006/PUU-IV/2006. Instead, he formed a new team of academics, diplomats, former military officers and state officials to examine past human rights violations through a non-judicial approach. Human rights activists and civil society organizations reacted to this development with sharp criticism, stating that it would not be effective to hold past human rights abusers accountable (Wahyuningroem 2023).

80 Marcus Mietzner, "Political Conflict Resolution and Democratic Consolidation in Indonesia: The Role of the Constitutional Court," *Journal of East Asian Studies* 10, no. 3 (2010): 409, http://www.jstor.org/stable/23418865.

6 Conclusion

In post-conflict settings, constitutional courts have important roles to play despite the complex and often competing challenges they face to institutionalize their legitimacy and entrench the rule of law while attempting to build bridges from conflict to peace. As Kim Lane Scheppele states, constitutional courts can also help shape collective memory about previous regimes of horror.[81]

The Constitutional Court of Indonesia has solidified its position among modern constitutional bodies. Instead of relying only on its own decisions or those of the Supreme Court, it has demonstrated its ability to carry out comprehensive global comparative analysis, referring to cases from other constitutional and international courts to help shape its jurisprudence. In this way, the Indonesian Court is ahead of a number of other apex courts in its willingness to consider constitutional issues through a global lens.[82]

At the 5th Congress of the World Conference on Constitutional Justice, held in Indonesia in October 2022, the 94 delegations in attendance acknowledged the relationship between constitutional justice and peace and affirmed that protection of human rights is a prerequisite to conflict resolution and sustained peace. The conference's Resolution stated that constitutional courts contribute directly to appeasing social tensions and maintaining social peace by curbing excessive political power and ensuring diversity, guaranteeing respect for the rule of law and honoring the trust people place in the law and courts.

---

81 Kim Lane Scheppele, "Constitutional Interpretation after Regimes of Horror" (SSRN Scholarly Paper. Rochester, NY, May 1, 2000), https://doi.org/10.2139/ssrn.236219 and Hailbronner, "Rethinking the Rise of the German Constitutional Court," 628.

82 Debate about the legitimacy of foreign and international law when interpreting the U.S. Constitution has taken place at the Supreme Court level for decades. Former Justice Antonin Scalia argued that reference to foreign constitutional law may be acceptable when writing a new constitution but not when interpreting an existing one. See Vicki C. Jackson, "Resisting the Transnational," in *Constitutional Engagement in a Transnational Era*, 17–38 (Oxford University Press, 2013). Former Justice Stephen Breyer takes a different approach, arguing that "local law is increasingly affected by what happens abroad. Lawyers, legislators, and judges to an ever greater extent must look beyond their own shores to answer questions of local law." Breyer states that in close to twenty percent of the Supreme Court's current caseload, it is necessary to consider approaches taken by courts in other countries to find appropriate solutions to current legal problems in the United States. See Stephen Breyer, "America's Courts Can't Ignore the World" *The Atlantic*, October 2018, https://www.theatlantic.com/magazine/archive/2018/10/stephen-breyer-supreme-court-world/568360/.

In meeting these goals, constitutional courts no longer need operate in isolation. Through information provided by CODICES, the database maintained by the Council of Europe's Venice Commission, and the World Conference on Constitutional Justice, among other resources, constitutional courts are now able to benefit from the individual and collective experiences of other apex courts operating in post-conflict contexts despite the diversity of legal systems and languages. These avenues of cooperation allow judicial cross-fertilization contributing to jurisprudence that supports democracy, human rights and the rule of law, which can be shared "from court to court, from country to country, from continent to continent".[83] As Vicki Jackson states, constitutional engagement "offers important insights for constitutional adjudication, both from a deliberative perspective concerned with improving. ... decision-making. ... and from a relational perspective in accommodating and mediating the developing relationships among and between constitutional and supranational legal systems."[84]

Bibliography

"2010 Annual Report." Constitutional Court of Kosovo, 2011. https://gjk-ks.org/wp-content/uploads/2017/11/Annual-Report-2010.pdf.

"Admissibility: As to the Prima Facie (Manifestly) Ill-Founded." Constitutional Court of Bosnia and Herzegovina, n.d. https://www.ustavnisud.ba/en/as-to-the-prima-facie-manifestly-ill-founded.

Aguilar, Paloma. "The Spanish Amnesty Law of 1977 in Comparative Perspective: From a Law for Democracy to a Law for Impunity." In *Amnesty in the Age of Human Rights Accountability: Comparative and International Perspectives*, edited by Francesca Lessa and Leigh A. Payne, 315–35. Cambridge: Cambridge University Press, 2012. https://doi.org/10.1017/CBO9781139177153.016.

Amendment to Article 79 of the Constitution regarding the concession of amnesties and pardons., No. 1, 6 March 1992, Constitution of Italy (1992).

83 Buquicchio, Gianni, and Schnutz Rudolf Dürr. "Judicial Cross-Fertilisation – Co-Operation between Constitutional Courts as a Means to Promote Democracy, the Protection of Human Rights and the Rule of Law" in *Liège, Strasbourg, Bruxelles: Parcours Des Droits de l'homme: Liber Amicorum Michel Melchior* (2011): 311–23.

84 Vicki C. Jackson, "Constitutional Adjudication in the U.S. Supreme Court: Why Engage the Transnational?" in *Constitutional Engagement in a Transnational Era*, 103 (Oxford University Press, 2013).

"Bali Communique – Constitutional Justice and Peace." World Conference on Constitutional Justice, October 6, 2022. https://www.venice.coe.int/files/2022_10_06_WCCJ5_Bali_Communique-E.PDF.

Breyer, Stephen. "America's Courts Can't Ignore the World." *The Atlantic*, October 2018. https://www.theatlantic.com/magazine/archive/2018/10/stephen-breyer-supreme-court-world/568360/.

Buquicchio, Gianni, and Schnutz Rudolf Dürr. "Constitutional Courts – the Living Heart of the Separation of Powers / the Role of the Venice Commission in Promoting Constitutional Justice." In *Human Rights in a Global World: Essays in Honour of Luis Lopez Guerra*, 515–44. Wolf Legal Publishers, 2018.

Buquicchio, Gianni, and Schnutz Rudolf Dürr. "Judicial Cross-Fertilisation – Co-Operation between Constitutional Courts as a Means to Promote Democracy, the Protection of Human Rights and the Rule of Law." In *Liège, Strasbourg, Bruxelles: Parcours Des Droits de l'homme: Liber Amicorum Michel Melchior*, 311–23. Anthemis, 2011.

Butt, Simon. "Indonesia's Constitutional Court: Conservative Activist or Strategic Operator?" Law Explorer, KnowledgeBase, October 8, 2016. https://lawexplores.com/indonesias-constitutional-court-conservative-activist-or-strategic-operator/.

"Constitutional Court Decides NPD-Party Ban Case." German Law Journal e.V., January 25, 2017. https://germanlawjournal.com/party-ban/.

Chestermann, Simon. "Justice and Reconciliation: The Rule of Law in Post-Conflict Territories." In *You, The People: The United Nations, Transitional Administration, and State-Building*, 154–82. Oxford University Press, 2004.

Cohen, Drew. "A Constitution at a Crossroads: A Conversation with the Chief Justice of the Constitutional Court of South Africa." *Northwestern Journal of Human Rights* 12, no. 2 (April 1, 2014): 132. https://scholarlycommons.law.northwestern.edu/njihr/vol12/iss2/1.

Constitutional Case No. C-370/06 (Constitutional Court of Colombia 2006).

Constitutional review of the Law, No. 04/L-209, on Amnesty, No. KO 108/13 (The Constitutional Court of the Republic of Kosovo September 9, 2013).

Dugard, Jackie. "Courts and Structural Poverty in South Africa: To What Extent Has the Constitutional Court Expanded Access and Remedies to the Poor?" In *Constitutionalism of the Global South: The Activist Tribunals of India, South Africa, and Colombia*, edited by Daniel Bonilla Maldonado, 293–328. Cambridge: Cambridge University Press, 2013. https://doi.org/10.1017/CBO9781139567114.011.

Farahat, Anuscheh. "The German Federal Constitutional Court." In *Constitutional Adjudication: Institutions*, Vol. III. Oxford: The Max Planck Handbooks in European Public Law, Oxford University Press, 2020.

Feldman, David. "Developments." *International Journal of Constitutional Law* 3, no. 4 (October 2005): 649–662.

Frei, Norbert, and Joel Golb. "The Amnesty Law of 1954." In *Adenauer's Germany and the Nazi Past: The Politics of Amnesty and Integration*, 67–92. Columbia University Press, 2002. http://www.jstor.org/stable/10.7312/frei11882.9.

Garlicki, Lech. "Constitutional Courts versus Supreme Courts." *International Journal of Constitutional Law* 5, no. 1 (January 2007): 44–68.

Gennusa, Maria Elena. "Constitutionalising the International Legal Order through Case Law – Judgment No. 238/2014 from the Italian Constitutional Court." *Cambridge Journal of International and Comparative Law* 5, no. 1 (2016): 139–152.

Gibson, James L. "The Evolving Legitimacy of the South African Constitutional Court." In *Justice and Reconciliation in Post-Apartheid South Africa*, edited by François du Bois and Antje du Bois-Pedain, 229–66. Cambridge Studies in Law and Society. Cambridge: Cambridge University Press, 2009. https://doi.org/10.1017/CBO9780511575419.

"Government Commits to Seeking a Ban of the Extreme Right-Wing National Democratic Party of Germany (NPD)." *German Law Journal* 1, no. 2 (2000): E3. https://doi.org/10.1017/S2071832200003102.

Hailbronner, Michaela. "Rethinking the Rise of the German Constitutional Court: From Anti-Nazism to Value Formalism." *International Journal of Constitutional Law* 12, no. 3 (July 2014): 626–49.

Hart, Vivien. "Democratic Constitution Making." Special Report 107. United States Institute of Peace, July 2003. https://www.usip.org/publications/2003/07/democratic-constitution-making.

Hirschl, Ran. "The Judicialization of Mega-Politics and the Rise of Political Courts." *Annual Review of Political Science* 11, no. 1 (June 1, 2008): 93–118. https://doi.org/10.1146/annurev.polisci.11.053006.183906.

Human Rights Watch. "Argentina: Amnesty Laws Struck Down," June 14, 2005. https://www.hrw.org/news/2005/06/14/argentina-amnesty-laws-struck-down.

Italy's Diplomatic and Parliamentary Practice on International Law. "CC Judgment 238/2014." Italyspractice, October 22, 2014. https://italyspractice.info/judgment-238-2014.

Jackson, Vicki C. "Constitutional Adjudication in the U.S. Supreme Court: Why Engage the Transnational?" In *Constitutional Engagement in a Transnational Era*, 103–31. Oxford University Press, 2013.

Jackson, Vicki C. "Resisting the Transnational." In *Constitutional Engagement in a Transnational Era*, 17–38. Oxford University Press, 2013.

Jackson, Vicki C. "What's in a Name? Reflections on Timing, Naming, and Constitution-Making." *William & Mary Law Review* 49, no. 4 (March 1, 2008): 1249–1305.

Kommers, Donald P., and Russel A. Miller. *The Constitutional Jurisprudence of the Federal Republic of Germany*. 3rd ed. Duke University Press Books, 2012.

Kranenpohl, Uwe. "Decision Making at the German Federal Constitutional Court." In *Constitutional Courts in Comparison: The US Supreme Court and the German Federal Constitutional Court*. Berghahn Books, 2016. https://www.jstor.org/stable/j.ctt1btbw22.11.

Landau, David. "Constitutional Backsliding: Colombia." In *Constitutionalism in Context*, edited by David S. Law, 497–516. Comparative Constitutional Law and Policy. Cambridge: Cambridge University Press, 2022. https://doi.org/10.1017/9781108699068.023.

Law 46/1977 of 15 October 1977 Of Amnesty (1977): 1–5.

Legge Costituzionale 6 marzo 1992, n. 1. (1992): 1–1.

McWinney, Edward. "The German Federal Constitutional Court and the Communist Party Decision." *Indiana Law Journal* 32, no. 3 (Spring 1957): 295–312.

Mietzner, Marcus. "Political Conflict Resolution and Democratic Consolidation in Indonesia: The Role of the Constitutional Court." *Journal of East Asian Studies* 10, no. 3 (2010): 397–424. http://www.jstor.org/stable/23418865.

O'Brien, James C. "The Dayton Constitution of Bosnia and Herzegovina." In *Framing the State in Times of Transition*, 332–49. United States Institute of Peace, 2010. https://www.usip.org/sites/default/files/Framing%20the%20State/Chapter12_Framing.pdf.

Order 29/1980, ECLI:ES:TC:1980:29A (Constitutional Court of Spain October 1, 1980).

Order 80/2021, No. 5781–2018 (Constitutional Court of Spain September 15, 2021).

Pavoni, Riccardo. "Simoncioni v. Germany." *American Journal of International Law* 109, no. 2 (April 2015): 400–406. https://doi.org/10.5305/amerjintelaw.109.2.0400.

Petersberg Agreement. 1 BVerfGE 351 (German Federal Constitutional Court 1952).

"Proceedings for the Prohibition of Political Parties." German Federal Constitutional Court, n.d. https://www.bundesverfassungsgericht.de/EN/Verfahren/WichtigeVerfahrensarten/Parteiverbotsverfahren/parteiverbotsverfahren_node.html.

Rosenfeld, Michel. "Judicial Politics versus Ordinary Politics: Is the Constitutional Judge Caught in the Middle?" Chapter. In *Judicial Power: How Constitutional Courts Affect Political Transformations*, edited by Christine Landfried, 36–65. Cambridge: Cambridge University Press, 2019. https://doi.org/10.1017/9781108348669.003.

Roznai, Yaniv. "Unconstitutional Constitutional Amendments—The Migration and Success of a Constitutional Idea." *The American Journal of Comparative Law* 61, no. 3 (2013): 657–719. http://www.jstor.org/stable/43668170.

Ruiz, Marian Ahumada. "The Spanish Constitutional Court." In *Comparative Constitutional Reasoning*, edited by András Jakab, Arthur Dyevre, and Giulio Itzcovich, 604–40. Cambridge: Cambridge University Press, 2017. https://doi.org/10.1017/9781316084281.018.

Sachs, Albie. "Karl Klare: The Person Who Helped Us See the Tree for the Wood." Northeastern University School of Law. Northeastern University School of Law, June 17, 2022. https://law.northeastern.edu/karl-klare-testimonial/.

Sachs, Albie. "War, Violence, Human Rights, and the Overlap between National and International Law: Four Cases before the South African Constitutional Court." *Fordham International Law Journal* 28, no. 2 (January 2005): 432–476.

Sapiano, Jenna. "Courting Peace: Judicial Review and Peace Jurisprudence." *Global Constitutionalism* 6, no. 1 (2017): 131–65. https://doi.org/10.1017/S2045381716000253.

Scheppele, Kim Lane. "Constitutional Interpretation after Regimes of Horror." SSRN Scholarly Paper. Rochester, NY, May 1, 2000. https://doi.org/10.2139/ssrn.236219.

Schwartz, Alex. "International Judges on Constitutional Courts: Cautionary Evidence from Post-Conflict Bosnia." *Law & Social Inquiry* 44, no. 1 (February 2019): 1–30.

Slye, Ronald. "The Cambodian Amnesties: Beneficiaries and the Temporal Reach of Amnesties for Gross Violation of Human Rights." *WIS. INT'L L. J.* 22 (January 1, 2004): 99. https://digitalcommons.law.seattleu.edu/faculty/552.

Sólyom, László. "The Constitutional Court of Hungary." In *Constitutional Adjudication: Institutions*, Vol. III. The Max Planck Handbooks in European Public Law. Oxford University Press, 2020.

"Statement by the Press Office of the Federal Constitutional Court." The Federal Constitutional Court, October 23, 1952. https://www.bundesverfassungsgericht.de/SharedDocs/Pressemitteilungen/EN/1952/bvg52-059.html.

"Statement by the Press Office of the Federal Constitutional Court." The Federal Constitutional Court, October 23, 1952. https://www.bundesverfassungsgericht.de/SharedDocs/Pressemitteilungen/EN/1952/bvg52-059.html.

Starita, Massimon. "Amnesty for Crimes against Humanity: Coordinating the State and Individual Responsibility for Gross Violations of Human Rights." *Italian Yearbook of International Law* 9 (1999): 86–112.

Stockmann, Petra and Hanns-Seidel-Stiftung. "The new Indonesian Constitutional Court: A Study into Its beginnings and First Years of Work." (2007).

Swart, Mia. "The Wouter Basson Prosecution: The Closest South Africa Came to Nuremberg?" *Heidelberg Journal of International Law* 68 (2008): 209–26.

Tame, Clare, and Sarah Pasetto, trans. "The Italian Constitutional Court." Constitutional Court of Italy, March 2020. https://www.cortecostituzionale.it/documenti/download/pdf/lacorte_depliant_EN.pdf.

The Asia Foundation. "Indonesia – The State of Violence and Conflict in Asia." The Asia Foundation, October 2017. https://asiafoundation.org/wp-content/uploads/2017/10/Indonesia-StateofConflictandViolence.pdf.

The Constitutional Court of the Republic of Indonesia. "History." The Constitutional Court of the Republic of Indonesia, n.d. https://en.mkri.id/profile/history.

"Truth Commission: Timor-Leste (East Timor)." United States Institute of Peace, February 7, 2002. https://www.usip.org/publications/2002/02/truth-commission-timor-leste-east-timor.

Tushnet, Mark, and Beatriz Botero Arcila. "Conceptualizing the Role of Courts in Peace Processes." *International Journal of Constitutional Law* 18, no. 4 (December 2020): 1290–1302.

Vigoriti, Vincenzo. "Italy: The Constitutional Court." *The American Journal of Comparative Law* 20, no. 3 (1972): 404–14. https://doi.org/10.2307/839312.

Virdaus, Saivol, Nasrulloh Ali Munif, and Zainal Arifin. "The Urgency of the Truth and Reconciliation Commission (KKR)." 560–67. Atlantis Press, 2021. https://doi.org/10.2991/assehr.k.211112.073.

Wahyuningroem, Sri Lestari. "Accountability Missing in Action." *Inside Indonesia*, February 7, 2023. https://www.insideindonesia.org/accountability-missing-in-action.

Zulueta-Fülscher, Kimana. "Interim Constitutions: Peacekeeping and Democracy-Building Tools." International IDEA, October 2015. https://www.idea.int/sites/default/files/publications/interim-constitutions-peacekeeping-and-democracy-building-tools.pdf.

CHAPTER 6

Religious Rights: Testing the Limits of Tolerance

Ann Black

Abstract

As guardians of the Constitution, the Justices of the Indonesian Constitutional Court play a pivotal role in ensuring national legislation complies with constitutionally guaranteed rights and freedoms. In a nation where belief in Almighty God is a pre-eminent constitutional tenet, the Constitutional Court is called on to uphold the religious and spiritual rights of all Indonesians, whether Muslim, followers of the five recognised religions, or animistic believers. In this chapter, two landmark judgments which go to the heart of religious practice in Muslim-majority democratic Indonesia are reviewed. The first is on the jurisdiction of Indonesia's Religious (Syariah) Courts and whether Islamic criminal law should be included in their competencies. The second determines whether beliefs of Indonesia's indigenous believers (*kepercayaan*) should be recognised alongside those of religion (*agama*) for purposes of identity cards, public services, and administration. Guided by the unifying spirit of the Pancasila, the Justices of the Constitutional Court take an integrative approach. The significance of this is highlighted in this chapter through comparative analysis with neighbouring Muslim-majority Brunei Darussalam and Malaysia. By adopting Masaji Chiba's model of legal pluralism, the significance of Pancasila as the nation's legal postulate shines through as a unifying, yet pragmatic, way to facilitate tolerance in a land of diversity.

Keywords

Almighty God – belief – legal postulate – Pancasila – religion – religious courts

1 Introduction

> This country, the Republic of Indonesia, does not belong to any group, nor to any religion, nor to any ethnic group, nor to any group with customs and traditions, but the property of all of us from Sabang to Merauke.
>
> President Sukarno, Speech at Surabaya, September 24, 1955

In August 1945, Indonesia was the world's most populous Muslim-majority nation, yet the spirit of unity and inclusion, as captured in Sukarno's words above, permeated its independence Constitution. Today, Indonesia remains the world's largest Muslim-majority nation, with eighty-seven percent (today over 240 million) of Indonesians identifying as Muslim.[1] Yet Islam does not feature in the Constitution, nor Syariah (as the law of Islam), nor secularism.[2] Instead the spirit that guides the nation lies in Pancasila, the Five Principles; the first of which is "Belief in the One Almighty God" (*ketuhanan*).[3] Religion and belief are integral to being Indonesian, and the carefully crafted simplicity of the first Pancasila principle resists categorisation, having been variously described as Indonesia's "the state religion";[4] creating a "Godly" constitution;[5] a symbiotic model ... [of a] "mutually influencing relationship",[6] "a guarantee of religious plurality";[7] and as the "grundnorm" which accepts "sacredness in the secular national legal system".[8] Indonesian scholar Dr Nadirsyah Hosen considers Pancasila a "compromise between secularism where no single religion predominates in the state, and religiosity, where religion (especially Islam) became one of the important pillars of state".[9] For Hosen, it is the "middle way".[10] This chapter will also argue that in pluralistic Indonesia, Pancasila is, in Chiba's legal pluralism theory, the nation's postulate as the "value principle" that directs, explains and justifies the operation of law[11] and informs Constitutional Court decisions.

---

1 See the Indonesian Government Portal for statistics on religious adherence at "Agama," Indonesia.go.id, Portal Informasi Indonesia [Indonesian Government Portal], htps://indonesia.go.id/profil/agama.

2 The Preamble of the Constitution of the Republic of Turkey states: "as required by the principle of secularism, there shall be no interference whatsoever by sacred religious feelings in state affairs and politics."

3 *Ketuhanan Yang Maha Esa* is also translated into English as "belief in the One and Only God" and "One Supreme God".

4 Nadirsyah Hosen, *Sharia and Constitutional Reform in Indonesia* (Singapore: ISEAS, 2007), 194.

5 Ahmad Rofii, "The Religiosity of the Indonesian Constitution: Article 29(1) and Its Interpretation," *Constitutional Review* 7, no. 2 (December 2021): 204.

6 Muchamad Ali Safa'at, "The Roles of the Indonesian Constitutional Court in Determining State-Religion Relations," *Constitutional Review* 8, no. 1 (May 2022): 113.

7 Discussed in Simon Butt, "Constitutional Recognition of 'Beliefs' in Indonesia," *Journal of Law and Religion* 35, no. 3 (2020): 451.

8 Ratno Lukito, "Mapping the Relationship of Competing Legal Traditions in the Era of Transnationalism in Indonesia," in *Pluralism, Transnationalism and Culture in Asian Law*, ed. Gary F. Bell (Singapore: ISEAS, 2017), 93–95.

9 Nadirsyah Hosen, "Can the Muslim World Borrow from Indonesian Constitutional Reform?: A Comparative Constitutional Approach," *Journal of Indonesian Islam* 1, no. 1 (2007): 94.

10 Hosen, "Can the Muslim World," 94.

11 Masaji Chiba, *Legal Culture in Human Society* (Tokyo: Shinzansha International, 2002), 69.

"Belief in the One Almighty God" sits alongside the co-principles of "just and civilized humanity", "national unity", "democracy guided by wisdom", and "social justice for all". Together, they make Pancasila an inspirational, integrative, and inclusive ideology designed to unite the many and diverse peoples of the former colonies of the Dutch East Indies. Given the multitude of islands, races, ethnicities, religions, languages, and ways of living, the founding fathers recognised the need for an integrative constitution rather than one accentuating difference through separate constitutional recognition. If in 1945, Islam was made the state religion or if the obligation for Muslims to follow Islamic law (the Jakarta Charter) had not been removed, the people of the archipelago that now comprise Indonesia may not have united.[12] By facilitating tolerance yet preserving the religious spiritual pulse of the nation, Pancasila makes possible *Bhinneka Tunggal Ika*: "unity in diversity" (Article 36 A).

The Pancasila spirit and its integrative role as a "unifying tool for the nation"[13] underpin the reasoning of the Constitutional Court in two essential judgments which will be analysed, followed by a brief comparison of other constitutional approaches in the region. The two cases reviewed in this chapter are exemplars of Indonesia's constitutional "middle way". This is clear when comparing Indonesia with two neighbouring Muslim-majority nations: Brunei and Malaysia. All three have much in common, yet their national postulates ensure different outcomes. The commonalities lie in a shared geography and history, in which early animism and *adat* (customary law and local wisdom) were subsequently informed by Hindu-Buddhist concepts and governance, which from the 14th Century were overlaid with Islam brought by Muslim traders. European colonisation followed as did significant Chinese immigration. After World War II, in the post-colonial era of nationalism differing visions of nationhood emerged including how to best manage religious plurality. The first to become independent was the Republic of Indonesia in 1945 and the last was the Sultanate of Brunei Darussalam in 1984. The Federation of Malaysia went through two stages with independence as Malaya in 1957, and then in 1963 as Malaysia, when the Bornean states of Sabah and Sarawak joined the Federation. Although a republic, a monarchical federation, and a sultanate, each has a Muslim (Sunni) majority (87%, 60% and 70% respectively); sizable religious and ethnic minorities including indigenous animistic non-Muslim citizens; and a formal plural legal system which retains former colonial law

12 Butt, "Constitutional Recognition," 451.

13 Law No. 7 of 1989 on Religious Courts [3.18].

(Dutch and English respectively) and enacted national laws for civil /secular courts, with Syariah law for religious courts.

2 Comparative Method

Legal pluralism whereby "two or more legal systems coexist in the same social field"[14] aptly applies in Indonesia, Malaysia, and Brunei, where one's religion determines the law to apply and the court able to adjudicate a matter. Professor Masaji Chiba's model for analysing legal pluralism serves as a comparative lens. Chiba's first level of law is "official law". The official law is the national statutes enacted by Indonesia's legislature – *Dewan Perwakilan Rakyat* (hereafter DPR) which are reviewable by the Constitutional Court, in particular Religious Courts Law (Law Number 7 of 1989) and the Population Law (Law Number 23 of 2006). Official law also encompasses provincial regulations, elucidations, Presidential and Ministerial decrees. In Malaysia and Brunei, there is court precedent in addition to legislation enacted by Malaysia's parliaments (Federal and State) and emergency orders of Brunei's Sultan.

Chiba's second level is "unofficial law". This is the law and rules not officially sanctioned by the state, but which have legitimacy through recognition and use by certain sectors in society. In Southeast Asia, *adat* as the traditional living law of many ethnic and rural communities operates as unofficial law that can surpass, or supplement and at times becomes "official" law. There is also religious law and rules to which members of non-Muslim communities may choose to adhere.[15] Fatwas are another form of unofficial law. As the legal scholarly opinions or rulings of the *ulama* – Islamic legal scholars – they guide individuals, non-government agencies, judges, legislatures, and executive governments and have potential to become "official" law when endorsed by the state. In Indonesia, the *Compilation of Islamic Law* developed with *Majlis Ulama Indonesia* (MUI), the Ministry of Religious Affairs and the Supreme Court became official law per the Presidential Instruction Instrument No 1 of 1991.

14 Sally Engle Merry, "Legal Pluralism," *Law and Society Review* 22, no.5 (1988): 870.

15 On "unofficial" law of minorities, see Gary Bell, "Religious Legal Pluralism Revisited – The Status of the Roman Catholic Church and her Canon Law in Singapore," *Asian Journal of Comparative Law* 7, (2012): 49–84.

The third category that is important in this chapter is "legal postulates". For Indonesia, this is Pancasila with "belief in One Almighty God" and the accompanying four tenets setting parameters for a democratic, inclusive, socially just, fair, and tolerant nation for all Indonesians whether in Aceh, Kalimantan, Java, Bali, or Papua. In direct contrast, is Brunei's postulate of *Melayu Islam Beraja* (MIB) or Malay, Islam, Monarchy, under which the state promotes one religion, one culture, and one political authority. This is to unite the country through monoculturalism. MIB aims to eliminate religious and ethnic diversity by absorbing minorities into Sunni Islam and Malay culture, with the Sultan's autocratic rule preventing democratic diversity and plurality of thought. In the MIB postulate, religious plurality is demonised as "a poison".[16] The legal postulate in Malaysia comes from the social contract negotiated for its 1957 independence constitution between the Malays as *Bumiputera* (sons of the soil)[17] and the Chinese, Indian and other minorities who were not. Because Malay is an ethnic and religious identity (Constitution Article 160) the social contract excluded the indigenous non-Muslim people of the Malay peninsula. A grant of *jus soli* citizenship was given to Chinese, Indians, and other non-Malays, to allow participation in Malaysia's democracy and society, but not as equals with the Malays. In exchange, Malays received constitutional privileges allowing for positive discrimination in law, education, and economic policies (Article 153);[18] for Islam, the religion of Malays to be the official "religion the federation" (Article 3(1)); and for the Malay Sultans to be state rulers with constitutional privileges (Article 3(2)).[19] *Bumiputera* priority was extended to non-Muslim "natives" in Sabah and Sarawak when they joined the federation in 1963. It can be seen in this chapter how the postulates of Pancasila, MIB and *Bumiputera* priority shaped constitutional design and subsequent judicial interpretation.

16 Azlan Othman, "Imams Warn against Deviationist Teachings," *Borneo Bulletin*, January 4, 2004, 3.

17 Bumiputera is derived from Sanskrit and indicates indigenous status akin to Indonesian *Pribumi*.

18 The New Economic Policy (NEP) grants Malays and Bumiputra preferential quotas for licenses, public service positions, shares, scholarships, university admissions, government contracts.

19 The Sultans form the Conference of Rulers. Any amendments to the constitution relating to the Social Contract require the consent of the Conference of Rulers and two-thirds parliamentary support.

3 Religious Courts

> Indonesia is a country with a belief in the one and only God who protects every believer in carrying out the teachings of their respective religions.
>
> Religious Court Case 19/PUU-VI/2008

In all three nations (as well as in neighbouring Singapore and the Philippines) "religious" courts are Syariah Courts. No other religion (Christianity, Hinduism, Buddhism) has its religious laws officially recognised or enforced by the state. Indonesia does this without a state religion and on the understanding that through Pancasila the state protects all believers and having religious courts for Muslims does not diminish this protection. Dr Hosen explains that as there is nothing in the Constitution requiring the "state shall not interfere in religious affairs, nor that religions shall not interfere in the affairs of the State",[20] it is constitutional for the religion of the majority, Islam, to receive special treatment. This allows the Indonesian government to provide religious courts, enact Islamic laws, and facilitate religious regulations for Islamic practices, *zakat* (alms), *waqf* (religious endowments), *hajj* (pilgrimage) and *halal* certification.

For non-Muslim minorities, civil laws apply, with disputes adjudicated in Indonesia's general civil courts.

3.1 *Religious Courts in Indonesia*

Article 49(1) of Law Number 7 of 1989 on the Religious Courts as amended by Law Number 3 of 2006 on Religious Courts (Religious Courts Law) sets out the nine competencies for Indonesia's Religious Courts:

> to examine, decide and resolve cases at the first level between people who are Moslems in the fields of a. marriage; b. inheritance; c. wills; d. grants; e. waqf; f. zakat; g. infaq; h. sadaqah; and i. sharia economic.

These competencies were reviewed by Constitutional Court for compliance with the Constitution's human rights guarantees. The Court's power to do so comes from Article 24(C)(1) of the Constitution and Article 10 of Law No 24 of 2003 on the Constitutional Court.

---

20 Hosen, *Sharia and Constitutional Reform*, 194.

3.2 *Decision number 19/PUU-VI/2008 (Religious Court Case)*

A petition for judicial review was brought by Suryani (the Petitioner) to the Constitutional Court to determine the constitutional validity of Article 49(1) as the Religious Court's competencies did not include Islamic criminal law (*jinayah*).

The Petitioner argued that this exclusion infringed on her right to religious freedom embodied in three constitutional provisions: first, Article 28E(1), which guarantees freedom "to embrace a religion and to worship according to that religion"; second, Article 28I(1) that the right to have religion "cannot be reduced in any circumstances" with (2) of the same Article extending this to "freedom from discriminatory treatment" and "protection against discrimination"; and third, Article 29(1), which situates the state as one "based on God Almighty" with (2) guaranteeing the "independence of each citizen to embrace their respective religions and to worship according to their religion and beliefs". Each constitutional guarantee, she submitted, was violated by omission of Islamic criminal law. By not enforcing Islamic criminal law, she argued, her constitutional right to perfect her religion to the "level of piety" required by Islam, was denied, and therefore was discriminatory.

The Petitioner called on the Constitutional Court to remedy the unconstitutionality of Article 49(1) by either revoking it, or by adding additional authority so that other aspects of Islamic law, specifically criminal law (*jinayah*), came within the Religious Court's jurisdiction.

Her petition was dismissed. There were three dimensions to the Constitutional Court's reasoning. The first was on the competency of the Religious Court's jurisdiction per Article 49; the second was the legitimate scope for Islamic law given Indonesia is a nation based on belief in one Almighty God; and third, whether the petitioner's religious rights in Articles 28E, 28I and 29(2) of the Constitution had, in fact, been infringed as claimed.

On the first issue of the competencies, the Justices of the Constitutional Court held they lacked authority to increase or add new competencies to Article 49, to allow for criminal law. Authority to do rests exclusively with the nation's legislators as Article 24(2) of the Constitution allocates judicial, not legislative, power to the Supreme Court and its four judicial bodies including the Religious Court.[21] Article 24A(5) specifies that the "composition, position, membership and procedural law of the Supreme Court and the judicial bodies under it *shall be regulated by law*" [italics added]. In essence, to be enforced,

21 Article 24(2) includes the general, military, and state administrative courts as under the Supreme Court.

Islamic law, like any other law, must be enacted by the legislature (the DPR) and not by the judges of either the Religious Court or the Constitutional Court. This is confirmed by Article 10 of the Constitutional Court Law, which does not authorise the court to "add to the contents of the regulations or become a positive legislature" but to adjudicate on the constitutionality of a law.[22]

On the second issue, as to whether the Pancasila's belief in "one Almighty God" mandates Islamic law to include criminal law (*jinayah*), the Constitutional Court affirmed that whilst Indonesia is "not a religious country based on one particular religion" it also is not a secular state that leaves "religious affairs entirely to individuals and society".[23] To be just and civilized, Indonesia seeks to protect "every believer in carrying out the teachings of their respective religions" and the way it does so is through the national official law. The Justices opined this enables the national law to be an "integration factor" that can unify the nation regardless of religion, ethnicity, or race.[24] Islamic law is one source of national law but so are customary and western law.

On the third issue, the Justices held that the petitioner's constitutional rights and freedom to embrace Islam and worship according to her religion, had not, in fact, been reduced by Article 49(1) of the Religious Courts Law, nor was it contrary to the cited Articles of the Constitution.[25]

3.3 *Analysis and Comparative Contextualisation*

Implicit in the Petitioner's grievance was that if Syariah covers all facets of a Muslim's life from birth to death it must include criminal law and punishments, many of which come directly from the Quran, and Sunna of the Prophet. For this reason, the state is not at liberty, as it did in Article 49(1), to pick and choose which aspects of Islamic law it recognises.

3.3.1 Islamic Criminal Law

At the time of Suryani's petition, no nation in Southeast Asia enforced classic Islamic criminal law in its entirety. Records show that even pre-colonial Southeast Asia rarely, if ever, implemented *hudud* punishments of stoning, amputations, or *qisas* executions. Across the wider Islamic world in 2006,

---

22 Judicial Review of Constitutional Court, Decision of Constitutional Court No. 19/PUU-VI/2008 [3.16] (The Constitutional Court of the Republic of Indonesia 2008).

23 Judicial Review of Constitutional Court, Decision of Constitutional Court No. 19/PUU-VI/2008 [3.18] (The Constitutional Court of the Republic of Indonesia 2008).

24 Ibid.

25 Judicial Review of Constitutional Court, Decision of Constitutional Court No. 19/PUU-VI/2008 [3.19] (The Constitutional Court of the Republic of Indonesia 2008).

only a handful of conversative mainly Middle eastern Muslim nations – Saudi Arabia, Iran, Iraq, UAE, Qatar, Afghanistan – and Pakistan, Sudan and parts of Nigeria fully applied classic Islamic criminal law with *hudud*, and *qisas* and *diyah* punishments. This contrasts with the almost worldwide preservation of family laws. Colonisers transplanted secular, universally applicable European criminal laws to their colonies, such as the Indonesian Penal Code (KUHP)[26] and in the former British colonies were variants of Macauley's Indian Penal Code (1860). Another factor in the limited use of Islamic criminal law was the increasing reach of international law human rights,[27] which conflicted with some Islamic criminal laws including *hudud* and *qisas* punishments. As well, influential Islamic scholars were engaged in reinterpretation of textual sources by going back "to the abundance of opinions found in the classical works on jurisprudence with the aim of selecting those that are most in conformity with the demands of modern society".[28] Dr Nadir Hosen, argued it was:

> possible to reform and reinterpret Islamic criminal law in a manner that is not only compatible with human rights principles but can also be justified under the Islamic legal tradition … one might argue that Western-inspired penal codes, which are already practiced in most Muslim countries, should be considered as Islamic. Consequently, the attempts of Muslim conservatives to restore the old Islamic criminal law could not be considered to be 'Islamic' and must be rejected.[29]

Indonesia was in step with contemporary Islamic jurisprudence and with international human rights obligations, both of which influenced "the landscape of the country's legal pluralism".[30] Given the three legal traditions (civil, Islamic and *adat*) it was pragmatic, Ratno Lukito argues, to choose Dutch penal law as the national criminal justice system, to avoid the "negative effects

---

26 It is noteworthy that a new Criminal Code was passed by the DPR in 2022 amid international and domestic controversy.

27 Indonesia signed the International Convention on Civil and Political Rights in 2006 and the Convention Against Torture and other Cruel, Inhuman or Degrading Treatment or Punishment in 1998. Brunei and Malaysia are not signatories. All three signed the Convention on the Elimination of all Forms of Discrimination against Women in 1984, with reservations.

28 Rudolph Peters, *Crime and Punishment in Islamic Law: Theory and Practice from the Sixteenth to the Twenty-first Century* (Cambridge: Cambridge University Press, 2005), 190.

29 Nadirsyah Hosen, "Islamic Criminal Law" in *Modern Perspectives on Islamic Law*, ed. Ann Black, Hossein Esmaeili and Nadirsyah Hosen (Cheltenham: Edward Elgar, 2013), 229.

30 Lukito, "Mapping the Relationship," 98.

of complicated penal plurality".[31] It was an integrative approach as Dutch penal law had universal application, and had become entrenched in people's perception of justice making it able to "uphold the ideals and values of the new national legal system."[32] Cognisant on the one hand of the practical difficulties of a dual criminal law, but aware, on the other, of pressing separatist demands in the devoutly conservative province of Aceh, a later grant of regional autonomy[33] empowered the Acehnese provincial government to enact more expansive Syariah criminal laws. In this compromise, the demands of Acehnese Muslim were met, but expansion of Islamic criminal law was regionally confined.

However, at the time the Petitioner brought the case, her views would resonate not only with the Acehnese, but with traditionalist Muslims including in neighbouring Brunei and the northern Malaysian states (Kelantan and Terengganu). *Parti Islam SeMalaysia* (PAS) governments dominated the two state's legislatures, which passed what were colloquially known as *hudud* acts in 1993 and 1999 respectively. The laws could not be applied as the punishments exceeded the maximum penalties permitted for state Syariah courts under the Malaysian Federal Constitution (Ninth Schedule)[34] but were a tangible manifestation of a growing desire for Syariah criminal law and Islamic theocracy in conservative parts of Southeast Asia. They were the forerunners of subsequent reforms expanding Syariah criminal jurisdiction.[35] The most recent iteration is the Kelantan Syariah Criminal Code (I) Enactment 2019, which expanded the number and types of criminal offences, but for constitutional limits stopped short, this time, of *hudud* and *qisas*. Human rights organisations, including Sisters in Islam,[36] Lawyers for Liberty,[37] and Universiti Malaya Student Union,[38] raised concerns about the Enactment's constitutionality and societal consequences for Malaysians. Arguing that as the Enactment is "contrary to

---

31 Ibid.

32 Ibid.

33 Law No.14 of 1999 on Implementation Privileges in the Special Province of Aceh.

34 Syariah Courts (Criminal Jurisdiction) Act 1965 (Act 355) limits the maximum penalty to six strokes of the cane, three years in prison, and a fine of up to 5,000 ringgit (equivalent to approximately US$1,200).

35 Kelantan Syariah Criminal Code (I) Enactment 2019 came into force November 2021.

36 SIS, "Kelantan Enactment Report," https://sistersinislam.org/wp-content/uploads/2022/03/Kelantan-Enactment-Report.pdf.

37 Lawyers for Liberty, "Defending Human Rights," https://www.lawyersforliberty.org/.

38 Universiti Malaya Student Union Discussion Paper "New Kelantan Syariah Criminal Code (I) Enactment 2019: Is it necessary?" December 2, 2021. Myumsu.com.

inclusive, progressive and tolerant Islam" it could escalate religious and ethnic tensions piercing Malaysia's "diversity and social harmony".[39]

On the issue of constitutionality, Malaysia Bar Association President Steven Thiru stated in 2015 that the then-proposed Enactment:

> goes against the secular structure of our Federal Constitution, which does not envisage a theocratic Islamic state, or a parallel criminal justice system where Muslims and non-Muslims are subjected to unequal treatment before the law ... Criminal law and procedure, and the administration of justice, are exclusively within the legislative competence of Parliament.[40]

Brunei went further. After the Sultan announced in 1996 that the new Syariah Courts were not just for implementing family laws but were to apply '*Qunan Jina'I Islam*' (an Islamic criminal law) in its entirety as required by Allah, the Almighty,[41] twenty-five years later he used his emergency powers to enact the Syariah Penal Code Order 2013, followed by the Syariah Penal Procedure Order 2018. *Hudud, qisas* and *diyah*, as well as *tazir* offences, many with the death penalty, including for apostasy and blasphemy (Section 107), apply to all in Brunei, including non-Muslims. With judicial review abolished,[42] it is not possible for persons adversely affected by these laws to seek redress.

3.3.2 Islam as Source of Law

The reasoning of the Constitutional Court affirmed that whilst Pancasila's "belief in one God" makes Indonesia a religious country, belief is not confined to one religion (of the majority).[43] Pancasila's other tenets for a just and civilized society require national law is to "protect every believer" and not to be based on the majority or minority of "followers of religion, ethnicity of race".[44]

---

39 Universiti Malaya.

40 Tan Yi Liang, "Kelantan Hudud is Unconstitutional and Discriminatory," *The Star*, March 20, 2015. https://www.thestar.com.my/news/nation/2015/03/20/malaysian-bar-statement-on-kelantan-hudud.

41 *Titah* (Royal Speech) delivered 16 July 1996, reported in *Borneo Bulletin*, July 17, 1996. *Titah* can be accessed from the Government of Brunei's website: http://www.rtb.gov.bn/PMO%20Pages/Titah-View.aspx.

42 Constitution Article 84(C).

43 Judicial Review of Constitutional Court, Decision of Constitutional Court No. 19/PUU-VI/2008 [3.16] (The Constitutional Court of the Republic of Indonesia 2008).

44 Judicial Review of Constitutional Court, Decision of Constitutional Court No. 19/PUU-VI/2008 [3.18] (The Constitutional Court of the Republic of Indonesia 2008).

Islamic law is a source of national law, but because it is not the only source, national law can be an "integration factor ... an adhesive and unifying tool for the nation".[45] For this reason, Indonesia's Religious Courts apply national statutes such as the laws concerning marriage, zakat and waqf enacted by the DPR[46] guided by the Compilation of Islamic Law[47] and the Compilation of Sharia Economic Law, not traditional *fiqh* with "*Al-Quran* and *Hadith* or other sources of Islamic law such as *Ijma, Qiyas, Istihsan, Istishab* or certain books of *fiqh*."[48] To unify and apply Islamic law consistently across the provinces of Indonesia, the Religious Courts are national courts under the "one roof"[49] of the Supreme Court of Indonesia, which is the administrative and final appeal court for decisions from Religious Courts, including for autonomous Aceh. The result is greater jurisprudential certainty and consistency. This contrasts with Malaysia's federal system, where Islamic laws enacted by each of the fourteen states can vary significantly, not only for criminal matters (apostasy laws, for example) but also in inheritance and family laws.[50] United under the "one roof" of Indonesia's Supreme Court, Religious Courts apply the same general civil rules of procedure and evidence,[51] as used in all other courts whereas Brunei and Malaysia use Syariah evidentiary and procedural laws in the religious courts and common law procedure and rules of evidence in the civil courts.

The inclusive model in Indonesia opens the doors of the Constitutional Court to Muslims and non-Muslims wanting to challenge national statutes for violation of religious rights. This is clear from the two cases in this chapter – the first brought by a Muslim Petitioner and second by non-Muslim Petitioners. This inclusive right-based model does not exist in Brunei, where no one can bring a case for constitutional review. In Malaysia, prior to 1988, the civil High Courts had jurisdiction over Syariah Courts with power to review

45 Ibid.

46 Law No. 1 of 1974 on Marriage; Law No. 38 of 1999 on Management of Zakat; Law No. 1 of 2004 on Waqf.

47 Presidential Instruction Instrument No. 1 of 1991.

48 Enden Haetami, "Islamic Law Enforcement Through Religious Courts in Indonesia," *ENDLESS: International Journal of Futures Studies* 2, no. 2 (2019): 76.

49 Raihan Azzahra and Farid Sufian Shuaib, "Religious Courts in Indonesia and Malaysia: History Structure and Jurisdiction," *Indonesian Comparative Law Review* 4, no. 2 (2022): 120.

50 To increase uniformity between states, the Federal Government set up a special department, *Jabatan Kehakiman Sharia Malaysia* (JKSM).

51 Religious Courts Law Article 54. Also see: Haetami, "Islamic Law," 77.

their decisions by *certiorari*.[52] However, Malaysia removed judicial review and appellate oversight in 1988 by adding (1A) to Article 121 of the Constitution, which reads: "[The High Court] shall have no jurisdiction in respect of any matter within the jurisdiction of the Syariah Courts." Since then, case law has prevented individuals seeking a civil court remedy if the issue falls within the ambit of Syariah, as specified in the Ninth Schedule.

4 Relationship Between Indigenous Beliefs (*Kepercayaan*) and Religion (*Agama*)

> To believe in a religion and to believe in beliefs is an inherent right of every person.
>
> BELIEFS CASE 97/PUU-XIV/2016 [3.13.1]

For millennia, animism was the dominant belief system across all Southeast Asia. Later, religions from outside the region came to dominate but did not fully extinguish indigenous beliefs and practices. Communities across Indonesia, Malaysia and Brunei keep to some pre-Islamic belief systems, also known as native or indigenous beliefs (*aliran kepercayaan*). Attaining legal recognition for believers and equivalency of beliefs with established religions has been an ongoing challenge. Ascertaining the rights of "believers" was at the heart of an important 2016 case heard by the Justices of Indonesia's Constitutional Court.

4.1 *Religion and Beliefs in Indonesia*

Chapter XI of the Indonesian Constitution is titled "Religion". It consists of Article 29, which serves two purposes: paragraph one (1) affirms the Pancasila principle that the "State is based upon the belief in the one Almighty God",[53] and paragraph two (2) guarantees "the freedom of religion for each citizen and to practice such religion *and* belief accordingly" [italics added]. Religion and belief stand together.

Hosen considers "belief in one Supreme God" to be Indonesia's state religion. This, he holds, does not mean that Indonesia mixes all religions into one shared

52 See Tsun Hang Tey, "Malaysia: The Undermining of its Fundamental Institutions and the Prospects for Reform," in *Law and Legal Institutions of Asia*, eds Ann Black and Gary Bell (Cambridge: Cambridge University Press, 2011), 232.

53 Article 29(1) makes atheism and agnosticism problematic in Indonesia. Although not officially banned, denying or questioning God's existence may incur blasphemy laws.

belief in one and the same God, nor does it mean that any religion based on belief in one God should be recognised as a religion in Indonesia. Instead, the state itself must determine which "religions" receive legal recognition and status as a religion.[54] Since, 1965, Presidential Decree No 1 of 1965 on Blasphemy (Later Law No 5 of 1969) identified six religions (*agama*): Islam, Catholicism, Christian (Protestantism), Buddhism and Hinduism and Confucianism.[55] Other religions such as Shintoism, Judaism, Taoism, Sikhism could be followed but lacked state recognition. Some small religious groups were subsumed within one of the official six.[56] The Indonesian Conference on Religion and Peace (ICRP),[57] estimates there are about 245 unofficial religions in Indonesia including adherents of traditional indigenous ancestral beliefs (*aliran kepercayaan*). Believers are considered part of Indonesia's cultural heritage, with animistic beliefs and worship falling short of requirements for "religion". This results in discrimination and marginalisation as "second class siblings" to followers of established religions.[58] The estimated 12 million[59] to possibly 20 million[60] believers come under the jurisdiction of the Ministry of Education and Culture, not the Ministry of Religious Affairs.

4.2 *Decision Number 97/PUU-XIV/2016 (the Beliefs Case)*

Each of the four Petitioners – a farmer, a student and two entrepreneurs (small business owners) – followed local indigenous beliefs based on the spiritual ways of their ancestors (*kepercayaan*).[61] They came from three different Indonesian provinces (East Nusa Tenggara, North Sumatra, and Central

---

54 On the history of recognition of a religion, see, Victor I.W. Nalle, "The Politics of Intolerant laws against Adherents of Indigenous Beliefs of *Aliran Kepercayaan* in Indonesia," *Asian Journal of Law and Society* 8. No. 3 (2021): 561.

55 Confucianism at times has been removed from the list, for example in 1967, Suharto's Presidential Instruction No. 14 of 1967. Abdurrahman Wahid rescinded this, enabling Confucianism to again have status as a religion.

56 Greek Orthodox are subsumed within Christian (Protestantism).

57 Indonesian Conference on Religion and Peace, "ICRP Homepage," https://www.icrp-online.com/.

58 Simon Butt, "Constitutional Recognition," 453.

59 The number of believers is difficult to quantify. The Ministry of Culture and Education estimates 12 million, whilst the Ministry of Home Affairs estimates far fewer. See, Johannes Nugroho, "A New Ray of Hope for Indonesia's Traditional Religious Beliefs," *Strategic Review*, March 4, 2019. https://sr.sgpp.ac.id/post/a-ray-of-hope-for-indonesias-traditional-religious-beliefs.

60 Paul Marshall, "The Ambiguities of Religious Freedom in Indonesia," *The Review of Religion and International Affairs* 16, (2018): 88.

61 The indigenous beliefs followed were Marapu, Parmalim, Ugamo Bangsa Batak and Sapto Dharma.

Java) and as believers had encountered various forms of discrimination. Their petition for judicial review centred on three Articles of the Population Administration Law[62] (Population Law) which, they claimed, breached their constitutional rights for equality under the law and for freedom of religion as guaranteed in Articles 28D, 28I and 27. In addition to their own testimony, the Petitioners submitted written supportive evidence from six witnesses and eight experts. The President, the DPR and the Indonesian Supreme Council for Belief in God Almighty also made submissions to the Court. This was destined to be a high-profile case.

The Population Law sets out the framework for a national civil registry recording biographic data and life events[63] of Indonesian citizens and residents. From this, each person is issued with an identifying number (NIK),[64] a Family Card (*Kartu Keluarga*, KK)[65] and an electronic (chipped) Identity Card (*Kartu Tanda Penduduk*, e-KTP).[66] Identification cards are required to access government services whilst the aggregated information in the registry aids in government planning for state services. The petitioners' concern in this case was with Articles 61(1) and (2) and Article 64(1) and (5) of the Population Law.

Article 61(1) sets out information that must be on the Family Card. Along with name/s, date and place of birth, gender, marital status, blood type, and occupation, is *agama* – religion. This posed a problem for indigenous faith believers as Article 61(2) stated that if it was not one of the six recognised in Indonesian law, the religion column was to be left blank. Article 64 applied to electronic Identity Cards (e-KTP), which had similar requirements. The Population Law indicated, however, that all persons once registered should receive the same services. The Petitioners gave evidence to the Court of discrimination and unequal treatment when the religion column was blank. This evidence included non-registration of believers' customary marriages, which in turn caused difficulties for their children to obtain birth certificates[67] and to access schools. When at school, Sapto Darmo believers were required to take subjects on Islam when those teachings were contrary to their own beliefs.[68] Burials and funerals

62 Law 23 of 2006 on Population Administration.

63 Law 23 of 2006 on Population Administration. Articles 1(17) and 58(2).

64 Law 23 of 2006 on Population Administration Article 1(12).

65 Law 23 of 2006 on Population Administration Article 1(13).

66 Law 23 of 2006 on Population Administration Article 1(14).

67 Judicial Review of Constitutional Court, Decision of Constitutional Court No. 97/PUU-XIV/2016 Marupu [3.5.2] (The Constitutional Court of the Republic of Indonesia 2016).

68 Judicial Review of Constitutional Court, Decision of Constitutional Court No. 97/PUU-XIV/2016 Sapto Darmo [3.5. 5] (The Constitutional Court of the Republic of Indonesia 2016).

had been disallowed at some public cemeteries.[69] Evidence was presented that a blank religion column had negative financial and commercial consequences including denial of jobs, non-receipt of wages when employed, and facing difficulties in obtaining capital and loans from banks.[70] Consequently, to avoid unequal treatment and discrimination, many indigenous believers had no option but to lie, put down one of the six official religions, unwillingly convert, or in some cases alleged they were forced by officials to choose a religion[71] rather than leave the religion column blank on their KK and e-KTP.

For the Petitioners, this was contrary to protections in the Indonesian Constitution, which recognised and gave equal status to both belief and religion making it discriminatory for identity cards to accept only state approved religions and not customary beliefs.

In their decision, nine Justices of the Constitutional Court unanimously declared the relevant sections of the Population Law "contrary to the Constitution of the Republic of Indonesia". They ruled that Article 61 (1) would conditionally have no binding legal force as long as it did not include the word 'belief', and that Articles 61 (1) and 64 (5) have no binding force.[72] This means that any statutes where 'religion' is used will be unconstitutional unless interpreted to also include 'beliefs'.

4.3 *The Reasoning of the Court*

The Justices focused on the relationship between 'religion' and 'belief' when used separately and conjunctively in the Constitution. For example, in Article 28E(1):

Every person is free to choose and to practice their choice of religion …

The next paragraph 28E(2) states:

> Every person has the right to freedom of *belief*, and to express thoughts and tenets, in accordance with their conscience. [Italics added]

69 Ibid.

70 Judicial Review of Constitutional Court, Decision of Constitutional Court No. 97/PUU-XIV/2016 Batak Nation's Ugamo [3. 5.4] (The Constitutional Court of the Republic of Indonesia 2016).

71 Judicial Review of Constitutional Court, Decision of Constitutional Court No. 97/PUU-XIV/2016 Parmalim [3.5. 3]; Batak Nation's Ugamo [3.5.4].

72 Judicial Review of Constitutional Court, Decision of Constitutional Court No. 97/PUU-XIV/2016 Verdict [5] (The Constitutional Court of the Republic of Indonesia 2016).

And Article 29:

> The state guarantees the freedom of religion for each citizen and to practice such religion *and* belief accordingly. [Italics added]

Use of the conjunction "and", the Court reasoned, "places the matter of 'belief' in equal proportion to 'religion'."[73] The Justices affirmed that the right "to believe in a religion and to believe in beliefs is an inherent right" of every Indonesian[74] not a gift from the state. They added that this right is more than a constitutional right that obliges the state to "to respect, to protect and to fulfil"[75] but a human right recognised in the spirit of universal freedom of religion as stated in the Universal Declaration of Human Rights (UDHR) and the International Covenant on Civil and Political Rights (ICCPR) (ratified by Indonesia in 2005). Whilst the two words may not be the same, both are equally "recognised for their existence". Employing lexical and contextual interpretation,[76] the use of "and" indicates cumulation, in the same way as "religion" and "belief" are formulated in the ICCPR. There was historic support too in the Court's review of the 1945 debates between the founding fathers which showed "belief" was not "meant to be something separate from religion" but was to ensure that believers of any religion were equally "guaranteed their right to practice according to their beliefs". Thus, if religion and belief are equally recognised and protected in the Constitution, then the differential treatment in the Population Law was discriminatory. The jurisprudence of the Court's earlier decisions[77] on discrimination was applicable as the Population Law had "treated the same thing differently, namely the citizens who believe in beliefs and the citizens who believe in religions that are recognised according to the Laws, in accessing public services".[78] Because Article 64(2) made it clear that religion was only to include recognised religions, the state failed to meet its obligation to guarantee the rights of adherents of beliefs:

---

73 Judicial Review of Constitutional Court, Decision of Constitutional Court No. 97/PUU-XIV/2016 [3.13.1] (The Constitutional Court of the Republic of Indonesia 2016).

74 Judicial Review of Constitutional Court, Decision of Constitutional Court No. 97/PUU-XIV/2016 [3.13.1] (The Constitutional Court of the Republic of Indonesia 2016).

75 The Indonesian Constitution Article 28I(4).

76 The three principles of contextual interpretation applied were *noscitur a sociis, ejusdem generis* and *expressio unius exclusion alterius* [3.13.2.1].

77 Decisions 070 PUU-II/2004 NS 27/PUU-V-/2007.

78 Judicial Review of Constitutional Court, Decision of Constitutional Court No. 97/PUU-XIV/2016 [3.13.2.3] (The Constitutional Court of the Republic of Indonesia 2016).

> This is not in line with the spirit of the 1945 Constitution which clearly guarantees that every citizen is free to embrace a religion and belief and to worship in accordance with that belief.[79]
>
> Article 61(1) and Article 64(1) is contrary to the Constitution Article 28I(2) as long as the word 'religion' is not interpreted to include 'belief'.[80]

The Justices also looked at the practical implications and benefits of allowing identifying information on the national register database. First, for the individuals, it equalises their right to services. The Population Law states that it fulfils "the needs of public services as an inherent right of every citizen" and Article 4 of the Public Services Law[81] requires such services be "based on, among other things, the principles of equality of rights and non-discrimination" meaning "no distinction between ethnicity, race, religion class, gender and social status".[82] Thus, indigenous believers should receive services in the same way as followers of Indonesia's six religions. Second, there is a national benefit. The e-KTP enables the creation of an accurate national population database to aid in fulfilling and regulating citizens' rights including for freedom of religion and belief. The Justices noted as the "the number of believers of beliefs is very large and diverse" it makes data on believers necessary for orderly government administration and service provision. This can only occur if believers can specify "believer" (*kepercayaan*) on the KK and e-KTP.[83] They do not, however, need to specify the name of a particular belief system.

4.4 *Analysis and Comparative Contextualisation*

The Beliefs Case again highlights how Pancasila's first principle, "Belief in Almighty God", endorses an integrative approach to religion which the Constitutional Court imbibes to ensure statutes comply with its inclusive spirit and aspirations for a united tolerant nation. The Constitution of 1945 did not posit an exact meaning for "religion" nor for "belief" nor did it limit guarantees for religious freedom to six state defined religions. "Religion" as belief in one God was protected, but left malleable for subsequent presidents,

---

79 Judicial Review of Constitutional Court, Decision of Constitutional Court No. 97/PUU-XIV/2016 [3.13.3] (The Constitutional Court of the Republic of Indonesia 2016).

80 Judicial Review of Constitutional Court, Decision of Constitutional Court No. 97/PUU-XIV/2016 [3.13.3] (The Constitutional Court of the Republic of Indonesia 2016).

81 Law Number 25 of 2009 on Public Services.

82 Judicial Review of Constitutional Court, Decision of Constitutional Court No. 97/PUU-XIV/2016 [3.13.1] (The Constitutional Court of the Republic of Indonesia 2016).

83 Judicial Review of Constitutional Court, Decision of Constitutional Court No. 97/PUU-XIV/2016 [3.13.5] (The Constitutional Court of the Republic of Indonesia 2016).

ministers, legislatures and judiciaries to refine and shape. Since independence, political debate on its meaning has been ongoing. The Minister of Religious Affairs Regulation No. 9 of 1952 held religion meant monotheism, requiring a holy book from divine revelation and a Prophet.[84] Twenty years later, due to political reasons[85] and the need to bring religion under the control of the state bureaucracy, Presidential Decree No 1/PNPS/1965 on Blasphemy decreed six official religions, which included polytheistic Hinduism, Buddhism and Confucianism, but omitted indigenous beliefs. People's Consultative Assembly (MPR) Decree No IVV/MPR/1978 confirmed *kepercayaan* was not a religion. Although the Constitutional Court in the Beliefs Case did not re-classify *kepercayaan* as a religion, nor was the Court asked to do so, it inclusively raised the status of "belief of believers" to be the equal of the six recognised "religions", for the purposes of public services and administration. Essentially it was a careful compromise. By equating "belief" with "religion", the six-decade long recognition of six religions could stand, whilst giving rights and legal standing to a small marginalised indigenous minority of "believers".

It was hailed as a landmark case in religious rights for Indonesians. Researcher Victor Nalle wrote how the Constitutional Court's "restoration of the rights of adherents of *Aliran Kepercayaan*" "shows proof of the importance of judicial avenues to challenge the intolerant and discriminatory laws and policies".[86] It was both a "watershed moment in Indonesia's history of religious freedom",[87] and "a new hope"[88] for believers, marking a "step in the recognition of the rights of indigenous believers" with a "chance to encourage reconciliation of *agama* and *kepercayaan* groups".[89]

Not all applauded the decision. MUI (the Indonesian Ulema Council), in an eight-point response criticised the Court's departure from the 1978 MPR ruling, stating MUI "deeply regretted the Constitutional Court decision" which was "inaccurate and hurts the feelings of religious people, especially Indonesian Muslims because the decision means aligning the position of *agama* and

84 Asep Sandi Ruswanda, "Indonesian Constitutional Court's Decision No 97/PUU-XIV/ 2016: A Change to Encourage Reconciliation between *agama* dan *kepercayaan* [Religion and Belief]," *RELIGI: Jurnal Studi Agama-Agama* 16, no. 1 (2020): 26.

85 See Nugroho, "A New Ray of Hope."

86 Nalle, 574.

87 Nugroho.

88 Ahmad Tholabi Kharkie and Fathudin, "The Constitutional Policy: State Recognition of the Believers in Indonesia," *Advances in Social Science and Humanities Research* 162, (2018) 144.

89 Ruswanda, 34.

kepercayaan".[90] Asep Sandi Ruswanda reviewed the varied reactions to the decision from the six established religions. MUI opposed it, Muhammadiyah had mixed feelings, the Buddhist organisation was neutral, and the Protestant Chairman was positive, hoping it could end religious discrimination. Self-interest led some Muslim and Hindu spokespersons to express concern that with the changes to the identity card, their number of adherents could decline.

As the Court's constitutional recognition of beliefs was limited to the facts of the case, scholars including Professor Butt noted that other non-recognised religions, such as Indonesia's Ahmadis, would not be covered even though they too experience similar identity card issues and consequences.[91] In addition, because the Constitutional Court's powers end with judicial review, with enforcement and implementation for the executive, the Court "cannot pursue government officials who refuse to comply with its decisions, or to invalidate regulations that are inconsistent" with it.[92]

4.4.1 Comparative Analysis across the Region

Identity cards are used by most Southeast Asian nations. Brunei requires ethnicity on its card and as Malay ethnicity is fused with Islam, authorities can reasonably ascertain religion. Since 1990, Malaysia's MyKad only requires Islam be displayed on the card so non-Muslim affiliation is assumed by the omission, although it is contained in the card's chip.[93] A separate identity code "for natives of Sabah and Sarawak" is used to confirm *Bumiputera* status.[94] An issue does arise when an identity card wrongly states the holder's religion as Islam, as removal of this error is difficult[95] due to Malaysia's firm stance on apostasy.

Although identity cards were the ignition point in the Beliefs Case, the broader issue of the status and protections for non-Muslim minorities, whether followers of a minority religion or indigenous believers recurs in pluralistic Brunei (30% non-Muslim) and Malaysia (40% non-Muslim). On this issue, the legal postulates of Pancasila, MIB and *Bumiputra* prioritisation inform how

90 Ibid., 27.

91 Butt, "Constitutional Recognition," 471.

92 Ibid., 472.

93 Ida Lim, "Why Islam is on Muslim Malaysians identity Card," *Malay Mail*, January 28, 2020. https://www.malaymail.com/news/malaysia/2020/01/28/why-islam-is-on-malaysian-muslims-identity-cards/1831992.

94 Ibid.

95 See Decision of Mahkamah Rayuan Malaysia, Lina Joy v. Majlis Agama Islam Wilayah [2004] 2 M.L.J. 119 (Mahkamah Rayuan Malaysia 2004).

each conceives of and manages religion in its plural context. Different postulates lead to different outcomes.

First, the Indonesian Constitution provides for "Belief in Almighty God" but does not prescribe an official (or six) religions, nor exclude believers. This integrative constitutional design allowed the Court to reach an inclusive decision in the Beliefs Case. In contrast, Brunei and Malaysia set Islam, (Article 3 in both Constitutions) as their nation's "official religion", which *ab initio* creates legal religious division. This division is used to legitimatise accrual of different rights based on majority versus minority. Although Article 3 extends a guarantee that "other" religions may be "practised in peace and harmony by the persons professing them" this is far from integrative equality.

For example, in Brunei, "practice in peace and harmony" is the only guarantee for religious freedom, but following MIB it is used by the Sultan (legislator, head of the executive and of Islam) for the benefit of Brunei's Muslim majority, not minorities.[96] It legitimises laws that ensure Muslims never encounter religious or cultural practices[97] or belief systems other than Islam, including at school.[98] Believers in Brunei[99] who follow pre-Islamic indigenous animistic practices of augury, *bomoh* (shamans and magic healers), and *keramat* shrines (sacred places believed to have supernatural powers),[100] are of special concern. Ensuring Muslims are not offended, confused or tempted to partake in "primitive" or "*kaffir*" practices, the state is preoccupied with their eradication and with facilitating conversions to Islam (*Dakwah* Propagation Unit). The Sultan condemns religious pluralism because it allows "deviant teachings about freedom of individuals to practice a religion of their choice", which, he argues, would pollute Brunei.[101] As Bruneian courts lack judicial review, no one can challenge Orders of the Sultan that arguably violate it.

96 See Ann Black, "Exporting a Constitutional Court to Brunei? Benefits and Prospects," *Constitutional Review* 8 no. 2 (December 2022): 361–391.

97 Fatwa (Siri 03/2005) reported in "Muslims Must not Follow Non-Islamic Celebrations," *Borneo Bulletin* December 28, 2014. Grand Mufti stated: "[B]elievers of other religions, according to Islam, may practise their religion, with the condition that the celebrations are not disclosed or displayed publicly to Muslims."

98 Compulsory Religious Education Act (Cap. 215).

99 Indigenous ethnic (described as racial) pluralism is acknowledged in the Constitution, and the Nationality Act (Cap. 15) but all seven indigenous "races" are categorised as "Malays."

100 Dominik Muller, "Sharia Law and the Politics of "Faith Control" in Brunei Darussalam," *Internationales Asienforum* 46 (2015): 329.

101 Othman "Steer clear".

Malaysia has additional guarantees of religious freedom (Article 11) and equality (Article 8),[102] however its courts have been at odds as to whether the "peace and harmony" provision in Article 3 is a right-protective provision for non-Muslims or designed to ensure Islamic Supremacy.[103] On the one hand, the High Court in the Meor case[104] held "Islam is not of the same status as the other religions; it does not sit side by side nor stand side by side. Rather, Islam sits at the top, it walks first, and is placed on a mantle with its voice loud and clear".[105] Justice Apandi also reasoned that Article 3(1) was for "the sanctity of Islam … to insulate [it] against any threat faced or any possible and probable threat".[106] Dr Neo sees these judicial interpretations as turning Article 3 "on its head"[107] to benefit the majority and not for the peace and harmony of other religions. On the other hand, Justice Ariffin in 2021 found that Article 3(1) does not allow the state to restrict religious freedom of minorities[108] and cannot override other constitutional protections as found in Article 11(1).

Second, unlike Indonesia's integrative design, where the word "believer" like "religion" was open and broad, allowing adjudicative latitude for the Constitutional Court in cases on religious rights, the *Bumiputera* postulate in Malaysia restricts the interpretative hands of the judiciary by linking "race" with religion for the Malays,[109] and with belief for the believers of Sabah and

102 Article 11(1) guarantees that "[e]very person has the right to profess and practise his religion and, subject to Clause (4), to propagate it." Clause (4) authorizes laws that "control or restrict the propagation of any religious doctrine or belief among persons professing the religion of Islam." Article 8 guarantees: "all persons are equal before the law and entitled to equal protection of the law".

103 On this issue see, Syed Fadhil Hanafi Syed A Rahman, "The Malaysian Federal Constitution: an Islamic or Secular Constitution?" *Constitutional Review* 5, no. 1 (May 2019): 134–162.

104 Decision of High Court of Seremban, Meor Atiqulrahman bin Ishak v. Fatimah bte Sihi [2000] 5 M.L.J. 375 (High Court of Seremban 2000); also, see: Decision of Mahkamah Rayuan Malaysia, Lina Joy v. Majlis Agama Islam Wilayah [2004] 2 M.L.J. 119 (Mahkamah Rayuan Malaysia 2004).

105 Translated and discussed in Jaclyn Neo, "What's in a Name? Malaysia's "Allah" Controversy and Judicial intertwining of Islam and Ethnic Identity," *International Journal of Constitutional Law* 12, no. 3 (July 2014): 759.

106 Decision of Court of Appeal Putrajaya, Menteri Dalam Negeri & Ors v. Titular Roman Catholic Archbishop of Kuala Lumpur [Allah case], [2013] 8 M.L.J. 890 [33] (Court of Appeal Putrajaya 2013).

107 Neo, "What's in a Name," 758.

108 Decision of High Court Malaysia, Jill Ireland Lawrence Bill v. Menteri Bagi Kementerian Dalam Negeri Malaysia, Judicial Review, High Court Malaya, No: R4(2)-25-256-2008. 17 March 2021. [194] (High Court Malaysia, 2021).

109 A "Malay" in Article 160 professes the religion of Islam, habitually speaks Malay language, and conforms to Malay customs.

Sarawak. Not all indigenous believers in Malaysia are equal. The indigenous non-Muslim people of the Malay peninsula are, in constitutional terms "aborigines" (Article 160) and not accorded the same legal recognition and advantages as the indigenous non-Muslims who constitutionally are "natives" of Sabah and Sarawak and thus *Bumiputera*. Article 161A sets out that natives must belong to one of the indigenous races of Borneo and if "of mixed blood" it must be exclusively from one of the qualifying races.[110] The result is that indigenous believers in Sabah and Sarawak have constitutional recognition with protection of their animistic beliefs and spiritual practices, whereas the indigenous believers on the Malay peninsula, the *Orang Asli,* do not. In line with the *Bumiputera* postulate, native customary law has become the basic law in East but not West Malaysia. Much of the customary *adat* is now codified[111] and is administered and enforced by Native Courts.[112] These courts determine who is, in fact, a "native". In 2022, a new Native Court's Ordinance was passed by the Sarawak Assembly to increase the jurisdiction of Native Courts to be "on par with the Syariah and Civil courts".[113]

Third, Pancasila's "Belief in one Almighty God" avoids other consequences that come with an "official" religion. Article 2 of Brunei's Constitution constructs Islam as "the Islamic Religion according to the Shafeite sect of Ahlis Sunnah Waljamaah", which undermines Islamic interpretative democracy. Without this fetter, Indonesia can embrace intra-Islamic plurality. Indonesian *ulama* have independence from government, can engage in collective ijtihad, and issue fatwas that may differ.[114] An official religion brings one state-approved form of Islam, and a state Mufti with definitive religious and legal authority. Otto, quoting Fuller, notes, "there is no one Sharia but rather many different, even contrasting ways to build a legal structure in accordance with God's vision for mankind. A single Sharia doesn't exist."[115] Brunei asserts there

110 Article 161A(6) indigenous to Sarawak are the Bukitans, Bisayahs, Dusuns, Sea Dayaks, Land Dayaks, Kadayans, Kalabits, Kayans, Kenyahs (Sabups and Sipengs), Kajangs (Sekapans, Kejamans, Lahanans, Punans, Tanjongs and Kanowits), Lugats, Lisums, Malays, Melanos, Muruts, Penans, Sians, Tagals, Tabuns and Ukits.

111 Native Courts Ordinance of 1992. See Tey, 223.

112 Native Court's website: https://nativecourt.sarawak.gov.my.

113 Chief Registrar Michael Dawi Alli, quoted in "Looking into the Establishment of the Native Court in Sarawak" *Dari RAKAN Sarawak* August 3, 2022. https://www.rakansarawak.com.

114 Nadirsyah Hosen, "Hilal and Halal: How to Manage Islamic Pluralism in Indonesia?" *Asian Journal of Comparative Law* 7 (2012): 111–126.

115 Jan M Otto, *Sharia: a Comprehensive Overview of the Legal Systems of Twelve Muslim Countries in Past and Present* (Leiden, Leiden University Press, 2012), 24.

is. Airing practices or Syariah interpretations outside what is sanctioned by Brunei's Sultan, Mufti and Ministry of Religious Affairs warrants criminal penalties, even the death penalty. State authorities including the Religious Police and the *Aqidah* (Doctrine/Faith) Control Section monitor for adherence "correct" Islam. To express an alternative view on a Quranic text, *hadith* or *ijma*[116] is deviationist and criminalised[117] as differing views on Islam are a "poison to security and could destabilise the country's peace and harmony creating havoc, foes and even spill blood (fighting) among Muslims".[118]

5 Conclusion

FOR JUSTICE BASED ON GOD ALMIGHTY

Each decision of the Indonesian Constitutional Court opens with the words above, in which God Almighty is acknowledged as a font for justice. The Indonesian Constitution recognises a neutral God, one for all believers, not just a God for Indonesia's Muslims. This comes from the Pancasila postulate or value principle, which distinguishes Indonesia from all other nations with Muslim majority populations. The significance of this is apparent in the two Constitutional Court cases on religion, reviewed by this chapter.

First, in the Religious Court Case, the Constitutional Court rejected the argument that Islamic criminal law was an imperative for the right to practice Islam, by affirming that justice in a plural nation required that "national law should not be based on the size of the large (majority) and small (minority) followers of religion, ethnicity or race" and instead be an "integration factor which shall be an adhesive and unifying tool for nation".[119] Citing Pancasila, the Justices concluded that national law must guarantee the ideological integrity and integration of the country's territory, as well as build religious tolerance that is just and civilised.[120] This is compared with two other plural nations, Brunei and Malaysia, where MIB and *Bumiputera* priority, led to Islam's

116 Azlan Othman "Imams remind Ummah against anti-Hadith groups" *Borneo Bulletin*, March 30, 2013.

117 Syariah Penal Code Order 2013, Section 209(1).

118 Othman, "Imams Warn."

119 Judicial Review of Constitutional Court, Decision of Constitutional Court No. 19/PUU-VI/2008 [3.18]. (The Constitutional Court of the Republic of Indonesia 2008).

120 Judicial Review of Constitutional Court, Decision of Constitutional Court No. 19/PUU-VI/2008 [3.19]. (The Constitutional Court of the Republic of Indonesia 2008).

elevation as their state religion. The consequential constitutional protections and benefits which flow to their Malay majorities has accentuated differences and fractured national unity. Similarly, in the Beliefs Case, the Justices of the Indonesian Constitutional Court determined that "Belief in Almighty God" could encompass more than Islam to allow accommodation of other religions and beliefs of its indigenous minority. This was in "line with the spirit of the 1945 Constitution, which explicitly guarantees that every citizen is free to believe in a religion and belief and to worship according to that religion and belief."[121] Both demonstrate the Indonesian "middle way". Courts cannot through their judgments alone end discrimination and marginalisation but their decisions, as seen in both cases, can provide a beacon for tolerance and inclusivity. Former Indonesian President Susilo Bambang Yudhoyono, when opening the World Movement for Democracy in 2010, saw tolerance and embrace of pluralism as the way forward: "The future belongs to those who are willing to responsibly embrace pluralism, openness and freedom. I say this based on the Indonesian experience."[122]

Bibliography

Azzahra, Raihan and Farid Sufian Shuaib. "Religious Courts in Indonesia and Malaysia: History Structure and Jurisdiction." *Indonesian Comparative Law Review* 4, no. 2 (2022) 115–130. http://dx.doi.org/10.18196/iclr.v4i2.15911.

Bell, Gary. "Religious Legal Pluralism Revisited – The Status of the Roman Catholic Church and her Canon Law in Singapore." *Asian Journal of Comparative Law* 7, (2012): 49–84.

Black, Ann Hossein Esmaeili and Nadirsyah Hosen. *Modern Perspectives on Islamic Law.* Cheltenham: Edward Elgar, 2013.

Black, Ann. "Exporting a Constitutional Court to Brunei? Benefits and Prospects." *Constitutional Review* 8 no. 2 (December 2022): 361–291. https://doi.org/10.31078/consrev826.

Butt, Simon. "Constitutional Recognition of 'Beliefs' in Indonesia." *Journal of Law and Religion* 35, no. 3 (2020): 450–473. http://doi.org/10.1017/jlr.2020.39.

Compulsory Religious Education Act Cap 215, Brunei Darussalam.

Constitution of Brunei Darussalam (1959).

121 Judicial Review of Constitutional Court, Decision of Constitutional Court No. 97/PUU-XIV/2016 [3.13.2.1] (The Constitutional Court of the Republic of Indonesia 2016).

122 Keynote Speech, Sixth Assembly, World Movement for Democracy. Jakarta 12 April 2010. https://www.setneg.go.id.

Constitution of the Republic of Indonesia (UUD NRI 1945).

Constitution of the Republic of Turkey (Law No. 2709 1982).

Decision of Court of Appeal Putrajaya, Menteri Dalam Negeri & Ors v. Titular Roman Catholic Archbishop of Kuala Lumpur [Allah case], [2013] 8 M.L.J. 890 [33] (Court of Appeal Putrajaya 2013).

Decision of High Court of Malaysia. Jill Ireland Lawrence Bill v. Menteri Bagi Kementerian Dalam Negeri Malaysia, No: R4(2)-25-256-2008. 17 March 2021 (High Court of Malaysia 2021).

Decision of High Court of Seremban, Meor Atiqulrahman bin Ishak v. Fatimah bte Sihi [2000] 5 M.L.J. 375 (High Court of Seremban 2000).

Decision of Mahkamah Rayuan Malaysia, Lina Joy v. Majlis Agama Islam Wilayah [2004] 2 M.L.J. 119 (Mahkamah Rayuan Malaysia 2004).

Federal Constitution of Malaysia (1957).

Government of Indonesia. "Indonesian Portal." Accessed January 30, 2023, https://indonesia.go.id/profil/agama.

Haetami, Enden. "Islamic Law Enforcement through Religious Courts in Indonesia." ENDLESS: *International Journal of Futures Studies* 2, no. 2 (2019): 71–81 https://doi.org/10.54783/endlessjournal.v2i2.105.

Hosen, Nadirsyah. "Can the Muslim world borrow from Indonesian Constitutional Reform?: A Comparative Constitutional Approach." *Journal of Indonesian Islam* 1, no. 1 (2007): 75–99. https://doi.org/10.15642/JIIS.2007.1.1.75-99.

Hosen, Nadirsyah. "Hilal and Halal: How to Manage Islamic Pluralism in Indonesia?" *Asian Journal of Comparative Law* 7, no.1 (2012): 111–126. https://doi.org/10.1515/1932-0205.1418.

Hosen, Nadirsyah. *Sharia and Constitutional Reform in Indonesia*. Singapore: ISEAS, 2007.

Indonesia.GO.ID, Portal Informasi Indonesia [Indonesian Government Portal]. "Agama." htps://indonesia.go.id/profil/agama.

Judicial Review of Constitutional Court, Religious Courts Law, No. 19/PUU-VI/2008 (The Constitutional Court of the Republic of Indonesia 2008).

Kelantan Syariah Criminal Code (I) Enactment 2019, Kelantan, Malaysia.

Kharkie, Ahmad Tholabi and Fathudin. "The Constitutional Policy: State Recognition of the Believers in Indonesia." *Advances in Social Science and Humanities Research* 162, (2018): 143–148. https://doi.org/10.2991/iclj-17.2018.30.

Law No. 1 of 1974 on Marriage.

Law No. 1 of 2004 on Waqf.

Law No. 14 of 1999 on Implementation Privileges in the Special Province of Aceh.

Law No. 23 of 2006 on Population Administration.

Law No. 25 of 2009 on Public Services.

Law No. 38 of 1999 on Management of Zakat.

Law No. 7 of 1989 on Religious Courts.

Lawyers for Liberty. "Defending Human Rights." https://www.lawyersforliberty.org/.

Lukito, Ratno. "Mapping the Relationship of Competing Legal Traditions in the Era of Transnationalism in Indonesia" in *Pluralism, Transnationalism and Culture in Asian Law,* edited by Gary F Bell, 90–115. Singapore: ISEAS, 2017.

Marshall, Paul. "The Ambiguities of Religious Freedom in Indonesia," *The Review of Religion and International Affairs* 16, (2018): 85–96. https://doi.org/10.1080/15570274.2018.1433588.

Merry, Sally Engle. "Legal Pluralism." *Law and Society Review* 22, no.5 (1988): 869–896.

Muller, Dominik. "Sharia law and the Politics of 'Faith Control.' In Brunei Darussalam," *Internationales Asienforum* 46 no.3/4 (2015): 313–345.

Nalle, Victor I.W. "The Politics of Intolerant law s against Adherents of Indigenous Beliefs of *Aliran Kepercayaan* in Indonesia." *Asian Journal of Law and Society* 8. no. 3 (2021): 558–576. https://doi.org/10.1017/als.2020.54.

Nationality Act (Cap 15) Brunei Darussalam.

Native Courts of Sarawak Website: https://nativecourt.sarawak.gov.my.

Native Courts Ordinance of 1992, Sarawak.

Neo, Jaclyn. "What's in a Name? Malaysia's 'Allah' Controversy and Judicial Intertwining of Islam and Ethnic Identity." *International Journal of Constitutional Law* 12, No. 3 (July 2014): 751–768. https://doi.org/10.1093/icon/mou050.

Nugroho, Johannes. "A new Ray of Hope for Indonesia's Traditional Religious Beliefs," *Strategic Review,* March 4, 2019. https://sr.sgpp.ac.id/post/a-ray-of-hope-for-indonesias-traditional-religious-beliefs.

Othman, Azlan. "Imams Warn against Deviationist Teachings." *Borneo Bulletin,* January 4, 2004, 3.

Peters, Rudolph. *Crime and Punishment in Islamic Law: Theory and Practice from the Sixteenth to the Twenty-first Century.* Cambridge: Cambridge University Press, 2005.

Presidential Instruction Instrument No.1 of 199.1.

Rahman, Syed Fadhil Hanafi Syed. "The Malaysian Federal Constitution: an Islamic or Secular Constitution?" *Constitutional Review* 5, no. 1 (May 2019): 134–162. https://doi.org/10.31078/consrev515.

Rankan09Sarawak. "Looking into the Establishment of the Native Court in Sarawak." *Dari RAKAN Sarawak* August 3, 2022. https://www.rakansarawak.com.

Rofii, Ahmad. "The Religiosity of the Indonesian Constitution: Article 29(1) and Its Interpretation." *Constitutional Review* 7, no. 2 (December 2021): 203–240. https://doi.org/10.31078/consrev722.

Ruswanda, Asep Sandi. "Indonesian Constitutional Court's Decision No 97/PUU-XIV/2016: A Change to Encourage Reconciliation between *Agama dan kepercayaan* [Religion and Belief]." *RELIGI: Jurnal Studi Agama-Agama* 16, no. 1 (2020): 18–41. https://doi.org/10.14421/rejusta.2020.1601-02.

Safa'at, Muchamad Ali. "The Roles of the Indonesian Constitutional Court in Determining State-Religion Relations." *Constitutional Review* 8, no. 1 (May 2022): 2548–3870. https://doi.org/10.31078/consrev815 https://doi.org/10.31078/consrev815.

SIS (Sisters-in-Islam). "Kelantan Enactment Report." https://sistersinislam.org/wp-content/uploads/2022/03/Kelantan-Enactment-Report.pdf.

Syariah Courts (Criminal Jurisdiction) Act 1965 (Act 355) Federation of Malaysia.

Syariah Penal Code Order 2013, Brunei Darussalam.

Syariah Penal Procedure Order 2018, Brunei Darussalam.

Tan, Yi Liang. "Kelantan Hudud is Unconstitutional and Discriminatory." *The Star*, March 20, 2015. https://www.thestar.com.my/news/nation/2015/03/20/malaysian-bar-statement-on-kelantan-hudud.

Tey, Tsun Hang. "Malaysia: The Undermining of its Fundamental Institutions and the Prospects for Reform." In *Law and Legal Institutions of Asia: Traditions, Adaptations and Innovations,* edited by Ann Black and Gary Bell, 212–262. Cambridge: Cambridge University Press, 2011.

Universiti Malaya Student Union. "New Kelantan Syariah Criminal Code (I) Enactment 2019: Is it necessary?" Discussion Paper, December 2, 2021. https://www.myumsu.com/discussion-series.

Yudhoyono, Susilo Bambang (President) Opening Speech, Sixth Assembly, World Movement for Democracy. Jakarta 12 April 2010. https://www.setneg.go.id/baca/index/welcoming_remarks_president_of_the_republik_of_indonesia_on_sixth_assembly_world_movement_for_democracy.

CHAPTER 7

The Recognition of Customary Land Rights at the Constitutional Court of Indonesia: A Critical Assessment of the Jurisprudence

Yance Arizona and Miriam Cohen

Abstract

This chapter analyzes the legal recognition of indigenous peoples' rights in Indonesia through a comparative and international law framework. The focus is on landmark cases from the Constitutional Court of Indonesia, which has had a significant role in defining the contours of indigenous peoples' rights within the country. The chapter discusses the development of jurisprudence concerning customary land rights and the impact of international law on indigenous rights in Indonesia. The examination includes the legal frameworks that protect indigenous peoples' rights internationally, including the International Covenant on Civil and Political Rights (ICCPR), the International Labor Organization Convention 169, and the United Nations Declaration on the Rights of Indigenous Peoples. In Indonesia, indigenous organizations have been advocating for a special law on indigenous peoples' rights since 2011. However, political support for such legislation has been lacking in Parliament. Through the analysis of landmark decisions, it becomes apparent that judicial rulings have a significant impact on the development of indigenous rights. The Constitutional Court of Indonesia has confirmed the need for a special law regarding indigenous peoples, but until such legislation is enacted, scattered laws in various sectoral areas, such as mining, forestry, and coastal fields, can be justified. The chapter concludes that international law has had a positive impact on the development of the Court's jurisprudence and the recognition of customary land rights within Indonesia. The Court's rulings have been inspired by international environmental law and the UNDRIP, and the Court looks to international law to further protect the rights of indigenous peoples. The Court's decisions have also generated legal reform and altered the concept of colonial law that is still inherent in national forestry law, strengthening the rights of indigenous peoples in Indonesia. Although the influence of landmark court decisions is still limited in Indonesia, the chapter finds that the Court's decisions have played a significant role in recognizing the customary rights of indigenous peoples in the country.

 | DOI:10.1163/9789004691698_008

Keywords

customary land rights – indigenous peoples – Indonesia – constitutional court – international law – UNDRIP

1 Introduction

Many states recognise indigenous rights in their laws or within their constitutional framework.[1] In Indonesia, however, the legal recognition of indigenous peoples' rights is problematic. At international meetings in the United Nations, the Indonesian Government consistently rejects the applicability of the concept of indigenous peoples in Indonesia. In fact, the Indonesian Constitution recognises customary law communities (*masyarakat hukum adat*) along with their traditional rights. Some derivative legislation also regulates various rights of customary law communities, including land and forest rights, cultures, education, and traditional Government.

The courts have become an important legal institution to settle actual problems encountered by indigenous peoples. Moreover, they also play a significant role in generating policy reform. A notable example is the High Court of Australia ruling in the case of *Eddy Mabo v Queensland*, involving indigenous peoples from Murray Island in 1992.[2] This court ruling refuted the *Terra Nullius* doctrine of the British colonialists by recognising the land rights of aboriginal peoples and Torres Strait islanders.[3] The decision marked a turning point, fostering a new political awareness within the Australian Government toward indigenous peoples. The Court decision was followed by the enactment of the

1 Kirsty Gover and Benedict Kingsbury, "Editorial Note in Indigenous Groups and the Politics of Recognition in Asia: Cases from Japan, Taiwan, West Papua, Bali, the Republic of China, and Gilgit," *International Journal of Minority and Group Rights* 11, no. 1–2 (2004): 1; James Anaya, *Indigenous Peoples in International Law* (New York: Oxford University Press, 2004), 57; Patrick Thornberry, *Indigenous Peoples and Human Rights* (Manchester: Manchester University Press, 2013), 317.

2 Sean Brennan, Megan Davis, Brendan Edgeworth, and Leon Terrill, "The Idea of Native Title as a Vehicle for Change and Indigenous Empowerment," in *Native Title from Mabo to Akiba: A Vehicle for Change and Empowerment?*, eds. Brendan Edgeworth, Leon Terrill, Megan David, and Sean Brennan (Sydney: Federation Press, 2015), 2.

3 Brendan Edgeworth, "The Mabo 'Vibe' and Its Many Resonances in Australian Property Law," in *Native Title from Mabo to Akiba: A Vehicle for Change and Empowerment?*, ed. Brendan Edgeworth, Leon Terrill, Megan Davis, and Sean Brennan (Sydney: Federation Press, 2015), 75–98.

Native Title Act in 1994 and the establishment of the Native Title Tribunal.[4] Over a decade later, on February 13, 2008, Australian Prime Minister Kevin Rudd delivered a national apology for the forced removal of aboriginal children from their families, commonly referred to as the stolen generation.[5]

Meanwhile, international law also protects the rights of minorities and provides some recognition for traditional indigenous titles.[6] The development of international law regarding indigenous peoples was initiated by the International Labour Organisation (ILO). Two conventions relevant to this issue are ILO Convention Number 107 on Indigenous and Tribal Populations (1957) and ILO Convention Number 169 on Indigenous and Tribal Peoples (1989).[7] The two conventions distinguish between indigenous peoples and tribal peoples, but they never received a great number of State ratification.[8] In the Indonesian context, the concept of tribal peoples better describes the condition of non-dominant cultural groups in society, a common occurrence in Asia and Africa. However, as international law has developed, the terms indigenous peoples (and indigenous rights) are used as a general term in many contexts.

The development of international law on indigenous peoples is also present in the realm of environmental law. The *Rio Declaration on Environment and Development* in 1992 substantiated the importance of the role of indigenous peoples in environmental protection. International agreements on climate change and biological diversity also emphasise the role and participation of indigenous peoples in climate change mitigation and conservation administration. Finally, the Conference of the Parties (COP15) to the UN Convention on Biological Diversity (CBD), which took place in Montreal, Canada, in December 2022, formulated several biological diversity conservation goals, one of which is targeting 30% of the earth's territory as conservation areas by

4 Ibid.

5 Full text of the national apology can be found here: "Text of the Apology to the Stolen Generations," Australian Government Department of Foreign Affairs and Trade, accessed February 22, 2023, https://www.dfat.gov.au/people-to -people/public-diplomacy/programs-activities/Pages/text-of-the-apology-to-the-stolen-generation.

6 Ronald Niezen, *The Origins of Indigenism: Human Rights and the Politics of Identity* (Berkeley, CA: University of California Press, 2003), 138; Kathleen Birrell, *Indigeneity: Before and Beyond the Law* (New York: Routledge, 2016), 75.

7 Anaya, *Indigenous Peoples*, 47.

8 Dwight Newman, "Chapter 1: Internationalization of the Law of Indigenous Rights," in *Research Handbook on the International Law of Indigenous Rights* (Cheltenham, UK: Edward Elgar Publishing, 2022), 2–8; see also, Ken Coates and Carin Holroyd, Chapter 4: The Emergence and Evolution of the Global Indigenous Rights Movement," ibid.

2030 with due recognition and involvement of indigenous peoples in conservation activities.[9] Additionally, regional human rights conventions and jurisprudence also recognise land titles.[10]

The most advanced development in international law regarding indigenous peoples is the *United Nations Declaration on the Rights of Indigenous Peoples* (UNDRIP), adopted by the United Nations in 2007. UNDRIP provides an international framework for indigenous rights. Indonesia supported the UNDRIP, although it refused the applicability of the concept of 'indigenous peoples' to the Indonesian context.

This chapter reflects on the contribution of the Constitutional Court of Indonesia (CCI) to the recognition of the rights of indigenous peoples, particularly regarding their customary land rights. Adopting a comparative approach, this chapter provides specific comments on three landmark judgements of the CCI while drawing references to international law. It also discusses how the CCI rulings correspond to international law on indigenous peoples' rights. This chapter thus analyses Indonesian law regarding indigenous peoples' rights from a critical assessment of the relevant jurisprudence.

2 The Constitutional Court and Customary Land Rights in Indonesia

2.1 *Indigenous Rights in Indonesia: A Background*

The Indonesian Government is inconsistent in the application and understanding of indigenous peoples within the Indonesian context. In international meetings, the Indonesian Government has repeatedly refused to state that indigenous peoples exist in Indonesia.[11] Governments from other Asian

---

9 See "COP15: Nations Adopt Four Goals, 23 Targets for 2030 In Landmark UN Biodiversity Agreement," Convention on Biological Diversity (cbd.int), accessed February 22, 2023, https://www.cbd.int/article/cop15-cbd-press-release-final-19dec2022.

10 Øyvind Ravna and Nigel Bankes, "Recognition of Indigenous Land Rights in Norway and Canada," *International Journal on Minority and Group Rights* 24, no. 1 (2017): 72.

11 The Government of Indonesia's denial of the applicability of the concept 'indigenous peoples' appeared in its ambiguous response to the United Nations in 2012, stating that: "The Government of Indonesia supports the promotion and protection of indigenous people worldwide. Given its demographic composition, Indonesia, however, does not recognise the application of the indigenous people concept as defined in the UN Declaration on the Rights of Indigenous Peoples in the country." See: Adriaan Bedner and Stijn van Huis, "The Return of the Native in Indonesian Law: Indigenous Communities in Indonesian Legislation," *Bijdragen tot de taal-, land- en volkenkunde* [*Journal of the Humanities and Social Sciences of Southeast Asia*] 164, no. 2 (2008): 165–193.

countries, such as India and Thailand, constantly repeat the same strategy.[12] In our view, this denial occurs because the Indonesian Government considers indigenous peoples a static concept that only fits into colonial settler countries. In fact, the development of international law has established the meaning of indigenous peoples so as to accommodate various subjects with different names and characteristics in different countries.

In the Indonesian context, the 1945 Constitution recognises a particular subject called customary law communities (*masyarakat hukum adat*), defined as a group of people who come from the same lineage, live in a particular geographical area, and have their own institutions and customary laws. Indigenous organisations and activists from Indonesia interpret customary law communities as indigenous peoples in the Indonesian context.[13] However, the Indonesian Government has never expressly justified such an interpretation. The Indonesian Government's denial of the concept of indigenous peoples is due to two main reasons. The first reason has to do with politics. It is feared that recognition of indigenous peoples may undermine the state's territorial integrity because one of the primary rights of indigenous peoples is self-determination. The second reason has to do with competition for natural resources. Recognition of indigenous peoples bears the implications of sharing resources. Meanwhile, the state wants to control natural resources' potential for national development fully.

The denial of the definition and concept of indigenous peoples leads to the lack of fulfilment of their rights, especially concerning the right to self-determination and the right to natural resources in their territories. In the Indonesian context, this has been happening systematically since the Dutch colonial era. This has been evident in Dutch colonial forestry regulations 1865 and Agrarian Law 1870.[14] The regulation introduced the principle that if land

12 Gerard Persoon, "Isolated Groups or Indigenous Peoples; Indonesia and the International Discourse," *Bijdragen tot de Taal-, Land- en Volkenkunde* [*Journal of the Humanities and Social Sciences of Southeast Asia and Oceania*] 154, no. 2 (1998): 281–304; Gover and Kingsbury, "Editorial Note in Indigenous," 1; Christian Erni (ed.), *The Concept of Indigenous Peoples in Asia: Resource Book*, IWGIA Document No. 123 (Copenhagen: International Work Group for Indigenous Affairs (IWGIA) and Asia Indigenous Peoples Pact Foundation (AIPP), 2008), n.p.; Rhett A. Butler, "In Landmark Ruling, Indonesia's Indigenous People Win Right to Millions of Hectares of Forest," Mongabay, accessed February 2, 2023, https://news.mongabay.com/2013/05/in-landmark-ruling-indonesias-indigenous- people-win-right-to-millions-of-hectares-of-forest/.

13 Adriaan Bedner and Yance Arizona, "Adat in Indonesian Land Law: A Promise for the Future or a Dead End?" *The Asia Pacific Journal of Anthropology* 20, no. 5 (2019): 416–434.

14 Nancy Lee Peluso, *Rich Forests, Poor People: Forest Access Control and Resistance in Java* (Los Angeles: University of California Press, 1992), 50.

ownership cannot be proven by a person, then the land becomes state land. This is what is known as the *domein declaration*. Most of these lands are forest lands. In addition, the *Forestry Law* also criminalises and restricts indigenous communities' access to live within forest areas.[15] Many people have experienced expulsion.[16] The colonial ruler only believed that government officials could control and manage forest areas and resources. Local people were considered a threat, even though most of them have lived in the forest areas for generations.

Although Indonesia became an independent country in 1945, the new *Forestry Law* created in 1967 inherited the colonial forestry legal regime against communities, particularly against indigenous communities who lived and depended on forest resources. Similarly, when the Government enacted a new forestry law in 1999, this law began to mention the existence of customary forests for indigenous peoples but still considered that customary forests were part of state forests, not as a separate category of rights.

Such forestry regulations have caused many forest and land tenure conflicts in Indonesia. This problem was never resolved because of the lack of legal protection for indigenous peoples' rights. At the same time, the Government continuously used state law as a base to expand its land claim toward indigenous territories. New hope came after the amendment of the 1945 Constitution (1999–2002). Political reforms in Indonesia in 1998 prompted the implementation of constitutional amendments. The People's Consultative Assembly, as the constitution-making body, added several new clauses that strengthened indigenous peoples' rights into the Constitution.

The second amendment to the 1945 Constitution in 2000 began to regulate indigenous peoples' rights more explicitly. Article 18B Paragraph (2) of the 1945 Constitution states that: "The State recognises and respects the customary law community units and their traditional rights as long as they are alive and following the development of society and the principles of the Unitary State of the Republic of Indonesia, which are regulated in law." In addition, Article 28I Paragraph (3) of the 1945 Constitution uses the term 'traditional communities': "The cultural identity and rights of traditional communities are respected in line with the development of times and civilisations." Although both provisions recognise the existence and rights of indigenous peoples with different

15 Ibid., 44.
16 Ibid.

names and some conditions, currently, the Constitution adopts indigenous rights provisions that can be used as a basis for reviewing national legislation.[17]

The case study on Indonesia in this chapter will focus on the definition and recognition of indigenous peoples' rights in the forestry and plantation sectors.[18] This is because the development of the *Forestry Law* is strongly influenced by colonial laws that discriminated against indigenous communities. While the *Plantation Law* is important because the current Government provides significant support to the establishment of plantation estate, especially for palm oil, this land expansion supported by the *Plantation Law* generates pervasive land conflict involving many indigenous peoples. Many forestry and plantation conflicts occur between indigenous communities against state agencies and corporations. Local communities involved in such conflicts refer to indigeneity as the basis for their land claims. Several Constitutional Court decisions have become landmark decisions related to the legal status and rights of indigenous peoples in these fields, which will be discussed in the following section.

2.2 *The Contribution of the Indonesian Constitutional Court to the Recognition of Indigenous Rights: An Overview of Leading Cases*

Two Constitutional Court rulings against the *Forestry Law* are landmark decisions whose significant influence goes beyond the realm of forestry issues. These two rulings generate a fundamental change in the core of colonial forestry law that has persisted in an independent Indonesia for decades. The first ruling is related to the status of customary forests, which the Government has ignored for many centuries. Meanwhile, the other ruling is related to eliminating the applicability of forestry crimes to communities living in forest areas for a long time and using forest resources for their subsistence needs. A Constitutional Court ruling related to plantations is also discussed in this section. This ruling limits the criminal provisions of the Plantation Law if the conflicted plantation land is attributed to the customary rights of indigenous peoples. The Constitutional Court suggested that in situations of land conflicts,

17 Yance Arizona, "Indigeneity in the Indonesian Constitution," in *Constitutional Democracy in Indonesia*, ed. Melissa Crouch (Oxford: Oxford University Press, 2022), 197–216.

18 We did not include the mining sector in the chapter. Although NGOs advocacy related to mining problems that violate indigenous community rights is common in Indonesia, no case in the Constitutional Court that supports the protection of indigenous peoples' rights in the mining sector has ever been granted. Conflicts between indigenous peoples, companies and governments are more prevalent in the forestry and plantation sectors.

TABLE 7.1 Constitutional Court ruling number 35/PUU-X/2012

Before the Constitutional Court ruling	After the Constitutional Court ruling
Article 1 point 6 of the Forestry Law "Customary forests are state forests located within the territory of indigenous peoples."	Article 1 point 6 of the Forestry Law "Customary forests are forests located within the territory of indigenous peoples."

criminal approaches must be set aside first to resolve conflicts over plantation land claims.

2.1.1 Separation of Customary Forest and State Forest (Case Number No. 35/PUU-X/2012)

The applicants in Case No. 35/PUU-X/2012 consisted of AMAN (the Alliance of Indigenous Peoples of the Archipelago), the Kuntu community and the Cisitu Kasepuhan community. AMAN is Indonesia's largest indigenous community organisation, consisting of more than 2,000 communities across the country. The main concern of this case is the legal status of customary forests within the scope of the *Forestry Law*. Historically, customary forests have been neglected by the colonial and subsequent national governments for centuries. The newest Forestry Law (Number 41/1999) began recognising customary forests, albeit with problematic provisions. Article 1 point 6 of the *Forestry Law* states, "Customary forests are *state* forests located within the territory of indigenous peoples." The provision stating that customary forests are part of the state's forests created a denial of the existence of customary forests. In fact, before the case was decided by the Constitutional Court, none of the customary forests had been granted recognition by the Government.

The applicants argued that the customary forests should be separated into a special forest category in contrast to state forests and rights forests (i.e., forest located in other type of land rights such as ownership rights and land use rights). In doing so, they asked the Constitutional Court to erase the word 'state' in Article 1 point 6 above, demanding the revision of the definition of customary forest. The applicants and the Government brought experts and witnesses to testify before the Court. In 2013, the Constitutional Court granted the application and redefined customary forest by establishing a clear separation between customary forests and state forests.

In its legal considerations, the Constitutional Court examined the Forestry Law provisions in light of the Constitution and international law. The Constitutional Court argued that the provision in question contradicted Article 18B (2) of the Constitution. Moreover, the Constitutional Court cited the 1992 *Rio Declaration on Environment and Development*, especially Principle 22, which states the importance of the role of indigenous communities in environmental management and protection. Consequently, the Government is required to support indigenous communities in their active participation in sustainable development. By referencing international instruments, the Constitutional Court aligned the concept of indigenous peoples used in international law with the customary law communities recognized in the Indonesian Constitution.

For AMAN and indigenous communities in Indonesia, the Constitutional Court's ruling is a significant victory. Hundreds of indigenous communities in various places put up signposts in the forests they traditionally occupy, bearing the inscription: "Based on the Constitutional Court Decision Number 35/PUU-X/2012, this customary forest is no longer a state forest." Indigenous peoples are demanding that the Government return about 40 million hectares of indigenous territories that the Government has already claimed as state forests.[19] The Minister of Environment and Forestry followed the Constitutional Court's decision by issuing a Ministerial Regulation on Customary Forests. However, the process for the return or determination of customary forests is not an easy one. The determination of customary forests by the Minister of Forestry entails a long and complex procedure.

As of 2022, the Minister of Environment and Forestry has only designated 148,488 hectares of customary forests for 105 indigenous communities. This is still very far from the target and the actual condition of customary forests. The Customary Territory Registration Agency (BRWA), an NGO that collects participatory maps made by indigenous communities, had recorded 26 million indigenous territories in Indonesia as of 2022. When comparing these figures, it is evident that the Government's efforts to establish customary forests as a follow-up to the Constitutional Court's decision remain very limited.

2.1.2 Exemption of Criminal Provisions for Indigenous and Local Communities (Case Number 95/PUU-XII/2014)

The second case is related to the judicial review of criminal provisions in the *Forestry Law* (Number 41/1999) and the *Law on the Prevention and Eradication of Forest Destruction* (Number 18/2013). The applicants, in this case, were ten

19 See Butler, "In Landmark Ruling."

parties consisting of indigenous communities, individuals, and NGOs. The applicants argued that the enactment of criminal provisions in the *Forestry Law* and the *Law on Prevention and Eradication of Forest Destruction* led to the criminalisation of communities living within and around forest areas. In Indonesia, many indigenous and local communities live around forest areas, which is illegal according to the *Forestry Law*. Statistics Indonesia (*Badan Pusat Statistik*, BPS) released census results stating that 31,957 (or 71.06%) of villages in Indonesia are located in the vicinity of forest areas. In 2014, the Ministry of Environment and Forestry (MoEF) conducted a forestry survey that found 32,447,851 people depend on forest resources for their livelihoods. Most of them are living in poverty. According to their local customs, they have been cultivating land and gathering products from the forests.

In Indonesia, land conflict is omnipresent. The NGO Agrarian Reform Consortium (*Konsorsium Pembaruan Agraria*, KPA) recorded 2,047 land conflict cases from 2015 to 2019. In 2019 alone, there were 279 land conflicts covering an estimated area of 734,239 hectares, affecting around 109,042 households in 420 villages across Indonesia. In 2021, the MoEF received 500 reports on land conflicts in the forestry sector. Only 54 of these have been solved between the conflicting parties.[20] The forestry tenure conflicts arise because of the *Forestry Law*, which ignores the existence of indigenous and local communities who have long inhabited the land that the Government later designated as forest areas.[21]

The applicants, in this case, asked the Constitutional Court to annul Article 50 paragraph (3) points *e* and *i* of the *Forestry Law*. However, the Constitutional Court decided that Article 50 paragraph (3) points *e* and *i* of the *Forestry Law* would be exempted for people who have lived in forest areas for generations and engage in activities such as tree cutting, harvesting, collecting forest products, and raising livestock in forest areas for non-commercial purposes. The Constitutional Court argued that people who live for generations in the forest need clothing, food, and shelter for their daily needs, and they must be protected by the state, rather than being threatened with criminal penalties.

---

20 "Jumlah Penanganan Pengaduan [Number of Complaint Handling]," Direktorat Jenderal Perhutanan Sosial dan Kemitraan Lingkungan Kementerian Lingkungan Hidup dan Kehutanan [Directorate General of Social Forestry and Environmental Partnerships Ministry of Environment and Forestry], accessed November 30, 2021, http://pskl.menlhk.go.id/pktha/pengaduan/frontend/web/index.php?r=site%2Fjumlahpenanganan-pengaduan.

21 Peluso, *Rich Forests, Poor People*, 44.

TABLE 7.2 The Constitutional Court ruling number 95/PUU-XII/2014

Before the Constitutional Court ruling	After the Constitutional Court ruling
Article 50 paragraph (3) letter *e* and letter *i* of the Forestry Law Article 50 paragraph (3) Every person is prohibited from: *e.* cutting down trees or harvesting or collecting forest products in the forest without holding any rights or license issued by the authorised agency; *i.* herding livestock within forest areas not specifically designated for such purposes by the authorised agency;	Article 50 paragraph (3) letter *e* and letter *i* of the Forestry Law Article 50 paragraph (3) Every person is prohibited from: *e.* cutting down trees or harvesting or collecting forest products in the forest without holding any rights or license issued by the authorised agency, *except for people who live for generations in the forest and if not intended for commercial purposes.* *i.* herding livestock within forest areas not specifically designated for such purposes by authorised officials, *except for people who live for generations in the forest and if not intended for commercial purposes;*

People who have lived in forest areas for generations, known as heredity communities, are not subjected to the criminal provision in the Forestry Law. The Constitutional Court stated that this exemption applies to people living within the forest, rather than communities located "around the forest area." The Constitutional Court did not specify the difference between people who "live within the forest" and people who are "around the forest area." However, to provide a clear understanding, the definition of "people living within the forest" must be linked to their livelihood, especially their dependence on the forest for their basic needs such as clothing, food, and shelter, as considered by the Constitutional Court. Therefore, people who live within the forest do not have to be a community whose houses are built within the forest but local community members whose livelihoods depend on forest land and resources. In short, only people with a strong life relationship with the forest, beyond economic relations, are exempted from the criminal provisions. Another criterion for the exemption is that local communities only use forest land and resources for non-commercial activities. This condition is essential to avoid the over-exploitation of forest resources by local community members, which can lead to forest degradation.

2.1.3 Restricting Criminal Provisions in Situations of Land Conflict between Indigenous Communities and Plantation Companies (Case Number 55/PUU-VIII/2010)

The petitioners in this case were four farmers and indigenous peoples: Japin, Vitalis Andi, Sakri and Ngatimin. The subject of the petition, in this case, relates to plantation criminal provisions in the *Plantation Law* (Number 18/2004) that are often imposed on indigenous and local communities in conflict with plantation companies. A common condition in Indonesia is that the Government grants concessions to plantation companies on land claimed by indigenous peoples. Granting plantation concessions is usually conducted without the consent and compensation of indigenous peoples. The problem is that when indigenous peoples fight for their rights, they are subject to criminal provisions because they disturb plantation activities carried out by companies.

The petitioners challenged the constitutionality of Article 21 of the *Plantation Law*, which stated that: "Everyone is prohibited from taking actions that result in damage to plantations and/or other assets, use of plantation land without permission and/or other actions that result in disruption of plantation business." As well as Article 47, which provides a penalty of 5 years in prison for people who violate Article 21 of the *Plantation Law*.

The Constitutional Court concluded that Article 21 and Article 47 of the Plantation Law, which have been used as the basis for criminalizing local and indigenous peoples who conflict with plantation companies, have the potential to be misused arbitrarily. In particular, the phrase "disturbing plantation business" in Article 21 of the *Plantation Law* can be interpreted very broadly by the police to arrest local and indigenous peoples. According to the Constitutional Court, this provision is contrary to the principles of a just rule of law, legal certainty, the principle of legality and the principle of predictability, as well as the protection of human rights in general.[22]

The Constitutional Court then decided that the implementation of criminal provisions in the Plantation Law must consider the context of plantation conflicts that occur between communities and plantation companies. Thus, if there are indigenous peoples' claims to conflicting land, what needs to be completed first is to resolve the conflict claims, not impose criminal provisions on

22 Yance Arizona, *Konstitutionalisme Agraria* (STPN Press, 2014), p. 253–9.

the community. Regarding the legality of plantation land, the Constitutional Court encourages the identification and mapping of customary territories claimed by indigenous peoples by the Government in advance. In other words, the actual confirmation of the existence of indigenous communities must first be carried out before haphazardly applying criminalization provisions in handling plantation conflicts.

3 A Comparative Assessment of Indigenous Rights

This section provides a comparative lens through which situate the contribution of the CCI in the recognition of indigenous title and customary law. The purpose here is not to conduct a thorough analysis of Canadian and international legal frameworks, but rather to provide a comparative prism through which the leading jurisprudence of the CCI on the topic can be viewed.

3.1 *Indigenous Rights in Canada: A General Overview of the Legal Framework*

"Indigenous peoples" in Canada include the Mi'kmaq, Mohawk, Anishnabe, Cree, Dakota, Piikani, Kainaiwa, Inuit, Dene, Haida nations.[23] The early Canadian settlers were mostly from France and England. Before the arrival of the settlers, the indigenous peoples had their respective laws, practices, customs, and traditions.[24] Over time, the relationship of coexistence evolved from trade alliances to land treaties. The land treaties were considered "private purchases of land from the Indigenous peoples" in the name of the British Crown, as noted in the *Royal Proclamation, 1763* after the conquest of New France.[25]

The *Constitution Act, 1867* (i.e., *British North America Act*) was based on a division of powers between the federal and provincial legislatures. Section 91(24) provides for "the exclusive Legislative Authority of the Parliament of Canada" over "Indians, and Lands reserved for the Indians." In doing so, the

23 OECD, "Overview of Indigenous Governance in Canada: Evolving Relations and Key Issues and Debates," in *Linking Indigenous Communities with Regional Development in Canada*, ed. OECD (Paris: OECD Publishing, 2020), 37–65.

24 John Borrows, "Indigenous Constitutionalism: Pre-Existing Legal Genealogies in Canada," in *The Oxford Handbook of the Canadian Constitution*, eds. Peter Oliver, Patrick Macklem, and Nathalie Des Rosiers, 1st ed. (Oxford University Press, 2017), 13–44.

25 Sébastien Grammond, "Treaties as Constitutional Agreements," in *The Oxford Handbook of the Canadian Constitution*, eds. Peter Oliver, Patrick Macklem, and Nathalie Des Rosiers, 1st ed. (Oxford University Press, 2017), 308–309.

Indian Act, 1876 dealt primarily with reserve lands and "Indian" status. From 1871 to 1921, the federal Government contracted a series of eleven treaties, commonly called the *Numbered Treaties,*[26] to acquire land of the indigenous peoples, mainly from the Prairies.[27] These treaties have been controversial because the latter claim they never intended "to surrender title to their lands."[28]

The Canadian judicial system first recognized "the binding force of treaty rights and Aboriginal title" in contemporary Canadian law.[29] Section 35(1) of the *Constitution Act, 1982* stipulates that "the existing aboriginal and treaty rights of the aboriginal peoples of Canada are hereby recognized and affirmed."

Section 35(2) defines "aboriginal peoples" as including "Indian, Inuit and Métis peoples," while Section 35(3) provides that "'treaty' rights includes rights that now exist by way of land claim agreements or [that] may be so acquired." The *Act* also introduces a commitment by the provincial and federal governments to "invite representatives of the aboriginal peoples of Canada to participate" in the constitutional conference concerning the amendment of Section 91(24) of the *Constitution Act, 1867* or Sections 25 and 35 of the *Constitution Act, 1982* (Section 35.1). While Section 35 does not expressly define indigenous rights, the evolving jurisprudence of the Supreme Court of Canada has clarified those rights to include the right to land, to hunt and fish, to establish treaties as well as a range of economic, cultural and political rights.[30]

Ravna and Bankes explain the approach to the recognition of aboriginal title as:

> the tribes, Indians, First Nations and Inuit have long been the subject of a special legal status in Canada. This is reflected in the terms of the Royal Proclamation of 1763, the pre-confederation (1867) version of the Indian Act, the "Indians" provision of the British North America Act, 1867 (which afforded the federal parliament the power to make laws in relation to Indians and land reserved for Indians), and the post-confederation versions of the Indian Act. Thus there is a long tradition of crafting special

26 Government of Canada, Crown-Indigenous Relations and Northern Affairs, "Indigenous Peoples and Communities," published January 12, 2009, https://www.rcaanc-cirnac.gc.ca/eng/1100100013785/1529102490303.

27 Grammond, "Treaties," 310–311.

28 Ibid, 311.

29 Jeremy Webber, "Contending Sovereignties," in *The Oxford Handbook of the Canadian Constitution*, eds. Peter Oliver, Patrick Macklem, and Nathalie Des Rosiers (Oxford University Press, 2017), 282.

30 Borrows, "Indigenous Constitutionalism," 35.

> legislative regimes and applying them to indigenous communities. A *sui generis* approach to the recognition of aboriginal title may fit well within this approach to law making and this intellectual tradition.[31]

Ravna and Bankes explain that "[d]eeply embedded in the modern aboriginal rights jurisprudence of the Canadian courts is the recognition that traditional lands were not just occupied at the time of settlement but they were occupied by indigenous societies living in accordance with their own laws."[32]

More recently, the Government of Canada has adopted the "Principles respecting the Government of Canada's relationship with Indigenous peoples" and an "Indigenous Justice Strategy"[33] to address systemic discrimination, in consultation with indigenous partners. Furthermore, the *United Nations Declaration on the Rights of Indigenous Peoples Act* received Royal Assent and came into force in Canada in 2021.[34] In June 2023, the Canadian Government released the UN Declaration Action Plan, which was developed in cooperation with First Nations, Inuit and Métis from across Canada.[35]

4 The International Legal Framework as Applied in the Indonesian Context

Indigenous peoples' rights are recognised within the framework of international law through various regional and international conventions and declarations. The international framework comprises the *International Covenant on Civil and Political Rights* (ICCPR) and the *International Labour Organization Convention 169 concerning Indigenous and Tribal Peoples and Independent Countries* (ILO 169), which provide protections for traditional aboriginal lands.

Indigenous rights have also been recognised gradually under the larger framework of international human rights conventions and mechanisms. Article 27 of the ICCPR recognises that ethnic, religious and linguistic minorities have the right to enjoy their culture. The Human Rights Committee, in its General Comment No. 23 (*Art. 27, CCPR/C/21, 8 April 1994*), has held that the

31 Ravna and Banks, "Recogniton of Indigenous," 115.

32 Ibid., 116-117.

33 Government of Canada, Department of Justice, "Indigenous Justice Strategy," accessed August 10, 2023, https://www.justice.gc.ca/eng/csj-sjc/ijr-dja/ijs-sja/index.html.

34 Government of Canada, "Implementing the United Nations," accessed May 10, 2023, https://www.justice.gc.ca/eng/declaration/index.html.

35 Ibid.

right to culture includes access to land, natural resources and fisheries essential for the livelihood of minorities. Indonesia and Canada are parties to the ICCPR, while ILO 169, which they have not ratified, imposes an obligation on states parties to recognize indigenous peoples' traditional land ownership.

Furthermore, regional human rights conventions have been interpreted to include the obligation for states to demarcate and grant legal titles to the lands of indigenous peoples within their territories.[36] In regional contexts, within the Inter-American system of human rights protection, the *American Convention on Human Rights*[37] as well as the *American Declaration on the Rights and Duties of Man*[38] have been interpreted by both the Inter-American Court of Human Rights and the Inter-American Commission of Human Rights in the context of recognising indigenous rights.[39] As such, the Inter-American Court of Human Rights has delivered significant decisions on indigenous rights.[40] Furthermore, as Newman states, there have been regional recognition of Indigenous rights, "with regional treaties on Indigenous rights being able to focus on issues that escape international attention and thus [are] ongoing complements to the globalized international body of Indigenous rights law, with the American Declaration on the Rights of Indigenous Peoples (ADRIP) being a key example."[41] More recently, the *United Nations Declaration on the Rights of Indigenous Peoples* recognized the rights of Indigenous peoples to their traditional lands, territories and resources, as stated in Article 26. The Declaration also addresses the recognition and adjudication of traditional indigenous lands claims.

The development of international law on indigenous peoples became the inspiration for indigenous peoples activists to encourage national legislative reform. In Indonesia, indigenous organizations are advocating the Government to create a special law on indigenous peoples' rights. They have been urging the Parliament since 2011,[42] and discussions on the bill addressing indigenous

36 Ravna and Bankes, "Recognition of Indigenous," 71–72.

37 Adopted at the Inter-American Specialized Conference on Human Rights, San José, Costa Rica, 22 November 1969, 1144 UNTS 123.

38 Adopted by the Ninth International Conference of American States, Bogotá, Columbia, 2 May 1948, OAS Doc. oea/Ser.L.V/ii.82 doc.6 rev.1 (1992), p. 17.

39 Ravna and Bankes, "Recognition of Indigenous," 71–72.

40 See Tom Antkowiak, "Rights, Resources and Rhetoric: Indigenous Peoples and the Inter-American Court" (2013) 35 *U Penn J Int'l L* 113.

41 Newman, "Chapter 1: Internationalization of the Law of Indigenous Rights," 3. See *American Declaration on the Rights of Indigenous Peoples*, OAS AG/RES.2888 (XLVI-O/16), adopted at the Organisation of American States 3rd plenary session, 15 June 2016.

42 Yance Arizona and Erasmus Cahyadi, "The Revival of Indigenous Peoples: Contestations over a Special Legislation on Indigenous Peoples," in *Adat and Indigeneity in Indonesia: Culture and Entitlements between Heteronomy and Self-Ascription*, ed. Brigitta

peoples' rights have been taking place for more than a decade. Up until now, a special law on indigenous peoples' rights has not materialized because of a lack of political support in the Parliament. Indigenous peoples' organizations hope that the Indigenous Peoples Bill will become a means to incorporate the latest advancements concerning indigenous peoples contained in international law.

In Decision Number 35/PUU-X/2012 regarding the *Forestry Law*, discussed in section 2 of this chapter, the CCI confirmed the need for the establishment of a special law on indigenous peoples as mandated by Article 18B (2) of the Indonesian Constitution. However, according to the Constitutional Court, the existing fragmented legislation on indigenous peoples, found in various sectoral laws, such as mining, forestry, and coastal regulations, could be deemed valid until the enactment of the special law.

The CCI also refers to international environmental law to strengthen the rights of indigenous peoples that have been included in the national Constitution. Furthermore, the Constitutional Court confirmed that the concept of indigenous peoples is commensurate with customary law communities in the Indonesian context. This CCI ruling gives a different notion to the general attitude of the Indonesian Ministry of Foreign Affairs when attending international meetings discussing indigenous peoples. The use of international environmental law instruments to strengthen indigenous peoples' rights is in line with the assumption that indigenous peoples are guardians of the environment.[43]

5 Conclusion

This chapter provided an assessment of Indonesian law concerning indigenous communities and land rights. Using international law as the lens through which the Indonesian leading cases were analysed, it can be seen that the judicial rulings have a major impact on the development of indigenous rights.

Developments in international law regarding indigenous rights have also had a significant impact in Indonesia. The jurisprudence of the CCI is inspired by international environmental law and the UNDRIP. Interestingly, the CCI looks to international law to further protect the rights of indigenous peoples which are protected in the Indonesian Constitution.

Hauser-Schäublin, Göttingen Studies in Cultural Property, vol. 7 (Göttingen: Göttingen University, 2013).

43 Anna L. Tsing, "Indigenous Voice," in *Indigenous Experience Today*, eds. Marisol de La Cadena and Orin Starn (London: Routledge, 2007), 48.

The Constitutional Court altered the concept of colonial law that is still inherent in national forestry law. In doing so, the Constitutional Court decolonized the inherent colonial elements in the law by strengthening the rights of indigenous peoples in Indonesia. The Constitutional Court resolved not only the concrete problems of injustice encountered by indigenous peoples but also generated legal reform. While in some countries, landmark court decisions can be followed up by the enactment of new legislation and institutions to realize indigenous peoples' rights, in Indonesia, such influences are still very limited.

The chapter has traced the major role that the CCI has had in defining the contours of indigenous peoples' rights within Indonesian society. It analyses the landmark decisions of the CCI, and concludes that international law has had a positive impact on the development of the Court's jurisprudence and the recognition of customary land rights within Indonesia.

Bibliography

Act on United Nations Declaration on the Rights of Indigenous Peoples Act, S.C. 2021, c. 14.

American Convention on Human Rights, Adopted at the Inter-American Specialized Conference on Human Rights, San José, Costa Rica, 22 November 1969, 1144 UNTS 123.

American Declaration on the Rights and Duties of Man, Adopted by the Ninth International Conference of American States, Bogotá, Columbia, 2 May 1948, OAS Doc. OEA/Ser.L.V/ii.82 doc.6 rev.1 (1992), p. 17.

American Declaration on the Rights of Indigenous Peoples, OAS AG/RES.2888 (XLVI-O/16), adopted at the Organisation of American States 3rd plenary session, 15 June 2016.

Anaya, James. *Indigenous Peoples in International Law*. New York: Oxford University Press, 2004.

Arizona, Yance. *Konstitutionalisme Agraria*. STPN Press, 2014.

Arizona, Yance. "Indigeneity in the Indonesian Constitution." In *Constitutional Democracy in Indonesia*, edited by Melissa Crouch. Oxford University Press, 2022.

Arizona, Yance. "*Rethinking Adat Strategies: The Politics of State Recognition of Customary Land Rights in Indonesia.*" PhD thesis, Leiden Law School, the Netherlands, 2022.

Arizona, Yance and Erasmus Cahyadi. "The Revival of Indigenous Peoples: Contestations over a Special Legislation on Masyarakat Adat." In *Adat and Indigeneity in Indonesia: Culture and Entitlements between Heteronomy and Self-Ascription*, edited by Brigitta Hauser-Schäublin, Göttingen Studies in Cultural Property, Vol. 7. Göttingen University, 2013.

Australian Government Department of Foreign Affairs and Trade. "Text of the Apology to the Stolen Generations." Accessed February 22, 2023. https://www.dfat.gov.au/people-to-people/public-diplomacy/programs-activities/Pages/text-of-the-apology-to-the-stolen-generation.

Baird, Ian G. "Indigeneity in Asia: An Emerging but Contested Concept." Asian Ethnicity 17, no 4 (2016): 501–505.

Bankes, Nigel. "The Implications of the Tsilhqot'in (William) and Grassy Narrows (Keewatin) Decisions of the Supreme Court of Canada for the Natural Resources Industries." *Journal of Energy and Natural Resources Law* 33, no. 3 (2015): 188–217. https://doi.org/10.1080/02646811.2015.1030916.

Bedner, Adriaan and Stijn van Huis. "The Return of the Native in Indonesian Law: Indigenous Communities in Indonesian Legislation." *Bijdragen tot de taal-, land- en volkenkunde* [*Journal of the Humanities and Social Sciences of Southeast Asia*] 164, no. 2 (2008): 165–193.

Bedner, Adriaan and Yance Arizona. "Adat in Indonesian Land Law: A Promise for the Future or a Dead End?" *The Asia Pacific Journal of Anthropology* 20, no. 5 (2019): 416–434.

Birrell, Kathleen. *Indigeneity: Before and Beyond the Law*. New York: Routledge, 2016.

Borrows, John. "Indigenous Constitutionalism: Pre-Existing Legal Genealogies in Canada." In *The Oxford Handbook of the Canadian Constitution*, edited by Peter Oliver, Patrick Macklem and Nathalie Des Rosiers, 1st ed., 13–44. Oxford University Press, 2017. https://doi.org/10.1093/law/9780190664817.003.0002.

Brennan, K., Megan Davis, Brendan Edgeworth and Leon Terrill (eds). "The Idea of Native Title as a Vehicle for Change and Indigenous Empowerment." In *Native Title from Mabo to Akiba: A Vehicle for Change and Empowerment?*, edited by Brendan Edgeworth, Leon Terrill, Megan David and Sean Brennan, Federation Press, 2015.

Canada. Indian Act, RSC 1985, c I-5.

Coates, Ken and Carin Holroyd, "Chapter 4: The Emergence and Evolution of the Global Indigenous Rights Movement" In *Research Handbook on the International Law of Indigenous Rights*. Cheltenham, UK: Edward Elgar Publishing, 2022.

"COP15: Nations Adopt Four Goals, 23 Targets for 2030 In Landmark UN Biodiversity Agreement." *Convention on Biological Diversity* (*cbd.int*). Accessed February 22, 2023. https://www.cbd.int/article/cop15-cbd-press-release-final-19dec2022.

D'andrea, Claudia. *Kopi, Adat dan Modal: Teritorialisasi dan Identitas Adat di Taman Nasional Lore Lindu Sulawesi Tengah* [*Coffee, Custom and Capital: Territorialization and Indigenous Identity in Central Sulawesi's Lore Lindu National Park*]. Yogyakarta: Sayogyo Institut, Tanah Air Beta, Yayasan Tanah Merdeka, 2013.

Delgamuukw v. British Columbia, [1997] 3 S.C.R. 1010 (1997).

Edgeworth, Brendan. "The Mabo 'Vibe' and Its Many Resonances in Australian Property Law." In *Native Title from Mabo to Akiba: A Vehicle for Change and Empowerment,* edited by Brendan Edgeworth, Leon Terrill, Megan Davis, and Sean Brennan. Birmingham: Federation Press, 2015.

Erni, Christian (ed). *The Concept of Indigenous Peoples in Asia: Resource Book.* IWGIA Document No. 123. Copenhagen: International Work Group for Indigenous Affairs (IWGIA) and Asia Indigenous Peoples Pact Foundation (AIPP). Denmark: International Work Group for Indigenous Affairs, 2008.

Gover, Kirsty Benedict Kingsbury. "Editorial Note in Indigenous Groups and the Politics of Recognition in Asia: Cases from Japan, Taiwan, West Papua, Bali, the Republic of China, and Gilgit." *International Journal of Minority and Group Rights* 11: 1–2.

Government of Canada. "Department of Justice – Principles Respecting the Government of Canada's Relationship with Indigenous Peoples." Accessed July 14, 2017. https://www.justice.gc.ca/eng/csj-sjc/principles-principes.html.

Government of Canada. "Implementing the United Nations Declaration on the Rights of Indigenous People Act." Accessed April 12, 2021. https://www.justice.gc.ca/eng/declaration/index.html.

Government of Canada, Crown-Indigenous Relations and Northern Affairs. "Indigenous Peoples and Communities." Published January 12, 2009. https://www.rcaanc-cirnac.gc.ca/eng/1100100013785/1529102490303.

Government of Canada. Department of Justice. 2017. "Indigenous Justice Strategy." Accessed February 10, 2017. https://www.justice.gc.ca/eng/csj-sjc/ijr-dja/ijs-sja/index.html.

Government of Canada, Indigenous and Northern Affairs. "The Numbered Treaties (1871–1921)." Published February 15, 2013. https://www.rcaanc-cirnac.gc.ca/eng/1360948213124/1544620003549.

Grammond, Sébastien. "Treaties as Constitutional Agreements." In *The Oxford Handbook of the Canadian Constitution*, edited by Peter Oliver, Patrick Macklem and Nathalie Des Rosiers, 257–278. 1st ed. Oxford University Press, 2017.

Guerin v. The Queen, 1984 CanLII 25 (SCC), [1984] 2 SCR 335 (1984).

Haddock, Leslie and Kent McNeil. *Bibliography on Indigenous Rights in Canada.* Toronto: York University, 2022.

Haida Nation v. British Columbia (Minister of Forests), [2004] 3 S.C.R. 511, 2004 SCC 73 (2004).

"Jumlah Penanganan Pengaduan [Number of Complaint Handling]." Direktorat Jenderal Perhutanan Sosial dan Kemitraan Lingkungan Kementerian Lingkungan Hidup dan Kehutanan [Directorate General of Social Forestry and Environmental Partnerships Ministry of Environment and Forestry], accessed November 30, 2021. http://pskl.menlhk.go.id/pktha/pengaduan/frontend/web/index.php?r=site%2Fjumlahpenanganan-pengaduan.

Macklem, Patrick. "The Form and Substance of Aboriginal Title: Assimilation, Recognition, Reconciliation." In *The Oxford Handbook of the Canadian Constitution*, edited by Peter Oliver, Patrick Macklem and Nathalie Des Rosiers, 325–48. Oxford University Press, 2017.

Newman, Dwight. "The Section 35 Duty to Consult." In *The Oxford Handbook of the Canadian Constitution*, edited by Peter Oliver, Patrick Macklem and Nathalie Des Rosiers, 349–66. Oxford University Press, 2017.

Newman, Dwight. *Research Handbook on the International Law of Indigenous Rights*. Cheltenham, UK: Edward Elgar Publishing, 2022.

Niezen, Ronald. *The Origins of Indigenism: Human Rights and the Politics of Identity*. Berkeley, CA: University of California Press, 2003.

OECD. "Overview of Indigenous Governance in Canada: Evolving Relations and Key Issues and Debates." In *Linking Indigenous Communities with Regional Development in Canada*, edited by OECD, 37–65. Paris: OECD Publishing, 2020.

Peluso, Nancy Lee. *Rich Forests, Poor People: Forest Access Control and Resistance in Java*. Los Angeles: University of California Press, 1992.

Persoon, Gerard. "Isolated groups or indigenous peoples; Indonesia and the international discourse." *Bijdragen tot de Taal-, Land- en Volkenkunde* [*Journal of the Humanities and Social Sciences of Southeast Asia and Oceania*] 154. no. 2 (1998): 281–304.

Ravna, Øyvind and Nigel Bankes. "Recognition of Indigenous Land Rights in Norway and Canada." *International Journal on Minority and Group Rights* 24, no. 1 (2017): 70–117.

REDD. "Indonesia's Response to the United Nations Human Rights Council Universal Periodic Review." Accessed March 7, 2021. http://redd-monitor.org/wp-content/uploads/2012/10/indonesias-response-tounpr.pdf.

Royal Proclamation of 1763. 1763. Primary Documents. October 7. https://primarydocuments.ca/royal-proclamation-1763/.

Schedule B to the Canada Act 1982 (UK), 1982, c 11 | The Constitution Act, 1982'. CanLII, n.d.

Senwung, Luk. "The Law of the Land: New Jurisprudence on Aboriginal Title." *The Supreme Court Law Review: Osgoode's Annual Constitutional Cases Conference* 67, no. 1–8 (2014): 289–317.

Slattery, Brian. "The Constitutional Dimensions of Aboriginal Title." *The Supreme Court Law Review: Osgoode's Annual Constitutional Cases Conference* 71, no. 1–3 (2015): 45–66.

The Constitution Act, 1867, 30 & 31 Vict, c 3, CanLII.

Thornberry, Patrick. *Indigenous Peoples and Human Rights*. Manchester: Manchester University Press, 2013.

Tom Antkowiak, "Rights, Resources and Rhetoric: Indigenous Peoples and the Inter-American Court" (2013) 35 *U Penn J Int'l L* 113.Tsing, Anna L. "Indigenous Voice." In *Indigenous Experience Today*, edited by Marisol de La Cadena and Orin Starn. London: Routledge, 2007.

United Nations. "Resolution Adopted by the General Assembly on 13 September 2007." Report, United Nation, 2007.

Webber, Jeremy. "Contending Sovereignties." In *The Oxford Handbook of the Canadian Constitution*, edited by Peter Oliver, Patrick Macklem and Nathalie Des Rosiers. Oxford University Press, 2017.

CHAPTER 8

The 'Right' to Free, Prior and Informed Consent: Evolving Customary International Law

George Barrie

Abstract

In the 1990s, international law experienced significant judicial development regarding claims by indigenous people, particularly in the Americas and then spreading to Africa. These claims were prompted by the increasing global demand for natural resources. This demand led to resource exploitation in territories traditionally occupied by indigenous peoples, who in most instances were heavily dependent on their natural environment. Such exploitation impacted severely on the lives of indigenous peoples, especially their rights to property, culture, religion, physical well-being, clean environment and the right to pursue their own priorities regarding their development – all rights emanating from the right to self-determination. This right to self-determination is a cardinal principle of international law and in an evolutionary way has given rise to the concept of Free, Prior and Informed Consent (FPIC). FPIC has been outlined in the UN Declaration on the Rights of Indigenous Peoples (UNDRIP) 2007, which in essence requires that indigenous peoples have the right to accept or reject decisions, especially regarding natural resource exploitation, that affect their lives or territories. UNDRIP is supported by various hard-law and soft-law international instruments. This chapter investigates how FPIC has developed into an emerging rule of customary international law and has resonated in jurisdictions such as Canada, Latin America and Africa – all areas with significant indigenous populations. In the concluding section, the chapter investigates the application of this emerging concept of FPIC by the Indonesian Constitutional Court. The view is expressed that this court sees FPIC as critical to resource development stakeholders – albeit in an implied manner – and sees FPIC as best practice for protecting the rights of indigenous peoples in natural resources projects.

Keywords

customary international law – free – prior and informed consent – indigenous people

 | DOI:10.1163/9789004691698_009

1 Introduction

In the 1990s, international law became an active field of judicial development, especially regarding claims of indigenous peoples at the national level. Such claims were wrapped in language drawn from the rapidly developing international law on self-determination. The shape that international law took during this period was extremely attractive to indigenous people, specifically with regard to land claims. Also during the 1990s, international law and municipal law converged with much of the judicial vocabulary channeled through international institutions. The field of indigenous peoples' rights travelled rapidly from a smattering of norms located in disparate instruments largely associated with the remit of the International Labour Organization (ILO) and as a dimension of minority rights, to being a distinct emerging field demanding the attention of the United Nations (UN). The imprimatur for the UN to become involved was the 1982 UN Working Group on Indigenous Populations, which reviewed developments pertaining to the promotion and protection of the human rights and fundamental freedoms of indigenous populations.

Thirty years later, in 2012, at its Sofia meeting, the International Law Association (ILA) adopted a resolution to produce a report on which rights of indigenous peoples had or had not developed into customary international law. One of the issues it was envisaged to address was that of *consultation* with indigenous peoples. Various articles in the 2008 United Nations Declaration on the Rights of Indigenous Peoples (UNDRIP)[1] make reference to such consultation, especially Article 19, which states:

> States shall consult and cooperate in good faith with the indigenous people concerned through their own representative institutions in order to obtain their free, prior and informed consent before adopting and implementing legislative or administrative measures that may affect them.

It is the purpose of this chapter to set out how the right of consultation and the concomitant right of free, prior and informed consent (FPIC) in decisions which affect indigenous peoples developed into customary international law. How this came about was an evolutionary process. This evolutionary process will be illustrated by reference to resolutions of international organs and case law emanating from Canada, Africa, and the Americas. Due to the constraints

1 UNDRIP is annexed to GA Res. UNGAOR 61st Sess. No 49, vol III, UN Doc A/61/49 (2008) 15. See in general George Barrie, "The United Nations Declaration on the Rights of Indigenous Peoples," *Tydskrif vir die Suid-Afrikaanse Reg* 2 (2013): 292–305.

of fitting above into a single chapter representing such a wide spectrum of jurisprudence relating to diversity and plurality, the chapter will be approached with a broad brush. Space does not allow for an in-depth discussion of the various aspects referred to, especially the case law, but it should at least whet the appetite of interested readers and lead them to more extensive sources.

The general introduction will be followed by sections – some more brief than others – on the meaning of UNDRIP and its legal status; defining indigenous peoples; decisions of Canadian courts; decisions of the African Commission on Human and Peoples' Rights (ACHPR); the role of the inter-American system of human rights; the introduction of FPIC into the Southern African legal lexicon; the role of customary international law; and finally a discussion of two Indonesian Constitutional Court judgements, Decision Number 35/PUU – X / 2012 and Decision Number 95/ PUU – XII / 2014.

2 UNDRIP

Indigenous rights are different from minority rights. Minorities have a right to their culture, education and religion, as indigenous peoples do. But there is a fundamental difference in that indigenous peoples, as distinct communities, have a right to self-determination and a profound relationship with traditional lands and territories. The rights of indigenous peoples to their lands, territories and natural resources and other ancillary rights flow from their right to self-determination.

This realization led to UNDRIP.[2] Article 3 of UNDRIP affirms that "Indigenous peoples have the right to self-determination. By that right they freely determine their political status and freely pursue their economic, social and cultural development." Article 26 of UNDRIP affirms that "Indigenous peoples have the right to the lands, territories and resources which they have traditionally owned, occupied or otherwise used or acquired." Article 10 affirms that indigenous peoples shall not be forcibly removed from their lands and territories and that "no relocations shall take place without the free, prior and informed consent of the indigenous people concerned." Article 32(2) emphatically requires states to "consult and cooperate in good faith with indigenous peoples concerned through their own representative institutions in order to obtain their

2 Margaret Beukes, "The Recognition of 'Indigenous Peoples' and Their Rights as 'People': An African First," *South African Yearbook of International Law* 35 (2010): 216–238.

free and informed consent prior to the approval of any project affecting their lands or territories and other resources."

An important characteristic of UNDRIP is its affirmation of the *collective* rights of indigenous peoples which are "indispensable for their existence, well-being and integral development as a peoples."[3] A 1989 UN report on racism[4] concluded that the effective protection of individual human rights and fundamental freedoms of indigenous peoples cannot be realized without the recognition of their collective rights. For the past five decades, the collective rights of indigenous peoples have been addressed by diverse UN human rights bodies, so it is exceedingly difficult for any UN member state to argue that the collective rights of indigenous peoples are not human rights.

UNDRIP did not create any new rights. It was the harvest of many seeds planted previously as it were. Its foundation stemmed from two conventions drafted by the ILO. First, mention must be made of the Protection and Integration of Indigenous and other Tribal and Semi-Tribal Populations in Independent Countries, known as Convention No. 107 of 1957. Second, most important was the Convention on Indigenous and Tribal Peoples No. 169 of 1989 (ILO Convention 169)[5] which came into force on 5 September 1991. Article 4 of ILO Convention 169 mandates that "special measures shall be adopted as appropriate for safeguarding the persons, institutions, property, labour, culture and environment" of indigenous and tribal peoples, and that "such special measures shall not be contrary to the freely-expressed wishes of the people concerned."

In addition, ILO Convention No 169 in Article 16(2) states that indigenous and tribal peoples shall not be removed from the lands they occupy. If necessary as an exceptional measure, such relocation shall take place only with the free and informed consent. Article 33 requires states to consult with indigenous peoples and ensure their informed participation in decisions pertaining to development, national institutions and programs, cultural protection and resources.

ILO Convention 169 Article 14 was a particular focal point for the elaboration of indigenous rights at international law, especially land rights. It states:

1. The rights of ownership and possession of the peoples concerned over the lands which "they traditionally occupy shall be recognized.

3 Preamble para. 22.

4 UN Doc E/CN 4/1989/22, para. 40(d), United Nations Commission on Human Rights, "Study of the Problem of Discrimination against Indigenous Populations" (Final Report Submitted by Mr. José R. Martínez Cobo, Special Rapporteur).

5 *ILM* 28, 1982 (1989).

In addition, measures shall be taken in appropriate cases to safeguard the right of the peoples concerned to use lands not exclusively occupied by them, but to which they have traditionally have access for their subsistence and traditional activities. Particular attention shall be paid to the situation of nomadic peoples and shifting cultivators in this respect.

2. Governments shall take steps as necessary to identify the lands which the peoples concerned traditionally occupy, and to guarantee effective protection of their rights of ownership and possessions.
3. Adequate procedures shall be established within the national legal system to resolve land claims by the peoples concerned.

During the 1990s and beyond, a series of communications and reports by UN human rights monitoring bodies consistently recognized indigenous peoples' right to their traditional lands and territories, as well as compensation for any expropriation. These recognitions were based on the understanding that such rights are integral to the collective human rights of indigenous communities, ensuring their ability to fully enjoy and practice of their unique cultures.

Reference to consultation, participation and consent of indigenous peoples regarding their development can also be found in the UN Declaration on the Right to Development,[6] which mentions in Article 2(3) that the right to development includes "active, free and meaningful participation in development."[7]

A further example is the UN General Assembly's Programme of Action for the Second International Decade of the World's Indigenous People.[8] One of the objectives of this Programme was in "promoting full and effective participation of indigenous peoples in decisions which directly or indirectly affect their lifestyles, traditional lands or territories, their cultural identity as indigenous peoples with collective rights or any other aspect of their lives, considering the principle of free, prior and informed consent."

This basically echoes the stance of the Committee on the Elimination of Racial Discrimination (CERD), which, in its General Recommendation XXIII

6 UN GAOR 41st Sess. Doc A/Res/41/128 (1986), "Declaration on the Right to Development," adopted by the United Nations General Assembly on December 4, 1986.

7 Pashuram Tomay, "An Overview of the Principle of Free, Prior and Informed Consent to Development," *Australian Indigenous Law Reporter* 9 (2005): 111–116; George Barrie, "International Law and Indigenous People: Self-Determination, Development, Consent and Co-Management," *Comparative and International Law Journal of Southern Africa"* 51 (2018): 171–184.

8 GA Res 50/174, "United Nations Declaration on the Rights of Indigenous Peoples," UN GAOR, 59st Sess., Supp. No 49, Vol 1, UN Doc A/61/49 (2005) 344.

on the Rights of Indigenous People, called on states to "ensure that members of indigenous peoples have equal rights in respect of effective participation in public life and that no decisions directly relating to their rights and interest are taken without their informed consent."[9]

The International Convention on Economic Social and Cultural Rights (1996) (ICESCR)[10] and the International Convention on Civil and Political Rights (1996) (ICCPR)[11] share a common Article 1 that affirms the rights of all peoples to self-determination. By virtue of this right, all peoples "freely determine their political status and freely pursue their economic, social and cultural development." In monitoring state compliance with the ICESCR, the Committee on Economic, Social and Cultural Rights (CESCR) has highlighted the need for states to obtain indigenous people's consent in matters of resource exploitation. For instance, in its 2001 Concluding Observations on the periodic report on Colombia, the CESCR noted with regret that the traditional lands of indigenous peoples have been reduced or occupied, without their consent, by timber, mining and oil companies, at the expense of the exercise of their culture and the equilibrium of the ecosystem.[12] Likewise, in 2004 the CESCR stated in relation to Ecuador that it was deeply concerned that natural extracting concessions had been granted to international companies without the full consent of the communities concerned.[13]

Despite UNDRIP being a non-binding declaration, it is not without any standard-setting significance. Its adoption was supported by 144 states, while 11 states abstained and four states voted against it. Those four states (Australia, Canada, the United States and New Zealand) subsequently endorsed UNDRIP. Due consideration must be given to the major influence on the development of international law by other UN declarations such as the Universal Declaration on Human Rights;[14] the Declaration of Legal Principles Governing the Activities of States in the Exploration and Use of Outer Space;[15] and the Declaration on the Granting of Independence to Colonial Countries and Peoples.[16] In Filartiga v. Pena-Irala[17] the US Second Circuit Court of Appeals declared that

9 UN GAOR, 52d Sess., Supp. no. 18, UN, Official Records: Supplement to the Official Records of the General Assembly.

10 993 UNTS 3 (1967).

11 999 UNTS 171 (1966).

12 UN ESCOR 2002 Supp. No. 2, UN Doc. E/2002/22, EC.12/2001/17, para. 761.

13 UN ESCOR 2005 Supp. No. 2, UN Doc. E/2005/22, EC.12/2004/9, para. 278.

14 GA Res. 217 A III of 10 Dec 1948.

15 GA Res. 1962 XVII 1963.

16 GA Res. 1514 XIV 1960.

17 Filartiga v. Pena-Irala, 630 F 2d 876, 882 (1980).

UN declarations are significant because they specify with great precision the obligations of UN member states. UNDRIP is unarguably such an international instrument that specifically addresses the obligations of states towards their indigenous peoples. In Simon v. Canada,[18] for instance, the Federal Court held that while UNDRIP does not create substantive rights, it nevertheless favors an interpretation that will embody its values.

3 Definition of Indigenous People

Having determined the legal status of UNDRIP, it is also opportune at this juncture to briefly define the term indigenous people. For purposes of this chapter, the following definition can be accepted as being authoritative.

This definition sees indigenous people as:

> Communities, people's and nations … which have a historical continuity with pre-invasion and pre-colonial societies, that developed on their territories, consider themselves distinct from other sectors of the societies now prevailing in these territories or parts of them. They form at present non-dominant sectors of society and are determined to preserve develop and transmit to future generations their ancestral territories, and their ethnic identity, as the basis of their continued existence as peoples, in accordance with their own cultural patterns, social institutions and legal systems.[19]

The term 'indigenous peoples' however has different nomenclatures in English. It is also synonymous with the term 'aboriginal peoples'. In this chapter, the terms are used generically depending on the context, be it indigenous/ aboriginal peoples in Canada, Africa, South America or Indonesia. While the terms 'indigenous' and 'aboriginal' are used interchangeably throughout this chapter, it is not the purpose of this chapter to engage in semantic debates about the connotations of these words. Attempting to determine who qualifies

---

18 Simon v. Canada, 2013 FC 1117, para. 121.

19 UN Doc E/CN 4 Sub 2/1983/21 Add 8. See in general Stephen Anaya, *Indigenous Peoples and International Law* (Oxford: Oxford University Press, 2004); Solomon Derso, *Perspectives on the Rights of Minorities and Indigenous Peoples of Africa* (Pretoria: Pretoria University Press, 2010); Alexandra Xanthaki, *Indigenous Rights and United Nations Standards* (Cambridge: Cambridge University Press, 2007) and Paul Mc Hugh, *Aboriginal Title* (*Oxford: Oxford University Press,* 2011).

as indigenous or aboriginal is an impossible task due to the passage of time. The reason being that the conquests or assimilation of the original inhabitants occurred hundreds rather than scores of years ago. The above definition appears to refer mainly to Western expansion and does raise questions regarding its applicability to pre-invasion and pre-colonial societies. It must be noted that neither ILO Convention 169 nor UNDRIP define 'indigenous people'.

4 Canadian Courts and the Duty to Consult Indigenous Peoples

Canadian courts have always accepted that they have a duty to consult indigenous peoples. This duty emanates from Section 35 of the Constitution Act 1982, which declares that "existing aboriginal and treaty rights of the aboriginal peoples of Canada are hereby recognized and affirmed." This section has been interpreted taking into account evolving international norms on this duty.[20] In R v. Sparrow[21] the Canadian Supreme Court referred to a duty to consult as emanating from Section 35 of the Constitution, which recognizes aboriginal rights. In this case, the 'duty to consult' was based on a constitutional imperative and had no international law connotation. After the *Sparrow* case, the developing customary international law duty of consulting aboriginal people in Canada merges with the Constitutional imperative of Section 35, albeit implicitly, and plays an important role in Canada endorsing UNDRIP in 2012.

The application of the duty to consult in Canadian courts was emphatically illustrated in the trilogy of cases: Haida Nation v. British Columbia (Minister of Forests),[22] Taku River Tlingit First Nation v. British Columbia (Project Assessment Director),[23] and Mikisew Cree First Nation v. Canada (Minister of Canadian Heritage).[24] It is outside the ambit of this chapter to discuss these and further cases decided by the courts in any detail and such cases will consequently only be discussed briefly.

In the *Haida Nation* case, the Supreme Court explained how the duty to consult applies to aboriginal people in Canada. In this case, the

---

20 George Barrie, "The Canadian Courts Approach to the 'Duty to Consult' Indigenous Peoples," *Comparative and International Law Journal of Southern Africa* 53 (2020): 1–20. See in general Dwight Newman, *Revisiting the Duty to Consult Aboriginal People* (Saskatoon: Purich, 2014).

21 R v. Sparrow, 1 SCR 1075 (1990).

22 Haida Nation v. British Columbia (Minister of Forests), SCC 73 (2004).

23 Taku River Tlingit First Nation v. British Columbia (Project Assessment Director), SCC 74 (2003).

24 Mikisew Cree First Nation v. Canada (Minister of Canadian Heritage), SCC 69 (2005).

government transferred a tree farm license to a large forestry corporation named Weyerhauser without consulting the Haida Nation. The Court held that the Haida Nation should have been consulted prior to the transfer of the license because the government was bound to act honorably in its relations with aboriginal people. This duty to consult, Chief Justice McLachlin held, arises when the government has knowledge of the potential existence of the aboriginal title to land and when the contemplated conduct might adversely affect such aboriginal title.

In the companion *Taku River* case, the Supreme Court held that the government had met the necessary consultation requirements after the Tlingit's concerns about the possible impacts of a 160 kilometer road through their traditional territory. The Court found that issues relating to wildlife migration and the environmental impact had been adequately consulted on. In the *Mikisew Creek* case, the aboriginal Mikisew Creek Nation protested that the location of a road near their reserve would adversely affect their traditional lifestyle because it intersected with a number of their trap lines and hunting grounds. The Supreme Court held in the circumstances there was a duty to consult and that there had not been adequate consultation. Consequently, the government was ordered to reassess its initial decision.

These three cases established a new legal doctrine relating to government consultation with aboriginal nations in matters that seriously impact their economic interests, natural resource developments and traditional way of life.

The impact of these three cases was manifested in 2010 in Rio Tinto Alcan v. Carrier Sekani Tribal Council.[25] The case concerned applications for renewals of energy production licenses at hydro-electric facilities powered by dams that had been built decades ago with no consultation and with clear impacts on the aboriginal nation in the area. Questions were raised as to the duty of utilities commissions and various administrative boards to consult with the relevant aboriginal peoples in such situations. The Supreme Court held that the government is constantly obliged to see that consultation occurs. It also importantly held that the duty to consult was not retrospective but a forward-looking duty that attaches to potential future impacts of decisions made in the present. Dene Tha' First Nation v. Canada (Minister of the Environment)[26] resonates with the principles established in the *Rio Tinto* case, emphasizing the forward-looking nature of the duty to consult. Justice Phelan used the example of government planning a gas pipeline. If a plan was envisaged and a roadmap was in

25 Rio Tinto Alcan v. Carrier Sekani Tribal Council, SCC 43 (2010).

26 Dene Tha' First Nation v. Canada (Minister of the Environment), FC 1354 (2006).

the *contemplation* of government officials, the court held that there should at that early stage be consultation with the affected indigenous nations.

What constitutes meaningful consultation was addressed in White River First Nation v. Yukon (Minister of Energy, Mines and Resources).[27] The Supreme Court saw it to be a form of consultation which generates an appropriate level of respect for aboriginal rights and comprises a genuine process for feedback that is appropriate in the circumstances and allows the government to take proper account of such feedback. It was also determined that meaningful consultation should adhere to principles of procedural fairness, including adequate notice and the opportunity for all parties to be heard (*audi alteram partem*). Meaningful consultation was also addressed in various further cases. In Ka'a'gee Tu First Nation v. Canada (Indian Affairs and Northern Development)[28] it was held that consultation must be ongoing, including during the final stages of the decision-making. Brokenhead Objiway Nation v. Canada (Attorney General)[29] concerned a set of oil pipelines, one of which was the Keystone Pipeline. Justice Barnes emphasized the principle that the duty to consult must be proportionate to the anticipated impact of a development or project on the asserted interests.

The views of the Canadian courts regarding the respective rights and duties of the federal and provincial governments, the aboriginal communities and industry stakeholders regarding consultation is encapsulated in Saugeen First Nation v. Ontario (Minister of Natural Resources and Forestry).[30] The case concerned the government's duty to consult with the Saugeen Objiway Nation (SON) regarding an application for a license for a quarry on SON traditional lands. The court decided that the duty to consult required the government to: (i) give notice to SON of the application for the quarry project; (ii) provide SON with details of the project; (iii) disclose details of government funding to obtain expert assistance for SON; (iv) communicate with SON about SON's concerns after having received expert advice; and (v) follow a reasonable process to complete adequate consultations and, where appropriate, accommodate SON's concerns.

Concerns have arisen in Canada as to whether the duty to consult implies a veto by aboriginal communities in authorizing development projects after

27 White River First Nation v. Yukon, YKSC 66 (2013).

28 Ka'a'gee Tu First Nation v. Canada (Indian Affairs and Northern Development) FC 764 (2007).

29 Brokenhead Objiway Nation v. Canada (Attorney General) FC 484 (2009).

30 Saugeen First Nation v. Ontario (Minister of Natural Resources and Forestry), 4 CNLR 213 (2017).

consultation. In the *Haida Nation* case, it was held that the duty to consult does not include an aboriginal power to veto any government decision. The 2009 Annual Report of the UN Special Rapporteur on the Situation of Human Rights and Fundamental Freedoms of Indigenous People[31] suggests that UNDRIP does not create a veto power but rather creates an obligation to consult in good faith. However, the 2013 Annual Report of the Special Rapporteur on the Rights of Indigenous Peoples,[32] though not specifically adopting a veto power, stated that aboriginal peoples have the right to withhold consent in resource developments in their traditional territories.

An analysis of the state practice outlined above concerning the duty to consult indigenous peoples in Canada found that while the concept of FPIC is not explicitly mentioned, it is implicitly recognized in the ongoing jurisprudential conversation. This is evident especially in activities with a particularly severe impact on the indigenous peoples' lives.

5 The African Commission on Human and People's Rights

The African Charter on Human and Peoples' Rights[33] (Charter) was designed to reflect the particular circumstances of Africa and is the founding document of the Organisation of African Unity (OAU). The Charter has special provisions drawn from indigenous customary laws. Besides referring to civil, political, social, economic and cultural rights, the Charter provides for so-called third generation rights. These rights relate to development, self-determination and the environment. The latter group of rights vest in the main in groups rather than in individuals.

Implementation of the Charter is supervised by the African Commission on Human and Peoples' Rights (ACHPR). The ACHPR is the key mechanism for ensuring observance of the Charter. States party to the Charter are obliged to submit reports to the ACHPR. Any state party may refer any alleged violation to the ACHPR. Significantly, the ACHPR may entertain petitions from individuals if the petitions refer to a special case that reveals a series of serious massive violations.

31 UN Doc A/HRC/12/34 (15 July 2009).
32 UN Doc A/HRC/24/41 (1 July 2013).
33 *ILM* 21, 58 (1982).

Social and Economic Rights Action Centre and the Centre for Economic and Social Rights v. Nigeria (Serac and CESR v. Nigeria)[34] (the *Ogoni* case) is a renowned decision of the ACHPR regarding state obligations under peoples' socio-economic and cultural rights and the Charter. It was alleged that oil resource exploitation in the Niger Delta had violated the rights of the Ogoni people by degradation of the environment and resulted in health problems. The ACHPR recognized the Ogonis as a distinct people entitled to the peoples' rights provisions of the Charter. Regarding Article 21, which guarantees the right to freely dispose of wealth and natural resources, the ACHPR found that the Nigerian government, by giving the green light to oil companies, had devastated the wellbeing of the Ogonis. Second, the ACHPR found that the government had not involved the Ogoni communities in decisions that affected their development in Ogoniland.

This interpretation of the Charter is not only in line with the related provisions Articles 8(2)(b), 25–29 and 32 of UNDRIP, but also with those on the right to free, prior and informed consent in important matters affecting their lives, as outlined in Articles 10, 11, 19, 28, 29 and 32. It is also worth noting that the decision erases any doubt as to whether peoples' rights provisions in the Charter are applicable to indigenous groups as the Ogonis were

In Centre for Minority Rights Development (Kenya) and Minority Rights Group International obo Endorois Welfare Council of Kenya v. Kenya (*Endorois* case)[35] the cause of action was Kenya's eviction of an indigenous community, the Endorois, from their ancestral land for the establishment of a game reserve. The Endorois were relegated to semi-arid land, which proved to be unsuitable for pastoralism. As a result of the loss of their ancestral land, their access to clean drinking water was severely undermined. Moreover, the strict conditions attached to the access to their ancestral land resulted in the curtailment of their traditional means of subsistence by grazing cattle. The Endorois were not only unable to access the healthy pastures around Lake Bogoria, their traditional home, but also the salt licks their cattle required. A complaint was lodged with the ACHPR against the Kenyan state by the Endorois.

The ACHPR found that the Endorois were a distinctive tribal community and that the alleged violations of the African Charter espoused by the Endorois went to the heart of indigenous rights – the right to preserve one's identity through identification with ancestral lands.

---

34 Communication No. 155/96 (2001); 10 IHRR 287 (2003). See Felix Nahinda, *Indigenousness in Africa* (The Hague: Springer, 2011): 196–198.

35 *ILM* 49, 859 (2010).

The main thrust of the complaints of the Endorois can be encapsulated in Articles 21 and 22 of the Charter. Article 21(1) provides that all peoples have the right "freely to dispose of their wealth and natural resources. This right shall be exercised in the exclusive interest of the people. In no case shall a people be deprived of it." Article 22 reads:

1. All people shall have the right to their economic, social, and cultural development with due regard to their freedom and identity and in the equal enjoyment of the common heritage of the mankind.
2. States shall have the duty, individually or collectively, to ensure the exercise of the right to development.

Regarding Article 21, the ACHPR held that Kenya had a duty to "evaluate whether a restriction of these property rights is necessary to preserve the survival of the Endorois community." Further, with reference to the African Commission's *Ogoni case*, the ACHPR held that a right to natural resources contained within their traditional lands vested in the indigenous people. The ACHPR was of the opinion that the *Ogoni case* made it clear that a "people" inhabiting a specific region within a state can claim the protection of Article 21.

The ACHPR subsequently concluded that in relation to Article 21, Kenya had not consulted with the Endorois community, who possess the right to freely dispose of their wealth and natural resources through consultation with Kenya. Consequently, Kenya was found to have violated Article 21.[36]

As evident from the above, Article 22 of the African Charter proclaims the right to development of peoples. This right to development is comprehensive and includes peoples' rights to their economic, social and cultural development. Kenya contended that this meant that the task of communities within a participatory democracy is to contribute to the wellbeing of society at large and not only to care selfishly for one's own community at the risk of others. This contention was rejected.

The ACHPR endorsed the sentiment expressed in the Report for the UN Working Group on Indigenous Populations[37] that "indigenous peoples are not coerced, pressurized or intimidated in their choices of development". The ACHPR referred to Article 2(3) of UNDRIP, which notes that the right to development includes active, free and meaningful participation in development. The ACHPR held that Kenya's consultation had not been sufficient and did not

36 *Endorois* case, para. 268.

37 UN Doc E/CN 4/ Sub /2AC 4/2004/4 para. 14(a).

obtain the FPIC of all the Endorois before designating their land as a game reserve and evicting them.

In a nutshell, the ACHPR held that any developments or investment projects that would have a major impact within the Endorois territory generated a duty not only to consult with the community, but also to obtain their FPIC according to their customs and traditions.[38]

6 The Inter-American System of Human Rights

The Inter-American system upholds and enforces human rights through the Inter-American Commission on Human Rights (Commission) and the Inter-American Court of Human Rights (IACrtHR). The human rights obligations of member states of the Organization of American States (OAS) are set out in the Charter of the OAS,[39] the American Declaration of the Rights and Duties of Man, and the American Convention on Human Rights (Convention). The Convention contains a comprehensive guarantee of civil, political, economic, social and cultural rights and provides for a system of individual applications leading to decisions by the Commission. Although Article 26 of the Convention obliges states to progressively realize second-generation rights, Article 21 specifically guarantees the right to property.

Only states and the Commission may refer cases to the IACrtHR – provided that the states in question have accepted the jurisdiction of the court. The court may give advisory opinions on the interpretation of the Convention. The IACrtHR has no jurisdiction to receive individual complaints. Only the Commission has compulsory jurisdiction over individual petitions, which it may then refer to the IACrtHR.

The IACrtHR in the case of the Mayagna (Sumo) Awas Tingni Community v. Nicaragua[40] and the case of the Moiwane Village v. Suriname[41] accepted the collective rights of indigenous peoples or tribal groups to the communal use of their property. In the *Awas Tingni* case, the court held that possession of land should suffice for indigenous communities lacking real title to obtain official recognition of that property.

38 *Endorois* case, paras. 290–291.

39 119 UNTS 3.

40 10 1 HRR 758 (2003).

41 IACrtHR (Series C) No 124.

This approach was borne out by the IACrtHR in the case of the Sawhoyamaxa v. Paraguay,[42] where it was ruled that indigenous peoples' collective notion of

> ownership of land does not necessarily conform to the classic concept of property, but deserves equal protection under Article 21 of the American Convention. Disregard for specific versions of use and enjoyment of property, springing from culture, uses, customs, and beliefs of each people, would be tantamount to holding that there is only one way of using and disposing of property, which, in turn, would render protection under Article 21 of the Convention illusory for millions of persons.

The case of Mary and Carrie Dann v. USA[43] concerned meetings conducted with an indigenous community 14 years after their property rights had been extinguished. One of the issues was whether the community really understood what the nature and consequences of the meetings were. The IACrtHR was of the opinion that the meetings held 14 years after the fact could not constitute effective participation. The IACrtHR emphasized that to have a process that is fully informed, a minimum requirement was obtaining the consent of all of the members of the indigenous community and providing them with an effective opportunity to participate individually or collectively.

Yakye Axa Indigenous Community v. Paraguay[44] concerned the restitution of traditional lands and communal resources to indigenous peoples. The return of alternative lands, the IACrtHR held, must be done by agreement with members of the indigenous peoples according to their own consultation and decision procedures.

In the case of the Saramaka People v. Suriname,[45] the IACrtHR had to consider the Saramaka, whose lands were given to mining and logging companies with no regard to their FPIC. The court ruled that large-scale development projects that might affect indigenous and tribal peoples' lands and natural resources requires their free, prior and informed consent in accordance with their customs and traditions. The court further ruled that the Saramakas receive a reasonable benefit from the development and that an environmental and social impact be undertaken under supervision of the state. Any consultation with the Saramakas, the court added, must be effective consultation and held in good faith.

42 IACrtHR (Series C) No 146, para. 120.
43 10 IHRR 1143 (2003).
44 15 IHRR 978 (2008).
45 16 IHRR 1045 (2009).

An important case related to a South American country, Peru, was a decision of the UN Human Rights Committee. This Committee was established under Article 28 of the ICCPR to consider complaints of human rights violations under the ICCPR by states parties of the ICCPR. In Poma Poma v. Peru,[46] the complainant owned an alpaca farm in the Tacna region of Peru where she and her children raised alpacas, llamas and other animals as their only means of subsistence. This farming activity was practiced according to the traditional customs of the family, who were descendants of the indigenous Aymara people, as part of their way of life for thousands of years. Between the 1950s and 1980s water diversion projects authorized by Peru reduced the water supply to the pastures and areas from where the water for human and animal consumption was drawn. This caused the drying out of the wetlands on which the complainant depended for grazing and underground springs. The situation further deteriorated in the 1990s when Peru drilled wells in the area, accelerating pasture drainage and degradation, resulting in the deaths of thousands of animals. This potentially deprived the indigenous community of their only means of survival.

The complainant alleged several violations of the ICCPR the most important being Article 27, which emphasizes the right to enjoy a particular culture which may consist of a way of life that is closely connected with a territory and the use of its resources. This provision is particularly relevant in the context of members of an indigenous community constituting a minority. Where this is the case, the Human Rights Committee held, the enjoyment of the rights associated with the community's traditional activities may require measures be taken by the state to ensure the effective participation of members of the community in decisions affecting them. It was not disputed that the complainant was a member of an indigenous people and that the raising of llamas constituted an essential element of her community's culture. It was uncontested that the degradation of the pastures was the direct result of the water diversion schemes and led to the death of thousands of head of livestock and the financial ruin of the community, including that of the complainant.

The UN Human Rights Committee took into account the failure of Peru to properly consult with the complainant and affected indigenous community, and to require impact studies to be undertaken by an independent body to determine the impact of the wells on the economic activities of the complainant and community. The nature and scope of the required consultation in the Committee's comments in paragraph 7.6:

46 UN Doc CCPR/C/95/D 1457/2006.

> In the Committee's view, the admissibility of measures which substantially compromise or interfere with the culturally significant economic activities of a minority of indigenous community depends on whether the members of the community in question have had the opportunity to participate in the decision-making process in relation to these measures and whether they will continue to benefit from their traditional economy. The Committee considers the participation in the decision-making process must be effective, which requires not mere consultation but the free, prior and informed consent of the members of the community. In addition, the measures must respect the principle of proportionality so as not to endanger the very survival of the community and its members.

A landmark decision of the IACrtHR is the Case of the Kichwa Indigenous People of Sarayaku v. Ecuador[47] (*Sarayaku people* case). This case was initiated *inter alia* by the Association of the Kichwa People of Sarayaku, which sued the state of Ecuador by submitting that a number of rights of the Sarayaku people as set out in the Convention had been violated, including the right to private property (Article 21); the right to life and personal integrity (Articles 4 and 5), and freedom of movement and residence (Article 22).

The Sarayaku people lived in different sectors of Pastaza province along the banks of the Bobonaza River in the Amazonian region of Ecuador, in an undivided parcel of land that was granted to them in 1992 by Ecuador. The Sarayaku comprised approximately 1,200 people divided in different groups. They carried out traditional activities such as collective family-based farming, hunting, fishing and gathering. In 2004, the Sarayaku people registered their parcel of land before the competent governmental authority, setting out the dimensions of their territory.

In 1996, Ecuador granted a concession to Petro Ecuador, the national oil company, and other consociated oil companies, to explore and exploit hydrocarbons in Block 23 of the Amazonian basin. Petro Ecuador never complied with its obligations to do an environmental impact assessment or to preserve the ecological balance in the surrounding areas of Block 23. Meetings held between the government and the Sarayaku people never reached any substantial common agreement. Petro Ecuador placed 1,433 kilograms of explosives on the surface and at deeper levels to continue their seismic operations, which damaged the Sarayaku peoples' sacred sites and environment. Despite the

47 IACrtHR (Series C) No 245.

police having been ordered to remove the explosives from Sarayaku territory by the end of 2009, only 14 kilograms had been removed.

The IACrtHR found that Ecuador had violated certain rights of the Sarayaku people such as the right to consultation, the right to property, and the right to life and personal integrity.[48] For present purposes, the court's views on the right to consultation of the Sarayaku people will be discussed in more detail. The IACrtHR held that the spiritual relationship between indigenous people and their land must be respected in a democratic society and can be safeguarded by their right to consultation. The court linked participation with consultation regarding measures likely to affect the rights of indigenous peoples. This relationship between consultation and participation the court saw as being recognized by ILO Convention No 169 and UNDRIP. The court significantly saw the obligation to consult as being not only a treaty provision "but also a general principal of international law".

The Court also in paragraph 167 gave more content to the right to consultation and participation of indigenous peoples:

> Given that the State must guarantee these rights to consultation and participation at *all stages of the planning and implementation of a project* that may affect the territory on which an indigenous or tribal community is settled, or other rights essential to their survival as a people, *these dialogue and consensus-building processes must be conducted from the first stages of the planning or preparation of the proposed measure, so that the indigenous peoples can truly participate in and influence the decision-making process,* in accordance with the relevant international standards. In this regard, the State must ensure that the rights of *indigenous peoples are not ignored in any other activity or agreement reached with private individuals, or in the context of decisions of the public authorities that would affect their rights and interests.*

After recalling its previous cases *Awas Tingni* (2001) and *Saramaka v. Suriname* (2001), and taking into account the ICCPR and the ICESCR, the IACrtHR concluded that Ecuador, by failing the consult the Sarayaku people on the execution of a project that would have a direct impact on their territory, failed to comply with its obligations under the principles of international law, and its

48 Alexandra Tomaselli and Frederica Cittadino, "Land Consultation and Participation Rights of Indigenous Peoples in the Jurisprudence of the Inter-American Court of Human Rights," in *Litigating the Rights of Minorities and Indigenous Peoples in Domestic and International Courts*, ed. Bertus de Villiers (Leiden: Brill, 2021), 149–178.

own domestic law. It further failed to adopt all necessary measures to guarantee the participation of the Sarayaku people, in accordance with their values, practices, customs and forms of organization, in the decisions made regarding matters that could have an impact on their territory, their life and their cultural and social identity. The court laid emphasis on common Article 1 of the ICCPR and the ICESCR, which declares that by virtue of the right to self-determination, all peoples freely determine their political status and freely pursue their economic development. Relative to Article 21 of the Convention – the right to property – it can be submitted that this clearly implies the right to free, prior and informed consent regarding decisions and actions taken which have an impact on the territory of indigenous peoples. The court, in coming to its conclusion, referred to the participation and consultation rights of indigenous people recognized in ILO Convention 169. In paragraph 161, it reiterated that "human rights treaties are living instruments, the interpretation of which must evolve over time."

Shortly after the *Sarayaku people* case, the Commission referred the case of the Kalina and Lokono Peoples v. Suriname[49] (*Kalina and Lokono* case) to the IACrtHR. The case stemmed from the unresolved land claims of the Kalina and Lokono peoples due to the actions and inactions of Suriname. From 1966 to 1998, the Wia Wia, Galibi and Wave Creek nature reserves were created by order of the president of Suriname. These nature reserves were partly located in the lands of the Kalina and Lokono indigenous peoples and were created without their consultation. Following on the creation of these nature reserves, the fishing and hunting activities essential for the spiritual and material development of the Kalina and Lokono were affected and they were forced to flee their traditional lands due to the internal conflict between some tribes and the military regime. Beside creating tourism projects on these reserves, Suriname in 1958 granted bauxite mining concessions to a company called Suralco until 2033. Some of these activities were planned to take place in parts of the Wave Creek reserve. The mining activities resulted in the prohibition of the Kalina and Lokono peoples to enter their traditional territory in the Wave Creek reserve and had a significant environmental impact, which further led to the decline of fishing and hunting. After failing to get recognition of their traditional ownership over the nature reserves, the Kalina and Lokono indigenous peoples submitted their claims to the Commission, which in turn referred the claims to the IACrtHR.

49 IACrtHR 2015 (Series C) No 309.

For our purposes we shall focus broadly on Article 21 of the Convention, which concerns the right to property, as well as the related participatory rights outlined in Article 23. The court concluded that Suriname violated Article 21 of the Convention by denying the Kalina and Lokono peoples access to some portions of their traditional land and preventing them from enjoying the benefits of the Galibi and Wave Creek reserves. Further, the court found that the mining operations restricted the indigenous people's rights to their collective property. Regarding Article 23, the court gave a restrictive interpretation to participation in that it only referred to "free, prior and informed consultation" without addressing the term 'consent'. Despite this restrictive interpretation of the participatory rights of the Kalina and Lokono peoples, the IACrtHR did conclude that Suriname did not meet the benchmark of effective participation because it failed to consult the Kalina and Lokono peoples prior to the commencement of the mining operations. Suriname was consequently ordered to pay reparations to reverse the negative effects of the mining operations.

In the *Kalina and Lokono* case, the IACrtHR in defining effective participation in paragraph 305 referred to Articles 18 and 19 of UNDRIP. The latter Article refers to "free and informed consent."

As was submitted (supra) at the end of the discussion of the *Sarayaku people* case, it is similarly submitted here that the court's conclusion in the *Kalina and Lokono* case implies consent as being an inherent part of FPIC.

7 South Africa

In Baleni and Others v. Minister of Mineral Resources and Others[50] (*Baleni* case), the Gauteng Division of the High Court of South Africa had to interpret the provisions of the Informal Protection of Land Rights Act 31 of 1996 (IPILRA). The applicants in the case were known as the Imizi. They had lived in an area known as uMgungundlovu, which is in the greater Xolobeni area, according to their customs and traditions for centuries. The respondents were Transworld Energy and Mineral Resources (SA) Pty (Ltd) (TEMR) and various government departments.

TEMR applied for mining rights in the Xolobeni area. The Imizi lived in close proximity to the proposed mining area and were unequivocally opposed to the proposed mining activities. Their opposition was due to the fact that they had family graves in the proposed mining area and considered them essential

50 2019 2 SA 453 (GP).

sites for their community rituals. According to their culture, the relationship between the living and the dead is intertwined. It was not disputed by TEMR that the Imizi had informal rights to the land as defined by the IPILRA and it was not disputed that they occupied the land according to their own laws and customs.

According to section 2(1) of the IPILRA, an informal holder of rights to land is one who uses or occupies land in terms of any tribal, customary or indigenous law or practice of a tribe. Section 2(1) further states that no person may be deprived of any informal right to land without his or her consent. Section 2(2) states that where land is held on a communal basis, a person may only be deprived of such land in accordance with the custom and usage of the community. Section 2(4) declares that 'custom and usage of a community' shall be deemed to include the principle that a decision to dispose of an informal right to land may only be taken after a majority holders have attended a meeting and they all had a reasonable opportunity to participate. The Imizi submitted that they had never consented to the proposed mining operations. TEMR submitted that according to the Mineral Resources Development Act 28 of 2002 (MPRDA), their only obligation was to consult with the Imizi before mining operations commenced, which they had done.

The court saw the Imizi as part of the uMgungundlovu community and being holders of informal rights to land as defined in the IPILRA. Consequently, their consent was necessary, as set out in section 2(1) of the IPILRA, before being deprived of their informal rights to land. The court found that the consent requirement of the IPILRA trumps the sole consultation requirement as required by the MPRDA.

The court referred to section 233 of the South African Constitution, which states that when interpreting legislation a court must prefer any reasonable interpretation that is consistent with international law. In applying the section 233 to the terms of the IPILRA, the court found that multiple instruments in international law required that communities such as the Imizi have the right to grant or refuse their free, prior and informed consent to any mining development that will significantly affect them.[51] These multiple instruments in international law the court held were:

1. General Recommendation No. XXIII on Indigenous Peoples, issued in terms of CERD.[52]

---

51 *Baleni* case, para. 78.

52 UN GAOR 52nd Sess., Supp. 18.

2. General Comment 21 of 2009 of ESCOR,[53] which states that states must take measures to recognize and protect the rights of indigenous peoples to own, develop, control and use their communal lands and resources. Where such lands or resources have been used or inhabited without their free and informed consent, take steps to return such lands.
3. The Poma Poma v. Peru decision.[54]
4. The *Endorois* case.[55]

The court held that although the African Charter does not expressly provide for the concept of FPIC, the *Endorois* case emphasized that no decisions may be made about indigenous peoples' land without their FPIC. The court[56] concurred with this finding of the ACHPR. The court accordingly held that customary communities not protected by law have the right to decide what happens with their land. As such they may not be deprived of their land without their consent. Where the land is held on a communal basis – as in this matter – the community must be placed in a position to consider the deprivation of their land and take a communal decision in terms of their custom whether they consent to a proposal to dispose of their rights to their land.

In Maledu and Others v. Itereleng Mineral Resources (Pty) Ltd and Another,[57] the South African Constitutional Court (CC) on a similar set of facts came to the same conclusion. In this case the CC concurred with paragraph 291 of the *Endorois* case that any development that would have a major impact on the territory of indigenous people generates a duty not only to consult the community but also to obtain their FPIC according to their customs and traditions.

8 Botswana

Roy Sesana Keiwa Setlhobogwa and Others v. The Attorney General[58] (*Sesana* case) concerned Roy Sesana, who was a member of the Kgei band of the San or Basarwa people whose ancestors were indigenous to the Central Kgalagadi

53 UNESCOR 2002 Supp. No 2.
54 UNDOC CCPR/C/95/D 1457 /2006.
55 *ILM* (49) 858 2010.
56 *Baleni* case, para. 82.
57 2019 2 SA 1 (CC).
58 BWHC 1 (2006). See N Olmsted, "Indigenous Rights in Botswana: Development, Democracy and Dispossession," *Washington University Global Studies Review* 3 (2004): 799–866.

region. Roy Sesana was a human rights activist and a member of the First People of the Kalahari (FPK). He acquired fame in the mid-1990s due to events surrounding the removal of his people from the Central Kgalagadi (Kahahari) Game Reserve (CKGR).

The applicants were part of a larger community of Botswana's San/Basarwa people representing approximately 3% of the national population. The High Court case was highly publicized and is still the longest and most expensive court case in Botswana's history.

The *Sesana* case dealt with the removal or relocation of members of the Basarwa/San from various settlements within the CKGR. These settlements had been created by the departing British colonial administration in 1961. The stated reason for the creation of the CKGR was to protect wildlife resources and the need to safeguard the traditional lifestyle of the Basarwas/San. A 1963 regulation on the control of entry into the CKGR declared that no person other than a member of Basarwa/San people indigenous to the CKGR shall enter the reserve without first having obtained a permit in writing from the district commissioner in Ghanzi. This regulation, it was submitted, implied a recognition of the historical right of the Basarwa/San as an indigenous people to access ancestral lands that they had occupied for more than 2,000 years.

The heart of the legal battle revolved around the relocation of about six Basarwa/San settlements or communities who, it was submitted, had lived in the CKGR for ages in harmony with the wildlife and nature. It was submitted that the relocation would disrupt their traditional lifestyle. Sesana brought an action before the court, requesting it to declare *inter alia* that the removal of the Basarwa/San from the CKGR was an unlawful dispossession of land and that the applicants should be reinstated in their possession. The High Court of Botswana court decided that the applicants were indeed deprived of their possession of land forcibly or wrongly and *without their consent.* Within the ranks of advocates of human rights, the ruling of the court was hailed as a significant victory for indigenous rights, not only in Botswana but also in Africa more generally.

9 Customary International Law

Customary international law plays a significant role in the international legal order.[59] While states give their express consent to be bound by a rule when they

59 Johan Dugard's, *International Law* (Cape Town: Juta, 2018), 30–41; TW Bennett and J Strug, *Introduction to International Law* (Cape Town: Juta, 2022), 14–26.

enter into a treaty, the consent of states to a customary rule must be inferred from their conduct. The two main requirements for a rule of customary international law to exist is the settled practice of states (*usus*) and the acceptance of an obligation to be bound by the rule (*opinio iuris sive necessitatis*).

Usus in the context of customary international law means the practice of states. This practice must be general and widespread. Such practice can be found in a variety of materials, including treaties, decisions of national courts, national legislation, government policy statements, opinions of government law advisers, reports of the International Law Commission (ILC), resolutions of international organizations, and comments of states on such resolutions and reports. According to Justice Conradie in the South African case S v. Petane,[60] one must consider the action and practice of states and not their promises or rhetoric, as customary international law is founded on practice, and not on preaching.

According to the International Court of Justice (ICJ), a practice must constitute a constant and uniform usage before it will qualify as a custom. This was held in the Asylum Case (Columbia v. Peru).[61] The ICJ relaxed this approach in the Case Concerning Military and Paramilitary Activities in and Against Nicaragua (Nicaragua v. USA),[62] where it held that a custom did not require absolute rigorous conformity with a rule. It is sufficient that the conduct of states should indicate a "general" or "widespread acceptance" of the rule. Universal acceptance[63] is not a requirement.

A further requirement for customary international law is that states must feel that they are under an obligation (*opinio iuris*) to be bound by the rule. As stated by Article 38(1)(b) of the Statute of the ICJ, states must be of the opinion that the custom is evidence of a general practice accepted as law.[64] Evidence of *opinio iuris* can be found in the same materials that are used for state practice. The difference being that for *opinio iuris* the search is for evidence that states feel bound or entitle to act in a particular way, not just for policy or political reasons but by virtue of the existence of a rule of customary international law.

Resolutions of international organizations, in particular political organs of the UN, can play an important part in the formation of customary international

60 S v. Petane, 3 SA 51 (C), 61 (1988).

61 Columbia v. Peru, ICJ Rep 266, 277 (1950).

62 Nicaragua v. USA, ICJ Rep 14, 98 (1986).

63 Judge Tanaka in South West Africa Cases (Ethiopia v. South Africa: Liberia v. South Africa) Second Phase 1966 ICJ Rep 169: 291.

64 North Sea Continental Shelf Cases (Germany/Denmark: Germany/Netherlands) 1969 ICJ Rep 176.

law – either as proof of practice (*usus*) or as *opinio iuris*. An accumulation of resolutions may be evidence of a collective practice of states. Where a resolution specifies that a practice is a rule of customary international law, such a resolution may also serve as *opinio iuris*. Measured against the requirements necessary for customary international law, FPIC is moving inexorably towards meeting such demands. There is a vast amount of literature on the subject animated by what academics are saying about UNDRIP. As stated by Dayo Ayoade,[65] FPIC is recognized as an emergent right under international law and is here to stay. This is borne out by the many references to case law in various countries referred to above and is not based on a utopian reading of the significance of these cases.

10 FPIC in Essence

What in a nutshell do above developments and decided cases say about the nature and extent of FPIC?

'Free' implies lack of coercion, intimidation or manipulation. Indigenous people are thus free to make their decisions in the ways and manners they wish, and according to their own norms and customary laws.

'Prior' implies that an indigenous community's consent must be obtained before a decision is reached on a project which affects the community's interests. This avoids a situation where indigenous communities only participate as rubber stamps.

'Informed' means that the indigenous people are provided with the full and comprehensive information that encapsulates the nature, size and scope of any proposed project, its purpose and duration; the likely impacts and the risks and benefits.

'Consent' is the collective decision of the affected communities. It is a combination of the elements of consultation and participation. It is important that the consent carries the interpretation of the term the indigenous people normally ascribe to it.

65 Dayo Ayoade, "Towards Free, Prior, Informed Consent in Natural Resource Development Projects," *South African Yearbook of International Law* 44 (2019): 2–15; Andrea Carmen, "The Right to Free, Prior and Informed Consent," in *Realizing the UN Declaration on the Rights of Indigenous People*, ed. Jackie Hartley (Saskatoon: Purich, 2010), 120–134.

11 Indonesia

How has FPIC impacted on decisions of the Constitutional Court of the Republic of Indonesia, The two decisions to be discussed will, like those previously discussed, be approached with a very broad brush, thereby avoiding the legal intricacies involved. The focus will be on the position of indigenous people in general and in what way, if any, FPIC was taken into account.

Decision Number 35/PUU-X/2012 concerned an application by way of petitions for a judicial review of mainly Law Number 41 of 1999 on Forestry (Forestry Law). It was contended that the Forestry Law for various reasons was in conflict with the 1945 Constitution of the Republic of Indonesia (Constitution). The focus of the discussion will mainly be on the comments of the Constitutional Court relating to the position of indigenous peoples in general in Indonesia.

The Court recognized the legal standing of all the Petitioners according to Article 51(1) of the Constitution. By virtue of Article 5(1)(c), Petitioner I was in alliance with indigenous communities who together fought for the rights of indigenous communities. By virtue of Article 51(1)(b), Petitioners II and III were indigenous community units: Petitioner II represented the Kenegerian Kuntu indigenous community and Petitioner III represented the Kasepuhan Cisitu indigenous community.

Since Decision Number 006/PUU-III/2005 and Decision Number 11/PUU-V/2007, the Petitioners have also complied with the five conditions for standing mandated by these two Decisions:

1. The existence of constitutional rights;
2. The constitutional rights are deemed to be impaired by the enactment of the Law for which judicial review is requested;
3. The loss of constitutional rights must be specific and actual or potential in nature, which may reasonably occur;
4. There is a causal relationship between the loss of the relevant constitutional rights and the enactment of the Law for which judicial review is being petitioned for;
5. There is a possibility that if the petition is granted, the loss of constitutional rights will no longer occur.

A brief precursor relating to the legal standing of indigenous peoples in Indonesia may be necessary before the gist is discussed. According to Article 18B paragraph 2 of the Constitution, "The state recognizes and respects entities of the *adat* (indigenous) law communities along with their traditional rights as long as these remain in existence and are in accordance with the development of community and the principles of the Unitary State of the Republic of Indonesia, are regulated by law."

According to Article 28I paragraph 3 of the Constitution "Cultural identities and rights of indigenous people are respected in accordance with the development of times/age and civilizations." In addition to these statutory provisions, evidence has been presented showing that indigenous communities, as population groups, have special characteristics as groups that have continuously inhabited areas for generations, maintaining cultural systems that bind various social groupings. (This evidence, set out in paragraph 3.9, was not rejected by the Court). This, in a nutshell, sets out how indigenous communities are constitutionally viewed in Indonesia.

Significantly, in paragraph 3.9, the Court recognized the petitioners as being indigenous and autonomous community groups in accordance with the Articles 3 and 4 of UNDRIP. This affirmed their right to self-determination and the freedom to pursue economic development, as well as their autonomy in internal affairs. Additionally, the Court in paragraph 3.9 made reference to ILO Convention 169.

The Court referred to the evidence presented, which demonstrated that indigenous communities have been among the victims of mining, forestry and plantation concessions. The Court also referred to international conventions aimed at protecting indigenous communities, including ILO Convention No. 1969 on Indigenous and Tribal Peoples in Independent Countries, which effectively protected and recognized indigenous communities.[66] Furthermore, the Court commented that the land conflicts with indigenous peoples in Indonesia went as far back as the Dutch East Indies colonial era, which had deprived indigenous peoples from enjoying their natural resources.

The Court emphasized that achieving social justice for all Indonesian people, as demanded by the Constitution, includes attaining the general welfare of all Indonesian people, comprising various groups and ethnicities with different religions, different customs and habits, and their respective traditional rights. Importantly, the Court, in paragraph 3.12.1, held that indigenous communities are constitutionally recognized and respected as rights holders, who also bear certain obligations. The Court saw indigenous communities as being legal subjects.

Returning to the Forestry Law, the Court held that three legal entities regulated forests. First, the state. Second, the indigenous communities. Third, the rights holders of land containing forests. The Court agreed with the petitioners

66 *ILM* 28, 182 (1989).

that indigenous people had no clarity regarding their specific rights relating to forests, distinct from mere land rights where forests exist. As a result, indigenous communities faced the risk of losing their rights to the forests that produce the natural resources for their livelihoods and sustenance. The Court held that this often occurred in an "arbitrary manner" that caused injustice and legal uncertainty for indigenous communities.

It is submitted that the fact that the Court saw arbitrariness as possibly leading to injustice and legal uncertainty, is a strong indication that the Court would have preferred the inputs or participation of the indigenous communities when it comes to disputes over forest lands. One of the issues raised by the Petitioners was that as mandated by the law, the state could grant rights to indigenous lands without first obtaining the approval of the indigenous communities who already lived on that land. Further, that the state was under no legal obligation to pay compensation. The Court here reacted by referring to the Earth Summit in Rio de Janeiro and Principle 22 of the Rio Declaration on the Environment and Development,[67] which stated that indigenous communities had an important role in environmental management because of their traditional knowledge and practices and should thus actively participate in the achievement of sustainable development. Such participation, as has been indicated above, is an element of FPIC.

Based on these considerations the Court held that regarding state forests, the state has full authority to make regulations. Regarding indigenous forests, however, the management is based in the residents who live there and who may control and cultivate the land according to their personal and family needs. Placing indigenous forests into parts of state forests, the Court held, was disregarding the rights of indigenous communities. 'Disregard' according to the Oxford Dictionary means "pay no attention to, to ignore." This rejection by the Court of any decisions which 'disregard' the rights of indigenous people is seemingly based on Article 18B paragraph 2 and Article 281 paragraph 3 of the Constitution, which recognize and protect indigenous forests. These articles were seen by the Court in paragraph 3.13.1 to be "living indigenous law" and clearly implied FPIC.

The Court held that in determining the boundary of state forest areas and indigenous forest areas, the decision should not unilaterally be taken by the state but based on Decision Number 34/PUU-IX/2011 it must be conducted with the participation of the stakeholders, which clearly include the people

67 See Patricia Birne and Alan Boyle, *International Law and the Environment* (Oxford: Oxford University Press, 2002), 79–177.

who live in the indigenous forests. It is submitted that here, the Court applied the principles of FPIC. In paragraph 3.13.2, the Court in so many words applied FPIC by stating that the status of indigenous forests or land may not be utilized for other purposes consequent on evictions without the permission of the indigenous people.

Decision Number 95/PUU-XII/2014 was also due to petitions for a review of Law Number 18 of 2013 on the Prevention and Eradication of Forest Destruction and Law Number 41 of 1999 (Forestry Law). It was contended that both these laws were in conflict with the Indonesian Constitution. FPIC did not in so may words feature as prominently in Decision 35/PUU-X/2012 discussed above, but the case's importance lies in the Court's overall awareness of the importance and recognition of indigenous peoples. Similarly by virtue of the provisions set out in the case just discussed, including Article 51(1) of the Constitution and Decision Number 006/PUU-III 2005 and Decision Number 11/PUU-V/2007, the Court accepted the standing of the petitioners.

Petitioner I was a citizen and member of the Gugak Malalo indigenous community. Petitioner II was a citizen and chief of Pekasa Customary Village, who lived with the indigenous people of Pekasa in a government-declared protected forest area. Petitioner III was a citizen and a member of the Dukuk Pidik indigenous people, who were farmers claiming an area managed by state-owned forestry company Perhutani. Petitioner IV was a member of the Kaspepuhan indigenous community. Petitioners V to X were NGOs focused on promoting human rights, forest conservation, agrarian justice and the protection of indigenous peoples.

The Petitioners submitted that both above laws were contrary to the Constitution and thus had no binding force in that they violated legal certainty, were discriminatory and restricted indigenous communities in fulfilling their daily needs. It was also submitted that the Government, due to its negligence, had failed clearly to designate the different categories of forests. It was contended that the criminal regulations regarding the forests were vague and did not comply with international standards. It was submitted that people who caused forest damage were not always held responsible and that there was no adequate environmental conservation and protection to cater for future generations. It was statistically proven that due to government negligence there had been massive forest degradation reaching 2 million hectares per year. This led to material losses, forest damage and the loss of a healthy and proper living environment, which impacted heavily on indigenous people living in the forests.

The Court was of the opinion that under the circumstances it had the right to intervene with the enforcement of environmental policies in accordance with the principles of sustainable and environmentally sound developments, including establishing and implementing criminal law provisions within the forestry sector. The Court held that the criminal provision, Article 50(3) of the Forestry law, that all people are prohibited from cutting down trees or harvesting or collecting forest products in the forests without having the right or permits from the authorized official, must not apply to people who for generations have lived in the forest, as long as the products were not intended for commercial purposes. The same applied, the Court held, to Article 50(3)(i) of the Forestry Law, which prohibited the grazing of livestock in forest areas without the competent authority. Here the Court held that this prohibition must not apply if the relevant livestock are for the daily needs of people who have lived in the forests for generations.

By implication, the Court held that these two prohibitions were arbitrary in nature by not taking the views of the indigenous people into consideration. The Court ordered that transitional provisions be made to avoid any legal vacuum, to guarantee legal certainty and provide legal protection to all affected parties. The affected parties in the case by implication were clearly the indigenous peoples of Indonesia. It is submitted that above two Constitutional Court cases must be read together and that the Court's remarks in Decision Number 35/PUU-X/2012, which clearly applied the principles of FPIC relating to indigenous people, is also applicable to Decision Number 95/PUU-XII/2014 as it relates to the interests of indigenous peoples of Indonesia. The two cases are companion cases and have contributed to the development of customary international law. FPIC, as a product of emerging customary international law, has decidedly influenced the approach of the Constitutional Court of Indonesia to matters affecting the lives of indigenous peoples.

12 Conclusion

FPIC in simple terms refers to the right of indigenous peoples to give or withhold their consent to any action expected to impact their lands, resources and rights. It is the product of various hard law and soft law international legal instruments such as ILO Convention 169 and UNDRIP. As we have seen, case law emanating from numerous countries and international tribunals has accepted FPIC as a necessary requirement in interactions between governments, investors and indigenous peoples. Relevant customary international law has developed in the direction that for all practical purposes, indigenous peoples are rightful 'owners' of their lands, territories and resources and this has created emergent standards critical to resource development projects. It is for states to ensure that FPIC becomes a condition precedent for natural resource developments and have a FPIC regime in place. As stated by Ayoade, the wheel has turned and there is no turning back.[68] It is important to reiterate that 'consent' in FPIC is a collective decision of the affected communities and is a combination of the elements of consultation and participation. 'Consent' must carry the interpretation of the term indigenous people normally ascribe to it. FPIC must be seen as a procedural requirement and not as an effective veto power, as it is not intended to block lawful activities. Courts and policymakers dealing with FPIC need to consider carefully all the complex dynamics associated with it and ensure that it continues developing in forms that will work well for all. FPIC is a complex doctrine that includes a number of related aims and aspirations. It has room to evolve and its ongoing development will take time. This development may prove to be an exciting and enriching experience for all indigenous peoples.

Bibliography

African Charter on Human and People's Rights *ILM* 21, 58 (1982).

Alcan v. Carrier Sekani Tribal Council, SCC 43 (2010).

Anaya, S. *Indigenous Peoples in International Law*. Oxford: Oxford University Press, 2004.

Asylum Case (Columbia v. Peru), 1950 ICJ Rep 266, 277.

Ayoade, D. "Towards Free, Informed, Consent in Natural Resource Development Projects." *South African Yearbook of International Law* 44 (2019).

Baleni and Others v. Minister of Mineral Resources and Others, 2 SA 453 (GP) (2019).

Barrie, G. "International Law and Indigenous People: Self-Determination, Development, Consent and Co-Management." *Comparative and International Law Journal of Southern Africa* 51 (2018).

Barrie, G. "The Canadian Courts' Approach, to the 'Duty to Consult' Indigenous Peoples." *Comparative and International Law Journal of Southern Africa* 53 (2020).

Barrie, G. "The United Nation Declaration on the Rights of Indigenous Peoples." *Tydskrif vir die Suid-Afrikaanse Reg* 2 (2013).

Bennett, TW and Strug. J. *Introduction to International Law*. Cape Town: Juta, 2020.

Beukes, M. "The Recognition of the Rights of 'Indigenous Peoples' and Their Rights as a People." *South African Yearbook of International Law* 35 (2010).

68 Dayo Ayoade, "Towards 'Free, Prior, Informed Consent' in Natural Resource Development Projects," *South African Yearbook of International Law* 44, no. 1 (2019): 12.

Birne, P and Boyle, A. *International Law and the Environment.* Oxford: Oxford University Press, 2002.

Brokenhead Objiway Nation v. Canada (Attorney General), FC 484 (2009).

Case Concerning Military and Paramilitary Activities in and against Nicaragua (Nicaragua v. USA), ICJ Rep 14, 98 (1986).

Case of the Kalina and Lekono People v. Suriname, IACrtHR (Series C) No 309 (2015).

Case of the Mayagna (Sumo) Awas Tingni Community v. Nicaragua, (10) IHRR 758 (2003).

Case of the Sawhoyamaxa v. Paraguay, IACrtHR (Series C) No 146 (2006).

Centre for Minority Rights Development (Kenya) and Minority Rights Group International obo Endorois Welfare Council of Kenya, *ILM* 49 (2010) 858.

Charter of the Organisation of American States, 119 UNTS 3.

Constitutional Court of Indonesia 2012. Decision Number 35/PUU-X/2012.

Constitutional Court of Indonesia 2014. Decision Number 95/PUU-XII/2014.

De Villiers, B. *Litigating the Rights op Minorities and Indigenous Peoples in Domestic and International Courts.* Leiden: Brill, 2021.

Dene Tha' First Nation v. Canada (Minister of the Environment), FC 1354 (2006).

Derso, S. *Perspectives on the Rights of Minorities and Indigenous Peoples of Africa.* Pretoria: Pretoria University Press, 2010.

Dugard, J. *International Law.* Cape Town: Juta, 2018.

Filartiga v. Pena-Irala, 630 F 2d 876 (1980).

Haida Nation v. British Columbia, SCC 73 (2004).

Hartley, J. *Realising the UN Declaration on the Rights of Indigenous Peoples.* Saskatoon: Purich, 2010.

International Convention on Civil and Political Rights (ICCPR), 999 UNTS 171 (1967). ILO Convention on Indigenous and Tribal People No 169 of 1989.

International Convention on Economic, Social and Cultural Rights (ICESCR), 1993 UNTS 3 (1967).

International Convention on the Elimination of Racial Discrimination (CERD), 660 UNTS 195, (1966).

Ka'a'gee Tu First Nation v. Canada, FC 484 (2009).

Kichwa Indigenous People of Sarayaku v. Ecuador, IACrtHR (Series C) No 245.

Maledu and Others v. Itereleng Mineral Resources (Pty) Ltd and Another, 2 SA 1 (CC) (2019).

Mary and Carrie Dann v. USA, (10) IHRR 1143 (2003).

McHugh, P. *Aboriginal Title.* Oxford: Oxford University Press, 2011.

Mikisew Cree First Nation v. Canada (Minister of Canadian Heritage), SCC 69 (2005).

Moiwane Village v. Suriname, IACrtHR (Series C) No 124 (2012).

Nahinda, F.W. *Indigenousness in Africa.* The Hague: Asser Press, 2011.

Newman, D. *Revisiting the Duty to Consult Aboriginal Peoples.* Saskatoon: Purich, 2014.

North Sea Continental Shelf Cases (*Germany / Denmark: Germany / Netherlands*), 1969 ICJ Rep 176.

Olmsted, N, "Indigenous Rights in Botswana." *Washington University Global Studies Review* 3 (2004).

Poma Poma v. Peru, UN Doc CCPR/C/95/D1457/2006.

R v. Sparrow, 1990 1 SCR 1075 (2004).

Report for the UN Working Group on Indigenous Populations UN Doc E/CN 4/Sub/ 2 AC 4/ 2004.

Roy Sesana Keiwa Setlhobogwa and Others v. The Attorney General, BWHC 1 (2006).

S v. Petane, 3 SA 51 (C) (1988).

Saramaka People v. Suriname, (16) IHRR 1045 (2009).

Sauglen First Nation v. Ontario, 4 CNLR 213 (2017).

Simon v. Canada, FC 1117 (2013).

South West Africa Cases (Ethiopia v. South Africa: Liberia v. South Africa) Second Phase), ICJ Rep 169, 291 (1966).

Tamarg, P. "An Overview of the Principles of Free, Prior and Informed Consent to Development." *Australian Indigenous Law Reporter* 9 (2005).

Tau River Tlingit First Nation v. British Columbia (Project Assessment Director), SCC 74 (2003).

The Social and Economic Rights Action Centre and the Centre for Economic and Social Rights v. Nigeria, ACHPR Comm. No 155/96 (2001).

Tomaselli, A and Cittadino, F. "Land consultation and participation rights of indigenous peoples in the jurisprudence of the Inter-American Court of Human Rights." In *Litigating the Rights of Minorities and Indigenous Peoples in Domestic and International Courts,* edited by De Villiers B. Leiden: Brill, 2021.

UN General Assembly's Programme of Action for the Second International Decade of the World's Indigenous People, UN Doc A/59/49 (2005) 344.

United Nations Declaration on the Rights of Indigenous Peoples, A/Res/61/295 (2007).

Universal Declaration on Human Rights, GA Res 217 AIII 10 Dec 1948.

White River First Nation v. Yukon (Minister of Energy, Mines and Resources), YKSC 66 (2013).

Xanthaki, A. *Indigenous Rights and United Nations Standards.* Cambridge: Cambridge University Press, 2007.

Yakye Axa Indigenous Community v. Paraguay, (15) IHRR 978 (2008).

CHAPTER 9

Collective Decision-Making versus Individual Rights: A Reflection on the 'Noken' Electoral System of Papua and the Operation of Native Title in Australia

Bertus de Villiers

Abstract

The electoral system is the principal mechanism through which ordinary persons can influence government policies and express their preferences for the governance of their country. In 2009, the Constitutional Court of Indonesia upheld a cultural practice called 'noken', whereby indigenous leaders in certain parts of Papua province can vote on behalf of their entire community in an election. This decision effectively abrogated the individual's right to vote as guaranteed by the Constitution, and instead allowed for a collective vote to be accepted. The Court decided, in a brief judgement, that the noken system was consistent with the Constitution; that it was a lawful manner to determine the popular vote; that it reflects the laws and customs of 'customary law societies'; and that the imposition of one-person, one-vote could cause conflict and disintegration in and between those traditional communities. This judgement sparked an ongoing debate between those who hold the view that the use of the noken system in democratic elections is unconstitutional, and those who argue that recognition of the noken system shows how modernity and traditionalism can be harmonised. In a similar vein, the High Court of Australia in 1992 changed the course of legal history in that country by acknowledging the existence of native title. This set Australia on an unprecedented path to recognise indigenous ownership of land. This chapter highlights the challenges experienced by Indonesia and Australia in balancing competing objectives when responding to claims to recognise indigenous rights: how to balance modernity and traditionalism? International law strives to achieve outcomes that on the one hand place the individual at the centre of political, social, cultural, and economic rights; while at the same time there is also recognition in international law that in traditional, indigenous societies the community is a *de facto* and even *de jure* bearer of rights, with individual rights only being exercised within the context of the laws, traditions, and customs of the community. These competing objectives are evidenced in the way the two countries have responded to noken and native title. This chapter examines three crucial issues regarding indigenous communities and their rights: how indigenous rights are proven;

how to determine the content of such rights; and how to establish the membership of indigenous communities.

Keywords

collective decision-making – customary law – electoral system – indigenous people – native title – noken – right to vote – self-determination

1 Introduction

The noken system, a traditional practice of Papua characterized by the use of the noken bag, has gained international recognition as an important cultural custom and practice. Since the Constitutional Court of Indonesia in 2009 recognised the noken system as a valid mechanism for expressing the political will of entire indigenous communities in democratic elections, its political use has been shrouded in controversy. Despite universal recognition of the cultural value of noken, its use for political purposes – specifically its reliance on a single individual, the so-called Big Man,[1] to express the vote of an entire community – remains a contentious issue. Some defend the practice as a bridge or even a 'bride'[2] between the past and modernity, while others criticise the practice as susceptible to abuse and incompatible with democratic elections. The controversy surrounding the political use of noken has not abated.

Like Indonesia, Australia has also been searching for measures to give recognition to traditional laws and customs of the Aboriginal people[3] within the context of a modern, liberal democracy.[4] In Australia, Aboriginal people exercise their voting rights in a manner consistent with the one-person, one-vote principle of the International Covenant on Civil and Political Rights (ICCPR).

1 'Big Man' can also be translated as an authoritative, reliable or trusted man. See C. Pamungkas, "Noken Electoral System in Papua: Deliberative Democracy in Papuan Tradition," *Jurnal Masyarakat and Budaya* 19 (2017): 226.

2 Pamungkas, 232.

3 It is acknowledged that there is no agreement in Australia about the term to refer to the indigenous peoples of the country. Whilst generally in statutes the term 'Aboriginal' is used, in the social and political context reference is also made to First People, First Nations, and Indigenous Peoples. For sake of consistency, I use the term Aboriginal.

4 Pamungkas cautions that the notion of 'deliberative democracy', as understood in the western philosophical tradition, is not necessarily an adequate instrument by which to measure the adequacies of the traditional decision-making by Papuans (see Pamungkas, 230).

However, when it comes to the management and control of their traditional native title rights and interests to their ancestral land (or 'country' as it is called by Aboriginal people) special measures have been enacted to recognise their traditional self-management and self-government processes through native title. These measures reflect the intent and principles contained in the Indigenous and Tribal Peoples Convention, 1989 (ILO Convention 169) and the United Nations Declaration on the Rights of Indigenous People (UNDRIP).[5] It must also be noted that despite the universal franchise extended to Aboriginal people in Australia, efforts are ongoing to enhance their voice in public policy. In this respect, recommendations have been made, but rejected by way of a referendum in October 2023, to create an Aboriginal Voice that could give advice to federal and state governments on matters that affect Aboriginal people.[6] These arrangements in Australia may not have been ideal, but within the context of a world searching for answers on ways to protect the rights and interests of indigenous people, the arrangements represent a useful case study of indigenous traditional rights and customs, indigenous self-determination, and indigenous self-definition.

In this chapter, I aim to accomplish three objectives: first, to analyse and evaluate the approach taken by the Constitutional Court of Indonesia in recognising the noken system for democratic elections; second, to examine relevant jurisprudence from Australia in regard to the rights of Aboriginal people to self-organise, to self-determine membership of communities, and to make decisions on behalf of the community; and third, to reflect on what insights can be gained from jurisprudence arising from the noken system and native title. Considering the theme of this book involves jurisprudential analysis, I will examine several court decisions in Indonesia and Australia that pertain to the sub-themes of self-determination, community self-definition, and resolution of membership disputes.

The methodology in this chapter combines a literature review and a comparative jurisprudential analysis. Sources from Australia and Indonesia are used to firstly provide a brief description of the noken and native title systems respectively, whereafter jurisprudential analysis takes place of important judgements that have been handed down to resolve disputes about the

5 The word 'intent' is used since Australia has not ratified ILO Convention169, and although Australia is a signatory to UNDRIP, it is not binding at law.

6 Bertus De Villiers, "An Ancient People Struggling to Find a Modern Voice – Experiences of Australia's Indigenous People with Advisory Bodies," *International Journal on Minority and Group Rights* 26 (2019): 1–21. Bertus De Villiers, "Seven Questions before the Voice Can Be Heard: Learning from the Past," *Brief* August (2022): 8–11.

practical application of the indigenous systems. Finally, a comparative analysis is undertaken to reflect on the practices and jurisprudence of the two countries in response to these indigenous systems, with similarity and differences in approaches being identified.

2 Background to the Political Use of Noken

The electoral system is *the* principal mechanism through which ordinary persons can influence policies and express their preferences about the governance of a country. It is through the conduct of regular elections that individuals can, within the privacy of their own mind, opinion, and beliefs, declare a choice of whom they want to represent them, what policies they prefer, and what direction they want to give to a country or a locality. It is not surprising that a wide variety of electoral systems, quotas, reserved seats, thresholds, and other special electoral measures have been designed to accurately reflect the opinion of voters in general, and more particularly in deeply divided societies, to protect the rights of ethnocultural minorities and indigenous people. Electoral systems have given rise to much experimenting and discourse, but no system is without its critics.[7]

The notion of one-person, one-vote is a basic and fundamental element of liberal democracies regardless of the electoral system used. Universal franchise is a *sine qua non* for democratic government. From that principle arises other important values, such as freedom of expression, freedom of association, organisation of political parties, principles of representation and accountability, checks and balances, separation of powers, and responsible government. All those laudable democratic principles hinge however on one essential requirement – the conduct of free and fair elections whereby each individual can by way of the privacy of the ballot box, express their personal preference about who should govern them. Sounds simple? No.

7 A. Geddis, "Indigenous People and Electoral Law," in *Comparative Electoral Law*, ed. J.A. Gardner (Cheltenham: Elgar, 2022), 71–89; D. Nurumov and V. Vashchonka, "Effective Participation of National Minorities in the Electoral Process," in *Effective Participation of National Minorities and Conflict Prevention*, ed. W. Romans, I. Ulasiuk, and A.P. Thomsen (Leiden: Brill, 2020), 197–214; ACE: Electoral College Network, "Electoral Systems," 2020, https://aceproject.org/ace-en/topics/es/esd/esd06/esd06c; E. Herron, R. Pekkanen, and M. Shugart, eds., *The Oxford Handbook of Electoral Systems* (Oxford: Oxford University Press, 2018); A. Lijphart, "Constitutional Design for Divided Societies," *Journal of Democracy* 2 (2004): 96–109; and D.L. Horowitz, "Electoral Systems: A Primer for Decision Makers," *Journal of Democracy*, no. 14 (2003): 116–32.

Whilst the principle of individual expression of political preference may be deeply embedded in liberal thought and practice, it is not necessarily shared by all traditional, tribal, indigenous, and ethnocultural minority communities. In fact, there are many indigenous communities and non-indigenous minorities who seek special measures in an electoral system to protect them against majoritarian outcomes.[8] The role of individual rights versus collective rights is often at the centre of debate about the protection of indigenous and minority rights. It is particularly in some indigenous communities that promoting individualism is often perceived as akin to undermining the collective interests of the community, while the notion of freedom of political expression is frequently frowned upon by indigenous communities as potentially eroding the very essence of the unity of the community, the tribe and its ancestry institutions, the traditional hierarchy and practices, and community traditions. To those indigenous communities who adhere to traditional customs, the relevance of international opinion and liberal political philosophy about the purported sanctity of individual rights as contained in international instruments, are far removed from the practical reality of their daily living in remote parts of the world, and not particularly relevant to the ancestral rules that apply to their tribe or community. To those indigenous communities the world is local, and their traditions are sacred. Not perfect, but essential for their local peace, order, and good government. This is not entirely surprising. Traditional and customary authorities have demonstrated their resilience by surviving many kinds of upheaval, domination, colonisation, conflicts, wars, and political instability. In short: what to the world seems a relic of the past, is to many traditional communities their world.

International law acknowledges and reflects this clash of modernity and traditionalism. On the one hand, instruments of international law such as the ICCPR emphasise the individuality of rights in general, and more specifically the individual right to freedom of thought, expression, belief, opinion, association, and opinion.[9] Particularly relevant for the purposes of this chapter is Article 25(b) of the ICCPR, which determines that voting in elections shall take

8 See the example in the European context, the recommendations that have been made about mechanisms and techniques to better protect the interests of ethnocultural minorities ("The Lund Recommendations on the Effective Participation of National Minorities in Public Life & Explanatory Note," OSCE HCNM, 1999, https://www.osce.org/files/f/documents/0/9/32240.pdf; and "The Ljubljana Guidelines on Integration of Diverse Societies," OSCE, 2012, The Ljubljana Guidelines on Integration of Diverse Societies | OSCE).

9 ICCPR, "The International Covenant on Civil and Political Rights" (United Nations office of the High Commissioner for Human Rights, 12 December 1966), arts. 18; 19; 21; 22, https://www.ohchr.org/en/professionalinterest/pages/ccpr.aspx.

place by way of 'universal and equal suffrage and shall be held by secret ballot, guaranteeing the free expression of the will of the electors'. The individuality of each person, regardless of any other consideration, is at the centre of these rights. On the other hand, the notion of community or peoples' rights within a collective context is also recognised by international law and practice. The ILO Convention 169[10] seeks to recognise and protect the traditional and customary rights of indigenous communities, for example, the right to self-determination, collective social and cultural rights, special measures for indigenous benefit, recognition of social and cultural practices, participating in decision-making, protection of the environment, due regard to traditional laws and customs, and the right to retain their own customary institutions.[11] The UNDRIP, which does not have the legal effect of treaty law but nevertheless represents a widely held international opinion and even a general, non-binding consensus, also recognises the rights of indigenous people to self-determination, freedom to pursue political status, autonomy of internal and local affairs, maintenance of political institutions, protection against assimilation, protection of customs, election of representatives in accordance with indigenous processes, maintaining political and customary institutions, and determination of membership.[12] Proponents of the recognition of noken as a lawful mechanism to determine electoral outcomes are adamant that noken is consistent with international norms to recognise the sovereignty and self-determination of indigenous people.[13] However, critics say using noken for political purposes is an abrogation of democratic constitutional rights and in breach of international law. Reconciling the *individuality* of liberal democratic thought with the *collective* nature of traditional customs, is clearly not straightforward.[14]

---

10 International Labour Organization, "C16-Indigenous and Tribal Peoples Convention," 1989 (No. 169)', 27 June 1989, arts. 1; 2; 4; 5; 7, https://www.ilo.org/dyn/normlex/en/f?p=NORMLEXPUB:12100:0::NO::P12100_ILO_CODE:C169.

11 ILO Convention 169 is the only legally binding international treaty on indigenous peoples, whilst UNDRIP is a non-legally binding declaration of the UN General Assembly. ILO 169 offers greater security as far as enforceability of rights are concerned, but since it has been ratified by only a few nations (23) its practical utility as a universal legal instrument, other than inspirational and as an interpretative guide, has been limited. Neither Indonesia nor Australia is not a signatory to ILO 169, but both countries have endorsed the non-binding UNDRIP.

12 UNDRIP, "United Nations Declaration on the Rights of Indigenous People," 2007, arts. 3, 5, 8, 11, 18, https://www.un.org/development/desa/indigenouspeoples/declaration-on-the-rights-of-indigenous-peoples.html.

13 B. Setyanto, J. Wiwoho, and M. Jamin, "General Election System in Papua Indonesia," *Systematic Reviews in Pharmacy* 11 (2020): 826.

14 Yunus seeks to find common ground between noken and the electoral college in the USA for presidential elections. Such a comparison stretches the limits of comparative law,

Critics argue that the political use of the noken system of Indonesia as a substitute for the popular vote cannot be upheld in the face of the guarantees of the ICCPR and the Constitution, while defenders of noken are of the view that legal pluralism demands that customs and traditions that are ancient in origin must be respected by contemporary society. According to the latter approach, which was adopted by the noken judgements of the Constitutional Court, the 'fragile nature' of peace and inter-community relationships at a local level in those isolated communities demand recognition of ancient customs such as noken.[15] The counterargument is, however, that the noken system is susceptible to fraud, manipulation, and it eliminates individual choice, which in turn undermines democratisation and may also lead to conflict and violence since there are inadequate checks and balances built into the noken system.[16]

The recognition of the noken system, practiced in remote mountainous parts of Papua province (in Highland Papua province) in Indonesia,[17] highlights the challenge to harmonise the principles of individual freedom to vote with the practical effects of the collective right of indigenous self-determination. Whilst in many indigenous and other minority religious and cultural communities there is some *informal* degree of internal, community adherence and compliance with traditional rules and customs to resolve *internal* community disputes in areas such as use of land, minor criminal matters and family disputes, the noken system as a cultural practice has been endorsed by the Constitutional Court of Indonesia as a valid way for a community to exercise its political right of voting collectively rather than by way of individual choice.[18] This was a transformative judgement about recognition of the rights

with little if any, commonality between the systems. A. Yunus, "Multilayered Democracy in Papua: A Comparison of "Noken" System and Electoral College System in the United States," *Hasanuddin Law Review* 6 (2020): 232–39.

15 IPAC, "Carving up Papua: More Districts, More Trouble." (Jakarta: IPAC, 2013), 11.

16 IPAC, 12.

17 "West Papua" has long been used by non-Indonesian academics to refer to Indonesian Papua – as it is the Western half of Papua island (also known as New Guinea). However, Indonesia in 2003 split its Papua province into West Papua and Papua provinces. Noken takes place in Papua (not West Papua). Also note that in 2022, Indonesia further divided Papua into new provinces – including Highland Papua, where most of the noken areas are located.

18 There are, in essence, two approaches possible under noken, namely where the leader votes on behalf of the community without them being required to vote at all; and where there is some voting by way of placing votes in the noken bag, but the leader determines the actual allocation of votes (Cillian Nolan, "How Papua Voted," New Mandala: New Perspectives on Southeast Asia, 17 April 2014, https://www.newmandala.org/how-papua-voted/). It is therefore not unfamiliar that a 100% voting turnout is recorded. It is perhaps not surprising that the Election Supervisory Agency (Bawaslu) recommended in

of indigenous people, and can be compared in its transformative impact with the recognition of native title in Australia in the seminal case of Mabo.[19]

Whilst there is agreement in Indonesia that the noken system is an unique cultural custom, the elevation of noken for purposes of one person expressing votes on behalf of an entire community in democratic elections has been the subject of intense discourse and disagreement since it was first recognised by the Constitutional Court in 2009.[20] The Constitutional Court has since then reaffirmed the use of noken for democratic elections in parts of Papua in several subsequent judgements.[21] The use of the noken system for purposes of a form of *en bloc* voting has given rise to polarising descriptions. For example, on the one hand, that it should be abolished because it causes manipulation of votes and conflicts with the democratic principles of the Constitution. On the other hand, proponents maintain that it is a bridge between traditional and modernity, that it is consistent with the plurality of Indonesia, that it encourages local involvement and participation, and that it recognises indigenous law and customs.

3 Noken System: Its Cultural Meaning and Political Use

The noken system relates to a wide range of cultural and traditional practices. There is no precise definition of noken that covers all its uses since the way

2016 that the noken system be abolished for purposes of democratic elections (Bawaslu, "Bawaslu Calls for Abolition of "Noken" Voting System in Papua," 16 March 2016, https://bawaslu.go.id/en/news/bawaslu-calls-abolition-%E2%80%98noken%E2%80%99-voting-system-papua). The Commission expressed concerns about the undemocratic nature of noken; the high number of disputes arising from Noken-elections; the use of noken for political purposes; and the human rights violations that accompany noken. The recommendation for the abolition of Noken for electoral purposes, was not accepted by government or parliament.

19 Mabo (2), Mabo v. Queensland (No 2) [1992] HCA 23, (1992) 175 CLR 1 (1992). Bertus De Villiers, "Breathing Life into the Constitution: The Transformative Role of Courts to Give a Unique Identity to a Constitution," *Constitutional Court Review*, 2023.

20 Noken-case, Constitutional Court No 47–18/PHPU.A/VII/2009 (Constitutional Court 2009).

21 See, for example, Noken-case, Constitutional Court Case No. 31/PUU-XII/2014, 11 March 2015 (Constitutional Court 2015); Noken-case, Constitutional Court No. 1/PHPU.PRES-XII/2014, 21 August 2014 (Constitutional Court 2014); Noken-case, Constitutional Court Number 14/PHPU.D-XI/2013, 11 March 2013 (Constitutional Court 2013); Noken-case, Constitutional Court Number 3/PHPU.D-X/2012, 17 February 2012 (Constitutional Court 2012).

the noken customs are applied differs between communities.[22] Each area, in effect, has its own application of noken. The system is particularly associated with the indigenous people in Papua, the easternmost region of Indonesia. The New Guinea region of which Papua is part, is extremely heterogenous with up to 260 ethnic groups, speaking around 1,797 languages and dialects. It is regarded as one of the most ethnically diverse and remote regions in the world. Many of these communities live in isolation from each other and Jakarta is for all practical purposes part of a distant world.

Papua is one of the special regions of Indonesia that in 2001 was granted special, asymmetrical autonomy.[23] Through decentralisation, the government sought to give greater recognition to local cultures and traditions through *adat* (traditional customs and practices). The decentralisation process has been described as a 'big bang autonomy experiment' that provides fertile soil for the revival of *adat* movements across Indonesia[24] and for the accommodation of legal plurality, particularly at a regional and local level.[25] Decentralisation was seen as a mechanism to deepen democracy, bring decision-making closer to the community, and give greater recognition to local cultures and traditions through *adat*.[26] Some observers are however sceptical about the purported benefits of decentralisation and say it has 'encouraged predatory behaviour in the form of corruption, collusion and nepotism at a regional level.'[27]

Generally speaking, those defending the use of noken say the recognition of *adat* in general and noken in particular, is consistent with Article 18B(2) of the Indonesia Constitution, which provides for the recognition of customary and traditional rights. Article 18B(2) considers indigenous communities as legal

22 Nolan, "How Papua Voted."

23 Bertus De Villiers, S. Isra, and Z. Mochtar, "Asymmetry in a Decentralised, Unitary State: Lessons to Be Drawn from the Experiences of Decentralisation to the Special Regions of Indonesia," *Journal on Ethnopolitics and Minority Issues in Europe* 18 (2019): 43–71. A.W. Soetjipto, "Journey to Justice: The United Nations Declaration on the Rights of Indigenous Peoples in the Context of West Papua," *Journal of ASEAN Studies* 10 (2022): 129–49.

24 Rudy, R. Perdana, and R. Wijaya, "The Recognition of Customary Rights by Indonesian Constitutional Court," *Academic Journal for Interdisciplinary Studies* 10 (2021): 309.

25 The use of noken in economic development has also been described as a 'creative economic potential', by linking traditionalism and modernism in the field of socio-economic developments. (B.N. Avianto et al., "Ethnotechnology Noken-Papua as Carrying Capacity for Enhancing Local Economic Development," *International Journal of Social Economics* 48 (2021): 1476–91).

26 T. Efriandi, *Decentralization and the Challenges of Local Governance in Indonesia* (Groningen, University of Groningen, 2021).

27 Y. Nugraha, "Legal Pluralism, Human Rights and the Right to Vote: The Case of the Noken System in Papua," *Asia-Pacific Journal on Human Rights* 22 (2021): 255.

entities that are entitled to maintain their traditional and cultural organisation and rights. Various judgements of the Constitutional Court have recognised *adat*, ranging from creation of special regions, recognition of the noken system, management of land, recognition of customary law and practices, and control of forests.[28] The concern is, however, that the recognition of noken by the Constitutional Court in 2009 as a substitute of a public participatory electoral processes has created a 'legal vacuum' that can easily be exploited by elites, since in the wake of the 2009 judgement there were no regulatory checks and balances on the exercise of noken.[29]

The noken system comprises cultural, traditional, and political elements. The cultural elements refer, amongst others, to the use of the noken bag as a representation of a cultural tradition for practical tasks like carrying food, parcels, good purchased at the market, small animals, and babies. The bag may also be worn during traditional festivities. The bag is woven from wooden fibre. Culturally, noken is associated with a prosperous life, fertility, and peace. The noken bag is made by indigenous Papuan women when they enter fertility and are ready for marriage. The noken bag also reflects on and represents the unique identity of the tribe or clan, and it could be used for purposes of exchange or barter.[30] The noken bag has been recognised by UNESCO as an Intangible Cultural Heritage in Need of Urgent Safeguarding.[31] UNESCO described the noken bag as follows:

> Noken is a knotted net or woven bag handmade from wood fibre or leaves by communities in Papua and West Papua Provinces of Indonesia. Men and women use it for carrying plantation produce, catch from the sea or lake, firewood, babies or small animals as well as for shopping and for storing things in the home. Noken may also be worn, often for traditional festivities, or given as peace offerings. The method of making Noken varies between communities, but in general, branches, stems or bark of certain small trees or shrubs are cut, heated over a fire and soaked in water.

---

28 Rudy, Perdana, and Wijaya, "The Recognition of Customary Rights by Indonesian Constitutional Court," *Academic Journal of Interdisciplinary Studies* 10, no. 3 (2021): 314–15.

29 T. Efriandi, O. Couwenberg, and R.L Holzhacker, "The Noken System and the Challenge of Democratic Governance at the Periphery," in *Challenges of Governance: Development and Regional Integration in Southeast Asia*, ed. R.L Holzhacker and W.G.Z. Tan (Springer, 2021), 68.

30 Pamungkas, "Noken Electoral System in Papua: Deliberative Democracy in Papuan Tradition," 223.

31 UNESCO-Noken, "Decision of the Intergovernmental Committee: 7.COM 8.3," 2012, https://ich.unesco.org/en/decisions/7.COM/8.3.

> The remaining wood fibre is dried then spun to make a strong thread or string, which is sometimes coloured using natural dyes. This string is knotted by hand to make net bags of various patterns and sizes. The process requires great manual skill, care and artistic sense, and takes several months to master.[32]

The political element of noken refers, amongst others, to local tribal consultation and decision-making through collective and inclusive processes within a customary context. It is said that the core of the noken system is a 'discursive and consultation practice to determine decisions' at a local level about the affairs of the community.[33] Traditionally, the noken system was solely used for tribal consultation and decision-making processes.[34] However, in 1971, the noken system was used for the first time to determine the outcome of popular, democratic elections.[35] The essence of the noken is that the leader, often referred to as Big Man, formulates the response of a community to an election by allocating seats or support in a manner that he deems reflective of the opinion of the entire community. The decision of the Big Man is final and represents the entire electoral district, albeit that there may have been some consultation by him preceding the allocation of votes.

The adaptation of noken to determine the result of modern elections, on the one hand, arguably aligns with the observation of the High Court of Australia that native title of Aboriginal people is not 'frozen in time' and can adjust to new circumstances *provided* that a causal link between traditional and contemporary practice is established.[36] On the other hand, critics are of

32 UNESCO-Noken, para. 1.

33 E. Chaidir, "The Constitutional Court Decision Regarding Disputes of Legislative Election; from a Progressive Law Enforcement to the Recognition of Customary Communities in Democracy," *Advances in Social Science, Education and Humanities Research* 358 (2019): 162.

34 Note how in the case of an election of a governor in Bali, the Constitutional Court had upheld bloc-voting on the basis that it is consistent with traditional custom. (Bali-case, Constitutional Court Number 62/PHPU.D-XI/2013, 20 June 2013 (Constitutional Court 2013). In Bali a system referred to as 'bonding' is followed whereby the leader or head of the family may cast a vote for other persons.

35 It must however be noted that when in 1969 a referendum was held to determine if Papua should become part of Indonesia, community representatives made the decision *without* a popular vote. (Pamungkas, "Noken Electoral System in Papua: Deliberative Democracy in Papuan Tradition," 224).

36 Yorta Yorta (HCA), Yorta Yorta v. Victoria [2002] HCA 58; (2002) 214 CLR 422 (2002). A traditional culture can 'evolve' into new customs and practices, but on the condition that there is an *established link* between the new practice and the original customs and practices

the view that the political use of noken as a substitute for democratic elections cannot be regarded as an 'evolution' of the traditional system, but that is it an imposition and abuse without an adequate link to traditional custom, and it is therefore improper and unconstitutional to employ a cultural and customary practice to substitute constitutional guarantees for democratic elections. To critics, noken ought to be limited to cultural and traditional deliberations akin to the tribal arrangements in Africa, but without noken being elevated as a substitute for democratic elections.

The political representation of noken is reflected in the authority of the leader, the so-called Big Man, whereby community decisions are articulated by him. The Big Man is not necessarily the traditional leader through ancestry, but rather an authoritative person that is entrusted by the community to speak on their behalf.[37] The Big Man articulates decisions of the community after consultation and deliberation.[38] The nature, extent and manner of consultation depends on the practices of each community.

In essence, each locality has its own use for the noken system, but the characteristic shared for the purposes of this chapter is that the vote of individual members of a community is superseded by the Big Man, who determines the vote of the entire electoral district.[39] The recognition of noken reflects the continuation of practices that existed during the colonial era, where local customs and practices, so-called *adat*, were acknowledged within a philosophical framework that embraced plurality of law.[40] The allowance of *adat* is consistent with contemporary law, recognising the coexistence of 'two bodies of norms' within the same state.[41] For a country so diverse as Indonesia, *adat*

(Yorta Yorta, Members of the Yorta Yorta Aboriginal Community v Victoria [1998] FCA 1606 (18 December 1998) (1998)).

37 B. Setyanto, J. Wiwoho, and M. Jamin, "Noken System in Indonesian General Elections," *Advances in Economics, Business and Management Research* 140 (2020): 728.

38 P. Tombi, "Noken in Positive Legal Framework in the 2020 Election of Regional Heads (Pilkada) in Indonesia," in *International Conferene on Law and Human Rights*, ed. B. Nainggolan and H. Panjaitan (Jakarta: CCER, 2021), 60–68.

39 S. Butt, *The Constitutional Court and Democracy in Indonesia* (Leiden: Brill, 2015), 170.

40 The plurality of law is linked to the concept "Pancasila" which is a foundation norm of the Constitution whereby all agencies must work together to achieve the goals of the state (Setyanto, Wiwoho, and Jamin, "Noken System in Indonesian General Elections," 729). This is not dissimilar to the way in which the non-constitutional term *Ubuntu* has been used in South Africa. (Bertus De Villiers, "Does a Constitution Have a Soul? The Role of Bundestreue in Germany and Ubuntu in South Africa to Give Life and Identity to a Constitutional Text," in *Navigating the Unknown – Essays on Selected Case Studies about the Rights of Minorities* (Leiden: Brill, 2022), 163–214).

41 G.R. Woodman, "The Idea of Legal Pluralism," in *Legal Pluralism in the Arab World*, ed. B. Dupret, M. Berger, and L. al-Zwaini (Amsterdam: Kluwer, 1999), 4.

is 'very important in everyday life; therefore one cannot be separated from *adat*'.[42] The application of the noken system to contemporary elections therefore maintains the traditional reliance on achieving consensus or consultation within the community, with the ultimate decision-making authority residing in the Big Man.[43] Critics respond, however, that when noken is applied as a substitute to democratic elections, the system denies the right of individual franchise based on a secret ballot as anticipated by international law, democratic theory and practice, and the Constitution of Indonesia.

4 Constitutional Court Recognition of Noken as Substitute for Popular Vote

It is said that the noken system was used for the first time in popular elections in 1971, but it was only in the 2009 elections that a dispute over its usage came before the Constitutional Court. The challenge specifically pertained to the application of the noken vote in the highland district of Yahukimo in Papua.[44] The Court decided, in a brief judgement, that the noken system was consistent with the Constitution, that it was a lawful manner to determine the popular vote, that it reflects the laws and customs of 'customary law societies', and that the imposition of one-person, one-vote could cause conflict and disintegration in and between those traditional communities.[45]

This judgement set up a debate that continues between those who hold the view that the use of the noken system for purposes of democratic elections is unconstitutional, and those who argue that recognition of the noken system shows how modernity and traditionalism can be harmonised.

---

42 L.T. Murray, "Masyarakat Adat, Difference, and the Limits of Recognition of Indonesia's Forest Zone," *Modern Asian Studies* 35 (2001): 646.

43 Nugraha, "Legal Pluralism, Human Rights and the Right to Vote: The Case of the Noken System in Papua," 259.

44 In this case, the noken system was used in Yahukimo District not only for cultural and traditional purposes such as carrying of food or crops, but also to be a repository for ballots in contemporary elections. It served in effect as a ballot box but with the important caveat that the vote was not cast in private; the votes were not counted by the Electoral Commission; and the Big Man apportioned the votes for the entire electoral district.

45 *Noken* case, Constitutional Court No 47-18 / PHPU.A / VII / 2009 paragraph 3.24. Critics say that local conflict created by noken is reflected in the high number of electoral disputes that arise after each election from the noken areas, whilst proponents retort by saying the peaceful resolution of those electoral disputes has confirmed the appropriateness of the decision by the Constitutional Court to recognise the system.

The Constitutional Court has followed up the 2009 judgement with several other judgements in which the noken system has been upheld. It can be said that recognition of noken is now embedded in the constitutional law of Indonesia. The approach adopted by the Court to interpret the Constitution has been described as a 'contextual' approach, recognising that the text should be understood within the context of the specific community it serves. Rather than strictly adhering to a text-based interpretation, the Constitution is viewed as a dynamic entity that can be adjusted to new circumstances. In subsequent judgements following the 2009 decision, the Constitutional Court also referred to Article 18B of the Constitution to better explain the rationale for the judgements. This further enhances the contextual approach adopted by the Court.

The Indonesian Constitution determines in Article 22E(1) that general elections "shall be conducted in a direct, general, free, secret, honest, and fair manner once every five years". The principle of one-person, one-vote cannot be expressed with greater clarity than in Article 22E, and yet, in the 2009 general election the question arose whether an election result based on collective decision-making according to the noken tradition, was lawful and valid under the Constitution.

In the 2009 dispute, it was acknowledged that the voting process did not comply with Article 22E(1) since the votes had been placed in the village noken bag and the outcome of the vote had been conveyed to the Electoral Commission by the leader on behalf of the community. There had been no counting of votes by the Electoral Commission. It was contended by the applicants that a vote expressed in this manner was inconsistent with the Law No. 10 of 2008 on General Elections of Members of the People's Legislative Assembly, Regional Representative Council, and Regional People's Representative Council (Legislative Election). The Court did not undertake an in-depth analysis of the noken system; however, it acknowledged the noken system contravenes Article 22E(1) as people do not vote individually, they do not enter a voting booth privately, and the leader decides the outcome of the vote instead of it being tallied by the Electoral Commission.[46]

Notable is that while the Constitutional Court's 2009 judgement accepted the practice of noken, it failed to examine its operation within the community, its impact on citizens' rights, checks and balances on the Big Man, the opinions of disenfranchised community members, the regions of application, and the fairness and transparency of noken procedures in relation to constitutional

46 A. Sodiki, "The Constitutionality of Election Model Society Yakuhimo," *Journal of Constitution* 6 (2009): 342–57.

guarantees. The Court also did not consider why some regions are bound by noken, or to what electoral areas noken applies. The Court essentially endorsed the noken system without any in-depth reasoning or expert evidence of why noken should be accepted regardless of its encroachment on constitutional guarantees of individual franchise.

The 2009 judgement can be regarded as principally informed by pragmatism, rather than an in-depth balance of competing considerations and proportionality between those of modernism versus traditionalism. Curiously, the Court did not in 2009 invoke Article 18B(2) of the Constitution, which it later relied on in subsequent judgements to justify the acceptance of the noken system within the framework of customary law and practice.

In a 2013 judgement, the Court dismissed evidence by a complainant that there was a conspiracy aimed at preventing the counting of all ballot boxes. The Court found that noken allowed for votes to be collectively cast and hence there was no requirement for each vote to be counted.[47] In a 2014 judgement concerning the noken system, the Constitutional Court again endorsed the practice whereby the electoral choice of an entire community could be based on the authority of the clan chief (*kepala suku*) 'who acts as the political representative of the community'.[48] This meant, in effect, that the Big Man could determine the outcome of an election, regardless of whether individuals cast their vote in the noken bag. The Big Man can allocate all votes to a single party, or divide them among multiple parties or candidates.

Critics observed that the reasoning employed in 2014 judgement eliminated any 'pretence' of public participation in elections within traditional communities.[49] Whilst the Constitutional Court in 2014 relied on the constitutional provision Article 18B (as mentioned above, in 2009 there was no reference by the Court to Article 18B),[50] it did not provide a detailed explanation as to why

47 *Noken* case, Constitutional Court Number 14/PHPU.D-XI/2013, 11 March 2013 paragraph 3.24.4.

48 *Noken* case, Constitutional Court Number 6-32/PHPU-DPD/XII/2014, 25 June 2014 (Constitutional Court 2014). In the 2014 election, 12 of the 16 highland districts used noken to cast the community vote.

49 IPAC Report, "Open to Manipulation: The 2014 Elections in Papua Province" (Jakarta: IPAC, 10 December 2014), 4.

50 *Noken* case, Constitutional Court No. 1/PHPU.PRES-XII/2014, 21 August 2014, paragraph 3.24.4.4. The Court declared that although the 'voting mechanism' through which votes are counted by way of 'community agreement' is not explicitly mentioned in the Constitution, the arrangement can be recognised pursuant to Article 18B(2) of the Constitution.

it found that the noken system complies with Article 18B or which regions and localities fall within the noken system. Article 18B provides as follows:

1. The State recognises and respects units of regional authorities that are special and distinct, which shall be regulated by law.
2. The State recognises and respects traditional communities along with their traditional customary rights as long as these remain in existence and are in accordance with the societal development and the principles of the Unitary State of the Republic of Indonesia, and shall be regulated by law.

The Court also did not thoroughly examine the reactions of individuals affected by the noken system, nor did it consider whether noken, as a cultural system, had genuinely evolved into a political system that supersedes universal democratic franchise guaranteed by the Constitution.

The reasoning of the Constitutional Court regarding the evolution of a cultural custom differs from the approach adopted by the High Court of Australia. The High Court of Australia has also accepted that a culture can evolve, but such evolution must be supported by an in-depth assessment of the evidence of each Aboriginal community that seeks to have their native title rights and interests recognised. As discussed below, Aboriginal communities are required to meet a standard of proof that shows they are related to the ancestral community that traditionally occupied the land, that they continue to practice the customs of that ancient community, and that they continue to function as a society. Most important for purposes of this chapter is that each Aboriginal community must, through evidence, prove the content of its 'bundle of rights' and that those rights continue to be practiced in contemporary society.[51] If the methodology of the High Court were to be applied to noken, one would expect those who rely on noken to replace democratic elections must be required to give evidence to the Court to explain how the traditional use of noken has evolved to also include contemporary democratic elections and what traditional and customary checks and balances apply to curb the powers and functions of the Big Man.

The Constitutional Court of Indonesia recognizes that the noken system presents an outcome based on community agreement as determined by the Big Man, as opposed to individual franchise. The Court in 2009 found that failure to acknowledge the noken system could result in conflict at the local level where the traditional custom is still practiced. The Electoral Commission

51 R. Bartlett, *Native Title in Australia* (Australia: LexisNexis Butterworths, 2020).

therefore had to give effect to the election results as presented to it by the Big Man. Curiously, the Court did not hear evidence and did not explain in its reasoning why it concluded that recognition of noken could prevent community violence, or why universal franchise as guaranteed by the Constitution could give rise to violence. One would have expected that such an important deviation from guaranteed constitutional rights would be accompanied by detailed reasoning and assessment of relevant expert and lay person evidence. It is also notable, when election outcomes since 2009 are assessed, that the noken results have given rise to the most disputes of election outcomes. In fact, some of the noken regions are rated the highest on the so-called vulnerability index for disputed elections.[52]

In order to give effect to the constitutional recognition of the noken system, the statute that precedes the holding of each general election was for the first time adjusted in 2019 to specifically regulate noken elections. The General Election Commission issued a declaration in 2019 to regulate the conduct of elections in Papua pursuant to noken.[53] The Declaration identified 12 areas where a noken result would be accepted. The Commission thereby solidified and clarified the use of the system for traditional voting. The noken system was defined by the Commission as a 'form of common agreement or acclamation' to conduct elections 'in accordance with customs, tradition, culture and local wisdom of the local populace.'[54] This is clearly a very wide, catchall description of noken, while allowing room for local communities to adapt and apply the system according to their specific practices.

It is for now established law and practice that the noken system is used in 12 areas for collective voting. In those areas, the individual right to vote cannot be exercised in any other way as through noken, and there is no provision for the application of noken to expire or to be reviewed in the future.

5 Noken Elections: the Aftermath of the 2009 Judgement

The noken judgements have given rise to polarising opinions and heated debates. The endorsement and criticism of the 2009 judgement and subsequent

52 Efriandi, Couwenberg, and Holzhacker, "The Noken System and the Challenge of Democratic Governance at the Periphery," 82.

53 Electoral Commission – Noken, "Guidelines for the Implementation of Voting with the Noken System in Papua Province," Electoral Commission, 2019, https://jdih.kpu.go.id/beritadetail-4a6454305277253344253344.

54 Electoral Commission – Noken, para. 23.

rulings are wide ranging, but the following main points are at the core of the ongoing debate:

Critics argue that the recognition of noken for electoral purposes is a fundamental breach of the Constitution and its use in democratic elections is inconsistent with the provisions of international law. The power of a 'small elite' has substituted the power of the general electorate.[55] In some villages, voting does not take place at all. On the other hand, the noken system allows for some form of elite bargaining whereby different interests are reconciled through community leadership in a manner consistent with traditional law and customs. The recognition of the noken system is in principle not dissimilar to other efforts internationally to give effect to group rights and collective interests through various forms of power sharing and elite bargaining. But the risk is that any consensus-driven process that lacks checks and balances and judicial supervision, may give rise to abuse. On the other hand, it is said that the recognition of noken reflects the principles contained in ILO Convention 169 and UNDRIP, which encourage respect for indigenous institutions and incorporate traditional and customary processes as checks and balances. Noken is therefore seen as an extension of 'local wisdom'.[56]

The concern by the Constitutional Court in 2009 that the non-recognition of noken could lead to violence and community conflict, has not been properly scrutinised by subsequent decisions to confirm the veracity of the finding. Whilst the concern may have merit, one would expect judicial reasoning based on evidence to explain why such a finding of fact is made and, on the balance, why a derogation of a constitutional right to individual franchise should be accepted. The converse may also be true, namely that the abrogation of the right to vote has created fertile soil for conflict and popular dissatisfaction as is evidenced in disputes arising from noken area elections. The deviation from the Constitution and international legal principles may not be justified by a purported fear of violence or unrest. But, on the other hand, noken is seen by locals as an 'instrument of harmony'.[57]

The outcome of noken elections has according to crtitics become arbitrary and unreliable due to the unsupervised discretion of the Big Man. This may lead to community conflict, which is what the 2009 judgement sought to prevent. The lack of public and judicial scrutiny of elections is undermining

---

55 IPAC, "Open to Manipulation: The 2014 Elections in Papua Province," 1.

56 Setyanto, Wiwoho, and Jamin, "General Election System in Papua Indonesia," 827.

57 B. Setyanto, J. Wiwoho, and M. Jamin, "Local Democracy: Election of Regional Head and Regional Deputy Head in the Noken System in Papua Indonesia," *International Journal of Innovation, Creativity and Change* 11 (2020): 358.

democratisation and leading to unreliable and arbitrary outcomes.[58] However, it is not clear what the impact would be if noken was entirely abolished, and the effect on traditional communities if they were exposed to free and open political activism. Many aspiring and emerging democracies have failed as a result of one-party dominance, or electoral violence and corruption. It is therefore not clear if the abolition of the noken system would enhance or erode local peace and stability. According to Sahabat, noken is a 'deliberative democratic system' wherein the will of a community is ascertained in a direct, traditional manner.[59] Pamungkas says that in the event of removal of community consensus decision-making, the community would become 'fragile and easy to be dominated by an oligarchy.'[60]

Reliance on noken outcomes has undermined the reliability of data of population size within the noken areas. This in turn has possibly negatively impacted on the ability of governments at all levels to properly plan for socio-economic development. On the other hand, there may be better ways to secure more accurate estimations of population size than through voter participation in elections. Those alternative avenues for population estimations ought to be explored, rather to rely on the purported shortcoming of noken as a rationale to abolish the system.

The inflation of population numbers in noken areas for the benefit of increasing representation and political influence, has arguably had the flow-on effect of additional funds being allocated to certain noken localities to the detriment of other local areas. As a result, the noken system has become a 'formidable obstacle to curbing corruption and improving governance'.[61] The counter to this concern is to ask whether there are any mechanisms by which the allocation of funds to local communities can be managed and assessed other than via the outcome of elections? Ultimately it may be erroneous to link dispersal of funds to any electoral system since there may be many reasons why persons vote or abstain from voting.

58 See the analysis by IPAC about the inconsistencies between actual outcomes of elections and 'real irregularities' that have arisen in some of the regions where Noken is practiced (IPAC, "Open to Manipulation: The 2014 Elections in Papua Province," 3). Nolan also observes about the 'dangers' lurking due to the lack of consistency between different approaches to Noken (C. Nolan, "Votes in the Bag? The Noken System and Conflict in Indonesia" (Jakarta: International Crisis Group, 2012), 2).

59 Sahabat, "Noken System Used to Ensure West Papua Led by Native," *West Papua Story* (blog), 5 January 2022.

60 Pamungkas, "Noken Electoral System in Papua: Deliberative Democracy in Papuan Tradition," 231.

61 IPAC, "Open to Manipulation: The 2014 Elections in Papua Province," 1.

It remains contested how the Constitutional Court or the Electoral Commission ascertains whether in a particular locality, noken is applied or not. One would expect that consistent with ordinary rules of evidence it is for a community to adduce evidence as to why their local traditions ought to be given effect rather than the norms prescribed in the Constitution. The burden of proof should be high since a derogation of a constitutional right should not be easy to achieve. The Electoral Commission has only since 2019 acknowledged the specific regions where noken elections are to be held. This is a closed list. Those regions are specifically identified based on adherence to traditional customs, remoteness, geographical isolation, and lack of human resources to conduct effective elections.[62] It is yet to be seen, however, if the number of regions that now use noken would decrease in years to come if communities reject noken or noken falls in disuse. One thing is clear, no new regions can be added to the 12 already acknowledged since the Court has ruled that regions that have never used noken, cannot revert to noken.[63]

6 Native Title Jurisprudence in Australia: a Few Comparative Judgements

The recognition of native title by the Mabo judgement in 1992 in Australia cannot be directly compared to the recognition of noken in democratic elections in 2009 in Indonesia.[64] Whilst native title relates to the recognition of customary rights to land of Aboriginal people, the right to vote of Aboriginal people is not dependent on their native title rights and interests. Aboriginal people were granted general franchise in 1962. There is no comparable traditional system of voting in Australia to noken in Indonesia, and there are no reserved seats for Aboriginal people as for the Māori in New Zealand.[65] The electoral system of Australia is for all practical and legal purposes a one-person, one-vote system.

Arising from the recognition of native title there are, however, some interesting Australian judgements that bear relevance to aspects of the operation of noken. It is the aim of this part of the chapter to briefly reflect on some of those Australian judgements. The judgements referred to are particularly relevant to

62 Tombi, "Noken in Positive Legal Framework in the 2020 Election of Regional Heads (Pilkada) in Indonesia".

63 Noken-case, Constitutional Court Case No. 31/PUU-XII/2014, 11 March 2015 at 34.

64 Mabo (2), *Mabo.*

65 A. Xanthaki and D. O'Sullivan, "Indigenous Participation in Elective Bodies: The Māori in New Zealand," *International Journal on Minority and Group Rights* 16 (2009): 181–212.

three dimensions that arise from the noken system, namely: (a) the threshold to *prove* native title; (b) the obligation on native title holders to prove the *bundle of rights* that they possess; and (c) the determination of the Aboriginality of a person in general, and more specifically, the *membership* of a person of native title community.

In the following part, each of these dimensions is briefly discussed with reference to the noken judgements of Indonesia, accompanied by an explanation of why the Australian jurisprudence is potentially relevant to the application of noken.

6.1 *Threshold for the Recognition of Native Title*

The question that arises in both jurisdictions revolves around determining when any indigenous community may receive special rights and privileges. What is the rationale for such special status, and are these special arrangements to be permanent, temporary or transitional?

In the 2009 noken judgement, the Constitutional Court of Indonesia did not explain why that particular community was entitled to use noken, nor did the Court lay down any guidelines for other noken communities about benchmarks to qualify for the use of noken in elections. There was also no legislative intervention in Indonesia to regularise or give effect to the 2009 judgement. It was only some years later that the Court indicated that only communities that had previously used noken could fall within the ambit of the 2009 judgement. The Electoral Commission identified in 2019, a decade after the 2009 judgement, the 12 regions to which noken would be applied both currently and in the future. It is not clear whether there would be scope in future for individuals from any of those 12 regions to challenge the ongoing application of noken, or whether those communities are for all practical purposes frozen in the noken system, meaning that their votes will be cast by the Big Man *en bloc* in perpetuity.

Turning to the recognition of native title in Australia: The entirety of Australia was regarded as *terra nullius* (no person's land) under common law when the British settled in 1788. The term *terra nullius* reflected the legal dogma that the continent was either uninhabited or, to the extent that there had been some human presence, the unsophisticated nature of the indigenous people rendered them incapable of recognition, negotiation or protection.[66] This dogma prevailed until the Mabo judgement of 1992 when the High Court of

66 S. Banner, "Why Terra Nullius? Anthropology and Property Law in Early Australia," *Law and History Review* 23 (2005): 95–131.

Australia for the first time held that native title continued to exist and is therefore recognised by common law.[67] It is, however, not simple for an Aboriginal community to have their native title rights recognised or restored. Success is often only achieved after a lengthy court and adversarial process.

The benchmarks to be met for an Aboriginal community to prove the ongoing existence of their traditional native title comprise, in essence, three elements: the community must prove that their apical ancestors exercised native title rights over the area that is now being claimed; they must prove that the current Aboriginal community continue to exercise native title rights in regard to that area and they must specify the exact nature of the rights they exercise; and they must prove that they continue to function as a traditional society.[68] In the Yorta Yorta judgement, the High Court of Australia interpreted the word 'traditional' to mean a society that is 'united in and by its acknowledgement and observance of a body of law and customs.'[69] This does not mean the contemporary laws and customs must be identical now as at the time of settlement, but that there must be a 'continuous existence' and a causal link of the traditional laws and customs to contemporary practices. Evolution of a cultural practice is therefore possible, but if a practice had been discontinued, it cannot be reactivated for purposes of a native title declaration. These benchmarks to prove native title are not easy to meet.[70]

There are some similarities and differences between Indonesia and Australia regarding the recognition of indigenous rights. For example, both countries require evidence of the existence of and adherence to a traditional custom; both countries have declared that only those communities that had a traditional custom can be recognised and new communities cannot be added to the list; both jurisdictions acknowledge that once the traditional custom is lost, it cannot be revived for purposes of noken voting or native title; and both countries allow for traditional customs to evolve from traditional into a contemporary context. The countries differ, however, in the process leading to recognition of special rights for an indigenous community. In Australia, Aboriginal people must prove their native title *and* the rights they assert attach to native title. This process to prove native title involves lengthy research, litigation, negotiation and court outcomes. The benefit of this laborious process is that the outcome is supported by findings of fact and cannot in future be challenged.

67 Mabo (2), *Mabo*.

68 Bartlett, *Native Title in Australia*, 156–228.

69 Yorta Yorta (HCA), Yorta Yorta v. Victoria [2002] HCA 58; (2002) 214 CLR 422.

70 N. Duff, *What's Needed to Prove Native Title? Finding Flexibility within the Law on Connection* (Canberra: AIATSIS, 2014).

In Indonesia there is ample anthropological evidence of the *cultural* use of noken, but recognition of the 12 areas where noken may be applied for electoral purposes was an administrative and even pragmatic outcome, rather than a court declaration or legislative outcome. There has not yet been a legal inquiry into communities where noken could potentially be used for purposes of vote counting; the response of communities; the impact on minorities, such as the rights of women; and the rules that would apply under noken.[71] It is perhaps not surprising that Efriandi concludes that arguments in favour of the retention of noken are 'not well-grounded'.[72] Indonesia's Constitutional Court has also not considered to the same level of detail as its Australian counterpart, the extent to which communities and individuals in those 12 areas support noken for electoral purposes, the views of dissenters, community compliance with noken, checks and balances on the Big Man, and whether the community continues to abide by noken. Another point of difference: in Australia, the Mabo judgement was followed by the enactment of the Native Title Act in 1993[73] to regulate all aspects of native title, while in Indonesia there has been no constitutional amendment or legislative framework to regularise noken, or to set out minimum requirements by which the reporting of votes could be scrutinised, or to explain if the noken system would apply in perpetuity, or for a transitional period. Noken continues to function to some extent in a legal vacuum since it lacks transparency and accountability.[74]

6.2 *Determining the Bundle of Rights of a Native Title Community*

In both countries, the package of rights that comprise noken or native title respectively, is undefined. There is no exhaustive definition of the customs of the respective communities, and it is often in the practical application of rules, traditions and practices that noken and native title are recognised. The Constitutional Court determined in 2011 that the definition of Papua people is based on the customs of each community and cannot be prescribed by

---

71 Y. Suryana, "The Relationship of Husband Authority to the Wife Political Rights," *Justitia Et Pax* 38 (2022): 1–23.

72 Efriandi, "Decentralization and the Challenges of Local Governance in Indonesia," 160.

73 Native Title Act, "National Native Title Act, 1993" (1993), https://www.legislation.gov.au/Details/C2019C00054.

74 Efriandi, for example, expresses concern that due to the vacuum, "there is no clear technical guidance on how consensus should be reached among the clan members, or how clan members who have different preference over the candidate can use votes directly at the polling station without being represented." (Efriandi, "Decentralization and the Challenges of Local Governance in Indonesia," 178).

government.[75] The two countries have, however, adopted different ways for the communities that claim special recognition, to prove the merit of their claim. In Indonesia, the 2009 case dealt with only the one community that was involved in the dispute, with no further guidance given by the Constitutional Court or parliament at the time to other communities that have relied on noken. It is only in 2019 that the Electoral Commission identified the 12 regions where noken would in future apply, but this was an administrative decision without any legal scrutiny or public enquiry of the views or opinions of the communities concerned. The exact manner how the noken vote are to be collected and seats allocated in future remains open and at the sole discretion of each regional community, which means independent scrutiny of noken in general and the Big Man in particular, is difficult or even impossible. This is a less than optimal outcome for stable electoral processes.

The Australian recognition of native title requires each Aboriginal community to prove all the elements of their bundle of rights, thereby implying that while native title is the general description of customary title, the exact nature and scope of rights must in each case be proven though community evidence of laws and practices. The specific rights forming part of the native title bundle of rights of a specific community may therefore vary from community to community.[76] The typical in the bundle are practices such as camping, hunting, fishing, resource utilisation, access control and taking care of country. The bundle of rights is ultimately set out in a legal instrument with the effect of a court order pursuant to the Native Title Act and the exercise of those rights are judicially reviewable.[77] The exercise of rights and recognition thereof by native title communities was described in the Mabo judgement as follows:

> The range of current estimates for the whole continent [at time of settlement] is between three hundred thousand and a million or even more. Under the laws or customs of the relevant locality, particular tribes or clans were, either on their own or with others, custodians of the areas of land from which they derived their sustenance and from which they often took their tribal names. Their laws or customs were elaborate and

75 Special Autonomy for Papua, Constitutional Court DCFVVt Number 029/PUU-IX/2011 (Constitutional Court 2011).

76 Wik, Wik Peoples v. The State of Queensland [1996] HCA 40, (1996) 187 CLR 1 (23 December 1996), High Court. (1996).

77 Bertus De Villiers, "Breaking New Ground for Indigenous Non-Territorial Cultural Self-Government: The Noongar Settlement in Australia," in *Navigating the Unknown – Essays on Selected Case Studies about the Rights of Minorities* (Leiden: Brill, 2022), 138–62.

> obligatory. The boundaries of their traditional lands were likely to be long-standing and defined. The special relationship between a particular tribe or clan and its land was recognized by other tribes or groups within the relevant local native system and was reflected in differences in dialect over relatively short distances. In different ways and to varying degrees of intensity, they used their homelands for all the purposes of their lives: social, ritual, economic. They identified with them in a way which transcended common law notions of property or possession.[78]

Indonesia and Australia face a similar question about the future of the traditional title that has been recognised by its highest courts. In the case of Indonesia, the use of noken is limited to 12 regions, but it is not clear whether in time to come the number of regions may reduce due to noken falling into disuse, or through rejection by communities. Whilst both countries accept that a custom can expand into a contemporary setting, the converse is also true, namely that a custom may become dormant, diluted, or rejected. There is no review mechanism in place in Indonesia to assess ongoing community support and compliance with noken. Ideally, a legislative act of parliament should regulate the operational aspects of noken and perhaps even identify reviews where the ongoing suitability of the system can be debated. The legislation may even identify a sunset date by which noken will cease to operate. The noken regions are now, in effect, locked into an arrangement whereby individual franchise is not only suspended, but the right to a personal vote is also, in effect, abrogated in perpetuity.

6.3 *Determining Who Belongs to the Indigenous Community*

Australia and Indonesia face the question of how to ascertain who belongs to an indigenous community, and to what extent the right to freedom of individual association should be the sole guide to ascertain membership, or should individual freedom of association be restricted through community decision-making?

In the case of Australia, the question is relevant because a person may claim to be part of a native title group while the community may dispute the claim; or a person may want to receive a benefit that is solely directed at Aboriginal people. In the case of Indonesia, *all* persons within a region are deemed by law to fall within noken election processes, even if they do not subscribe, adhere or practice noken, or even if they are not otherwise part of the local indigenous

---

78 Mabo (2), *Mabo* paragraph 37.

community. Individuals therefore cannot opt out of political use of noken for purposes of electoral choice, and even those who are part of the indigenous community who wish to cast an individual vote, cannot achieve their desire. This means that individuals residing in the 12 regions have no expectation, now or into the future, of their constitutional right to individual suffrage being recognised.

The Australian courts have consistently relied on a three-pronged test to test the claim of a person to be Aboriginal, namely descent, personal identification, and community acceptance.[79] In the Mabo judgment, the High Court of Australia endorsed the three-pronged approach, weighing the individual's claim of aboriginality against the community's response to the individual's assertion, and considering the descent of the person. The Court emphasised the need to examine all evidence of association and then make a finding of fact whether a person is indeed of aboriginal descent and, if so, whether the person is accepted by the specific community or parts of the community as part of the native title group. Importantly, the Court observed that evidence of acceptance by the community is not restricted to a specific checklist or fixed criteria, but that the test includes *all* relevant information of association. The Court summarised its approach as follows:

> Membership of the indigenous people depends on biological descent from the indigenous people and on mutual recognition of a particular person's membership by that person and by the elders or other persons enjoying traditional authority among those people.[80]

In the 2010 Aplin judgement in Australia, the question arose as to how disputes about the assertion of a person that they form part of an Aboriginal native title group (which is in effect a sub-group of the larger aboriginal community) ought to be resolved. The Court declared that it is primarily the responsibility of the indigenous community to determine whether a person is a member of the group, but the Court noted that such a decision cannot be made arbitrarily. The decision of the community must be informed by fact and in accordance with the standards and processes of traditional laws and customs that apply to that community. The Court acknowledged that acceptance of membership by a community is "inherent in the nature of a society", but that

79 Tasmania-case, Commonwealth v. Tasmania (1983) 158 CLR 1 (1983).

80 Mabo (2), *Mabo* paragraph 70.

the *subjective assertion* of membership may be adequate for a community to accept a person.[81]

In the Love judgment of 2020 in Australia, Justice Nettle succinctly summarised the requirement for aboriginality as follows: being of Aboriginal descent, identifying as a member of an Aboriginal community, and being recognised as a member of an Aboriginal community.[82]

The approach adopted by the Australian courts in regard to Aboriginal membership disputes is not without criticism since the question remains: who makes a decision on behalf of the Aboriginal community in general or more specifically the native title community, what level of support is required for acceptance of an individual who claims membership, what evidence is relied upon, what weight is to be attached to the opinion of expert witnesses who appear in court proceedings but who are often non-Aboriginal, and what factors are conclusive to determine membership? In a similar vein, in Indonesia there is no mechanism for a person to opt out of the political use of noken, even if they do not otherwise adhere to noken culturally or worse, even if they are not a member of the local indigenous community.

7 Conclusion

This chapter has highlighted the challenges experienced by both Indonesia and Australia in reconciling their conflicting objectives in response to claims to recognise indigenous rights: how to balance modernity and traditionalism? International law strives to achieve outcomes that on the one hand place the individual at the centre of political, social, cultural, and economic rights; while at the same time there is also recognition in international law that in traditional, indigenous societies the *community* is a *de facto* and even *de jure* bearer of rights, with individual rights only being exercised within the context of the laws, traditions, and customs of the community. These competing objectives are evidenced in the way the two countries have responded to noken and native title, respectively.

The Constitutional Court of Indonesia in 2009 endorsed for the first time the use of noken for purposes of democratic elections, but without any in-depth analysis of evidence why a constitutional right should be abrogated;

81 Federal Court of Australia, Aplin on behalf of the Waanyi Peoples v. Queensland, FCA 625, 2010, para. 256 (Federal Court of Australia 2010).

82 Love, Love v. Commonwealth of Australia and Thoms v. Commonwealth of Australia [2020] HCA 3. (High Court 2020).

whether the recognition of noken is to endure in perpetuity; when a community can revert to noken; whether noken is at all reviewable to ensure that community traditions are indeed adhered to by the Big Man; or what solace is given to those who do not want to be bound by the Big Man's allocation of votes. Ideally, the 2009 judgement should have been followed up by parliament with an electoral act outlining the use and reliance of noken, similar to how the Australian parliament responded with legislation to the Mabo judgement. As a result, noken continued to be recognised in the wake of 2009, but in a policy and legal vacuum. It was only in 2019 that the Electoral Commission designated the regions where noken would apply, but as has been discussed, this was principally an administrative decision without giving communities an opportunity to be consulted about their views of noken being imposed on them. The outcome of this decade-long development is that noken is limited to 12 areas, but with the application of noken entirely in the hands of local leaders, while there is no indication that noken would be reviewed from time to time.

It is shown how Australian jurisprudence may be relevant to the noken debate since in Australia native title of an Aboriginal community is only determined after extensive research, expert and community evidence, and a court declaration; the specific rights of the native title holders are ascertained through their evidence of ongoing cultural practices, and any evolution that has occurred must be explained; and no person can against their will be 'classified' as being part of a native title community. Importantly, the recognition of native title does not affect any civil and political rights, such as the right to vote, of Aboriginal people.

In summary, the recognition of noken and of native title were transformative judgements in Indonesia and Australia. The Mabo judgement has internationally become one of the most cited cases of any Australian court. The noken judgements of Indonesia's Constitutional Court have the potential to also become groundbreaking in its effort to strike a balance between modernity and traditionalism. Both judgements highlight the importance of accommodating traditional customs and use, while at the same time subscribing to universal democratic norms. It sounds simple, but in practice it is not.

Bibliography

ACE: Electoral College Network. "Electoral Systems." 2020. https://aceproject.org/ace-en/topics/es/esd/esd06/esd06c.

Avianto, B.N., D. Marjanto, U. Sudrajat, and K. Julizar. "Ethnotechnology Noken-Papua as Carrying Capacity for Enhancing Local Economic Development." *International Journal of Social Economics* 48 (2021): 1476–91.

Banner, S. "Why Terra Nullius? Anthropology and Property Law in Early Australia." *Law and History Review* 23 (2005): 95–131.

Bartlett, R. *Native Title in Australia*. Australia: LexisNexis Butterworths, 2020.

Bawaslu. "Bawaslu Calls for Abolition of "Noken" Voting System in Papua." 16 March 2016. https://bawaslu.go.id/en/news/bawaslu-calls-abolition-%E2%80%98noken%E2%80%99-voting-system-papua.

Butt, S. *The Constitutional Court and Democracy in Indonesia*. Leiden: Brill, 2015.

Chaidir, E. "The Constitutional Court Decision Regarding Disputes of Legislative Election; from a Progressive Law Enforcement to the Recognition of Customary Communities in Democracy." *Advances in Social Science, Education and Humanities Research* 358 (2019): 161–66.

De Villiers, B. "An Ancient People Struggling to Find a Modern Voice – Experiences of Australia's Indigenous People with Advisory Bodies." *International Journal on Minority and Group Rights* 26 (2019): 1–21.

De Villiers, B. "Breaking New Ground for Indigenous Non-Territorial Cultural Self-Government: The Noongar Settlement in Australia." In *Navigating the Unknown – Essays on Selected Case Studies about the Rights of Minorities*, 138–62. Leiden: Brill, 2022.

De Villiers, B. "Breathing Life into the Constitution: The Transformative Role of Courts to Give a Unique Identity to a Constitution." *Constitutional Court Review* 9, no.1 (2023).

De Villiers, B. "Does a Constitution Have a Soul? The Role of Bundestreue in Germany and Ubuntu in South Africa to Give Life and Identity to a Constitutional Text." In *Navigating the Unknown – Essays on Selected Case Studies about the Rights of Minorities*, 163–214. Leiden: Brill, 2022.

De Villiers, B. "Seven Questions before the Voice Can Be Heard: Learning from the Past." *Brief* August (2022): 8–11.

Decision of Constitutional Court of the Republic of Indonesia, Bali Case, Constitutional Court Number 62/PHPU.D-XI/2013, 20 June 2013. (Constitutional Court of the Republic of Indonesia 2013).

Decision of Constitutional Court of the Republic of Indonesia. Constitutional Court Case No. 31/PUU-XII/2014, 11 March 2015 (Constitutional Court of the Republic of Indonesia 2015).

Decision of Constitutional Court of the Republic of Indonesia. Constitutional Court No. 1/PHPU.PRES-XII/2014, 21 August 2014 (Constitutional Court of the Republic of Indonesia 2014).

Decision of Constitutional Court of the Republic of Indonesia. Constitutional Court No 47–18 / PHPU.A / VII / 2009 (Constitutional Court of the Republic of Indonesia 2009).

Decision of Constitutional Court of the Republic of Indonesia. Constitutional Court Number 3/PHPU.D-X/2012, 17 February 2012 (Constitutional Court of the Republic of Indonesia 2012).

Decision of Constitutional Court of the Republic of Indonesia. Constitutional Court Number 6–32/PHPU-DPD/XII/2014, 25 June 2014 (Constitutional Court of the Republic of Indonesia 2014).

Decision of Constitutional Court of the Republic of Indonesia. Constitutional Court Number 14/PHPU.D-XI/2013, 11 March 2013 (Constitutional Court of the Republic of Indonesia 2013).

Decision of Constitutional Court of the Republic of Indonesia. Constitutional Court Number 029/PUU-IX/2011 (Constitutional Court of the Republic of Indonesia 2011).

Decision of Federal Court of Australia, Aplin on behalf of the Waanyi Peoples v. Queensland, FCA 625, 2010, para. 256 (Federal Court of Australia 2010).

Decision of Federal Court of Australia. Members of the Yorta Yorta Aboriginal Community v. Victoria [1998] FCA 1606 (18 December 1998) (Federal Court of Australia1998).

Decision of High Court of Australia, Love v. Commonwealth of Australia and Thoms v. Commonwealth of Australia [2020] HCA 3 (High Court of Australia 2020).

Decision of High Court of Australia, Mabo v. Queensland (No 2) [1992] HCA 23, (1992) 175 CLR 1 (High Court of Australia 1992).

Decision of High Court of Australia. Commonwealth v. Tasmania (1983) 158 CLR 1 (High Court of Australia 1983).

Decision of High Court of Australia. Wik Peoples v. The State of Queensland [1996] HCA 40 (1996) 187 CLR 1 (23 December 1996) (High Court of Australia High Court 1996).

Decision of High Court of Australia. Yorta Yorta v. Victoria [2002] HCA 58; (2002) 214 CLR 422 (High Court of Australia 2002).

Duff, N. *What's Needed to Prove Native Title? Finding Flexibility within the Law on Connection*. Canberra: AIATSIS, 2014.

Efriandi, T. "Decentralization and the Challenges of Local Governance in Indonesia." University of Groningen, 2021.

Efriandi, T., O. Couwenberg, and R.L. Holzhacker. "The Noken System and the Challenge of Democratic Governance at the Periphery." In *Challenges of Governance: Development and Regional Integration in Southeast Asia*, edited by R.L. Holzhacker and W.G.Z. Tan, 65–85. Springer, 2021.

Electoral Commission – Noken. "Guidelines for the Implementation of Voting with the Noken System in Papua Province." Electoral Commission, 2019. https://jdih.kpu.go.id/beritadetail-4a6454305277253344253344.

Geddis, A. "Indigenous People and Electoral Law." In *Comparative Electoral Law*, edited by J.A. Gardner, 71–89. Cheltenham: Elgar, 2022.

Herron, E., R. Pekkanen, and M. Shugart, eds. *The Oxford Handbook of Electoral Systems*. Oxford: Oxford University Press, 2018.

Horowitz, D.L. "Electoral Systems: A Primer for Decision Makers." *Journal of Democracy*, no. 14 (2003): 116–32.

ICCPR. "The International Covenant on Civil and Political Rights." United Nations office of the High Commissioner for Human Rights, 12 December 1966. https://www.ohchr.org/en/professionalinterest/pages/ccpr.aspx.

International Labour Organization. "Indigenous and Tribal Peoples Convention, 1989 (No. 169)." 27 June 1989. https://www.ilo.org/dyn/normlex/en/f?p=NORMLEXPUB:12100:0::NO::P12100_ILO_CODE:C169.

IPAC. "Carving up Papua: More Districts, More Trouble." Jakarta: IPAC, 2013.

IPAC. "Open to Manipulation: The 2014 Elections in Papua Province." Jakarta: IPAC, 10 December 2014.

Isra, S., B. de Villiers and Z. Mochtar. "Asymmetry in a Decentralised, Unitary State: Lessons to Be Drawn from the Experiences of Decentralisation to the Special Regions of Indonesia." *Journal on Ethnopolitics and Minority Issues in Europe* 18 (2019): 43–71.

Lijphart, A. "Constitutional Design for Divided Societies." *Journal of Democracy* 2 (2004): 96–109.

Ljubljana Guidelines. "The Ljubljana Guidelines on Integration of Diverse Societies." OSCE, 2012.

Murray, L.T. "Masyarakat Adat, Difference, and the Limits of Recognition of Indonesia's Forest Zone." *Modern Asian Studies* 35 (2001): 645–76.

Native Title Act. National Native Title Act 1993 (1993). https://www.legislation.gov.au/Details/C2019C00054.

Nolan, C. "How Papua Voted." *New Mandala: New Perspectives on Southeast Asia*, 17 April 2014. https://www.newmandala.org/how-papua-voted/.

Nolan, C. *Votes in the Bag? The Noken System and Conflict in Indonesia*. Jakarta: International Crisis Group, 2012.

Nugraha, Y. "Legal Pluralism, Human Rights and the Right to Vote: The Case of the Noken System in Papua." *Asia-Pacific Journal on Human Rights* 22 (2021): 255–86.

Nurumov, D., and V. Vashchonka. "Effective Participation of National Minorities in the Electoral Process." In *Effective Participation of National Minorities and Conflict Prevention*, edited by W. Romans, I. Ulasiuk, and A.P. Thomsen, 197–214. Leiden: Brill, 2020.

Organization for Security and Co-operation in Europe. "The Lund Recommendations on the Effective Participation of National Minorities in Public Life." 1999. https://www.osce.org/files/f/documents/0/9/32240.pdf.

Pamungkas, C. "Noken Electoral System in Papua: Deliberative Democracy in Papuan Tradition." *Jurnal Masyarakat and Budaya* 19 (2017): 219–35.

Rudy, R. Perdana, and R. Wijaya. "The Recognition of Customary Rights by Indonesian Constitutional Court." *Academic Journal for Interdisciplinary Studies* 10 (2021): 308–18.

Sahabat. "Noken System Used to Ensure West Papua Led by Native." *West Papua Story* (blog), 5 January 2022. https://westpapuastory.com/noken-system-used-to-ensure-west-papua-led-by-native/.

Setyanto, B., J. Wiwoho, and M. Jamin. "General Election System in Papua Indonesia." *Systematic Reviews in Pharmacy* 11 (2020): 825–28.

Setyanto, B., J. Wiwoho, and M. Jamin. "Local Democracy: Election of Regional Head and Regional Deputy Head in the Noken System in Papua Indonesia." *International Journal of Innovation, Creativity and Change* 11 (2020): 353–66.

Setyanto, B., J. Wiwoho, and M. Jamin. "Noken System in Indonesian General Elections." *Advances in Economics, Business and Management Research* 140 (2020): 725–30.

Sodiki, A. "The Constitutionality of Election Model Society Yakuhimo." *Journal of Constitution* 6 (2009): 342–57.

Soetjipto, A.W. "Journey to Justice: The United Nations Declaration on the Rights of Indigenous Peoples in the Context of West Papua." *Journal of ASEAN Studies* 10 (2022): 129–49.

Suryana, Y. "The Relationship of Husband Authority to the Wife Political Rights." *Justitia Et Pax* 38 (2022): 1–23.

Tombi, P. "Noken in Positive Legal Framework in the 2020 Election of Regional Heads (Pilkada) in Indonesia." In *International Conferene on Law and Human Rights*, edited by B. Nainggolan and H. Panjaitan, 60–68. Jakarta: CCER, 2021.

UNDRIP. "United Nations Declaration on the Rights of Indigenous People." 2007. https://www.un.org/development/desa/indigenouspeoples/declaration-on-the-rights-of-indigenous-peoples.html.

UNESCO-Noken. "Decision of the Intergovernmental Committee: 7.COM 8.3." 2012. https://ich.unesco.org/en/decisions/7.COM/8.3.

Woodman, G.R. "The Idea of Legal Pluralism." In *Legal Pluralism in the Arab World*, edited by B. Dupret, M. Berger, and L. al-Zwaini. Amsterdam: Kluwer, 1999.

Xanthaki, A., and D. O'Sullivan. "Indigenous Participation in Elective Bodies: The Maori in New Zealand." *International Journal on Minority and Group Rights* 16 (2009): 181–212.

Yunus, A. "Multilayered Democracy in Papua: A Comparison of "Noken" System and Electoral College System in the United States." *Hasanuddin Law Review* 6 (2020): 232–39.

CHAPTER 10

Constitutional Approaches to Diversity and Non-discrimination in Multi-level States: Indonesian and South African Jurisprudential Perspectives

Nico Steytler

Abstract

This chapter examines the Indonesian Constitutional Court's decision on the strict requirements for the candidates running for governor and deputy governor in the Special Region of Yogyakarta, which had limited the field of eligible candidates to only two men. The Court upheld the unique qualifications based on traditional leadership positions but invalidated national legal provisions that added discriminatory requirements based on gender. Notably, this decision paves the way for a woman to become the provincial governor of Yogyakarta. Although the governor and deputy governor must still be the Sultan of Ngayogyakarta Hadiningrat Sultanate and the Duke of Pakualaman, respectively, a requirement that they have wives was found to contravene the prohibition of gender discrimination. The Court's decision raises broader questions about the balance between autonomy and national unity, particularly in relation to decentralization, diversity, and a bill of rights. How is the balance struck between autonomy and national unity as expressed in a bill of rights? The Indonesian Constitutional Court's decision offers a comparative perspective on how the South African Constitutional Court has addressed similar questions. In both Indonesia and South Africa, a bill of rights serves as a crucial check on imbalanced power dynamics between sub-national entities by limiting their autonomy. The impact of the bill of rights on traditional leadership and customary law has already been observed in South Africa, where customary law must be allowed to align with the demands of non-discrimination on the basis of gender.

Keywords

customary law - Duchy of Pakualaman - constitutional court of Indonesia – gender equality – Kingdom of Yogyakarta – South African constitutional court

1 Introduction

After the end of the authoritarian rule of Indonesia's long-serving President Soeharto in 1998, the amendments to the 1945 Constitution ushered not only democracy and a bill of rights but also a system of decentralisation.[1] It was an asymmetrical system; as of late 2022, there were 38 provinces, of which nine had a special status.[2] The six provinces with indigenous Papuans are accorded 'special' status of governance. The Capital Region of Jakarta, which enjoys a 'special' status due to its role as the country's capital, remains so despite a 2022 parliamentary decision to relocate the capital to Kalimantan, as the process is still in its early stages. A region with a 'privileged' status is the Special Region of Yogyakarta, where the Kingdom of Yogyakarta (Ngayogyakarta Hadiningrat Sultanate and Duchy of Pakualaman) is recognized within a republican Indonesia. The ninth province with special status, that of Aceh, has both a special and privileged status on the basis of religion.[3] The asymmetrical system flowed from both the founding of the Republic of Indonesia in 1945 and subsequent conflicts.[4] Central to the post-1998 dispensation is that 'Indonesia is a law-based state' (Article 1(3)).

One key to the rule of law is the Constitutional Court of Indonesia, established in 2003, which has, among others, the final power of decision in reviewing laws against the Constitution (Article 24C). The distribution of powers in the decentralised system, as in other non-centralised systems, is a likely area for contestation between the orders of government. The Constitutional Court in Case Number 88/PUU-XIV/2016 grappled with the constitutionality of a national law (Law No. 13/2012 on the Special Region of Yogyakarta)[5] that prescribed the requirements to be a candidate for the governor and deputy governor of the Special Region of Yogyakarta. In addition to the requirement of having to be the Sultan of Ngayogyakarta Hadiningrat Sultanate and the Duke

1 Simon Butt, "Central-local Relations in Indonesia: Reforming the Integrationist State," in *Central-Local Relations in Asian Constitutional Systems*, ed. Andrew Harding and Mark Sidel (Oxford and Portland, OR: Hart, 2015), 85–104.

2 Saldi Isra, Bertus de Villiers, and Zulkarnaini Arifin, "Asymmetry in a Decentralized, Unitary State: Lessons from the Special Regions of Indonesia," *Journal on Ethnopolitics and Minority Issues in Europe* 18, no. 2 (2019): 43–71.

3 Simon Butt, "Provincial Asymmetry in Indonesia: What is so 'Special' about it? A Country Study of Constitutional Asymmetry in Indonesia," in *Constitutional Asymmetry in Multinational Federalism: Managing Multinationalism in Multi-tiered Systems*, ed. Patricia Popelier and Maja Sahadžić (Cham: Palgrave Macmillan, 2021), 227–254.

4 Saldi Isra, Bertus de Villiers, and Zulkarnaini Arifin, "Asymmetry in a Decentralized," 49-50

5 Indonesian Constitutional Court, Decision Number 88/PUU-XIV/2016 on August 31, 2017.

of Pakualaman, respectively, such persons also have to 'submit a curriculum vitae that contains, among others, educational history, occupation, siblings, wife, and children'. The Court found that the latter requirement was not only an infringement by the centre in the constitutional domain of the Special Region, but the reference to a 'wife' (indirectly requiring that the candidate be a male) contradicted the anti-discrimination clause of the post-amendment Indonesian Constitution.

The judgment dealt with issues important for Indonesia, but also raises matters of general interests for other jurisdictions where the relationship between decentralisation, diversity and a Bill of Rights is at stake. The case brings to the fore the important question of the scope or ambit of the autonomy of a region that enjoys a special protected status in a decentralised system. Moreover, how is the balance to be struck between local autonomy and national unity as expressed in a bill of rights?

From a comparative perspective it is useful to examine how the South African Constitutional Court has addressed similar questions. South Africa is selected as a comparator as it shares many common features with Indonesia. Like Indonesia, the new democratic constitutional dispensation, which came about in 1994, sought to transform the country from a minority authoritarian regime to one based on constitutional supremacy and the rule of law. Given its diversity, the constitution-makers eschewed the adoption of a federation (and avoided the term 'federalism' altogether), much like Indonesia,[6] and constructed a very centralised multilevel system. Like the Indonesian Constitution's emphasis on the 'unitary' nature of the state, outlined in section 1(1), the 1996 South African Constitution declares that South Africa is '*one*, sovereign, democratic state' (emphasis added). In the 1993 Constitution, very asymmetrical arrangements were made to accommodate two troublesome ethnic groups – the Zulu and the Afrikaner nationalists.[7] Traditional authorities were accommodated, and in the case of one province – KwaZulu-Natal – the Zulu monarch had to be recognized in an otherwise republican system. The motto on the country's crest is '*! ke e: /xarra //ke*', written in the Khoisan language of the /Xam people, literally meaning diverse people unite,[8] which

6 Anthony Reid, "Indonesia's Post-Revolutionary Aversion to Federalism," in *Federalism in Asia*, ed. Baogang He, Brian Galligan, and Takashi Inoguchi (Cheltenham: Edward Elgar, 2007), 144–164.

7 Nico Steytler and Johan Mettler, "Federal Arrangements as a Peacemaking Device during South Africa's Transition to Democracy," *Publius: The Journal of Federalism* 31, no. 4 (2001): 93–106.

8 Jaap de Visser and Nico Steytler, "'!ke e:/xarra //ke': Old Diversities and New Responses in the Quest for Unity in South Africa," in *Revisiting Unity and Diversity in Federal Countries: Changing*

echoes the Indonesia motto of *Bhinneka Tunggal Ika*, translated as 'unity in diversity' (Article 36A). Finally, the South African Constitutional Court, too, has dealt with the issue of reconciling diversity and unity at subnational level.

Despite these similarities, the jurisprudence of the two courts shows differences, but these are accounted for by the different processes of forming the countries. In the case of Indonesia, the Kingdom of Yogyakarta joined the newly independent state of Indonesia, while the South African provinces were formed through a process of disaggregation that was embedded in the constitution itself. In terms of the relationship between diversity and the Bill of Rights, the South African Constitution is explicit in stating that traditional leaders and customary law are also subject to the demands of the Bill of Rights, a matter on which the Indonesian Constitution is not clear.

Section 2 of this chapter commences with an analysis of the Constitutional Court's judgment in Case Number 88/PUU-XIV/2016.[9] On the basis of the issues identified in the judgment, the focus of Section 3 is the jurisprudence of the South African Constitutional Court on these issues. Section 4 seeks to draw the relevance of this comparative exercise to the fore.

2 Constitutional Court of Indonesia: Decision 88/PUU-XIV/2016

The Constitutional Court of Indonesia issued Decision 88/PUU-XIV/2016 in response to a case brought by three sets of petitioners. The first set consisted of gender activists who claimed standing because Law No. 13/2012 on the Special Region of Yogyakarta provided in Article 18(1)(m) that a candidate for the governorship or deputy governorship must, in addition to being the sultan or duke, also 'submit a curriculum vitae that contains, among others, educational, history, occupation, siblings, wife, and children'. They based their standing thus on their interest in gender equality as protected in the bill of rights in a number of provisions. The second set of petitioners were businessmen who argued that their interests were affected by the possibility that a permanent vacancy may occur because the sultan and the duke may not meet the requirements of Article 18(1)(m). Such a vacancy may result in poor governance and service delivery, which may affect their lives and businesses. The third set of petitioners were two persons who were part of the households of the sultan and duke, respectively, and had a direct interest in the matter. The

Concepts, Reform Proposals and New Institutional Realities, ed. Alain-G. Gagnon and Michael Burgess (Leiden and Boston: Brill Nijhoff, 2018), 5–26.

9 Indonesian Constitutional Court, Number 88/PUU-XIV/2016, sec. 2.

Constitutional Court had little difficulty in admitting the arguments of the first set of petitioners because the gender activists had a real interest in the matter, as did the third set. The second set of petitioners' arguments about their interests were dismissed as they could not specify which of their constitutional rights could possibly be harmed.

The Court's judgment hinged on a particular reading of Article 18(1)(m): did it impose an obligation on any candidate for the two positions to have, in fact, 'siblings, a wife, and children'? If so, it would mean that a woman would be excluded from standing as a candidate (because she has no wife) or a man who had no siblings or children. The Court found that Article 18(1)(m) did indeed impose such substantive requirements.

A different reading of Article 18(1)(m) would, however, have solved some of the constitutional problems but not all of them. A preferable reading is that Article 18(1)(m) imposes only the duty to submit a curriculum vitae (CV). What then follows is a list of items of information that should be included, 'among others', 'educational history, occupation, siblings, wife and children'. First, the list is not a closed list of 'requirements' but merely gives examples of what should be included in the CV. The Court's reading has the effect that any other 'requirement' could be added under the term 'among others', which is untenable where the Constitution itself requires legal certainty, namely in Article 28D(1). Second, the named item of information cannot be seen as requirements. For example, the words "educational history" cannot be read as a requirement for specific educational qualifications, but merely as information about a candidate's educational background. Similarly, the word "occupation" cannot be regarded as a requirement, as everyone has an occupation of some kind. The requirement lies in the information about a candidate's particular occupation. According to the common law maxim of *eiusdem generis* (the restriction of general words by reference to other words in their immediate vicinity),[10] the remaining words (siblings, wife and children) can only refer to information items. In this case, the question is whether the candidate has siblings, a wife or children – yes or no – and if so, who they are. Third, the other provisions in Article 18(1) do impose real requirements, such as being the sultan or the duke (Article 18(1)(c)).

On the basis of the finding that Article 18(1)(m) did indeed impose requirements, the Constitutional Court invalidated the provision on three grounds. The first reason was that Article 18(1)(m) unnecessarily intervened in the constitutionally protected domain of the Special Region, and was thus void

10 G.E. Devenish, *Interpretation of Statutes* (Cape Town: Juta, 1992).

for such intervention. This argument stands on two legs. First, the appointment of a governor and a deputy governor was a privilege that originated from the founding of the Indonesian Republic in 1945. The Kingdom and Duchy preceded the Dutch colonisation era and were still in existence when the Japanese invasion came to an end in 1945 and independence was proclaimed. In a typically 'coming together' federation, the voluntary joining of the two entities preserved their governance system, including the appointment of the sultan and the duke as governor and deputy governor, respectively.

The second leg of the argument is that this 'special and distinct' status of the Special Region of Yogyakarta, captured in Article 18B of the Constitution and ensuing legislation, implicitly exempts the region from democratically electing the executive. The right of participation in democratic government is not found in the chapter on human rights (chapter XA). In the provisions dealing with the central and subnational governments, the requirements for democratic government are entrenched. Article 22E(1) provides that 'General elections shall be conducted in a direct, general, free, secret, honest, and fair manner once every five years', a rule which also applies to the Regional People's Representative Councils (*Dewan Perwakilan Rakyat Daerah*), which is again asserted in Article 18(3). Moreover, 'Governors, Regents (*bupati*) and Mayors (*walikota*), respectively as head of regional government of the provinces, regencies and municipalities, shall be elected democratically' (Article 18(4)). In an exception to the general rule in Article 18, Article 18B states the following:

1. The State recognises and respects units of regional authorities that are special and distinct, which shall be regulated by law.
2. The State recognises and respects traditional communities along with their traditional customary rights as long as these remain in existence and are in accordance with the societal development and the principles of the Unitary State of the Republic of Indonesia, and shall be regulated by law.

The recognition of the region of Yogyakarta as 'special and distinct' then implicitly exempts the region from electing the governor and deputy governor democratically. As it is a requirement that the candidate for the two posts must be the sultan and duke, respectively, no other candidate is qualified. Who the sultan or duke may be at any given time is determined by the custom prevailing in those hereditary families. The Court concluded that the state had no constitutional right to intervene in imposing other requirements for who should be entitled to be the sultan or the duke (para. 3.13(7)).[11]

The second ground of invalidity is based on the resultant 'legal uncertainty' which this particular reading of Article 18(1)(m) may cause. The requirement, set in Article 18(1)(c) that the governor and deputy governor must be the sultan and duke, respectively, clashes with the requirement set in Article 18(1)(m) imposing further requirements. As the list of requirements in Article 18(1)(a) to (n) are cumulative, it is possible that the sultan may not meet the Article 18(1)(m) requirements. The potential for legal uncertainty looms very large, and the resultant deadlock 'can even develop into a dangerous political crisis' (para. 3.13(10)).[12] Again, as argued above, a harmonious reading of Article 18(1)(m) would have avoided the possibility of such legal uncertainty.

The third ground is that the impugned provision contradicts the constitutional commitments on non-discrimination and gender equality. The reference to a 'wife' implies that the candidate must be a male, and therefore the provision is in direct conflict with both the Constitution's provision asserting equality as well as Indonesia's international commitments under the Convention on the Elimination of All Forms of Discrimination against Women (CEDAW), which the country ratified and incorporated into domestic legislation. Although Article 28I(3) provides that 'The cultural identities and rights of traditional communities shall be respected in accordance with the development of times and civilisations', the Court nevertheless applied the general limitation clause contained in Article 28J(2), which reads:

> In exercising his/her rights and freedoms, every person shall have the duty to accept the restrictions established by law for the sole purposes of guaranteeing the recognition and respect of the rights and freedoms of others and of satisfying just demands based upon considerations of morality, religious values, security and public order in a democratic society.

Finding that no justification for the gender-discriminatory provision was proffered, Article 18(1)(m) was also invalidated on this ground. The Court was emphatic that 'in a democratic Indonesian society, there are no moral ideas, religious values, security, or public order that are impaired or violated' if women become the candidate for Governor or Deputy Governor of the Special Region of Yogyakarta (para. 3.13(11)).[13]

---

11 Indonesian Constitutional Court, para. 3.13(7).
12 Ibid., para. 3.13(10).
13 Ibid., para. 3.13(11).

The question that the Court did not address is whether the internal process of appointing a new sultan or duke according to tradition was compliant with the anti-discrimination commitment. Yet, at that time the sultanate itself was already moving away from patrilineage. According to Indonesian media reports, Sultan Hamengkubuwono X, who has only daughters, had changed the name of the sultanate to a gender-neutral term, which would pave the way for his eldest daughter to become the next sultan.[14] This provoked much opposition from conservative members of the royal family, including the sultan's siblings, who argued that a female sultan would threaten their values, tradition and palace laws. They threatened that should the daughter assume the throne, she would be evicted from the palace.[15] A legal tussle seems on the cards.

The situation in Yogyakarta raises a broader question of how to balance the 'unitary' nature of a country, which is often based on a uniform set of fundamental norms such as the Bill of Rights and other democratic values, against the recognition of the asymmetrical provisions that accommodate special cases of diversity. These issues, although not necessarily in the same context, have also been raised in the South African Constitutional Court, which has come up with a number of answers that may be of interest to Indonesian courts grappling with similar questions.

3 South African Jurisprudence

3.1 *Introduction to South African Constitutional Jurisprudence*

One of the foundational values of the South African state is the 'supremacy of the constitution and the rule of law' (section 1(c)). Standing as the guardian of the Constitution and its values is the Constitutional Court, which is the final interpreter of the Constitution.[16] With its independence strongly buttressed in the Constitution, the Court has played a fundamental role in shaping the new democratic South Africa. From the outset, it had to deal with difficult issues, such as the constitutionality of the death penalty, giving meaning to

---

14 Veronica Pengilley, "Feminist or Capitalist? Behind the Move to Install a Woman as Sultan of Yogyakarta," Southeast Asia Globe, published March 29, 2018, https://southeastasiaglobe.com/feminist-capitalist-move-woman-sultan-yogyakarta/.

15 BBC News, "Sultan of Yogyakarta: A feminist Revolution in an Ancient Kingdom," BBC News, published June 1, 2018, accessed February 23, 2023, https://www.bbc.com/news/world-asia-43806210.

16 Since 2012 it is also the final arbiter on all matters of law (Constitution Seventeenth Amendment Act, 2012).

socio-economic rights, and developing a brand of transformative constitutionalism.[17] It was also the final bastion of protecting the rule of law against the onslaught of 'state capture' by former president, Jacob Zuma.[18] It developed new remedies to vindicate the bill of rights against violations, and steer the country towards rule-based solutions to the many challenges it faces.

One such task is to give life to the federal arrangements. As a compromise between the liberation movement, the African National Congress (ANC), which favoured centralism, and the minority parties, which advocated federalism, nine provinces were established, which were in 2000 subdivided into 287 municipalities. The powers of the provinces include both exclusive powers (listed in Schedule 5A) and concurrent powers shared with the national government (listed in Schedule 4A). Local government powers are also protected in Schedules 4B and 5B. In interpreting the provisions relating to decentralisation, the Court has arguably leaned towards centralism at the expense of interpreting provincial autonomy generously.[19] In the *Certification* judgment,[20] the Court opined that the Constitution's statement that South Africa is 'one, sovereign, democratic state' (as stated in section 1), gave the Constitution a 'unitary emphasis.'[21]

3.2 *Decentralisation and Asymmetry to Accommodate Diversity*

Given the high level of conflict leading up to South Africa's first democratic elections in April 1994, asymmetry was prevalent in constitutional arrangements of the interim Constitution of 1993, all in an effort to appease two possible spoilers of the transition to democracy: Zulu nationalists, represented by the Inkatha Freedom Party (IFP) of Chief Buthelezi, and Afrikaner nationalists. In March 1994, less than two months before the first democratic elections, the interim Constitution was amended to entice the IFP into participating by extending the scope of provincial autonomy to allow for the drafting of a provincial constitution with 'legislative and executive structures and procedures' that differed from those prescribed in the interim Constitution. While

---

17 Sandra Liebenberg, *Socio-Economic Rights: Adjudication under a Transformative Constitution* (Cape Town: Juta, 2010).

18 Economic Freedom Fighters v Speaker of the National Assembly and Others; Democratic Alliance v. Speaker of the National Assembly and Others, [2016] ZACC 11 (March 31, 2016).

19 Nico Steytler, "The Constitutional Court in South Africa: Reinforcing an Hourglass System of Multi-Level Government," in *Courts in Federal Countries: Federalists or Unitarists?* ed. Nicholas Aroney and John Kincaid, 328–366 (Toronto: University of Toronto Press, 2017).

20 Certification of the Constitution of the Republic of South Africa, 1996, [1996] ZACC 26 (September 6, 1996).

21 Ibid., para. 287.

this did not occur, a deal with the Afrikaner nationalists was more successful. To placate those Afrikaners who threatened to disrupt the elections and the new state, special asymmetrical provisions were included for the possible establishment of a *Volkstaat* (people's state) based on language and ethnicity. The Constitutional Principles also included the requirement that if such a *Volkstaat* were to be established prior to the final Constitution, it would be recognized in that Constitution.[22] To bring the Zulu-nationalists into the election and end the violence in that province, a concession was made two days before the election day that a provincial constitution may, where applicable, provide for 'the institution, role, authority and status of a traditional monarch in the province'. In an asymmetric arrangement, such recognition was mandatory in the province of KwaZulu-Natal (Constitution of South Africa Second Amendment Act, 1994).[23]

A key element of the interim Constitution of 1993 was a set of Constitutional Principles to which the 'final' Constitution, which had to be drafted within two years after the election, had to comply with. The Constitutional Court was given the task to certify whether there was compliance or not. In reviewing the Constitution, the Court was forthright about the anti-democratic nature of the following provision: 'In a purely republican democracy, in which no differentiation of status on grounds of birth is recognised, no constitutional space exists for the official recognition of any traditional leaders, let alone a monarch.'[24] However, the inclusion of the traditional monarch in the Constitutional Principles made this un-democratic feature possible.

3.3 *Limits to Diversity: Provincial Constitutions Complying with the Constitution*

Provincial constitutions were conceived of as providing a vehicle for some provincial diversity in governance structures.[25] When the IFP won the KwaZulu-Natal provincial election in 1994, they proceeded with the adopting of a provincial constitution. The draft KwaZulu-Natal Provincial Constitution

22 When it was found that there was no area whether Afrikaners were in the majority and no such *Volkstaat* could be established, these provisions proved to be of transitional value only.

23 Nico Steytler and Johan Mettler, "Federal Arrangements," 96-98.

24 Certification of the Constitution of the Republic of South Africa, 1996, [1996] ZACC 26, para. 195 (September 6, 1996).

25 Nico Steytler, "Subnational Constitutionalism in South Africa: An empty promise," in *Routledge Handbook of Subnational Constitutions and Constitutionalism*, ed. Patricia Popelier, Giacomo Delledonne, and Nicholas Aroney, 224–241 (London and New York: Routledge, 2021).

(KZN PC) manifestly fell outside the parameters of the permissible constitutional space; it sought to create a federal system which was not provided for. First, it defined KZN as 'self-governing' and based on the 'principle of federal partnership'. Second, it included a Bill of Rights with rights relating to fair trials, labour, and states of emergency which fell outside the list of provincial functional areas. Third, it established a provincial constitutional court and a provincial police force, again matters falling outside its jurisdiction. To save the Bill's obviously unconstitutional provisions, two legal techniques were employed: first, through a consistency clause, only provisions consistent with the national Constitution would be valid; and, second, through a suspensive clause, provisions in conflict with the national constitution did not apply until the Province was empowered by the national Constitution to enact them. Ironically, despite being a late addition to the election as a political sweetener, there was no recognition of the Zulu monarch, King Goodwill Zwelithini, because by that time the ANC had won over the King to their camp and ruptured the political relationship between the monarch and Buthelezi.[26]

When the draft KZN PC came before the Constitutional Court for certification that it complied with the national Constitution, the Court had little hesitation in rejecting it.[27] The Court held that the provincial legislature could not increase its own powers vested in it by the interim Constitution: 'a province cannot by means of the bootstraps of its own constitution confer on its legislature greater powers than those granted it by the interim Constitution.'[28] Moreover, the consistency and suspensive clauses could not immunize the Bill from the Court's scrutiny; the Court must be able to certify that each and every provision was compliant with the national Constitution. The provincial legislature could however include their own bill of rights, provided it did not detract from any of the rights in the national Bill of Rights, but it could add more rights. However, such additional rights could be included only within the functional areas of provincial competences.

The only two areas in which provincial constitutions are permitted to be different are, first, in respect of legislative and executive structures and procedures of a province and, second, in respect of the institution, role, authority and status of a traditional monarch, where applicable. None of the provisions that differed from the national Constitution, could be justified by these exceptions. The Court stated:

26 Nico Steytler, "Subnational Constitutionalism," 224-241

27 Certification of the Kwazulu-Natal Constitution, [1996] ZACC 17 (September 6, 1996).

28 Ibid., para. 8.

> whatever meaning is ascribed to 'structures and procedures' they do not relate to the fundamental nature and substance of the democratic state created by the interim Constitution nor to the substance of the legislative or executive powers of the national Parliament or Government or those of the provinces.[29]

The interpretation of different 'legislative and executive structures and procedures' came pertinently to the fore when the Western Cape provincial legislature, also under opposition party control, sought to adopt a provincial constitution. When the draft provincial constitution came before the Constitutional Court for certification, the question was whether the size of the legislature and a proposed electoral system could be justified as 'a legislative structure or procedure.'[30]

Determining the size of the provincial parliament was an easy question. In terms of the interim Constitution, the size of the provincial legislature was 42 members, which the Provincial Constitution (PC) repeated. However, the 1996 Constitution provided that the size is determined by the Electoral Commission in terms of a population formula. The Court found that this was indeed a change of the legislative structure which is constitutionally permitted.

The real test came with regard to a unique electoral system for the Western Cape. The national Constitution (NC) provides for a provincial electoral system as 'prescribed by national legislation' which 'results, in general, in proportional representation' (section 105(1)(a) and (d)). The NC provided for a closed party-list system of proportional representation. Given the lack of accountability that such a PR system facilitates, as elected representatives are not answerable to any geographical constituencies, the WC PC provided for an electoral system based on a combination of both a proportional representation (PR) and constituencies. Under clause 14, the electoral system should be 'based predominantly on the representation of geographic multi-member constituencies; and results, in general, in proportional representation'. Was the introduction of a constituency element a 'legislative structure or procedure'? The Court thought not. For the provision went beyond 'form' to the 'substance' of the legislative structure; the former entailed 'no more than a difference regarding the nature and the number of the elements constituting the legislative structure'.[31] The Court reasoned that the test is not 'whether the regulation of that matter can

29 Ibid., para. 5.

30 Certification of the Constitution of the Western Cape, 1997, [1997] ZACC 8 (September 2, 1997).

31 Ibid., para. 49.

have some bearing on the representation in a legislative structure, but whether it bears on the structure itself'.[32] This test would, of course, not help the Court much should the WC PC have included a second house, necessitating a new electoral process.[33] The judgment hollowed out the prospect of allowing for greater diversity and experimentation. As I wrote: 'a parsimonious application of the exception was given, which in effect suffocated the little life there may have been in provincial constitutions.'[34]

3.4 *Limits to Diversity: Policy Asymmetry and Compliance with the Bill of Rights*

Although the scope for asymmetrical provisions in provincial constitutions is limited, there is some constitutional space for difference in the policy areas falling within the legislative domain of provinces: their exclusive and concurrent powers. The list of exclusive powers is short and contains functions of little importance, including: abattoirs, ambulance services, libraries other than national libraries, liquor licenses, museums other than national museums, provincial planning, provincial cultural matters, provincial sport, provincial roads and traffic (schedule 5). Moreover, the national parliament may even intervene in these areas in qualified circumstances (section 44(2)).

Real substantive matters lie in the concurrent lists of competencies shared by the national and provincial governments. Schedule 4 includes a sizeable list of important policy areas such as education, health services, housing, social welfare, agriculture, environment, indigenous law and customary law, traditional leadership, tourism, trade, as well as casinos, racing, and gambling. If a provincial law conflicts with a national law, there is a generous but qualified override clause in favour of the national law (section 146).

Within this constitutional framework, provinces have a free hand to develop their own policy frameworks and enact legislation as they see fit for purpose. There is, however, an important general restraint: any legislation must be compliant with the Bill of Rights. Given South Africa's long and brutal history of racial discrimination during apartheid and patriarchy, two foundational constitutional values are 'non-racialism and non-sexism' (section 1(2) Constitution). Equality and non-discrimination are thus given pride of place in the Bill of Rights as being the first right listed. Section 9 reads:

---

32 Ibid.

33 Christina Murray, "Provincial Constitution-Making in South Africa: The (Non)Example of the Western Cape," *Neue Folge Jahrbuch des offentlichen Rechts* 49 (2001): 481–512.

34 Nico Steytler, "Subnational Constitutionalism," 237.

1. Everyone is equal before the law and has the right to equal protection and benefit of the law.
2. Equality includes the full and equal enjoyment of all rights and freedoms. To promote the achievement of equality, legislative and other measures designed to protect or advance persons, or categories of persons, disadvantaged by unfair discrimination may be taken.
3. The state may not unfairly discriminate directly or indirectly against anyone on one or more grounds, including race, gender, sex, pregnancy, marital status, ethnic or social origin, colour, sexual orientation, age, disability, religion, conscience, belief, culture, language and birth.

A general limitation clause permits limitations to the enumerated rights. The Bill of Rights, including the equality clause, binds all legislatures, including the provincial legislatures (section 8(1)). Many provincial laws dating from the apartheid era were still on the statute books after the commencement of the democratic dispensation and obviously fell foul of the non-discrimination clause. The *Zondi*-case[35] illustrates the Constitutional Court's approach to non-discrimination when it invalidated a provincial law originating from the apartheid era in the province of KwaZulu-Natal. The Pounds Ordinance of 1947 allowed for, among other things, the immediate seizure and impoundment of trespassing animals by a landowner without notice to the livestock owner (unless the livestock owner happens to be a neighbour), the assessment of damages caused by the stray animals by 'two disinterested persons', who had to be voters or landowners, and the payment of impoundment fees and damages by the livestock owner. This process required no intervention of court processes. The Ordinance was thus challenged on the basis that it (a) denied a livestock owner his or her right of access to the courts (section 34 Constitution), and (b) was discriminatory on the basis of race as the persons who were usually subject to the Ordinance were landless African people.

Denying a livestock owner access to the courts as a normal course of action during the impounding process, rendered the Ordinance invalid. Equally fatal was the discriminatory effect of the Ordinance. Whether the law is discriminatory, the Constitutional Court held, requires an assessment of its purpose and effect.

35 Zondi v MEC for Traditional and Local Government Affairs [2004] ZACC 19 (15 October 2004)

> If a statute has a purpose that violates the Constitution, it must be held to be invalid regardless of its actual effects. The effect of legislation is relevant to show that although the statute is facially neutral, its effect is unconstitutional. This will be the case where, for example, the legislation has a discriminatory impact on a particular racial group.[36]

First, the requirement that 'two disinterested persons', assessing the damage caused by the stray livestock, had to be voters, who at the time were confined to white persons, was deliberately racist, and thus deemed invalid. Second, the effect of the Ordinance was also racist given the context of the apartheid policy which was based on the denial of land rights to African people. The Court noted: 'Because African people were confined to small, overcrowded and often desolate areas, they had insufficient grazing land for any livestock that they were allowed to keep. By contrast, white farmers owned vast amounts of land which was adequate for farming, grazing and irrigation.'[37] The effect of the Ordinance was that it affected primarily Africans as a group, and was thus racist in purpose and effect, and thus invalid on this basis as well.

Any policy choice reflecting provincial diversity, but which does not affect a right in the Bill of Rights is permissible. The case of *Weare*[38] elucidates this point well. As racing, gambling, and gaming are concurrent functional areas, KwaZulu-Natal legislation provided that a juristic person may not hold a licence to carry on the business of bookmaking; only natural persons may hold bookmaking licences in the province. On this point, the province differed from the other provinces where juristic persons may do so too. A bookie taking bets on horse racing complained that he was discriminated against in KwaZulu-Natal because he could not ply his trade as a juristic person, as elsewhere in the country. The complaint of a bookmaker was thus one of discrimination, contrary to section 9(1) of the Constitution.

The Constitutional Court held, that since provinces have the right to regulate their own gambling industries, there could be no objection in this case to the KwaZulu-Natal law simply on the ground that it is different to that in other provinces: 'the fact that there are differences between the legal regimes in provinces does not in itself constitute a breach of section 9(1)'. The Court elaborated also on the difference between section 9(1)[39] – general equality clause – and section 9(3), the anti-discrimination clause:

---

36 Ibid., para. 90.
37 Ibid., para. 39.
38 Weare and Another v. Ndebele NO and Others, [2008] ZACC 20 (November 18, 2008).
39 Ibid., para. 70.

> Whereas the core of section 9(1) is the idea that no-one is above or beneath the law and that all persons are subject to law impartially applied and administered, the core of the right against discrimination in section 9(3) is dignity. Differentiation becomes unfair discrimination when it is based on grounds that have the potential to impact upon the fundamental dignity of human beings.[40]

In this case, the complainant could not muster an argument for how the differentiation could affect his dignity.

3.5 *Limits to Legal Pluralism: Customary Law and the Bill of Rights*

A further source of diversity at the community level has been the constitutional recognition of customary law and traditional leadership. South Africa's 1996 Constitution provides in section 211(1): 'The institution, status and role of traditional leadership, according to customary law, are recognized, subject to the Constitution.' In the case of customary law, the courts must apply it, 'subject to the Constitution and any legislation that specifically deals with customary law' (section 211(3)). Moreover, when a court develops 'the common law or customary law', it 'must promote the spirit, purport and objects of the Bill of Rights' (section 39(2)).

During the *Certification* hearings before the Constitutional Court, the argument from traditional leaders was that the Bill of Rights, in particular the provisions on non-discrimination on the basis of gender, would undermine the patriarchal principles which underly much of customary law.[41] The Court acknowledged this but subjecting indigenous law to the Bill of Rights was part and parcel of the new democratic deal struck in 1993. The alignment of customary law to the Bill of Rights through the former's interpretation thus became a task also of the courts.

In the case of *Shilubana*[42] the validity of the appointment of a woman as traditional leader of the Valoyi traditional community was contested for being in conflict with the custom of patrilineage. After the advent of democracy in 1994, the Royal House of the Valoyi decided to adapt their custom of appointing only males as chief of the community by appointing Ms Shilubana, the daughter of an erstwhile Chief. The appointment was made with the explicit aim of bringing their customary law of succession into line with the Bill of the

40 Ibid., para. 72.

41 Certification of the Constitution of the Republic of South Africa, 1996, [1996] ZACC 26, para. 200 (September 6, 1996).

42 Shilubana and Others v. Nwamitwa, [2008] ZACC 9 (June 4, 2008).

Rights and the rule against gender discrimination. A competing claim for the chieftainship from a cousin was based on the argument that the customary law was clear: the chieftainship goes to the eldest son of the previous Chief, and that the adaptation of this custom to the contrary was thus wrong and the appointment of Shilubana void. Moreover, an organisation of traditional leaders argued that because gender discrimination is an essential part of the institution of traditional leadership, it is not unfair discrimination in terms of section 9(3). The first issue for decision was the development of a community's customary law. The Court was clear that customary law was not static:

> where there is a dispute over the legal position under customary law, a court must consider both the traditions and the present practice of the community. If development happens within the community, the court must strive to recognise and give effect to that development, to the extent consistent with adequately upholding the protection of rights. In addition, the imperative of section 39(2) must be acted on when necessary, and deference should be paid to the development by a customary community of its own laws and customs where this is possible, consistent with the continuing effective operation of the law.[43]

Customary law is thus dynamic and the Court held 'a community must be empowered to itself act so as to bring its customs into line with the norms and values of the Constitution'.[44] The Court thus endorsed the development of the community's customary law in line with the Bill of Rights.

The Constitutional Court has also gone a step further by itself bringing customary law into line of the Bill of Rights. The *Bhe*-case[45] concerned constitutional challenges to the validity of two related laws: first, section 23 of the Black Administration Act and its regulations, which regulated the winding up of African estates according to what it called 'Black law and Custom', and second, the African customary law rule of male primogeniture in the context of the law of succession. In this matter, the Constitutional Court heard three cases together as they each related to intestate succession under African customary law. In the first case the application was made by Ms Bhe on behalf of her two minor daughters. She argued that the Black Administration Act and the rule of male primogeniture unfairly discriminated against her daughters as they prevented her daughters from inheriting from their deceased father's

43 Ibid., para. 49.

44 Ibid., para. 73.

45 Bhe and Others v. Khayelitsha Magistrate and Others, [2004] ZACC 17 (15 October 2004).

estate. Similarly, in the second case, Ms Shibi was for the same reasons unable to inherit from her deceased brother's estate. The third case was brought by NGOs as a class action on behalf of all women and children who were prevented from inheriting by the Black Administration Act and the customary law rule of male primogeniture.

In dealing with these applications, the Court struck down the impugned provisions of the Black Administration Act on the basis that they breached the non-discrimination provision in section 9(3) of the Constitution, and were not 'reasonable and justifiable in a democratic society based on dignity, equality and freedom' (section 36 Constitution). The Court also considered the African customary law rule of male primogeniture. It noted that it has 'over time become increasingly out of step with the real values and circumstances of the societies they are meant to serve and particularly the people who live in urban areas'.[46] The Court thus found that the rule of primogeniture could not be reconciled with 'current notions of equality and human dignity as contained in the Bill of Rights'.[47] Not only did the rule constitute unfair discrimination contrary to section 9(3) of the Constitution, it also violated the rights of women to dignity, contrary to section 10 of the Constitution. On this point customary law had to be developed to be non-discriminatory on intestate inheritance. The Court's ruling has, however, been slow in working down to the 'living' customary law at community level.[48]

3.6 *Mediating Diversity through Intergovernmental Relations*

Although the system allows for diversity in approaches to policy and legislation, conflicts will inevitably arise when provinces exercise their powers in the policy areas they share with the national and local governments. Having foreseen this eventuality, South Africa's constitutional framers specifically opted for cooperative federalism. The Constitutional Court noted that the Constitution embodies not 'competitive federalism', but rather 'a new philosophy' of cooperative government.[49] The Constitution thus imposes a duty on all government 'to cooperate with one another in mutual trust and good faith'

46 Ibid., para. 82.

47 Ibid., para. 95.

48 Christine O.J. Himonga, "The Advancement of African Women's Rights in the First Decade of Democracy in South Africa: The Reform of the Customary Law of Marriage and Succession," *Acta Juridica* 82 (2005): 234–252; Sindiso Mnisi Weeks, "Customary Succession and the Development of Customary Law: The Bhe Legacy," *Acta Juridica* (2015): 215-255.

49 Certification of the Constitution of the Republic of South Africa, 1996, [1996] ZACC 26, para. 268 (September 6, 1996).

(section 41(1)(h)). Cooperative government also includes the duty of 'avoiding legal proceedings against one another' (section 41(1)(h)(vi)). The courts may enforce this duty by referring a dispute back to the parties if the parties have not made every reasonable effort to solve the dispute by non-litigious means (section 41(3) and (4)). The Constitutional Court thus noted that disputes should, where possible, 'be resolved at a political level rather than through adversarial litigation'.[50] The Court has taken compliance with this duty seriously, holding that a court would 'rarely decide an intergovernmental dispute unless the organs of state involved in the dispute have made every reasonable effort to resolve it at a political level'.[51]

4 Discussion

The Indonesian Constitutional Court's case Number 88/PUU-XIV/2016 raised two interrelated questions of general concern. The first concerns the scope and ambit of autonomy of a region that enjoys a special protected status. How, then, within a unitary state structure, are asymmetrical elements to be accommodated? Flowing from the first, the second question is how a bill of rights constrains diversity. How is the balance struck between autonomy and national unity as expressed in a bill of rights?

In comparing the Indonesian jurisprudence to the South African counterpart, a number of similarities and differences are evident. First, while the Indonesian Constitution has made asymmetrical decentralisation arrangements a permanent feature, similar provisions in South Africa's interim Constitution proved only to be temporary. Moreover, the scope for diversity for provincial constitutions has been narrowly defined by the South African Constitutional Court.

Second, in both countries the bill of rights has been a key constraint on autonomy and hence also on asymmetry. As in the case of Indonesia, both national and provincial laws in South Africa are subject to the rigours of the Bill of Rights, which then play a unifying function by defining the core values of a nation. It is only beyond the platform of the fundamental rights that diversity can flourish.

Third, the impact of the bill of rights on traditional leadership and customary law has already been witnessed in South Africa. In a remarkable

50 Ibid., para. 291.

51 National Gambling Board v. Premier of KwaZulu-Natal and Others, 2002 (2) BCLR 156 (CC), para. 14.

coincidence, traditional authorities in both South Africa and Indonesia have themselves initiated the process of aligning tradition with the demands of non-discrimination on the basis of gender. The South African Constitutional Court has affirmed this development of customary law in the recognition of a non-sexist chieftainship of the Valoyi community, a matter which may come up in any legal battle of whom may succeed the current sultan of Yogyakarta. The Indonesian Constitutional Court may come to a similar result.

In conclusion the relationship between decentralisation, including its asymmetrical expressions, and a bill of rights requires close scrutiny.[52] A national bill of rights has the effect of centralising power and standardising subnational conduct.[53] A bill of rights, which captures core values, consolidates national identity to the detriment of regional identities by creating a sense of common citizenship. Where social and economic rights are included in a bill, this justifies federal intervention to ensure uniformity of services: national social solidarity is preferred over the protection of subnational autonomy. By virtue of being fundamental and universal, fundamental rights do not admit local exceptions. Further, where a constitutional court invalidates a law of one subnational government, the same rule applies to all subnational governments which sets a single standard.

The question, then, is how diversity, which decentralisation protects and promotes, could be balanced with the uniform protection of human rights. The usual answer from the human rights lobby is that human rights set a minimum floor of rights on which subnational units may improve. This was the view of the South African Constitutional Court; provincial constitutions may not detract from the national Bill of Rights but may expand on them. This solution has its own weaknesses.[54] Where more than one human right is involved, there is often a tension between them; an increase in the right to equality may be a regression on cultural and religious rights.

52 Nico Steytler, "The Constitutional Conversation between the Federal Structure and a Bill of Rights," Institute of Federalism, Fribourg, Working Paper Online No 2, 2015, https://www.unifr.ch/federalism/en/assets/public/files/Working%20Paper%20online/02_Nico%20Steytler.pdf.

53 José Woehrling, "Federalism and the Protection of Rights and Freedoms: Affinities and Antagonism," in *Political Liberalism and Plurinational Democracies*, ed. Ferran Requejo Coll and Montserrat Caminal di Badia (London, New York: Routledge, 2011), 139–156.

54 E.M. Belser, "Why the Affection of Federalism for Human Rights is Unrequited and how the Relationship could be Improved," in *The Principle of Equality in Diverse States: Reconciling Autonomy with Equal Rights and Opportunities*, ed. E.M. Belser et al. (Leiden and Boston: Brill, 2021), 62–100.

John Kincaid, writing from a federal perspective, asks how individual liberty could be balanced with a communitarian liberty of a subnational unit.[55] Which powers of communitarian liberty are to be tolerated and which are to be rejected for unduly infringing on individual liberty? He thus poses the question: '[W]hich rights should be treated as fundamental, universal, and uniform and which rights can be subjected legitimately to variations among communities of people holding diverse values?'[56] This has also been the approach of courts internationally, that a stricter level of compliance is required for some fundamental rights while with others a greater margin of appreciation is allowed.[57] There is thus a search for a balance between the universality of rights and subnational diversity.

The first element of this balance is that local diversity is not seen per se as discriminatory or objectionable. What else goes into the balancing act? The balance may be located in the interpretation of the right itself; the proportionality test for limiting rights balances individual rights against legitimate state interests. In the case of subnational governments, the value of subnational diversity and interests can then be considered appropriately. Also, the different dimensions of implementation – respect, protect and fulfil – are relevant. In the balancing act, most often the bill of rights predominates, resulting in the centralisation of power and the standardisation of diversity. How the balance will be struck depends, ultimately, on a number of factors, including the text of the constitution, the political and historical context of the decentralisation system, and the existence or absence of a consensus on the norm in question.

Bibliography

BBC News. "Sultan of Yogyakarta: A Feminist Revolution in an Ancient Kingdom." BBC News, published June 1, 2018. https://www.bbc.com/news/world-asia-43806210.

Belser, Eva Maria. "Why the Affection of Federalism for Human Rights is Unrequited and how the Relationship could be Improved." In *The Principle of Equality in Diverse States: Reconciling Autonomy with Equal Rights and Opportunities*, edited by Eva Maria Belser et al., 62–100. Leiden and Boston: Brill, 2021.

Bennett, T.W. *Customary Law in South Africa*. Cape Town: Juta, 2004.

Bhe and Others v. Khayelitsha Magistrate and Others, [2004] ZACC 17 (15 October 2004).

55 J. Kincaid, "Values and Value Tradeoffs in Federalism," in *Federalism, vol. 1, Historical and Theoretical Foundations of Federalism*, ed. J. Kincaid (Los Angeles: SAGE, 2011), 241–257.

56 J. Kincaid, "Values and Value," 252–3.

57 E.M. Belser, "Why the Affection," 91–100.

Butt, Simon. "Central-local Relations in Indonesia: Reforming the Integrationist State." In *Central-local Relations in Asian Constitutional Systems*, edited by Andrew Harding and Mark Sidel, 85–104. Oxford and Portland, OR: Hart, 2015.

Butt, Simon. "Provincial Asymmetry in Indonesia: What is so 'Special' about it? A Country Study of Constitutional Asymmetry in Indonesia." In *Constitutional Asymmetry in Multinational Federalism: Managing Multinationalism in Multi-tiered Systems*, edited by Patricia Popelier and Maja Sahadžić, 227–254. Cham: Palgrave Macmillan, 2021.

Certification of the Constitution of the Republic of South Africa, 1996, [1996] ZACC 26 (September 6, 1996).

Certification of the Constitution of the Western Cape, 1997, [1997] ZACC 8 (September 2, 1997).

Certification of the Kwazulu-Natal Constitution, [1996] ZACC 17 (September 6, 1996).

De Visser, Jaap and Nico Steytler. "'!ke e:/xarra //ke': Old diversities and New Responses in the quest for unity in South Africa." In *Revisiting Unity and Diversity in Federal Countries: Changing Concepts, Reform Proposals and New Institutional Realities*, edited by Alain-G. Gagnon and Michael Burgess, 5–26. Leiden and Boston: Brill Nijhoff, 2018.

Devenish, G.E. *Interpretation of Statutes.* Cape Town: Juta, 1992.

Economic Freedom Fighters v. Speaker of the National Assembly and Others; Democratic Alliance v Speaker of the National Assembly and Others, [2016] ZACC 11, (March 31, 2016).

Himonga, Christine O.J. "The Advancement of African Women's Rights in the First Decade of Democracy in South Africa: The Reform of the Customary Law of Marriage and Succession." *Acta Juridica* 82 (2005): 234–252.

Isra, Saldi, Bertus de Villiers, and Zainal Arifin. "Asymmetry in a Decentralized, Unitary State: Lessons from the Special Regions of Indonesia." *Journal on Ethnopolitics and Minority Issues in Europe* 18, no. 2 (2019): 43–71.

Kincaid, John. "Values and Value Tradeoffs in Federalism." In *Federalism, vol. 1: Historical and Theoretical Foundations of Federalism*, edited by John Kincaid, 241–257. Los Angeles: SAGE, 2011.

Liebenberg, Sandra. *Socio-economic Rights: Adjudication under a Transformative Constitution.* Cape Town: Juta, 2010.

Murray, Christina. "Provincial Constitution-Making in South Africa: The (Non)Example of the Western Cape." *Neue Folge Jahrbuch des offentlichen Rechts* 49 (2001): 481–512.

National Gambling Board v. Premier of KwaZulu-Natal and Others, 2002 (2) BCLR 156 (CC).

Pengilley, Veronica. "Feminist or Capitalist? Behind the Move to Install a Woman as Sultan of Yogyakarta." Southeast Asia Globe, published March 29. 2018. https://southeastasiaglobe.com/feminist-capitalist-move-woman-sultan-yogyakarta/.

Reid, Anthony. "Indonesia's Post Revolutionary Aversion to Federalism." In *Federalism in Asia*, edited by Baogang He, Brian Galligan, and Takashi Inoguchi, 144–164. Cheltenham, UK: Edward Elgar Publishing, 2007.

Shilubana and Others v. Nwamitwa, [2008] ZACC 9 (June 4, 2008).

Steytler, Nico and Johan Mettler. "Federal Arrangements as a Peacemaking Device During South Africa's Transition to Democracy." *Publius: The Journal of Federalism* 31, no. 4 (2001): 93–106.

Steytler, Nico. "Subnational Constitutionalism in South Africa: An Empty Promise." In *Routledge Handbook of Subnational Constitutions and Constitutionalism,* edited by Patricia Popelier, Giulio Delledonne, and Nicholas Aroney, 224–241. London and New York: Routledge, 2021.

Steytler, Nico. "The Constitutional Conversation between The Federal Structure and a Bill of Rights." Working Paper Online No. 2. Institute of Federalism, Fribourg, 2015.

Steytler, Nico. "The Constitutional Court in South Africa: Reinforcing an Hourglass System of Multi-Level Government." In *Courts in Federal Countries: Federalists or Unitarists?* edited by Nicholas Aroney and John Kincaid, 328–366. Toronto: University of Toronto Press, 2017.

Steytler, Nico. "The Relationship between Decentralisation and Constitutionalism in Africa: Concepts, Conflicts, and Hypotheses." In *Decentralisation and Constitutionalism in Africa*, edited by Charles M. Fombad and Nico Steytler, 25–52. Oxford: Oxford University Press, 2019.

Weare and Another v. Ndebele NO and Others, [2008] ZACC 20 (November 18, 2008).

Weeks, Sindiso Mnisi. "Customary Succession and the Development of Customary Law: The Bhe Legacy." *Acta Juridica* (2015): 215–255.

Woehrling, José. "Federalism and the Protection of Rights and Freedoms: Affinities and Antagonism." In *Political Liberalism and Plurinational Democracies*, edited by Ferran Requejo Coll and Montserrat Caminal di Badia, 139–156. London, New York: Routledge, 2011.

CHAPTER 11

The Australian Experience: Constitutional Courts – The Rule of Law

Robert French AC

Abstract

The role of the Constitutional Court of Indonesia is transformative. It is engaged in the process of nation-building and in the scope of limits of is powers. Its endeavours in this respect are much to be admired.

The High Court of Australia is the final appeal court for all Australian courts. It determines constitutional questions which come before it and has an entrenched judicial review jurisdiction in relation to the exercise of power by Commonwealth officials.

The two institutions have different histories and assume somewhat different roles in their home societies. Both, however, are key to the maintenance of the rule of law.

Keywords

democratic law-making – representative democracy – Australia – high court – constitutional court – religious courts – United Nations declaration on the rights of indigenous people – constitutional questions – rule of law – implied freedom of political communication – indigenous land rights – Mabo

1 The Constitutional Court of Indonesia – An Admiring Reflection

As a broad proposition, constitutional courts police the boundaries of democratic lawmaking and determine whether laws or proposed laws exceed constitutional limits. They may be authorised to go further and determine when lawmakers have failed to do what they are required by a constitution to do and instruct them accordingly. The limits which they police are often expressed in language which offers choices about its interpretation – constructional choices. The limits of power imposed by such constitutions may be uncertain. The decisions of constitutional courts are often inherently contestable because reasonable minds might come to different conclusions about the interpretation of a

 | DOI:10.1163/9789004691698_012

broadly worded provision. This has been the experience from time to time in Australia. The area of constructional choice is widened when a court is invited to draw an implication from the text and structure of a constitution.

The role of a constitutional court in responding to novel questions where the meaning of the constitution is uncertain, is challenging enough in a long-standing representative democracy such as Australia, where such questions do not arise with great frequency. Australia's *Constitution* came into effect in 1901 and reflected long-established conventions, institutional arrangements and concepts taken from the United States Constitution and from the United Kingdom system of responsible government. It was embedded in the common law. The self-governing colonies that became the States of Australia already had local constitutions in place, which reflected broadly understood institutional relationships between the legislature, the executive and the judiciary.

The Constitutional Court of Indonesia came into existence in a post-conflict society in 2003. It has established itself and carried out its work in circumstances far more challenging than those confronting its Australian counterparts. The Court has formal responsibilities under Art 24C(1) of the Indonesian Constitution. It reviews laws, including Interim Emergency Laws for their constitutional validity. It adjudicates on disputes about constitutional authority between State institutions. It can determine whether a political party should be dissolved, where that party employs violence so as to undermine the democratic order. It can decide disputes about the results of general elections. It can rule upon alleged violations of the Constitution by the President or the Vice-President.

These areas of jurisdiction conferred upon the Court which was created in 2003 in a post-conflict setting, meant that it was inevitable that the Court should play a key role in the process of ongoing nation-building. The term 'transformative constitutionalism', coined by Bertus de Villiers in the first chapter of this excellent book, is apposite.

There were a number of precedents for the Court to draw upon in defining its role. Examples are set out and discussed in Professor Warren's chapter on the Court as a post-conflict institution. The decisions of the Court in determining transitional justice issues are said to have been consistent with outcomes and analytical approaches taken by similar courts. It has explicitly relied upon comparative law from other post-conflict constitutional courts.

Adjudication on Australia's *Constitution* has often been concerned with the distribution of legislative powers between the Commonwealth Parliament and the States. The Commonwealth Parliament has enumerated, albeit non-exclusive, legislative powers which can be exercised concurrently with the States subject to a rule of primacy that Commonwealth laws will override inconsistent State laws. The Australian federal model, which has generated torrents of judicial ink since the commencement of the Federation, appears almost banal in its simplicity when compared with Indonesia.

Indonesia has 38 Provinces, nine of which have a special status, including the capital region of Jakarta – the latter perhaps analogous to the Australian Capital Territory in which the national capital, Canberra, is located. The Indonesian system is described by Professor Nico Steytler as 'asymmetrical', flowing from the founding of the Republic of Indonesia in 1945 and subsequent conflicts. As he observes, the distribution of powers in this decentralised system is a likely area for contest between orders of government. The Constitutional Court has had to grapple with such contests. That is notwithstanding the Indonesian Constitution's emphasis on the 'unitary' nature of the State in Art 1(1) of the 1945 Constitution. Interesting comparisons are drawn in Professor Steytler's paper between Indonesia and South Africa in this context.

As if decentralisation did not provide sufficient challenge, there is the question of the role of religion and religious rights in the Republic of Indonesia. Ann Black points out that Indonesia is the world's largest Muslim nation with 87%, over 207 million Indonesians, identifying as Muslim. Despite that, Islam does not feature in the Constitution, nor does the law of Islam. Nor does secularism for that matter. 'Belief in one Almighty God' (*ketuchanan*) is the first principle of Pancasila – the spirit that guides the nation. So Black observes that by facilitating tolerance but preserving the religious spiritual pulse of the nation, Pancasila makes possible 'unity in diversity'. There are religious courts which determine cases at first instance between Muslims in the fields of marriage, inheritance, will, grant, waqf, zakat; infaq; sadaqah; and Sharia economics. In its decision in the Religious Courts case, the Constitutional Court reviewed those competencies for consistency with human rights guarantees under the Constitution. That case, and the Beliefs Case discussed in Ann Black's chapter, highlight the complexities of the jurisdiction exercised by the Constitutional Court over the sprawling, populous and diverse archipelago that is Indonesia.

The Court has actively engaged in the recognition of indigenous rights discussed in Chapter 7 by Dr Cohen and Dr Arizona. In Case No. 35/PUU-X/2012, the Court was concerned with the legal status of customary forests within the scope of the Forestry Law. While that Law recognised customary forests, it described them as 'state forests located within the territory of indigenous peoples'. Indigenous applicants applied to the Constitutional Court to have the word 'State' in Article 1(6) of the Forestry Law deleted. The Court granted their application and thus changed the definition of 'customary forest' by separating such forests out from State forests. That decision was a straightforward but good example of the relatively more expansive role of the Constitutional Court of Indonesia in judicial review of legislation than that of its Australian counterparts. A more positively proactive approach was reflected in Decision No. 95/PUU-XII/2014, which was concerned with criminal provisions in the Forestry Law and the Law on the Prevention and Eradication of Forest Destruction. The Court carved out an exception from a prohibition against cutting down trees or harvesting or collecting forest products in the forest without having permission from authorised officials. The exception, inserted by a process of quasi-legislative drafting on the part of the Court, was 'for people who lived for generations in the forest and are not intended for commercial purposes'. A similar exemption was carved out in relation to a prohibition against herding livestock within forest areas.

As Drs Cohen and Arizona observe, developments in international law regarding indigenous rights have had a significant impact in Indonesia. The Constitutional Court's jurisprudence has been informed by international environment law and the United Nations Declaration on the Rights of Indigenous People. The Constitutional Court is described as having:

> resolved not only the concrete problems of injustice encountered by indigenous peoples but also generated legal reform.

Against this backdrop of transformative constitutionalism and a significant role in ongoing nation-building, judicial constitutionalism in Australia presents a rather unexciting contrast. That said, there are some important common elements of the kind that confront constitutional courts around the world. However, Australia's *Constitution* being largely bereft of express human rights guarantees and not importing norms derived from customary international law or Conventions, is not prone to give rise to as many occasions for conflict about fundamental values as the more expansive constitutional jurisdictions of other countries. Constitutional adjudication in Australia, however, is central to the operation of the Federation and the rule of law generally.

2 Constitutional Adjudication in Australia

Australia is a federation. The *Commonwealth Constitution* came into effect on 1 January 1901 as part of an Act of the United Kingdom Parliament. It created a new polity, the Commonwealth of Australia and legislative executive and judicial branches of government for that Commonwealth.

The High Court, Federal, State and Territory Courts in Australia can all hear and determine constitutional questions. However, the High Court is the highest constitutional court and also the final appeal court on all matters, constitutional and otherwise, from State, Territory and Federal Courts.

Under section 71 of the *Constitution*:

> The judicial power of the Commonwealth shall be vested in a Federal Supreme Court, to be called the High Court of Australia, and in such other federal courts as the Parliament creates, and in such other courts as it invests with federal jurisdiction.

Section 73 confers appellate jurisdiction on the High Court to hear and determine appeals on federal courts or courts exercising federal jurisdiction or of the Supreme Court of any State. Its judgment in all such cases is final and conclusive. The High Court also has original jurisdiction conferred on it directly by section 75 of the *Constitution*. It has additional original jurisdiction which the Parliament may confer on it by virtue of section 76. Curiously, that additional original jurisdiction includes, in section 76(i), jurisdiction in any matter 'arising under this Constitution, or involving its interpretation'. The Parliament can also make laws defining the jurisdiction of any federal court other than the High Court and investing any court of a State with federal jurisdiction under section 77.

Before Federation on 1 January 1901, the States of the Commonwealth were self-governing colonies, each with its own statutory constitution authorised by laws of the United Kingdom. Under those constitutions, the self-governing colonies had their own judicial systems, including Supreme Courts. Those State constitutions and laws made under them were continued in force by the *Commonwealth Constitution* in sections 106, 107 and 108.

The High Court, for which the *Constitution* provides in section 71, was established by legislation under the *Judiciary Act* 1903 (Commonwealth). That Act conferred upon the High Court additional original jurisdiction 'in all matters arising under the Constitution or involving its interpretation.' The same Act conferred the same jurisdiction on the courts of the States and the courts of the Territories. Following the creation of the Federal Court of Australia in 1976, it also had jurisdiction conferred upon it in matters arising under the Constitution or involving its interpretation. The effect of these provisions is that a constitutional question can be raised and decided in proceedings in any State or Territory court or in the Federal Court of Australia or in the original jurisdiction of the High Court. As the ultimate appeal court from the Federal Courts and the State and Territory Courts of course the High Court determines constitutional questions arising on appeals. Important constitutional matters are frequently taken directly to the High Court, in its original jurisdiction, where the validity of a law is to be challenged. Where there are factual matters to be determined before a constitutional question can be answered, the High Court will often remit the matter to a State or Federal court to determine those factual issues. Often, however, in constitutional adjudication, the High Court proceeds upon the basis of facts which have been agreed between the parties.

A safeguard provision, section 40, provides that where any cause or part of a cause 'arising under the Constitution or involving its interpretation' is pending at any time in a court other than the High Court, it may be removed into the High Court under an order of the High Court.

Without further exploring the procedural complications of constitutional jurisdiction in Australia, it may be seen that constitutional jurisdiction exists throughout the whole judicial system with the High Court serving as the ultimate decider.

3 The Constitutional Court: Policing the Limits of Power and Upholding the Rule of Law

A key role of constitutional courts is to maintain the rule of law by policing the limits of power. In Australia, all official power is found either in a statute conferring that power or in the *Constitution* of the Commonwealth or of a State. The meaning of the term 'rule of law' is much debated. A core element of it is that nobody, private citizen, public official or government, is above the law.

Under the *Commonwealth Constitution*, with its division of law-making power between the Commonwealth and the States, the limits it imposes on those powers and its separation of the judicial from the legislative and executive branches of government, there is no such thing as unlimited official power. Section 75(v) of the *Constitution* has the effect of conferring original jurisdiction on the High Court to judicially review decisions or conduct of Commonwealth Ministers and officers for jurisdictional error. Broadly speaking, that covers conduct in excess of constitutional or statutory powers. Former Chief Justice Gleeson described it as providing in the Constitution a 'basic guarantee of the rule of law'. Because it is a constitutional provision the jurisdiction it confers on the Court cannot be removed by anything other than a constitutional amendment. It is thus proof against attempts to place Commonwealth executive action beyond legal scrutiny and challenge.

A similar protection has been implied by the High Court from the *Constitution* as applying to the traditional supervisory jurisdiction of the Supreme Courts of the States.[1] That is to say they have, by implication, an entrenched constitutional jurisdiction to review exercises of official power for jurisdictional error. Moreover, the continuing existence of the State Supreme Courts has been held to be constitutionally entrenched, again as a matter of implication from the provisions of the *Commonwealth Constitution*. The Court has also held that the courts of the States cannot be made subject to the direction of the executive governments of the States.[2] Nor can they have imposed on them, or conferred on their judges, functions which are incompatible with their essential characteristics. Those essential characteristics include decisional independence, open hearings, procedural fairness and publicly available reasoned decisions. The foundation of these implied protections for State courts is Chapter 3 of the *Commonwealth Constitution* which allows the Parliament to invest them with federal jurisdiction. They have to be fit repositories for federal jurisdiction. The result of all of this is that Australia enjoys a pervasive constitutional protection for the rule of law concerning the exercise of official power, both legislative and executive, which enables its limits to be policed and enforced on the application of persons affected by its exercise.

In Australia, the core elements of the rule of law include specific propositions relevant to the exercise of official powers which provide a degree of protection for human rights and freedoms:

1. All official power derives from rules of law found in the Commonwealth and State Constitutions or in laws made under those Constitutions.
2. There is no such thing as unlimited official power, be it legislative, executive or judicial.
3. The powers conferred by law must be exercised lawfully, rationally, consistently, fairly and in good faith. Failure to comply with those requirements can constitute jurisdictional error and make the purported exercise of the power invalid.
4. The courts have the ultimate responsibility of resolving disputes about the limits of official power and in so doing they, like those whose decisions they review, must act lawfully, rationally, consistently, fairly and in good faith and within the proper limits of their constitutional function.

The Australian courts have adopted certain key rules for statutory interpretation that are consistent with the democratic process and, to the extent possible, protective of common law rights and freedoms. They are:

1 Kirk v. Industrial Court of New South Wales (2010) 239 CLR 531.

2 International Finance Trust Co Ltd v. New South Wales Crime Commission (2009) 240 CLR 219.

1. Laws made by the Parliament are to be interpreted in accordance with their text, context and purpose, and in accordance with common law and statutory rules of interpretation understood by those who draft the laws and, by attribution, by the parliaments which enact them.
2. Laws made by the Parliament are to be interpreted where interpretive choices are open on the text so as to avoid or minimise their impact on common law rights and freedoms. That principle is commonly referred to as the 'principle of legality'.

The claim can properly be made that the rule of law in Australia is well-established. It is an assumption on which the *Australian Constitution* is based.[3] We cannot say that it can be taken for granted. Indeed, it is important that it never be taken for granted. There are to be found in contemporary democratic societies, men and women of action and emphatic opinion in government and outside it who are impatient with the rule of law and the constraints it imposes on legislative and executive powers and who regard courts, in the words of one distinguished Australia academic 'as an inconvenient differentiation of government'. Much depends upon the culture of the society. This is particularly so in the absence of constitutional guarantees of human rights and freedoms. And even where such rights and freedoms are guaranteed, those guarantees may not be proof against an inimical societal or political culture.

4 Human Rights under the *Australian Constitution* and Statutes

The words 'rights' and 'freedoms' attach, in our ordinary speech, to individual men and women. The usage reflects the idea in international law of human rights and freedoms as aspects of the dignity and equality of every human being. The *Australian Constitution* does not provide expressly or by implication general guarantees of human rights and freedoms. There are, however, several provisions which incorporate limited guarantees. Briefly they are:

- Section 51(xxiiiA), which empowers the Commonwealth Parliament to make laws about medical and dental services but expressly precludes civil conscription, such as forcing doctors or dentists to work for the government under a national health system.

3 *Australian Communist Party v Commonwealth* (1951) 83 CLR 1.

- Section 51(xxxi) which, in effect, requires that any law of the Commonwealth Parliament with respect to the acquisition of property from any State or person must provide that the acquisition of property be on just terms.
- Section 75(v), which entrenches judicial review of decisions of Commonwealth officers.
- Section 80, which requires trial by jury for an offence against a law of the Commonwealth which is tried on indictment.
- Section 92, which guarantees freedom of interstate 'trade, commerce and intercourse'. The latter part of that guarantee applies to freedom of movement across State boundaries and was relied upon to strike down national security regulations in 1945.[4]
- Section 116, which prohibits the Commonwealth from making any laws for establishing any religion or imposing any religious observance or prohibiting the free exercise of any religion. It also provides that no religious test shall be required as a qualification for any office or public trust under the Commonwealth.
- Section 117, which prohibits discrimination between the residents of States.

The High Court has also held that there is an implied freedom of political communication under the Constitution. It is implied, among other things, from the provisions of sections 7 and 24 of the Constitution, which require that Senators and Members of the House of Representative be chosen directly by the people. It has been much litigated in challenges to laws which burden freedom of speech in various ways. It does not create a personal right or freedom but imposes limits on the law-making power of Parliament and on the common law. Political speech can be burdened for a legitimate purpose consistent with Australia's representative democracy if the burden is reasonable and appropriately adapted to meet that legitimate purpose.

There are many statutes which embody protections for human rights and freedoms in particular contexts, reflecting Australia's adherence to a number of international conventions. These include the *Racial Discrimination Act* 1975. Because that is a Commonwealth law made to give effect to the Convention for the Elimination of All Forms of Racial Discrimination, it prohibits discriminatory action at both Commonwealth and State level. The Commonwealth law has primacy under section 109 of the *Constitution* over any inconsistent State law. To that extent, human rights protections against forms of discrimination in Australia can be regarded as constitutionalised. There are also many such laws at State and Territory level and three Australian jurisdictions have

4 Gratwick v. Johnson (1945) 76 CLR 1.

adopted Human Rights Acts which require those State and Territory statutes to be interpreted consistently with fundamental human rights and freedoms and for pubic authorities to have regard to them in exercising their powers.

5 The Common Law

Statute apart, many of the things we think of as basic rights and freedoms come from the common law. The common law is also used to interpret Acts of Parliament and regulations made under them so as to avoid or minimise intrusion into those rights and freedoms. That is done against the backdrop of the supremacy of Parliament. Parliament can, by using clear words for which it can be held politically accountable, qualify or extinguish those rights or freedoms except to the extent that they are protected by the Constitution.

The common law rights and freedoms include the following: personal liberty, freedom of movement, freedom of speech, freedom of association and assembly, freedom of religion, immunity from deprivation of property without compensation, the presumption of innocence, the privilege against self-incrimination, legal professional privilege, the right to a fair trial, and the right to procedural fairness in administrative decision-making and judicial processes.

Restrictions on rights and freedoms may be imposed by democratic processes – by laws enacted by the Parliament. They may also be imposed by delegated legislation and legislative instruments made by Ministers or public officials under the authority of Acts of Parliament. The mere fact that a law adversely affects a right or freedom does not mean that the rule of law is somehow undermined. There is, however, a need for a continuing societal, parliamentary and official culture of scepticism about laws that seek to reduce any freedoms or the existence or exercise of any rights.

The rule of law is perhaps the most important protection of rights and freedoms. In the end, however consistently with the rule of law, statutes can be enacted by parliaments driven by short-term political imperatives which erode although perhaps only in a piecemeal way elements of those rights and freedoms. Over time, and cumulatively, this can be a process of death by a thousand cuts. Ultimately, the only legal limits imposed on parliaments are those derived from a written constitution policed by an independent and authoritative constitutional court. The damage to infringements on rights and freedoms may be mitigated by the way in which the court uses common law principles to interpret statutes so as to mitigate or avoid such infringements. But that approach is only possible where the language of the statute allows for an interpretive choice.

6 Recognition of Indigenous Land Rights

It was an important development of the common law in Australia that allowed for the recognition of traditional rights and interests of indigenous people in their land and waters – native title. That recognition was effected by the decision of the High Court in *Mabo v Queensland (No 2)* in 1992.[5] The decision led to legislation to provide a mechanism under Commonwealth law for facilitating recognition of such common law rights and interests and for protecting them against uncompensated extinguishment or impairment. Although an important common law development, it might be said to have a small 'c' constitutional dimension. It reflected a departure from a false understanding of the basis upon which Australia had been settled and of the absence of any cognisable legal systems among traditional societies of Australia's indigenous people.

The *Mabo* case had significant political impacts as did some follow-up decisions. There was public criticism of the Court from interest groups who thought they would be affected adversely by the decisions. In deciding *Mabo*, the High Court was not determining a political question. Typically, as a constitutional court, the High Court does not determine political questions but legal questions. But its decisions may have political consequences and it is all too easy in such cases for critics of such decisions to characterise them as exercises in judicial 'activism'. Ultimately, the legitimacy and authority of constitutional courts in the area of questions of political significance will depend upon the legitimacy and rigor of their reasoning and their respect for the other branches of government.

7 Conclusion

The development of the Constitutional Court of Indonesia has compressed into a very short period, a kind of historical evolution that has proceeded over centuries in other representative democracies with written constitutions. The complexities of the society in which the Constitutional Court of Indonesia

5 Mabo v. Queensland (No 2) [1992] HCA 23; (1992) 175 CLR 1.

must uphold the rule of law and its Constitution should evoke an appropriate sense of modesty in those of us who live under considerably less challenging regimes.

Bibliography

Australian Communist Party v. Commonwealth (1951) 83 CLR 1.

Gratwick v. Johnson (1945) 76 CLR 1.

International Finance Trust Co Ltd v. New South Wales Crime Commission (2009) 240 CLR 219.

Kirk v. Industrial Court of New South Wales (2010) 239 CLR 531.

Mabo v. Queensland (No 2) [1992] HCA 23; (1992) 175 CLR 1.

Index

www.ingramcontent.com/pod-product-compliance
Lightning Source LLC
LaVergne TN
LVHW012053011026
849162LV00018B/228